The
Food of
China

The
Food of
China

E. N. ANDERSON

Yale   *New*
University   *Haven and*
Press   *London*

Published with assistance from
the Louis Stern Memorial Fund.

Designed by Jo Aerne and set in Galliard
type by Eastern Graphics, Binghamton,
N.Y. Printed in the United States of
America by The Murray Printing Company
Westford, Massachusetts.

*Library of Congress Cataloging-in-
Publication Data*
Anderson, E. N., 1941–
The food of China.
Bibliography: p.
Includes index.
1. Food habits—China.   2. Agriculture—
China—History.   3. Cookery, Chinese—
History.   4. China—Social life and
customs.   I. Title.
GT2853.C6A53   1988   641.3'00951
87–29466
ISBN 0–300–03955–7 (alk. paper)

The paper in this book meets the guidelines
for permanence and durability of the
Committee on Production Guidelines for
Book Longevity of the Council on Library
Resources.

10   9   8   7   6   5   4   3   2   1

Dedicated to the hungry people of the world, in the hope that China's experience in feeding one-fourth of humanity will be made more widely useful through this book

Contents

Preface

In a world where hunger is all too common, China manages to feed one-fourth of the human species on a relatively small area of cultivable land. This success is due, in part, to an efficient socialist government. However, it also depends on China's agricultural system, which is not only productive but also —at least in principle—sustainable. China's agriculture does not depend on machines and chemicals so much as on highly productive crop varieties, recycling of nutrients, efficient use of water resources, and highly skilled intensive labor by hundreds of millions of peasant cultivators. As modern industrial agriculture changes, due to rising energy costs and massive poisoning of soil and water, the Chinese option will become more attractive. The future of humanity probably depends on combining Chinese-type intensive agriculture with the techniques of the "high-tech" era.

Therefore, several years ago, I began research into the development of agriculture in traditional China. My hope is that modern governments and individuals will learn from the Chinese some lessons about how development can take place.

I began with the plausible assumption that China developed its agriculture to feed its teeming millions. However, I found that many of the key innovations were made before China's population became large and dense. Indeed, it now appears that high population density led to more intensification but relatively less innovation than China had known in its less populous days (Chao 1986; Elvin 1973). This is not to deny the importance to China's agriculture of population pressure, or, more exactly, of high effective demand for food. However, the need for food can be met several ways: for example, by expansion and conquest, by out-migration, by overdependence on one staple crop (as in Ireland before the Great Famine), or by infanticide. All these were tried at various times in Chinese history. China's basic solution, however, was to develop an intensive, highly diversified, sustainable agriculture. Why was this option picked?

China's varied ecology permitted, even encouraged, a diverse farming system. Relatively high levels of trade, even in prehistoric times, led to the rise of a highly "rationalized" market system soon after civilization began. This, in turn, caused governments to be concerned about the availability of food—

not just for the citizenry, but for military security. Armies had to be fed; besieged cities had to have provisions. Thus, by the time China's imperial age dawned, a well-developed agricultural policy existed, and the government was committed to giving agriculture a high priority. This policy was successful. In agricultural productivity, China was far ahead of any other civilization until relatively modern times.

Chinese fascination with food, cuisine, and elaborate dining came from other sources. Ritual and ceremony institutionalized social codes surrounding recognition of honor and status. Respect for the old and for elite individuals was expressed in feasts. The gods, those "collective representations" of the community, also insisted on the best; they ate the subtle essence of the foods sacrificed to them, while the human community shared the material portion. Moreover, China early developed a medical science in which nutrition played the most important role. Many foods were eaten and many crops grown solely for their medical and nutritional values (real or alleged).

These belief systems led to demands on the food production system. Even the poor wanted gourmet fare, at least for New Year and for their aged parents' birthdays. Even the healthy wanted to keep themselves in shape by eating bean soup, chicken with ginger, or sea cucumbers. Minor crops of nutritional value thus remained in cultivation.

Imperial China displayed the paradox of a highly evolved food production system and a hungry populace. This was partly due to the importance attached to having as many children as possible—sons were the only security for one's old age. The elite also attempted to squeeze whatever they could from the people, often driving them below the margin of subsistence. The food system continued to intensify, as peasants tried to keep up.

No simple determinist explanation can account for the Chinese food system. It was the product of human choice—the countless decisions of emperors and peasants, businessmen and housewives, doctors and fishermen.

In this book I offer a general overview of Chinese food and discuss some of the problems we encounter in explaining how it came to be what it is today. Many questions remain. We still know very little, for example, about yields in traditional times, but recent work by Wen and Pimentel (1986a, 1986b) suggests that yields were even higher than we thought. If these scholars are correct, China's food system was considerably more effective than we realized. We need to know more about demography; recent work by Skinner (1986) suggests that Chinese census figures for the old days may have been quite inflated. We also need to know more about taxes and land tenure in imperial China and how they affected production. We need to know more about the origins of the whole system (Keightley 1983). We must learn about influences from western Asia, about medical science, about aesthetics and epicureanism, and about regional variation in practices. But I rest confident that the main outlines of Chinese food history are now clear.

This book is not a complete survey of Chinese food: there is no reason to repeat the excellent histories provided by Bray (1984), Chang (1977b), Young (1984), and others, or surveys of the contemporary nutritional scene such as those of May (1961), Whyte (1972, 1974) and Croll (1983). I do not attempt to survey the changes in agriculture since the modern industrial world came to China in the early nineteenth century: that would require another book far longer than this one. My concern is strictly with the traditional system, and I leave its modern transformations to those who are better qualified to discuss them. My book does not contain a comprehensive bibliography; I cite only easily available sources used for specific points in the text. In particular, for better or worse, I barely mention the Chinese literature (partly for lack of easy access to libraries). I am currently working on projects to extend this enterprise in some of these directions. This book is a way station.

Acknowledgements

This book owes its existence to hundreds of people on several continents. I take this opportunity to thank, deeply, all those who are not mentioned by name here. I have not forgotten you! Only the pressures of space prevent me from naming you all.

A prior and special debt is owed to my former wife and co-worker, Marja L. Anderson, and to my three children—Laura, Alan, and Tamar—who suffered years of fieldwork and enjoyed thousands of wonderful meals with me. This book owes much to Marja's aid, experience, and thought.

Of the many who have helped me in research, I remember especially Choi Kwok-tai and his family, especially Cecilia Choi Lau; Wang Chun-hua; Ch'ng Teng-liang; Kwok Wai-tak; John Ho; and Ali bin Esa. To them and many others I am deeply grateful.

I also owe a debt to my teachers, especially Brent Berlin, Peter Boodberg, Nick Colby, Wolfram Eberhard, Douglas Oliver, and Edward Schafer.

Among colleagues and friends that helped and sustained me in research, my love and thanks go to my parents, and to David Akers-Jones, Stanley and Anne Bedlington, Francesca Bray, Paul and Sally Buell, Chi-yun Chen, Alan Fix, Hill Gates, Chester Gorman, Philip Huang, Judit Katona-Apte (for, among other things, calling me to action toward explaining Chinese foodways), Michael Kearney, Carol Laderman, Victor Lippit, Robert and Katherine Martin, Sucheta Mazumdar, James and Helen McGough, Carole Nagengast, Jacqueline Newman, Marjorie Topley, Barbara Ward, Christine Wilson, Billy Wen-chi Young, and many, many others.

Thanks also to Ellen Graham and Stephanie Jones for sympathetic editing, and my eternal gratitude to Joye Sage and a multitude of typists and assistants for dealing with an unruly manuscript.

This research was funded by the University of California, the U.S. National Institute of Mental Health and the National Science Foundation, and the World Health Organization. My hope is that this book will prove useful in moving us toward a better world food system, and thus will—in part—repay the taxpayers who were, ultimately, my supporters.

Chronology

6000–6500 B.C. (approx.) First known agriculture in China: Millet in the north

5000 B.C.(approx.) First rice: Ho-mu-tu, Yangtze Delta

4000 B.C. Cultivation widespread and well established; several plant and animal species

3000 B.C. Agriculture universal in easily-cultivated parts of China; social differentiation; large villages, often with defensive arrangements; moves toward civilization

2000 B.C. Civilized society in North China and Manchuria; roughly the beginning of the Hsia Dynasty

By 1500 B.C. Shang Dynasty (traditionally began ca. 1751; perhaps actually 1500–1600)

By 1028 B.C. Chou Dynasty (traditionally began 1122; now a range of dates, all later, proposed)

480 B.C. Chou breaks down into the Warring States

221 B.C. Ch'in unifies China, creating Chinese Empire

207 B.C. Fall of Ch'in

206 B.C. Han Dynasty takes control

179–87 B.C. Chinese imperial agricultural policy takes shape (emperors Wen, Ching and Wu)

220 A.D. Fall of Han

220–265 A.D. Three Kingdoms period

265–420 A.D. Chin Dynasty (China not truly unified)

420–589 A.D. Six Dynasties

589–618 A.D. Sui Dynasty; China reunited

618–907 A.D. T'ang Dynasty; splendor and flourishing trade, especially with central and west Asia

907–960 A.D. Five Dynasties; China splits into warlord-dominated regions (actually many more than five separate courts)

960–1279 A.D. Sung Dynasty

937–1125 A.D. Liao Dynasty; Altaic-speaking rulers occupy some of northern China

1125 A.D. Chin Dynasty (Tungus-speaking rulers) conquers Liao

1126 A.D. Chin conquers Sung and takes all of northern China; Sung survives in south

1234 A.D. Mongols conquer Chin, take northern China

1279 A.D. Yüan Dynasty; Mongols conquer Sung, control all China

1368 A.D. Fall of Yüan, rise of Ming

1368–1644 A.D. Ming Dynasty

1644–1911 A.D. Ch'ing Dynasty

The Natural Environment

China's natural landscape is one of the world's most dramatic, ranging from the peak of the world's highest mountain (Jolmolungma or Everest, usually given as 29,141 feet high) to one of the lowest subaerial depressions (Turfan, ca. 900 feet below sea level) and from tropical rainforest in the south to frozen glacial caps on the high Himalaya. No other country approaches this range. China's endowment of plant and animal species is equally spectacular. The mountains of southwest China have the highest floral diversity of any temperate region in the world. The forests of Southeast Asia—which extend north to China, though not in their richest manifestation—are more diverse still; only the tropics of South America have a more varied vegetation. When the glaciers swept south in the Pleistocene, the forests of North America and Europe were forced into the Caribbean and Mediterranean seas, and the forests of Asia and western North America were driven into desert mountains. Only in China did they find a broad corridor where they could refuge until the climate ameliorated; and even many favored northern areas of China stayed relatively warm. Thus much vegetation that was once widespread in the rest of the world now survives only in China: such plants include the gingko and dawn-redwood. Moreover, China's mountainous terrain leads to geographical diversity, encourages speciation. A complex history of climatic change and consequent repeated migrations and fragmentations of vegetation cover have given China its rich heritage of plants. Nowhere else in the temperate zone has humanity had such a range of potential foods on which to draw. The Chinese have rarely been uninterested in new foods, and their position between the fantastic vegetational riches of Southeast Asia and the ancient agricultural cradle of the Near East has been the world's best for borrowing. (For general accounts of China's geography, see Buchanan 1970; Buchanan, Fitzgerald, and Ronan 1981; Tregear 1980; Tuan 1969.)

Other than true arctic and equatorial, China lacks one climate-type of great agricultural significance: the Mediterranean. Agriculture occurred first in Mediterranean lands, but many of the world's early major food crops were never important in China. Occupying the east coast and interior of the continent of Asia, China receives most of its rain from the summer winds that blow toward the northeast from the Pacific: the summer monsoon. In the far western areas of Central Asian China, the monsoon barely penetrates, and there the vanishingly small amounts of rain are apt to come in the winter, but the rest of China is entirely a summer-rain country. Rains in other seasons are appreciable in the moister regions, but only a small fraction of the total rainfall occurs in the cooler half of the year.

China has five great realms:

North China includes the zone of dry farming that was the heartland of China's civilization: the Yellow River plains and the hills around them.

Northeast China (Manchuria) is an area of subarctic forests and cold winters but also of fertile river valleys.

Central Asian China, the deserts and semideserts of Inner Mongolia, Sinkiang and the immediate border regions, are areas too dry for much unirrigated farming, thus given over to nomadic herding or to intensive irrigation in oases.

South China, from the Tsinling Range and its continuations (on the north side of the Yangtze Valley) southward, includes the Yangtze and the hilly and mountainous country where rice is the staple food.

Tibet, in the broad geographic sense (including most of the province of Tsinghai and bits of Szechuan and Yünnan, as well as Tibet Province), is the vast high desolate plateaus and mountain ranges of China's southwest. Much of this area is so cold and dry as to be utterly uninhabitable.

North China is the best known part of China archeologically and historically, and it contains the cradle of Chinese culture, including the earliest agricultural sites. It is an area of little rain, almost all falling in the warm half of the year. Winters are cold, bitter, dry, and dusty. The center of North China is the vast alluvial plain of the Yellow River, across which "China's Sorrow" wanders, bearing much mud and little water for so long a stream, since it drains desert and semiarid regions. It has often changed its course, frequently because of human activity: the dikes are raised, the riverbed aggrades until it is higher than the land, and then either a flood or—frequently—deliberate military action breaches the dikes. The resulting floods not only have devastated the land; they have also created large salt wastes in the lower valley, which are only now being reclaimed. (Some are in partly cut-off arms of the sea, thus especially salty.) Surrounding the great plain, and (apparently) occupied earlier, are high, rugged hills. These usually have a thin soil cover, but in the northwest—Kansu, Shensi, Shansi, and immediately neighboring areas—they are covered with loess, vast deposits of windblown soil. Most of the soil was blown in from the steppes of Mongolia during the cold, dry periods of the Pleistocene, when the hills were even more barren than they are now. Much moving of dust by the wind still goes on. The loess is deep (hundreds of feet in some areas) and very fertile; it holds water well. It tends to erode by shearing off vertically, so the loesslands feature steep cliffs and flat hills and valleys—the basis of the terracing that now occupies much of the landscape. The yellowish color of the loess and the alluvium derived from it gave the river its name and colored much of Chinese literature. "Heaven is dark, earth is yellow," begins the standard school primer of dynastic China; brown was and is regarded as a shade of yellow rather than as a separate color.

The vast majority of the people of North China live on the alluvial plain and the surrounding hills, especially the loess hills of the northwest and the rocky hills of Shantung. There are higher mountains and dry rolling country in the high west. The mountains and hills were once forested, but no one knows how extensive forests were in the loesslands; estimates range from almost entirely forested to almost entirely steppe. The former is difficult to believe, for the area is dry and fire-prone, in fact a very close climatic and geographic analogue to the prairies and plains of the central United States, where trees were confined to gallery forests on streams and scattered stands on the higher, rockier hills. Such must have been the case in China as well. Early historical records tell us that the alluvial plain was once covered with a vast riparian forest of water-loving trees, marshes, and swamps. Once again, we do not know how extensive it was. There is not one square inch of natural cover in North China; most of the land is under intensive cultivation, with no "wild" vegetation except a few weeds. Natural forests were cut centuries ago, and trees survive only around temples and shrines or as windbreaks and plantations, hence the difficulty of reconstructing past cover. Analysis of ancient pollen is providing a start in this direction.

North China was the native home of many of the key Chinese food plants, including millets, soybeans, the Chinese cabbages (including oilseeds), and peaches. These still survive in wild or weedy forms. Sheep are native and may have been domesticated here independently of their early Near Eastern domestication. The agriculture of North China today, however, is dominated by borrowed plants, including wheat, maize, sorghum, rice, cotton, and sesame.

Northeast China was occupied until recently primarily by Tungus-speaking and other non-Han peoples. Much of it is mountain country, forested with spruce, fir, birch, larch, pine, and other cold-weather trees. Its center consists of wide river plains, grass, and marshland. These are now cultivated, maize and sorghum being among the main crops; they are comparable to the plains of Manitoba and the Dakotas. The northeast was a marginal area through much of China's history.

Central Asian China includes the areas too dry for significant rainfed agriculture. (There is a little rainfall agriculture in northwestern Sinkiang and Inner Mongolia.) The lands are primarily desert or dry steppe suitable for extensive grazing, and barren, rugged mountains. Montane forests occur only in climatically favored areas such as the middle elevations of northern Sinkiang. Some of the driest and most barren country in the world is found in the Takla Makan Desert, where virtually no rain falls. Sizable rivers drain from the mountains surrounding the desert basins of Sinkiang, and the Yellow River flows through some of this region: irrigated farming is intensively practiced. During much of China's history, however, unsettled conditions led to disintensification of this agriculture. Central Asian China (and neighbor-

ing areas now in Mongolia and the USSR) has been the home base of Mongol, Turkic, and other groups who rode out in great waves of nomad conquest, occupying all
or part of China, but eventually losing hold and retreating or being absorbed by the
Chinese. Large populations of these peoples still exist, forming the majority in most
areas outside of cities and the main southeastern agricultural parts of the region.
The great Silk Road ran across Central Asia, from Lanchow and Yümen via the
Tarim Basin (skirting the Takla Makan to north or south) and then crossing the
mountains to Farghana, Samarkand, and points west (Boulnois 1963; Schafer 1963).
This road, with other parallel or confluent routes, was China's main artery of communication with the outside world throughout most of its history. Trade to the
south was never very significant. Traffic with India came mostly via Afghanistan and
joined the Silk Road near Balkh. The sea routes were less important than the land
until recent centuries. For many millennia—since early prehistoric times—China's
outside influences came primarily through this vast dry land of scattered oases or
through the more northern steppes and forest-steppes of Siberia. Central Asia served
as a vast filter: only what could easily cross the desert routes and steppes stood a
good chance of penetrating the Middle Country.

South China is currently the home of a large majority of the country's population
and an even greater percentage of its food production. The landscape is one of rugged high hills broken by alluvial valleys, of which by far the largest is the Yangtze-
Huai Plain. (The valley of the West River and its tributaries in the far south is a very
long second.) High plateaus such as those of Yünnan and Kweichow, and hilly basins, of which the most important is the warm, foggy Red Basin of Szechuan, are
also important food production areas. Only the Red Basin challenges the river and
coastal plains as a food production center. The region is warm with heavy rain in
summer, always ample, and in the western mountains superabundant—the southwest region of South China is not far from some of the wettest places on earth, the
hills of east India and west Burma. The natural cover of the region is mostly evergreen or monsoon subtropical forest. Fully tropical forests occur in the far south, and
incredibly rich forests in the west. In contrast to North China, South China still has
much forestland. Though most of it is degraded and abused, reforestation and restoration are taking place today. Soils are those of warm, wet, forested country: highly
leached, acidic, red and yellow soils from which water has taken most of the nutrients, and rich alluvial valley soils where nutrients are redeposited. In a few areas of
rich parent rock, notably the Red Basin, the hill soils are less wretched, but by and
large the valleys are richer than the hills, and they have become increasingly so in recent centuries because of slope erosion caused by farming and deforestation. Thus
people have concentrated in the alluvial lands.

South China is the great domain of rice. On steep slopes and in other areas unsuitable for rice, maize and root crops are grown. The highest areas produce wheat and
barley, which are also grown in rotation with rice in the cooler parts of this area—
especially on the Yangtze-Huai Plain. The wheat and barley grow in the win-

ter and ripen in spring; then the rice is put in. The rainfall regime is convenient for this—dry in winter, wet in summer, as the respective crops demand. Farther south, rice is grown year-round by double-cropping, or even triple-cropping in the far southeast. South China also boasts a great diversity of minor crops and an exceedingly efficient cropping and farming system based on wet-growing not only paddy rice, but also other water crops from watercress to pond fish.

Tibet is a vast plateau ringed and interrupted by the highest and wildest mountains on earth. Much of the plateau is over sixteen thousand feet above sea level. All of it is high and cold, most too high for agriculture and much utterly uninhabitable. The lower and warmer areas in the south and east produce barley, buckwheat, radishes, onions, and a few other crops—even some rice in the extreme southeast. Most of the population in these areas lives by farming. Much of the unfarmable land is ranged by nomadic herders of sheep, yaks, and other animals. The yak, Tibet's native species of cow, is a special blessing; most of inhabited Tibet would be uninhabitable, or nearly so, without it. It supplies milk, meat, and labor power. Even so, the whole of the Tibetan plateau region in China has only a few million inhabitants—fewer than some of the individual cities of the lowlands (Ekvall 1968; Snellgrove and Richardson 1968; Tucci 1967).

On the whole, then, China consists of the densely inhabited and agriculturally rich lands of North and South China, surrounded by wild and sparsely populated country which until recently was occupied by predominantly non-Han populations. Speakers of Chinese languages refer to themselves as "Han," after the Han Dynasty. Over fifty other languages are also found in China; their speakers are the non-Han people. (In addition, there are Chinese-speaking Muslims, who are usually called Hui, not Han.) The non-Han peoples, Hui included, live primarily in the northeastern, Central Asian, and Tibetan regions and in the tropical and semitropical mountains of the south. The densely populated areas are included in the Eighteen Provinces of Chinese tradition; the rimlands make up nine more provinces (counting Taiwan). Through most of Chinese history, only the Eighteen Provinces and parts of Central Asian China figured prominently, and even within these there were many marginal areas. Indeed, the three southwesternmost provinces, Yünnan, Kweichow, and Kwangsi, were through much of Chinese history more remote and less well known than Tibet and Central Asia. Thus, there has always been a striking contrast between the dense, long-settled parts of the Eighteen Provinces and the rest of China.

Last and not least, China is a land of disasters (the classic account is Mallory 1926). South China is favored in this regard, with nothing worse than floods and coastal typhoons to concern it, and with the phenomenally stable and productive wet-rice system to support it. Few general famines have occurred in South China except as adjuncts to war and political trouble (all too frequent in themselves, to be sure). The rest of China is plagued by droughts, floods, earthquakes, and other disasters that wreak havoc with food production and disrupt the economy. The world's most dreadful natural catastrophes have occurred in China: the Shensi earthquake of the Ming Dynasty killed 830,000 people; the Tangshan earthquake of 1976 killed or injured perhaps 600,000; an endless cycle of droughts and floods meant a famine somewhere in North China virtually every single year of record; the hard winters of the northeast and Central Asia often exterminated nomads' herds. China's instability is due primarily to two factors. The first is the monsoon: if the rains extend farther north than usual and are heavy, floods occur; if they do not reach far enough or come at odd times, droughts devastate the land. The second is the continuing pressure of the Indian subcontinent, which is being dragged inexorably northward by movements in the earth's crust and is being crammed under the huge rocky mass of Asia. The result is the fantastic Himalayan front, where the land is folded and wadded like a rug pushed against a wall; the high plateau and mountain country behind it; and the great breaks, tears, and rents in Central Asia as far east as North China, where the earthquakes occur as the land is squeezed up and out between India and the ancient, rigid, mountainous plate to the north in Siberia. In addition, mountains are actively being built in much of China: a stop-action camera with a period of a million years between frames would record something like the breakup of the ice on a northern river in spate. The lowlands of northern and central China are geosynclinal troughs, probably sinking—certainly sinking where the rivers are weighing them down with millions of tons of alluvium. These tectonic forces are not always slow. The Himalayas of Tibet have risen mostly within the past few million years. Displacements of many feet occur in major earthquakes. Silting up of river mouths happens so fast that Tientsin changed from a port to an inland city in recent history—and Shanghai continues as a port thanks only to artificial dredging. Whole farming districts have been added steadily, as marshes fill or open coastal seas fill with alluvium until they can be reclaimed as islands or new extensions of the coast. Areas built up by riverine silt are extremely fertile, except where sea water has been trapped and has evaporated to leave salt. Even the salty lands are now being reclaimed.

Few peoples have transformed their countries' landscapes more thoroughly than the Chinese. Rather than geographic determination of human fate, China illustrates human determination of geographic fate. For millennia before Mao urged the people to "struggle against nature," the Chinese were diking, draining, irrigating, terracing, deforesting, reforesting, reclaiming, and otherwise making their world. Much of China is now as purely a human creation as the Dutch polders (of which the proverb says, "God made the world, but the Dutch made Holland"). Even before the Chinese reworked their landscapes on this massive scale, the natural environment proved a facilitating rather than a limiting factor. The rich vegetation permitted (but did not force) people to domesticate a great variety of foods. The fertile bottomlands and plains, isolated and guarded by mountains and deserts, permitted (but did not force) a rich civilization to rise. The barriers allowed this civilization to maintain its integrity and separateness, but they were not so rigid as to shut out foreign influence or so numerous as to fracture the Chinese realm into many small states. China had its centuries of disunion, but, unlike Europe, it never broke up permanently into many small, distinct nations. This fact again was not determined solely by geography; surely China's internal barriers are as rugged as Europe's.

The Chinese were, and are, adept at making the land serve their ends rather than allowing it to constrain them. The land provided opportunities that were generally seized. It provided obstacles that in the long run have been overcome. No one farms high Tibet or grows bananas in Manchuria, and everywhere the accommodation of humans to climate, soil, and relief is marked, but within these limits China shows that cultural ecology is a matter of human response to human needs and desires, using the landscape as a means—not a matter of geographic determination of culture. The landscape provides opportunities and shaping forces, but the actual fate of humanity in that landscape is determined by human choices that are constrained more by social and historic factors than by natural ones.

2 Prehistory and the Dawn of History

Chou-k'ou-tien and Pre-agricultural Humans in China

Peking Man (*Homo erectus pekinensis*, formerly *Sinanthropus pekinensis*) was first found at Chou-k'ou-tien near Peking, in caves filled with limestone. Other specimens of early Chinese hominids have been discovered since then (Binford and Chuan 1985; Chang 1977a, 1986; Chia 1975; Jia 1980). At Chou-k'ou-tien, where finds are dated to about 500,000 B.C., hackberry fruits may indicate that early hominids took an interest in edible plant products, or they may be there by chance. There are many bones in the caves, especially those of deer. Although some of the bones seem to represent human food, most were brought in by hyenas and wolves, which spent more time in the cave than did hominids. In addition, a vast mass of bones of small animals, especially rodents such as mole rats, was apparently left by wolves. The bones are broken and often burned—representing early evidence for human use of fire, though surely humans had been using fire for long ages before. Much of the fire at Chou-k'ou-tien appears nonhuman in origin, but at least some human use of fire is probable.

The story enshrined in popular literature that Peking Man practiced cannibalism is incorrect; there is no evidence for cannibalism at Chou-k'ou-tien. Binford and his co-workers (Binford and Chuan 1985; Binford and Stone 1986a,b) point out that the skull damage previously thought to suggest cannibalistic practices was actually inflicted by predators, probably hyenas.

At Chou-k'ou-tien and elsewhere in China and Southeast Asia there is a great wealth of stone tools: large flakes of hard rock chipped to create a sharp edge, small cores, and hacked and broken pebbles. The tools of Pleistocene East Asia have usually been described as crude, simple, and primitive, but they are about as sophisticated as other tools of that age. Their makers were obviously skilled in handling hard, difficult rock, and the tools seem well adapted to their uses. Beside their obvious importance in hunting game, the tools must have been useful for chopping and shaping plant materials such as bamboo, vines, and wood.

A few finds, widely scattered in both space and time, bridge the gap from Peking Man to the present. Individuals resembling Neanderthal Man, dating from 50,000 to more than 100,000 years ago, have been found at Ma Pa near Canton, among other sites. By 50,000 B.C., in nearby parts of Central Asia, Neanderthals had developed a rather sophisticated culture: they built houses, had complex stone tool technologies, and practiced fairly elaborate burials. At Teshik-Tash in the USSR not far west of China, a Neanderthal boy was found surrounded by bear skulls and covered with red ochre; at Shanidar Cave in Iran, Ralph Solecki found burials in which the dead had been covered or decorated with medicinal plants, presumably part of a ritual to restore life or preserve the survivors. Thus, by fifty thousand years ago, in areas near China and no doubt in China too, people were beginning to treat plants and animals as more than mere food.

It is often assumed that man (note the sex) was basically a hunter until the rise of agriculture. This is incorrect. Humans are omnivores, as is shown by our nutritional needs, behavior patterns, and universal ethnographically recorded lifeways. Compared to most of the animal kingdom, humans have rather strange dietary requirements, which by and large we share with other primates. We cannot manufacture vitamin C, unlike most animals, but must consume it. We need unusually large amounts of protein and cannot synthesize as many of the amino acids as some mammals can. We are big animals and have huge brains to support; thus we need to eat a great number of calories. Before vitamin pills, the only way humans could ensure good health was to eat a varied diet. Groups of humans have survived on diets consisting almost exclusively of flesh (Eskimos), grain (Chinese), fruit, and so forth—almost every possible specialization is found somewhere—but always at the cost of sparse populations or constant threat of famine or ill health. Primary meat eaters have been rare and marginal since the huge Pleistocene species that supported them died out, and they were probably rare and marginal in the Pleistocene too, since the Pleistocene flora was as rich as the animal life and would surely not have been ignored by groups that could take advantage of it. The meat of land animals supplies little vitamin C, as well as too much saturated fat and other chemicals, for humans to survive exclusively on it. Yet humans cannot digest long-chain carbohydrates (cellulose, lignin, etc.) or handle tannins and other chemicals common in mature plant tissues. We are limited to soft, tender foods, to fats, sugars, starches, and proteins: seeds, fruits, young tender leaves and shoots, roots, and animals. Such foods are maximally present in recently cleared areas growing back up to mature plant communities. Areas recently burned or flooded are particularly rich; a burn that has been growing up for a year or two is ideal. All human groups know fire, and most use it to clear the land for food production or similar purposes. It thus seems highly probable that our combination of high intelligence, exceedingly flexible behavior and social systems, and wide nutritional requirements was formed as we adapted to the drying of Africa and other lands in the Miocene and Pliocene, becoming fire-followers and pioneers.

The First Agriculture

Perhaps the most momentous step in human history was the decision to plant and cultivate food. Yet for millions of years, humanity had found enough food for its needs and wants. The fact that plants grow from seeds, cuttings, or offsets is known to most hunters and gatherers; no one living in the wild can remain ignorant of it for long. Thus agriculture must not have been invented or discovered so much as *decided on*. Many people have assumed that population pressures forced the Chinese to develop elaborate agriculture. The truth is more complex. (The following account draws principally on An 1982; Andersson 1934, 1943; Bray 1984; Chang 1977a, 1986; Cheng 1959; Ho 1975; Kao 1978; Meacham 1975, 1977; Pearson 1981; Shangraw 1978; Watson 1969, 1971.)

Agriculture began first not in East Asia but in the Near East and neighboring southeastern Europe, where dogs were tamed by 14,000 B.C.; wheat, barley, sheep, and goats well before 10,000 B.C.; and cattle, pigs, chickpeas, lentils, and probably several other foods by 5000–6000 B.C. The date palm, too—the first tree crop— may have been domesticated by this time. (Domestication means genetic change from wild-occurring populations; the domesticated population is a deliberate or accidental product of human selection. For general accounts of early agriculture, see Bender 1975; Harlan 1975; Reed 1977; Zohary 1973.) Soon after, cultivation arose in North America, where the first known domesticates were chiles and squash in Mexico, and in South America, where Peruvian lima beans had been developed by about 8000 B.C. The coincidence in time is interesting, as is the early domestication of leguminous seeds in all areas (beans in Mexico were earlier than soybeans in China). Agriculture was independently invented in the New and Old World.

Meanwhile, pottery was invented in East Asia. For decades, anthropologists believed that pottery and agriculture arose together, along with polished and ground-stone tools, as part of a Neolithic complex. The first pottery did indeed appear at the same time as the first agriculture—but halfway around the world, in Japan, where the earliest Jomon pottery dates to before 10,000 B.C. In China and northern Southeast Asia, pottery very similar to the Jomon appeared before 7000–8000 B.C. (Chang 1987).

The earliest known agriculture in China was in the north, especially in the loesslands and neighboring areas. Consistently, from the beginnings of agriculture through the early civilizations, the center of action seems to be the Wei River Valley in Shensi and the Yellow River area downstream from the Wei through the Central Plain. However, the rest of China was never far behind, and at least one other important center is known in the Yangtze delta country. Others are suspected to lie somewhere in the south.

From 6500 to 5000 B.C., the P'ei-li-kang and related cultures occupied the loesslands, with domesticated foxtail millet (*Setaria italica*), panic millet (*Panicum miliaceum*), pigs, dogs, and chickens (Chang 1986). All are clearly local domesticates, except the dogs (human companions since long before) and possibly the chickens, which very likely came up from the south. By 5000 B.C., other Neolithic cultures flourished from Manchuria to Vietnam, and the Yang-shao Culture had brought spectacularly beautiful painted pottery and large settlements into the picture in the loesslands. Contemporary cultures throughout North China were not far behind, if they were behind at all. The general picture is one of steady development in each region, with a great deal of mutual influence but without evidence of migration or replacement by alien peoples.

I will discuss Pan-p'o Village as a typical Neolithic community, because it is the best described in the available literature and because I have visited it. Pan-p'o had farming by perhaps 6000 B.C., though its agriculture is better known from its Yang-shao phase, beginning by 5000 B.C. Pan-p'o lies near Sian, the provincial capital of Shensi. Significantly, many of the important cities of China's earliest dynasties were also near Sian, the site of the great city of Ch'ang-an, China's capital in the T'ang Dynasty. This spot is almost exactly in the center of the country (although it is often referred to as being in the west, since it is west of the ancient core of China). Sian lies some twelve hundred feet above sea level in the valley of the large Wei River, which drains the north side of the Tsinling Mountains and the rough, dry loess country north of them. Thus it is just on the cold, dry side of China's great ecological divide, but in a warm area—very hot in summer. Rainfall is low, slightly under 20 inches per annum, but the hills get more, and the high Tsinling is wet. Sian is in a rain-shadowed dry pocket, but near it flow the great Wei and several smaller tributaries draining north from the moist Tsinling massif. Thus the area is on balance well watered.

At Pan-p'o today, workers excavate new areas using tools that differ from those of the original farmers there only in the material of which they are made. The modern tools are in no sense primitive: rather, the Pan-p'o people were advanced, expert toolmakers. Not far off lie many other early farming villages, although none has been shown to be quite so old as Pan-p'o. Just down the Wei, nearer to its junction with the Yellow River, lie the sites of the Miao-ti-kou culture, only slightly later in date and very similar in all respects to the Pan-p'o sites, except that flower designs replaced the fish designs on Pan-p'o pottery. The first crop at Pan-p'o was millet; pigs and dogs were raised apparently from the beginning. The pigs (like sheep, which came later) were apparently domesticated locally, independent of Near Eastern domestications (Ho 1975). Chickens, probably domesticated in South China and imported, soon followed. Wild jungle fowl (ancestors of chickens) may have naturally occurred north of Pan-p'o. The millets used were *Setaria italica*, Italian or foxtail millet, probably a domesticated form of the wild grass *Setaria viridis* (= *S. lutescens*), and *Panicum miliaceum*. Their ancestors occur in dry, temperate areas all over the Northern Hemisphere and are often found as wild-gathered grain in archeological sites. The domestications of *S. italica* and probably *P. miliaceum* were achieved in China. The genetic changes that make a wild crop into a domesticated one almost certainly occur over a wide area in which incipient cultivation is going on. Dozens or hundreds of sites are probably involved, covering in this case perhaps all of central China, or all the loesslands, or all of some other large region.

The folk of early China did not, of course, confine themselves to such a narrow roster of foods. They ate bamboo shoots, persimmons, grass seeds, walnuts, pine nuts, chestnuts, mulberries, and such wildlife as fish, clams, mussels, and various species of deer. Storage jars full of seeds are a common find; they include small covered jars and round jars slotted like piggybanks. (Could this be the origin of the piggybank?) Mortars and pestles, manos and metates were used to grind seeds. At Pan-p'o as at other sites, the percentage of obviously cultivated food increases relative to wild and wild-type foods as time goes by.

Later came cattle and horses. *Brassica* (Chinese cabbage) seeds are found in pots at Pan-p'o by 4000 B.C., but sheep, horses, and panic millet are not so easy to date. The first two are found at Pan-p'o but they were probably wild game: their bones are few and show no evidence of domestication. The only other early evidence of these three foods together was at one site, Ching Village in Shansi, excavated a long time ago under less than ideal archeological conditions (Bishop 1933; Ho 1975). Sheep were soon domesticated, but the goat did not arrive from its native Near East until the Miao-ti-kou II culture, about 2500 B.C. (Ho 1975). Panic millet appeared in Europe by 4000 B.C. (Hubbard 1980); it may have spread through Central Asia from China. To round out the picture, hemp or *Cannabis sativa*, better known to the modern world as marijuana, was evidently grown. The Chinese used it primarily as an edible seed and clothing fiber plant. (They were, of course, aware of its other qualities. It has been used in China as an anesthetic or a pain-reliever, and the *Pen-ts'ao Kang-mu*, Li Shih-ch'en's great herbal of 1593, comments that it "makes one see devils.") Chinese hemp is by far the earliest known cultivated hemp in the world.

Mulberries and silkworms were known at Pan-p'o; a cut silkworm cocoon has been found. There is no conclusive evidence that silkworms were domesticated, but most authorities assume they were. If so, this was another first—the earliest known domestication of an insect. (The honeybee was brought under human control only thousands of years later.) It seems quite possible that other crops were grown too; minor vegetable and medicinal crops would leave very little archeological record. Mallow (*Malva*), for instance, would be a likely bet; it was the major vegetable in early historic China.

There is difference of opinion among archeologists concerning the question of how these Neolithic peoples farmed and what kind of country they had. Ho (1975) suggested that they practiced settled upland farming in sagebrush-grassland steppe. Others hold that the land was forested and the farmers practiced slash-and-burn agriculture. Ho (1984) responded by pointing out that the sites are on river and stream banks, often pedestaled now by subsequent erosion. We know that the mountains must have been wooded, the alluvial plains also, but the pediments and plateaus were very likely open country. Moreover, the fire-setting and fire-following propensities of humankind—especially hunters and simple farmers—must have guaranteed a great deal of burning, leading to much open country. Grasslands formed by constant firing have been widespread in China throughout recorded time. Finally, the area in question is climatically similar to the prairies and high plains of the United States, where the Pawnee and their neighbors practiced farming in flood-opened alluvial lands.

Large farming villages were widespread in China by 4000 B.C. The diet was rich and varied: wild foods supplemented millet and animals, and a few vegetables flavored the pot. Foods were boiled, roasted, and probably steamed. The lovely painted pottery looks very much like the contemporary wares of the Near East and Central Asia, and scholars from Andersson (1934) on have postulated a relationship between them. Others disagree (Ho 1975). To my eye, the resemblance is unmistakable; indirect contact across the steppes and deserts seems impossible to deny. Influences no doubt flowed in both directions.

The southerly realms also contributed to China's historic culture. A particularly famous site is Spirit Cave, in north Thailand, where plant remains dating as far back as 7000 to 9000 B.C. were excavated by Chester Gorman (1970; cf. Solheim 1970). Claims that these remains included agricultural or cultivated materials have not stood the test of time. But the Ma-chia-pang and Ho-mu-tu people of the Yangtze Delta appear to have been the first known rice farmers. Both long grain (*ch'ien* or *indica*) and short grain (*keng* or *japonica*) rices occur, indicating that this basic division of rices into two categories was incipient before 5000 B.C.

The rich environment of China's early Neolithic was apparently improving; around 6000 B.C., a wetter, warmer period replaced an earlier climate as harsh as that of today. The Pan-p'o villagers shared a world with much game, wild fruits, nuts, fish, and greens, and for a millennium or two, agriculture supplied only a tiny percentage of their livelihood. They did not turn to domestication out of necessity. Why, then? Carl Sauer (1952), in a purely speculative chapter whose purpose was simply to challenge current thinking, put forth an outrageous but notably insightful hypothesis of agricultural invention. We know from modern experience that people living on the margin of real want do not experiment: they cannot afford to. Much more innovation takes place among the rich than among the poor; to see this, one need only compare the agricultural research establishments of the United States or France with those of Bangladesh or Haiti, or the research devoted to beef and lamb for the rich with that devoted to barley, millet, manioc, and other crops used mostly by the poor—even after the considerable self-conscious effort to rectify this situation in the last few years.

Moreover, claimed Sauer, many people without the blessings of state and civilization have rarely been in want or in dire straits. Famine, desperate poverty, and their accompanying problems may be creations of the state, with its taxes, wars, and legally maintained social inequalities (cf. Sahlins 1962).

This theory renders unviable the many theories of agricultural invention and development based on necessity—which, as Sauer says, is no mother of invention. In recent years, archeologists have favored the theory of Ester Boserup (1965), who suggested that population pressure leads to pressure on the food base, forcing people to innovate or starve. This population pressure model has often been combined with a theory which claims that the extinction of many animal species in the late Pleistocene (perhaps with human hunting as a factor) created a food shortage, which caused people to shift to vegetable sources of food. Mark Cohen (1975) provides a particularly good and detailed analysis from this point of view.

But this model cannot be correct for China. In fact, the hunting and gathering peoples who invented agriculture must have controlled their numbers by internal regulation, war, or migration, as all such groups seem to do (Cowgill 1975); if they had faced real pressure on the resource base they would have fallen back on these solutions or suffered famine rather than innovating. In North China, in contrast to Boserup's theory, agriculture began when the climate and environment were improving and developed as climate continued to improve. But on the other hand, farming is so universally considered less fun than hunting and gathering that many or most farming peoples, notably including the Chinese and the Near Easterners who spun tales of the Garden of Eden, have tales of the fall of humanity from a state of farmless grace to a world of "earning . . . bread by the sweat of [the] brow."

What is needed is an explanation of why people came to want more plant and animal foods *close to home.* The earliest agriculture would not have led to any spectacular increase in the actual yields of foods; only selective breeding over years or centuries would do that. Rather, people must have begun farming out of a desire to control the location of foods. Mark Cohen's case, that the extinction of much of the world's large fauna at the end of the Pleistocene forced people to emphasize plants more, is complicated by the fact that agriculture appears early in areas where food plants were increasing in abundance. The late Pleistocene die-off was not very marked in the Near East, the highlands of Mexico, or upland Southeast Asia; it was very pronounced in the American West, northern Europe, and other areas which had no early agriculture. Thus the die-off is clearly not an adequate explanation of agriculture by itself.

Richard MacNeish (1977) stressed the importance of trade in agricultural origins: all over the world, agriculture occurred first at foci of trade and communication, crossroads and heartland sites. There are two reasons why people at a trade node would have been apt to cultivate early: they would have been abreast of new developments, including any new information about plants and their uses, and they would always have wanted something at hand to trade. The trade induction model explains why agriculture arose at trade nodes and rarely elsewhere, why it spread along trade routes, and why it never arose or appeared early in populous and climatically favorable cul-de-sacs, such as southern Australia, southern South America, most islands, and many coastal areas. (In East Asia, Japan was such a cul-de-sac. It had a dense, settled population, pottery, and other Neolithic characteristics very early indeed, but no obvious agriculture developed there until a few hundred years B.C.) Currently existing cultures on the southern edge of China show a pattern of trade and raid. Farming groups with good soil intensify their agriculture to produce trade goods and also to keep their fields close to home for maximum protection from raiding (Furer-Haimendorf 1962).

I believe, then, that the ancient inhabitants of China took up agriculture during a period of increasing richness in the environment. The end of the Pleistocene may have forced them to turn to plants more than before, but they began deliberate farming after they had already adjusted to this and built up the stability that seems necessary for experimentation. Those living in areas rich in plant foods traded such foods with other people who had, perhaps, better animal or mineral resources. To have these plants ready at hand and to protect them from raids, the plant-food traders encouraged food plants to grow close to their villages. Perhaps at first they merely cared for plants that grew from dropped seeds, but soon the advantages of deliberate planting were realized.

As far as we know, the early Neolithic cultures in China arose and flourished in areas where trade nodes have always been: Sian, the nearby junction of the Wei and Yellow rivers, and the Yangtze delta area. Perhaps other foci remain to be discovered, but there is increasing evidence that areas historically marginal and isolated from major routes of trade were marginal prehistorically as well.

China's progress from about the fourth millennium B.C. to the second is evident in its increasing population, the increasing complexity of its material culture, the differentiation of burials as social disequalities grew, and, not least, in the increasing dependence on agriculture and the rapid expansion and improvement thereof (Bray 1984; Chang 1977a). Advanced and diverse tools of polished stone were used in farming: mattocks, reaping knives (often small and semilunar like the metal rice-reapers of modern Southeast Asia), and tools ancestral to the modern Chinese cleavers, picks, and so forth. Grains abound in archeological sites. Preeminent among these are *Setaria* millet in the north and rice in the south, but trade, and the southward spread of millet, ensured the wide distribution of both grains. Rice was farmed from Taiwan to central India before 2500 B.C. Rice grown on dry, unirrigated ground, as it is today in the mountains of Southeast Asia, requires about 80 inches of rainfall well distributed over its growing season. Since by 2500 and even as early as 3000 B.C. rice was cultivated well outside regions with such high levels of precipitation, it must have been wet-grown, either by irrigation or in managed wet areas. Rice flourishes best in areas that are inundated and then dry off as the grain matures (the grain rots if it falls into standing water), so the earliest irrigation of rice was surely accomplished by digging ditches to enlarge seasonally inundated small water meadows and sloughs where rice grows naturally. The old theory that rice was once a "weed in taro fields" is unlikely to be true. It grows poorly in permanently wet fields, where it is choked out by taller and more aggressive plants, including taro, a ferocious weed in modern rice fields.

Water buffaloes, apparently domesticated, appeared by 2500 B.C. One famous site has produced such bizarre seeds as melon, sesame, broad bean, and peanut, leading to some highly irresponsible claims about their presence in ancient China. However, the first three are known to have been historic introductions from the Near East (Laufer 1919) and the fourth is a South American plant introduced into China in the late sixteenth or early seventeenth century.

Life in Neolithic China must have been very much like that in the non-state cultures of modern Southeast Asia. Warlike headhunters and intensive cultivators, brilliant artists and choreographers of ritual, but without formalized government or writing, these people persist from India and Burma far out into Indonesia and in isolated parts of Taiwan. Smaller and weaker groups, who cannot increase their wealth by means of warfare, are forced to farm more intensively and trade actively. Universal in the region is a pattern of leadership in which the most able settler of disputes and arranger of social affairs acquires much prestige and often wealth, validates his status by giving merit feasts, and eventually becomes the node of a redistributive system. He organizes feasts and festivals for which others offer goods to be eaten or handed out. (These merit feasts can be much like American Indian potlatches.) The local leader in Chinese society today arises and increases his power by the use of the same skills—he is an arbiter and the organizer of festivities. The men found with so many grave goods in the richer late Neolithic burials surely did likewise; they were probably senior men in patrilineal groups. Of course a pattern of warfare, trade, and redistribution provides a powerful stimulus for agricultural intensification.

It is possible that the Neolithic North Chinese were matrilineal and "matriarchal," however that oft-misused term is understood. Many archeologists in contemporary China support this position, because it fits the evolutionary scheme supported by Marx and Engels. Scholars outside China usually disagree. In fact there is absolutely no evidence either way. Early Neolithic graves suggest an egalitarian society. Individuals were buried separately (or in small same-sex groups) with a few grave goods. The Pawnee Indians of North America, a matrilineal group (Weltfish 1965), lived a life rather like that suggested by the archeological remains at Pan-p'o, but many of their neighbors, such as the Omaha, were patrilineal.

There is little doubt that at least some of the Neolithic peoples, most likely those in the Wei and Yellow river valleys and the North China Plain, spoke languages ancestral to the Sino-Tibetan phylum. South China was presumably inhabited by speakers of ancestral Thai-Kadai languages (Benedict 1942), as well as the ancestors of the Yao, the Hmong (Miao) and perhaps some of the Austronesian peoples. Along what is now the north border of China, Altaic speakers must have differentiated into ancestors of today's Mongols, Turkish, Tungus, Koreans, and Japanese. In ancient times, the Chinese were only one among many peoples, not the dominant majority that they are in the region today. Anyone looking at the area in 3000 B.C. might have picked the Thai, Miao, Yao, or some other group as the people "most likely to succeed." (There were, of course, no self-conscious nationalities at that time; the defensive arrangements and other archeological findings show that every village or group of villages was an independent polity.) Progress in prehistoric China seems to have been a matter of many small inventions by peoples of many linguistic backgrounds in many areas of East Asia. Archeology is revealing to an increasing degree that important innovations and developments were made widely in China and that local traditions progressed in roughly parallel step, everyone borrowing from everyone else to produce the similarities that define what Chang has called the "Lungshanoid horizon" (Chang 1977a).

Agriculture spread to Manchuria by perhaps 3500 B.C. and a millennium later gray cord-marked pottery extended all across Siberia from Manchuria to Europe. By the late Neolithic, agriculture and stock-breeding flourished in west China, notably in the Ch'i-chia culture, with its sophisticated gray pottery and focus on animal rearing. By then, agriculture must have extended from China to the Near East in a solid line. The abundance of cattle and horses in China attests to this, as does the occurrence of cultivated millets in the western world. Wheat and barley, unknown in the Chinese Neolithic sites but well established at the dawn of history, must have come in about this time. They had been established in Afghanistan and neighboring areas on or near China's frontier about 5000 B.C. and must have been at least occasionally introduced into China far back in the Neolithic. (There is wheat in a Lungshan site, but it is in a jar dating from the historic period, buried intrusively there; Ho 1975:73.) Wheat and barley are adapted to winter-rainfall climates, and the nearly rainless belt across far western China evidently slowed their spread; to the Chinese they must have seemed inferior to the millets, adapted to the hot, rainy summers of the area. Wheat and barley thus became popular only when they reached areas with good moisture even in winter. Later, water-conserving techniques were used to grow them, and the Chinese decided to grow both winter and summer crops, rotating winter wheat and barley with summer millets and buckwheat, and much more recently with sorghum and maize. The development of the skills and techniques necessary to implement this cycle, and of crop strains adapted to it, must have taken a long time; only a high population density would have made so much effort worthwhile. Indeed, wheat and barley may have been unimportant until taxes and levies forced people to increase their agricultural yields. Thus we cannot reason from the absence of wheat and barley in Neolithic sites that they were unknown; they may have been known as rare imports or curiosities but rejected as crops.

In the south, the Lungshanoid cultures grade into the vast undifferentiated mass of archeological material known as Hoabinhian. Hoa Binh is a site in Vietnam that gave its name to the entire Mesolithic and early Neolithic tradition in Southeast Asia, encompassing ten thousand years of progress in an area of several hundred thousand square miles.

Population increase was obviously important in this period, yet why did it occur? If it was a natural response to agriculture, why did it not center in the south, where rice and root crops provided a far more productive and secure base than did millets in the dry north? Population increase must have been more the result than the cause of growing cultural complexity in the core region. It seems to have led to increasing dependence on agriculture via the depletion of game and game habitats and the availability of more labor for farm work, but population increase itself must be explained, given the well-known tendency of simple agricultural societies to limit their populations. Lungshan populations were much smaller than their agriculture could support; China in the twentieth century still depends on much the same crops in an agricultural system often called (if not very accurately) Neolithic, and there is little question that the Lungshanians could have sustained more people than they did. Population increase explains little in this case.

A possible scenario for population increase assumes an existing pattern of conflict, which intensified with rising production and—in a word—greed. People wanted more and were willing to raid as well as trade: as Sahlins (1972) reminds us, robbery is nothing but a limiting case of trade, in which the payment is particularly low—that is, nonexistent. Increasingly complex production and increasingly serious warfare led to a greater need for social control. The gap between powerful and weak members of society widened. The powerful figures of the village might have been the military leaders, the most successful social arbiters, or the rich. Those who gained power by one means bolstered it with others: rich people strove for political success, politicians strove for wealth, and so on. I suspect that in an expanding economy, with many opportunities to increase wealth, it is the rich who take power and then move to consolidate their political hold. In a static economy, good talkers and managers—politicians and statesmen—take power and then strengthen it by acquiring wealth. In a situation of war, military leaders take over and acquire both political and economical power. Probably all of these routes to success were taken in the Lungshan villages; in each community, power seekers likely followed complex patterns, simultaneously employing various strategies. The net result was increasing stratification of society as a by-product of increasing economic activity.

With the growing concentration of power, the egalitarian village community, in which everyone had equal access to communally owned means of production, became a thing of the past. With it went many of the factors that hold down population. No longer did people feel so thoroughly in control of their situation. No longer could they get by with small households poor in labor power. More labor and production was needed, and the only way to get it was to increase the family's labor force. Thus began the vicious circle of China's economic history: advances in food production led to population growth; growing population created demand for more food and thus for agricultural intensification. After the state appeared, taxes and imposts made it still more difficult for the peasants to survive. They could not save wealth; they could only invest in children, to work with them and to support them in old age.

The Shang Civilization

Civilization began in the Near East by 3000 B.C., in China before 2000 B.C. The earliest well-known Chinese civilization was that of the Shang Dynasty, traditionally dated 1766–1122 B.C., now believed by most scholars to have been somewhat later;

presently proposed dates vary between the traditional ones and about 1500–1000 B.C. Before the Shang was the shadowy Hsia Dynasty, traditionally dated from the 2200s B.C. Until recently this dynasty was considered mythical, but several cities or large towns from that period, in the area that later became Shang, have been found, along with a goodly number of beautiful bronze vessels. So a Bronze Age civilization did flourish in central North China, and it is duly designated Hsia. (On the dawn of Chinese civilization, see Barnard 1972; Chang 1986, 1977b, 1979, 1983; Cheng 1960; Keightley 1978, 1983; Li 1977; Wheatley 1971; Willets 1965.)

A far more surprising find has recently been made in southern Manchuria. Here, large settlements, sizable temples, diverse and excellent art, and advanced jade carvings indicate that the Hungshan culture was a nascent civilization even earlier than Hsia (Fang and Wei 1986; Guo 1986; Sun and Guo 1986). Materials there take us back to 3500 B.C. and earlier; the beginnings of the large settlements may have been before 3000 B.C., as early as the Mesopotamian city-states (which were, however, more advanced at that time). This culture flourished in an area historically occupied by Altaic speakers (Tungus, Korean, and others), and it appears non-Chinese to my eyes—certainly different from—but in contact with—the Yang-shao and Lungshan cultures of central North China that led to Hsia. Finds of large towns in the Lungshan area, however, indicate that Hungshan was not unique, and that we still have much to learn about the dawn of civilization in China.

We have no recorded history or long written works dating from the Shang, but we do have vast masses of documents, most of them the famous oracle inscriptions on scapulas and tortoise or turtle shells. Predicting the future in Shang, as in some places almost to this day, was done by heating these objects until they cracked and reading prophecies from the cracks. Since the questions and answers were inscribed on the bones and shells in sophisticated writing that is now decipherable, we have excellent records of some aspects of life in Shang, especially the chief concerns of the royal court. Among these concerns hunting and astronomy figured notably.

The Shang civilization created splendid artworks, especially cast bronzes, and built large cities. It occupied the heartland of China, from the middle Yellow River north almost to Peking, east into Shantung, and south into Kiangsi. The area actually ruled by the Shang Dynasty was probably that of the richest finds and largest cities: the pivotally important triangle of lowland that extends up the Yellow River from the North China Plain to the area just northwest of Loyang. This region centers on the great historic cities of Loyang and Chengchou. An early Shang capital has been found near the former, and the latter in fact rests on a Shang capital (possibly Ao, occupied in the middle period of the dynasty), which underlies a startlingly large area of modern Chengchou, including Jen-min Park and the central market areas. In the market, one can still find many brittle, gritty, ash-glazed pottery kettles virtually identical in every respect to those of Shang. They are still common and ordinary pieces of kitchenware, so ideally suited to local cooking that they need no improvement. The Shang capital migrated north to Hsiao-t'un near Anyang—here the dynasty built its final and most splendid city, Yin. The outlying areas of civilization, from Hopei to Shantung to Kiangsi, are culturally distinct enough to imply other dynasties' local reigns (Chang 1979).

Shang civilization depended on many varieties of foxtail and panic millets and on rice, wheat, and barley. There is some slight evidence for double-cropping, presumably of the millets, as the long growing season of primitive varieties of rice would not have permitted it. During Shang, China was warmer and moister than it is now; elephants, tapirs, rhinoceri, and other tropical and subtropical fauna flourished in the central plains. The climatic difference, however, was not great enough to allow rice to grow outside swamps or irrigated areas. The region receives 20–50 inches of rain per year today, the core around the Yellow River 20–30 inches; dry rice requires about 80 inches or more per growing season. Obviously even double the rainfall would not permit it to flourish, and the area did not receive that much rain during Shang. There is some evidence for irrigation in the Shang period; there was also no shortage of riverine lagoons that would have been ideal for broadcast rice. Very likely a range of techniques was used, from simple broadcast seeding of natural sumps through cultivation of water meadows to actual irrigation of prepared paddies. The one thing certain is that the frequent textbook allusions to dry rice growing in Shang are wrong.

Aside from the grains, we also know of meat in the Shang diet. In addition to the pigs, dogs, chickens, sheep, goats, cattle, and horses already available, water buffaloes (believed to be a local species, now extinct) came into domestication. *Elaphurus* (Pere David's Deer) bones are so common as to suggest taming of this animal as well (Li 1977). Hunting was practiced on a vast scale, netting every sort of game from elephants and rhinoceri to rabbits and deer. Fish and turtles of every sort were eaten. Presumably the sacrificial animals that gave up their shoulderblades and shells wound up in the stew pot. Trade brought some exotic artifacts to the area; central China was scoured for turtles, and some species found originated from South China. Marine shells and whale bones indicate trade with people on the coast.

One must assume that vegetable foods were equally diverse and eclectic, but vegetable remains from Shang sites have been very incompletely analyzed and published. The vegetable materials from Yin were destroyed in World War II before they had been analyzed (Li 1977). Early Chou literary remains demonstrate the broad familiarity with vegetal foods that we would expect from the Shang people, and probably reflect conditions unchanged from that period. There is need for both archeological studies and up-to-date analyses of the oracle bone inscriptions. The inscriptions mention wheat (*mai*; probably the character also referred to barley) and millets (*shu* and *su*), rice, fodder, and a few important food trees: chestnut, mulberry (primarily used for silk production), apricot, and jujube. The characters for fruit (*kuo*) and for plucking (*ts'ai*) were established (Gibson 1937). All these characters were recognizably pictographic in Shang script. The mentions of the apricot tree are puzzling: the domesticated apricot is generally thought to be a native of West and Central Asia, while China has its own apricot species, the *mei* (*Prunus mume*, usually mistranslated "plum"). But the mei does not appear in the Shang script, while the apricot does. Sorghum was not mentioned in the inscriptions, despite a few publications to the contrary (Anderson and Buell MS; Hagerty 1940).

We have a quantity of food and drink vessels dating from the Shang Dynasty, the magisterial review of which by Barnard and Tamotsu (1975) has yet to be superseded (see also Chang 1979). They concluded that bronze was invented in the Shang Dynasty heartland independently from the earlier invention of the alloy in the Near East.

The chief conclusions about food that emerge from studying the types and quantities of pottery and bronze vessels are: (1) Food preparation and service was ritualized, regulated, and complex. (2) The rituals were a matter of enormous importance; the welfare of the entire civilization was evidently thought to depend on the sacrifices and other rituals being performed correctly, which meant above all the right arrangement of vessels and food. Modern Chinese worship rites (*paipai*) continue this tradition but are evidently less elaborate than the Shang rituals. (3) Ale was central to the Shang. (*Chiu*—"alcoholic liquid" in modern Chinese—meant ale or beer in early historic times, not wine as usually translated.) They had a reputation as heavy drinkers, and according to the Book of History their Chou successors made a number of laws against heavy drinking specifically to protect their own dynasty from going the way of Shang, whose overthrow they attributed to its alcoholic excesses. This story is supported by the quantity of huge drinking vessels that survive. Legend claimed that the last pre-Shang ruler had "a lake of beer and a forest of meat"—the latter interpreted as a forest hung with drying meat strips.

Food seems to have been divided into *fan*, "grain foods," and *ts'ai*, "dishes"; presumably there was an additional category of snacks (Chang 1977b, esp. pp. 23-51). The *fan*, typically a thick porridge, was boiled or steamed; the *ts'ai* were usually rich stews. Roasted and grilled meat was probably also common. In addition to food crops, hemp and silk were important as fiber; probably other fiber plants were grown as well, since we know of several in the following dynasty.

Shang farming technology was not significantly different from that of the late Neolithic. In spite of the onset of the Bronze Age, which brought a dramatic increase in the size and sophistication of the metal inventory, farm tools were still made of stone, bone, and wood and were confined to simple digging sticks, reaping knives, hoes, spades, sickles, mortars and pestles, and the like. Large digging sticks may have been dragged, serving as primitive plows. Fishhooks, nets, and stone arrowheads—the rich had bronze ones—were also part of the food acquisition system. Irrigation seems indicated by extensive ditches—even if the ones at Hsiao-t'un were moats, they imply thorough knowledge of the technique of leading water by trenching. The presence of rice as a major crop implies water control, and small-scale local irrigation is probable, given the splendor and urban focus of Shang civilization, but we have no good evidence of it. Large-scale irrigation works were apparently absent. The Bronze Age civilization of China was thus based on a quite simple technology, and one not significantly changed from that of previous centuries.

According to Karl Wittfogel (1957) the centralized bureaucratic state system characteristic of China and much of Asia—in which the state, headed by a single imperial person, owned and disposed of land—was maintained by, and to a great degree was a product of, central control of irrigation, brought about by the need to construct huge-scale irrigation works. But this hypothesis has fared poorly (Chang 1979; Eberhard 1977; Wheatley 1971). The consensus among contemporary scholars is that in the Old World control over irrigation was usually decentralized, that the state was well established before the rise of large-scale irrigation systems, and that irrigation agriculture had little or nothing to do with the development of highly centralized government. Wittfogel's hypothesis is clearly untenable for China. The Shang civilization does not seem to have had large irrigation works, which are not found in China until the third or fourth century B.C.; previous works were not much bigger than the irrigation systems of several native North American cultures, such as that of the Owens Valley Paiute, who lacked not only states but even domesticated plants (Lawton et al. 1976).

On the other hand, the high productivity of traditional agriculture certainly played an enabling role in the rise of the state. We are far beyond the naive belief that people first generate a "surplus" and then invent cities and elites to use it up. Rarely do people produce a lot of food (or other material) that they have no plans for using, and if they did, they would certainly think of more immediately gratifying uses than support of the tax collectors, armies, and predatory lords that represented the state to Chinese peasants throughout history. Yet, obviously, no such features of society could arise unless the agricultural system had the potential to support them. This potential was clearly translated into reality when political conditions demanded.

The importance of trade in the Shang civilization is discussed by Chang (1975), who argues that trade was much more important than most authors have implied. The flow of tortoise shells to the Shang capitols, the presence there of whale bones and other exotica, and the wideflung cultural similarities throughout China during Shang times all indicate broad, important economic contact. Most trade was with other relatively advanced societies. A glance at any map shows how natural a focus for trade is the middle Yellow River. Rice and salt were extensively traded. Increasing agricultural activity no doubt led to a greater demand for salt, which by Shang times was already vital for preserving foods. The well-known significance of "salt and iron" as trade items in later times must have been foreshadowed to some extent by the importance during Shang of salt and ores.

It is perhaps worth mentioning that Shang influence did not extend directly to the New World. Similarities between Shang and American Indian cultures are due to indirect contacts via the Bering Strait, or simply to independent development. The importance of jade in Shang and the contemporary Olmec civilization, for instance, is due not to mutual influence but to the fact that jade is a hard, tough, beautiful stone, valued in all cultures that know it. Alleged similarities in art styles are too vague to be credible. No food plants crossed the Pacific, as they would surely have done if contact sufficient to spread art styles had been maintained. Direct Chinese contact with the New World had to await European voyagers in the fifteenth century.

Meanwhile, with the rise of civilization, the whole structure of leadership changed. In an egalitarian society of small communities, the leader is usually either the head of a kinship group or the best arbiter—preeminently a political figure. But as material wealth increases, specialization arises, and trade intensifies, possession of wealth becomes more important. In a static economy, especially in a small society, leadership goes to the person who can best dispose of wealth—typically in great redistributive feasts or other deeds of magnanimity and generosity.

Kings seem to have arisen from the late Neolithic lineage structure. They were the senior men of the most powerful lineage—or pair of lineages, since a dualistic organization with two intermarrying lineages or lineage segments appears to have dominated the Shang dynasty (Chang 1979). The kings of Shang and its neighbor states were not mere political figures. They had to organize and keep functioning a complex and very active economy and for this they needed a constant flow of wealth into their coffers—not just foods brought in by free tribesmen as time and opportunity offered, but a reliable influx to support the court, the military, and the religious establishment with its fantastic scale of sacrifices. Thus from simple redistributors, taking in food and giving it out again in roughly equal portions and to roughly the same people who had provided it, kings became administrators, taking wealth from the whole body politic and distributing it to the favored few and their military protection. Taxes and imposts had come to East Asia, along with archives and laws (Posner 1972).

More controversial is the importance of slavery in Shang society. The Communist historians have felt that they must postulate Shang as a slave society, simply because in the Marx–Engels scheme of things slavery is the first stage of labor management in the state (Hsu 1979). In fact there is very little evidence one way or another. What there is seems to suggest that the Shang masses were not as free as birds (or as free as primitive cultivators) but neither were they the chattel slaves of classical Rome or the early American South. They had rights, possessions, and some sort of status as humans. They were *chung*, common people (Li 1977). State and commoners together created a highly distinctive and rather isolated civilization.

3 The Crucial Millennium: Chou through Han

The Chou Dynasty

No difference between late Shang and early Chou agricultural technology or production has been convincingly demonstrated. A Neolithic technology persisted; peasants' tools were almost all made of stone, bone, and wood, and crops consisted of the millets and coarse vegetables of earlier ages. Social organization was apparently still a rather inchoate feudalism. Chang (1977a) has pointed out that increasing social complexity and wealth during this period were not accompanied by much technological progress: wealth was accumulated at the expense of the poor.

Soybeans seem to have been introduced to China by about 1000 B.C., but they were not popularized until the early Eastern Chou period (Ho 1975); they seem to have come from the Jung people, northern and northeastern neighbors of the Chinese, who may have been Tungusic or Altaic and were perhaps related to or descended from the Hungshan. Domestic soybeans, *Glycine max*, are descended from the wild *G. max var. ussuriensis*, native to northeast China from Peking and the hills west and southwest of it up through Manchuria.

Cast iron appeared shortly after Eastern Chou came into being; wrought iron came later (Barnard and Tamotsu 1975). Iron revolutionized farming, although like all true revolutions, this was a slow and gradual process. Well before the end of the Chou Dynasty, iron was widely if sparsely used for farming tools. This new technology had fateful consequences. On the one hand, China's population could expand, given the new productivity incident on superior agricultural tools. On the other hand, the government could control the people far more thoroughly, by controlling the iron trade and equipping mass armies with really deadly weapons. (Bronze was too expensive for widespread use and brittle for tools and weapons, so earlier armies had fought with rather primitive material.)

The creative ferment of the latter half of the Chou Dynasty has left a strong mark on the fields of ethical and political philosophy. Foremost in importance, at least for China's future, was the Confucian school. K'ung Fu Tzu (Latinized as Confucius—*Tzu* means "master"), who lived from 551 to 479 B.C., remains a somewhat shadowy figure. We know him primarily from the Analects, a short collection of anecdotes about him and tag lines attributed to him, not from any coherent work of his. According to unconfirmed tradition, he compiled the Book of History (all we have of a vast and flourishing mythological tradition), the Book of Changes (*I Ching*), the Book of Songs, various books of rites, and the Spring and Autumn Annals of the State of Lu, his home state. The Book of Songs includes over three hundred traditional songs of the Chou Dynasty that make hundreds of references to food items and paint a fairly full picture of the agriculture of the age. The songs seem to have been creations of the peasants but in many cases they were sophisticated by court poets; some were probably court creations modeled after folk forms. They reflect, by and large, the world of the sixth century B.C. and earlier.

Farming seems to have been concentrated in the fertile bottomlands, as earlier, but it was expanding into all habitats. The songs talk of clearing artemisia (mugwort, wormwood, sagebrush), thistles, and other weedy plants more than they talk of woodland, so most of the good farmland must have been cultivated; the peasants usually reclaimed old fallow land rather than clearing virgin soil. Expansion onto the dry uplands probably also occurred, but these lands are most often associated in the songs with fallow-land weeds. The songs often contrast towns and croplands and *shan* and *tse*. Usually translated "mountains and marshes," these terms evidently mean something more like "wild uplands and wild bottomlands"—Derk Bodde (1981) has pointed out that many of the *tse* were dry rather than marshy. The fact that much of this most fertile of all soil types was still wild in the middle Chou indicates relatively little population pressure on the land. A great variety of wildlife still existed there, especially deer (which thrive in fallow land), but hunting was already a sport of the rich rather than a method of subsistence for the poor. Wild animals were still major crop pests, as several of the songs remark. Evidently the land was well peopled, and wild areas were few, but there was nothing like the dense population of Han and later times.

Fiber crops were silk, hemp, and kudzu (Keng 1974; Li 1974). The staple food was unquestionably millet. By now many varieties of both *Setaria* and *Panicum* were cultivated. Some were "glutinous" (sticky). Several, particularly some of the sticky varieties, were used especially for brewing. Other species of millets may also have been grown. Barley and wheat were much less important; but rice was very important—surprising in view of the dry climate of the Chou homeland. Various beans were also considered staples. A wide range of vegetables, fruits, and other plant foods were utilized; many were probably gathered wild.

The Book of Songs mentions at least forty-four definite or probable food plants; the Bible, by contrast, names only twenty-nine. The songs also mention all the common domestic and wild game animals, as well as several species of fish. A connoisseurship of fish, as today, led to preference for fish from certain sources; Chou Hung-Hsiang (pers. comm.) singles out Song 138, in which *fang*-fish (usually translated "bream") and carp from particular rivers are favored.

The following list of definite or probable food plants in the songs is adapted from Hsüan Keng (1974):

Grains

Broomcorn or panic millet *(Panicum miliaceum)*, *shu* and *ch'i*

Barley *(Hordeum vulgare)* and wheat *(Triticum aestivum)*, *mai*. Keng
doubts the presence of wheat but it is now well established for Chou.

Rice *(Oryza sativa)*, *tao*.

Foxtail millet, *(Setaria italica)*, *su* and *liang*.

Vegetables

Kudzu *(Pueraria lobata)*, *ke*. Translated "dolichos" in older literature. True
dolichos may have been present in South China at this time, but it has a
different Chinese name. Keng lists kudzu as a fiber plant, but he points
out that the shoots, leaves, and tuberous roots are edible, and it was unquestionably a food as well. Common people made and wore kudzu-
fiber clothing. Kudzu-fiber shoes are implied by the songs to be of high
quality.

Hemp *(Cannabis sativa)*, *ma*. Also primarily a fiber plant, but the seeds
were eaten. Its use as a drug is not mentioned in the songs but was
known by Han times and probably by Chou as well. It has never been a
significant indulgent in China.

Chinese cabbages *(Brassica spp.)*, *feng*. Keng claims that the turnip *B. rapa*
was the species known; this is surely incorrect. *B. chinensis* in its various
forms, and perhaps other species, were used. The radish *(Raphanus
sativus)* is almost surely implied by some references, although Keng
does not mention it.

Chinese chives *(Allium tuberosum)*, *chiu*. Miscalled leek *A. odorum* by
Keng.

Daylily *(Hemerocallis flava)*, *huan* and *huan-tsao*. The modern daylily, a ge-
netically complex cultigen of obscure origin, may already have been developed by Chou.

Chinese celery *(Oenanthe javanica)*, *ch'in*, possibly also *Cryptotaenia
canadensis*.

Bottle gourd *(Legenaria siceraria)*, *hu*. This was primarily an industrial
plant, as its name implies, but the young fruits were widely eaten.

Melon *(Cucumis melo*, probably var. *conomon)*, *kua*. Other melons were unknown at the time.

Soybean *(Glycine max)*, *shu*.

Lotus *(Nelumbo nucifera)*, *ho*.

Vegetables not certainly mentioned as food plants in the Book of Songs but commonly eaten in later times and almost certainly eaten in Chou:

Yarrow *(Achillea sibirica* and/or *A. millefolium)*, *shih*. Originally medicinal;
this may well have led to its use as an oracle plant. It sank back in later

times to a medicine. The shoots are occasionally used as food, although they were not considered very good.

Mugwort *(Artemisia vulgaris)*, *fan*. Young shoots are eaten. It is used as a flavoring herb today in Korea.

Motherwort *(Leonurus sibiricus)*, *tui*. A very common roadside weed, used as a medicine and regarded as a cure-all to this day.

Mallow *(Malva verticillata)*, *kuei*. Clearly a major food in the Chou; Li (1969) regards this as the most important vegetable in ancient China. Chinese cabbage would have been a strong competitor; contrary to Li's claim, oil is not needed to cook cabbage; it is usually eaten boiled or steamed today.

Huanlan (Metaplexis stauntoni).

Plantain *(Plantago major* var. *asiatica)*, *foúyi*. Another primarily medicinal plant with minor food use in recent times, probably in Chou as well.

Poke *(Phytolacca acinosa* var. *esculenta)*, *fu.*

Huo (Rhynchosia volubilis).

Sow thistle *(Sonchus oleraceus)*, *ch'i*. A weed of fallow land and other cultivated places; very commonly mentioned in this context in the Songs. It was also evidently eaten widely.

Cocklebur *(Xanthium strumarium)*. The young shoots are widely eaten today and no doubt were also eaten in Chou.

Grass-leaved sweetflag *(Acorus gramineus)*, *p'u*. Possibly includes cattail *Typha latifolia*.

Water plantain *(Alisma plantago)*, *hsü.*

Water-shield *(Brasenia schreberi)*, *mao*. Frequently mentioned in Chou texts as a food, especially in the context of a famous delicacy, water-shield stew.

Water fern *(Marsilea quadrifolia)*, *p'ing.*

Floating heart *(Nymphoides peltatum)*, *hsing-ts'ai.*

Elm *(Ulmus* spp.*)*, *yü*. Young leaves, bark, and seeds were eaten in later times and presumably also in Chou.

Bamboo *(Bambusa* spp. and perhaps other genera*)*, *chu*. The shoots are mentioned in the songs as a common and relished food.

Fruits and Nuts

Peach *(Prunus persica)*, *t'ao*. Native to China; other native species presumably used.

Plum *(Prunus salicina)*, *li*. This native Chinese species, different from the European species, is often mentioned in the songs.

Japanese or Oriental apricot, flowering apricot, mume, mei, "plum" *(Prunus mume)*, *mei*. This favorite plant of Chinese artists and poets was an important fruit plant in the songs. Almost invariably mistranslated "plum" or "prune" in Western literature, it is a species of apricot, closely related to the western *P. armeniaca*. Keng thinks the latter (*hsing*) might also have been found in China, but it is not mentioned by name in the songs.

Chinese jujube, "Chinese date" (*Ziziphus jujuba* and *Z. spinosa*), *tsao* and *chi*, respectively. The commonest and most widespread fruit in North China; the commonest woody plant in abandoned fields and other rough, cleared, dry, difficult habitats. An exceedingly popular food from the Neolithic to this day, mentioned in the songs along with other fruits.

Raisintree (*Hovenia dulcis*), *chü*. Cultivated for its fruit clusters. The stems, not the fruit, are eaten; they taste like very good raisins.

Hazelnut (*Corylus heterophylla*), *chen*.

Chinese chestnut (*Castanea mollissima*), *li*. Mentioned in four songs along with other forest or nut trees, in contexts implying it was an important food.

White Mulberry (*Morus alba*), *sang*. Primarily used for raising silkworms, but the fruits were also evidently eaten.

Pine (*Pinus* spp.), *sung*. Mentioned as a forest tree; the nuts were presumably eaten.

Oak (*Quercus* spp.), *li*. Also a forest tree whose seeds were eaten.

Brown pepper, Chinese prickly-ash (*Zanthoxylum piperitum* and also *Z. simulans* and others), *chiao*. The chief spice mentioned in the songs, evidently very widely used for spicing food, perfuming households, and so on. The fruits look like brown peppercorns but the plant is unrelated to either black or red peppers. It appears in songs primarily in metaphoric context: the small fruits grow twinned on a short stalk, the whole looking like miniature male genitalia; thus it is the standard trope for the male organs in the songs and other early Chinese poetry. (The double meaning of "spicy" may be known worldwide.)

Quince, Chinese (*Chaenomeles japonica*), *mükua*.

The anonymous authors of the Songs were good ecologists, noting such things as the wasps catching caterpillars to feed their larvae and the connection of heavy dewfall and luxuriant artemisia growth (song 173; I assume this is one of the species that can absorb dew, as those in southern California). They were also supreme poets. The spectacular and rich ecological tapestry in the songs is rhetorical. In the songs we have the first known example of quatrains with four-stress lines, the first two lines describing some biological phenomenon (usually botanical), the second two paralleling it with some powerful emotional concern of the poet, usually romantic and frequently erotic. Granet (1930, 1932) has convincingly argued that this form originated in the festivals of marriageable young people: the girls teased the boys with qua-

trains, the boys responded with their own. This custom—quatrains and all—
persists in contemporary South China and Southeast Asia. It survives among
the remote and conservative Hakka people, whose "mountain songs" (*shan ko*) are all
of this style. It also exists among the Vietnamese, and among the Malays now in a
form modified by puritanical Islam, the *pantun*.

Among the longer songs are odes that embody origin myths. One of these tells
the story of Prince Millet, founder of the Chou lineage. Not only did he send "the
fine cereals . . . black millet, doublekernelled black millet, millet with red sprouts,
with white sprouts" (Karlgren 1950:201), he also brought soybeans. This indicates
that soybeans were so ancient by middle Chou as to be embodied in origin myths;
very early Chou seems the latest possible time for their introduction. A number of
these longer songs speak of drought as the worst of catastrophes. In song 265, a "la-
ment for our times" of the sort found in the literature of all ages, the rapacity of the
elite is compared to drought.

A number of plants are paired in the songs, coupled in parallel lines or listed together in one line: bamboo and pine, kudzu and lien creeper, wheat and barley (this
is significant, as they were the winter-grown, alien grains), millet and rice (the
summer-grown natives), jujube and mei (both thorny upland fruit trees—each of
these is also paired with mulberry), hare and pheasant, and so on. Other materials
and non–food plants are also paired, for example, metals and jade, poplar and wil-
low. Trees such as oak, pine, and chestnut are often mentioned in connection with
mountain areas. The plant most often mentioned in the songs is artemisia. Many different varieties are named; evidently this genus was eminent ecologically as well as
poetically, an impression confirmed by pollen studies of Neolithic and early dynastic
China (Ho 1975, Tuan 1969).

In the two and a half centuries after Confucius, many other schools of philosophy
arose, presenting a variety of ethical and logical systems, all contending for the ap-
proval of rulers and use in government and politics. All early Chinese philosophy
was, ultimately, political philosophy: its goal was to produce and maintain a well-run
state with what the Mohist sages, like modern economists, described as maximum
benefit and minimal harm to the people. The disciples of the Confucian school faced
challenges that had not occurred to their teacher: they had to build a coherent system
and defend it against sharp attacks. The most formidable contender from among the
so-called "hundred schools" was Legalism, which argued for strong rule by law and
an active policy of agricultural development.

Other challengers included mysticism, which in the early Chinese context assimilated to philosophical Taoism, rather ascetic in its approach to food. Fine eating and
fancy technology are condemned in the *Tao Te Ching* (of unknown authorship) and
the *Chuang Tzu* (written by Chuang Chou in the third or fourth century B.C.; there
have been many later additions). (Giles 1926; Graham 1981; Waley 1939, 1958). A considerable body of Chou literature has been lost; some survives as later increments to

the *Chuang Tzu*, some in the Han Dynasty compilation Lieh Tzu (Graham 1960). Meanwhile, Mo Ti taught universal love and Yang Chu taught egotism; Mo tended toward extreme austerity regarding food, Yang toward hedonism. Chou science included a medical and nutritional component; this and its folk manifestations were to have a profound effect on food in China—as profound, I believe, as a belief system has ever had on a culture's foodways. But these posed no direct threat to the Confucian system; rather, they were complementary.

Significantly, all the schools discussed agriculture, food, and food policy. Agriculture was considered the most important work of the state and its citizens. Famine and war meant that food was a central concern of all. More than that, however, gourmetship was a part of life, even for the peasants: the songs contrast the ale, good grain, and meat of feast days with the coarse foods ordinarily eaten. The elite, of course, had long loved fine food. In the West, puritanical tradition has greatly interfered with enjoyment of food as well as other pleasures of the body. It is not clear why such an ideology did not take hold in China, given Taoist and Mohist calls for simplicity.

Among Confucians, Mencius is most famous for teaching the essential goodness of human nature; he argued that people naturally have good instincts (Lau 1970). His chief opponents in his own time were the Taoists, who taught that good and evil are human-imposed categories and thus do not refer to anything basic, and that humans are too malleable to have a specific nature. Later, Hsün Tzu argued that human nature is evil, with greed and selfishness at its core. *Good* and *evil* in the context of late Chou morality corresponded roughly to *altruism* and *selfishness*: the good person worked to help others, whether from spontaneous human decency (as Mencius argued) or from enlightened self-interest or good education, while the evil person followed something like the modern creed of "do unto others before they do unto you." Pursuit of one's own benefit or profit (*li*) was evil; pursuit of benefit for others was good. This implies a widely shared view that the world was a zero-sum game, an "image of limited good" found often in modern China and in many other peasant societies (Foster 1965). Indeed, life for people in feudal societies does normally follow such a pattern. Mencius describes the good ruler as one who is good to his subjects, which at first involves self-sacrifice (e.g., remittance of taxes that could be spent on luxuries) but later pays off in the prosperity and strength of the state and the consequent increase in its and its ruler's wealth and security. But Mencius stresses that one should not be good just for reward or expect a reward for being good. The true Confucian heroes are those who gave their lives for the sake of a principle.

Like other Confucians, and indeed like most Chinese philosophers of his time (notably the Legalists), Mencius took agriculture to be the basic industry, ranking crafts, manufacturing, and trade lower. In this he was followed by China's rulers and elites in all ages. This did not mean that peasants had high prestige; they suffered the mixture of scorn and grudging respect that has been the farmers' lot in many cultures. But the state accorded high priority to agriculture because of Confucian teachings.

The first passage in Mencius' book makes his basic point: consider how to be good, not how to get profit—even your state's profit. Goodness is summed up by *jen* and *li*: benevolence and righteousness. Steadfastness and responsibility, altruism and mutual aid are implied in these words. Mencius immediately goes on to note that only a person with clean conscience can really enjoy the deer, fish, and turtles in his parks, or have them in abundance. Then follows one of the most astonishing passages in all philosophical literature, in which Mencius launches a direct frontal attack on the policies of the sovereign he is serving. His explicit language must have risked his life. The passage is crucial for an understanding of China's food policy then and since:

If you do not interfere with the busy season in the fields, then there will be more grain than the people can eat; if you do not allow nets with too fine a mesh to be used in large ponds, then there will be more fish and turtles than they can eat; if hatchets and axes are permitted in the forests on the hills only in the proper seasons, then there will be more timber than they can use. When the people have more grain, more fish and turtles than they can eat, and more timber than they can use, then in the support of their parents when alive and in the mourning of them when dead, they will be able to have no regrets over anything left undone. This is the first step along the Kingly way.

If the mulberry is planted in every homestead of five mu of land, then those who are fifty can wear silk; if chickens, pigs and dogs do not miss their breeding season, then those who are seventy can eat meat; if each lot of a hundred mu is not deprived of labour during the busy seasons, then families with several mouths to feed will not go hungry. Exercise due care over the education provided by the village schools, and discipline the people by teaching them the duties proper to sons and younger brothers, and those whose heads have turned grey will not be carrying loads on the roads. When those who are seventy wear silk and eat meat and the masses are neither cold nor hungry, it is impossible for their prince not to be a true King.

Now when food meant for human beings is so plentiful as to be thrown to dogs and pigs, you fail to realize that it is time for garnering, and when men drop dead from starvation by the way-side, you fail to realize that it is time for distribution. When people die, you simply say, "It is none of my doing. It is the fault of the harvest." In what way is that different from killing a man by running him through, while saying all the time, "It is none of my doing. It is the fault of the weapon." Stop putting the blame on the harvest and the people of the whole Empire will come to you. (Lau 1970:51–52)

One theme that emerges from these paragraphs is resource conservation: Mencius was a conservationist like Confucius, but a far more systematic one. His famous simile for human nature is Ox Mountain, once verdant and lush with forest, but then stripped by firewood cutters and overgrazed, and now an eroded waste. Similarly, a bad person is only a good one managed unwisely. In Mencius' view, conservation is desirable but should not be pushed too far, nor should agricultural modernization. He scathingly criticizes kings who punish poaching as seriously as murder (Lau 1970:61–62) and those who develop agriculture purely to enrich the state rather than to help the people (Lau 1970:124)—the slap is at the Legalists as well as at Confucians gone wrong. It is all right for the king to have hunting parks, but the people should be able to get some wood and game there. As for food, Mencius points out, "in governing the Empire, the sage tries to make food as plentiful as water and fire. When that happens, how can there be any amongst his people who are not benevolent?" (Lau 1970:187). Mencius is not just saying that well-fed people are better behaved—his main point is that they have the sage/ruler's good example. Nothing was more important in Confucian statecraft than the concept that the ruler sets the standard for his people to follow.

Mencius' interest in food continually comes through in his work. Probably his most famous line reads, "fish is what I want; bear's palm is also what I want. If I cannot have both, I would rather take bear's palm than fish. Life is what I want; dutifulness is also what I want. If I cannot have both, I would rather take dutifulness than life" (Lau 1970:166). In the same passage, he says, "here is a basketful of rice and a bowlful of soup. Getting them will mean life; not getting them will mean death. When these are given with abuse, even a wayfarer will not accept them; when these are given after being trampled upon, even a beggar would not accept them." He goes on to say how much more surely he would refuse an unworthy offer of high position.

The Confucian answer to incipient puritanism is found in the *Li Chi*. This enormous and heterogeneous work was almost lost in the Burning of the Books that occurred during the Ch'in Dynasty. Texts found in fragmentary state in Han times were reconstructed as well as possible. My nonscholarly impression is that the Han editors did a fine job—an honest one, with minimal "fixing up," and that retained some of the arrangement, though many commentaries are now taken as part of the text. The *Chou Li* and the *Li Chi*, as well as the Book of Songs, tell us much about Chou Dynasty feasts and sacrifices. Sacrifices were chickens, pigs, dogs, sheep, and oxen, in descending order of abundance; fish, especially fine fat carp; vegetables, both fresh and pickled; grain, specifically the finer kinds of millet; and ale, again the finer grades. Dogs were a common and highly favored food at this time. (At present, dogs are no longer eaten in North China and only rarely in the south.)

Sacrificial rites are described in the *Li Chi*, including the foods used and offered (Legge 1967:459–464 lists almost all the foods used in Chou, although "maize" in that list is a mistranslation for a variety of millet). Agricultural and conservation activities are prescribed for the ruler to order and oversee. Warring States and Han philosophers editing the sections of the *Li Chi* dealing with rituals were under pressure from Taoists, Mohists, Legalists, and others to justify their practices in practical, realistic terms. Their first and most important justification was conservation, which we have met already in the writings of Confucius and Mencius. Rituals and other usages of food were intended to preserve the food supply and regulate its distribution, particularly wild animals and fish, the stocks of which were being rapidly depleted in Chou while the population was growing. The ruler and the court gentlemen were admonished to be careful with the supplies.

The ruler of a state, in the spring hunting, will not surround a marshy thicket, nor will Great officers try to surprise a whole herd, nor will (other) officers take young animals or eggs. In bad years, when the grain of the season is not coming to maturity, the ruler at his meals will not make the (usual) offering of the lungs, nor will his horses be fed on grain. His special road will not be kept clean and swept, nor even at sacrifices will his musical instruments be suspended on their stands. Great officers will not eat the large grained millet. (Legge 1967:1:106)

To hunt without observing the rules (for hunting) was deemed cruelty to the creatures of Heaven.

The son of Heaven did not entirely surround (the hunting ground); and a feudal prince did not take a (whole) herd by surprise. (220–21)

The prescribed activities for the months include taboos on destructive activities. In the first month, "nests should not be thrown down; unformed insects should not be killed, nor creatures in the womb, nor very young creatures, nor birds just taking to the wing, nor fawns, nor should eggs be destroyed" (256). Failing to observe these and the other seasonal recommendations not only wasted game but also disrupted cosmic harmony and order:

If in the first month of spring the governmental proceedings proper to summer were carried out, the rain would fall unseasonably, plants and trees would decay prematurely, and the states would be kept in continual fear. If the proceedings proper to autumn were carried out, there would be great pestilence among the people; boisterous winds would work their violence; rain would descend in torrents; orach, fescue, darnel, and southernwood would grow up together. If the proceedings proper to winter were carried out, pools of water would produce their destructive effects, snow and frost would prove very injurious, and the first sown seeds would not enter the ground. (257)

A materialist theory of social evolution lies behind much of the *Li Chi*:

In all their settlements, the bodily capacities of the people are sure to be according to the sky and earthly influences, as cold or hot, dry or moist. Where the valleys are wide and the rivers large, the ground was differently

laid out; and the people born in them had different customs. Their temper-
aments, as hard or soft, light or grave, slow or rapid, were made uniform
by different measures; their preferences as to flavours were differently
harmonised. . . .

The people of those five regions—the Middle states, and the Zung, Mi,
(and other wild tribes round them)—had all their several natures, which
they could not be made to alter. The tribes on the east were called I. They
had their hair unbound, and tattooed their bodies. Some of them ate their
food without its being cooked. (228–29)

Other barbarians too ate uncooked food or did not have grain staples. We need not
believe the ethnography here. What is important is that environmental influence on
culture is postulated and differences in foodways recognized. The evolution of rituals
is also covered in the *Li Chi*:

At the first use of ceremonies, they began with meat and drink. They
roasted millet and pork; they excavated the ground in the form of a jar, and
scooped the water from it with their two hands; they fashioned a handle of
clay, and struck with it an earthen drum. (Simple as these arrangements
were), they yet seemed to be able to express by them their reverence for
Spiritual Beings.

(By and by), when one died, they went upon the housetop, and called
out his name in a prolonged note, saying "Come back, So and So." After
this they filled the mouth (of the dead) with uncooked rice, and (set forth
as offerings to him) packets of raw flesh. (368–69).

The above quote describing the origins of rituals is attributed to Confucius. The *Li
Chi* continues discussing the origin of society:

"Formerly the ancient kings had no houses. In winter they lived in caves
which they had excavated, and in summer in nests which they had framed.
They knew not yet the transforming power of fire, but ate the fruits of
plants and trees, and the flesh of birds and beasts, drinking their blood and
swallowing . . . the hair and feathers. They knew not yet the use of flax and
silk, but clothed themselves with feathers and skins.

"The later sages then arose, and men (learned) to take advantage of the
benefits of fire. . . . They toasted, grilled, boiled, and roasted. They produced must and sauces. . . . They were thus able to nourish the living, and
to make offerings to the dead; to serve the spirits of the departed and
God."

In all these things we follow the example of that early time.

"Thus it is that the dark-colored liquor is in the apartment (where the
representative of the dead is entertained); that the vessel of must is near its

(entrance) door; that the reddish liquor is in the hall; and the clear, in the (court) below." (369–70)

The *Li Chi* goes on to describe the origins of other sacrificial rituals. (Sometimes the relation between the origin and the current ritual is unclear; this is probably due to text corruption and poor translation rather than to lack of clarity in the original.) Note, however, that the description of social evolution is clearly pure speculation, not a true report of ancient times, as some naive scholars have considered it.

The other great class of functional explanations for ritual includes the theory that the purpose of ritual is to express, inculcate, and (in general) communicate the social order or important components thereof, and to tell people how and when to do things. Durkheim's (1961) concept of ritual as an expression of the group's solidarity, and the idea of ritual as a communication system conveying information about the economy and society, are parts of this view. The authors of the *Li Chi* were aware of this function of ritual, and in this passage they explain some of the symbolism of the rituals. Those who originated the ceremonies did so to make "a distinction for nearer and more distant kinship, and for ancestors the remote and the recent, and teaching the people to go back to their oldest fathers, and retrace their beginnings, not forgetting those to whom they owed their being" (2:221). At appropriate seasons, in rituals continued right up to the end of the Chinese Empire in 1911, the emperor performed token plowing and the empress silkworm care. The *Li Chi* explains, "the son of Heaven himself guided the plough. . . . The prince of the states guided the plough . . . not because the son of Heaven and the princes had not men to plough for them, or because the queen and the princes' wives had not women to tend silkworms for them; it was to give the exhibition of their personal sincerity. Such sincerity was what is called doing their utmost" (2:238). The rites were thus intended to convey to the populace the fact that the rulers took these activities as basic. They also conveyed, expressed, or communicated the social hierarchy.

The mysterious Book of Changes (*I Ching*) and other early works all refer to the contrast of *yang* and *yin*. Yang is the bright, dry aspect of the cosmos; the character originally meant the sunny south-facing slope of a hill. Yin is the cool, dark, wet aspect; the character originally meant the shady north face. Maleness was associated very early with yang, femaleness with yin; men were thought to have more yang energy and were encouraged to conserve it; females had more yin energy, which they could give forth safely. Fire is yang, water yin. The famous Great Unity Diagram describes the relation of yang and yin. In the Taoist cosmology (greatly simplified), the Tao, an abstract first principle, begat unity; unity begat yang and yin; and the interpenetration of these produced the universe and all in it. At some uncertain time in the early history of China, Taoists added to the concepts of yang and yin the theory known variously as the Five Goings, Five Evolutive Phases, or Five Elements. ("Five Goings" is the literal translation; "going" can mean either a process or a way followed. The second is Manfred Porkert's [1974] neologistic rendering. The third is the traditional English translation.) The Five are Earth, Wood, Fire, Metal, and Water. They create each other in the order given—earth grows trees, which produce fire, which smelts metal, which causes dew to congeal—and destroy each other in reverse order.

The five phases were then associated with everything else imaginable: five colors, five tastes, five smells, five larger bodily organs, five smaller bodily organs, five limbs of the body, and everything else that could be forced into a set of about this size. The Five Tastes, for example, are sour, bitter, sweet, piquant (or hot, as pepper), and salt; the Five Smells are rancid, scorched, fragrant, rotten, and putrid. Porkert has explained in detail how this system was used in understanding disease, which was associated with phases and seasons (discussed further below).

The Ch'in and Han Dynasties

In the Ch'in and Han dynasties, China's agriculture took shape. Most important in this period was the formulation, primarily during the early reigns of Han, of a comprehensive agricultural development policy by the imperial government. This policy was maintained throughout the history of China—often it was only a pious hope, but sometimes it was seriously followed.

This policy led to a real Green Revolution in China—the world's first. From late Chou to mid-Han, yields and technology substantially increased. The main features of the policy were (1) relatively moderate land taxes; (2) maintenance of a class of independent small farmers (either freeholders or relatively secure tenants); (3) agricultural extension and government compilation of agricultural textbooks and encyclopedias; (4) public works, including irrigation systems and ever-normal granaries; (5) famine relief; and (6) concern with medicines and herbs as well as with food. Government action toward these goals was often blocked or limited by large landlords and by the tendency of pressing issues, such as military campaigns, to suck away time and money. However, agriculture flourished in Han, population expanded, and China's agricultural and medical lore was codified. This took place in a context of urbanization and market development; peasants and farmers near cities became highly market oriented and well integrated into an emerging cash economy. All these things were crucial in shaping the unique course of China's agricultural development from Han until the present.

In 221 B.C., the Ch'in state conquered all of China. From the point of view of agriculture and food, Ch'in's important action after its unification of China was imposition of Legalist rule, which placed high priority on agriculture and food production, viewing them as the key to strengthening the state. Thus in the great suppression of books that took place in 213 B.C., the only categories explicitly spared were agriculture and medicine. (Anyone familiar with censorship can guess the outcome: those books are among the worst preserved of pre-Han literature.)

Only a few years after the First Emperor was laid in his tomb, the Ch'in Dynasty collapsed. In 206 B.C., Liu conquered the capital, the strategic city of Ch'ang-an (now Sian), and declared the Han Dynasty. Profiting by Ch'in Shih Huang Ti's mistakes and his own native caution, Liu set up a framework that allowed the Han to last for four hundred years—the longest lasting of any Chinese dynasty, though the rule was interrupted by one successful coup and several periods of disorganization and loss of real dynastic control. Just as Ch'in gave the West the name China, Han gave to all Chinese the identity "people of Han," still used in China to distinguish ethnic Chinese from minority peoples. The story of Han Dynasty agriculture has been told by Hsu Cho-yun (1978, 1980), William Crowell (1979), and others (Anderson 1987; Bray 1980, 1984; Chen 1984; Loewe 1968; Pirazzoli-T'Serstevens 1982); its food has been discussed by Ying-shih Yu (1967, 1977) and Wang Zhongshu (1982). But the best stories are found in the writings of the Han historians themselves: Ssu-ma Ch'ien (Watson 1967; Sima 1974) and the Pan family (Dubs 1938–55; Swann 1950; Watson 1974b). They were great writers and strikingly objective observers, considering that they were virtually inventing systematic interpretive history for China and were involved in the politics of their times.

The world's first census (2 A.D.) counted sixty million Chinese. The population had shrunk to about sixteen million by 280 (Bielenstein 1974). The capital cities at the height of their power may have had populations of a million each, counting suburbs and suburban villages. Their planning, in this age of urbanization and urban increase, was careful and detailed. In the periods of unrest, though, the cities were particular targets, and strife and siege virtually depopulated them on various occasions. Agriculture became more intensive to support the growing urban populations. Taxes and rents were kept low to encourage agriculture, but even relatively low payments were a hardship for the peasants on their small landholdings. Moreover, the landholdings were shrinking: partible inheritance has always been preferred in China, and as population grew landholdings inevitably declined. Great families and even the smaller landlords were thus often able to increase their holdings at the expense of the small peasants. Modern authors stress the relatively low taxes, relatively low incidence of landlordism and high rents, and relative stability of the peasant economy, but the word *relative* covers up many things. The peasants of Han Dynasty China were faced with the problem of wringing more productivity out of the land. Taxes and rents were often collected in kind, and far from cities the subsistence sector presumably dominated farming; rural farmers felt primarily the pressure to increase food crop production. But peasants near cities also needed cash. Buying and selling of food were important in the economy of the period.

The core areas fed very dense populations; Hsu calculates densities (for various marquisates) of up to 207 persons per square kilometer, though by contrast much of the empire was virtually without population. In these areas, there was considerable pressure on cultivated land (1980:17–20). The average household of about five people farmed approximately 70 Han mu (one Han mu was approximately one-ninth of an acre). Families served as units of production and consumption and often tried to be self-sufficient: one relatively affluent family had a rule that family members should eat or wear nothing they did not produce (Chú 1972:286–87).

Emperor Wen—perhaps the most conscientious ruler China ever had, given to public self-reprimand that would do credit to an official under Mao Tse-Tung—in 167 B.C. tried to do away with land taxes and taxes on produce. This measure was short-lived, but Wen's successor, Ching, in 155 B.C. reduced taxes from one-fifteenth to one-thirtieth of the crop, "possibly the lowest rate a farmer ever had to pay in Chinese history" (Hsu 1980:16). The taxes crept back up again after this, and the official memos do not tell the whole story, for local officials inevitably took more than they were supposed to. But throughout Han taxes stayed exceedingly low by the standards of feudal societies. Even during Eastern Han they hovered around 10 percent.

Land was often taken and redistributed during Han. This did not always involve the government's robbing the gentry: emperors even redistributed land from their beloved hunting parks on occasion. Hsu points out that in Eastern Han there was only partial opening up of land to settlers, and no new concessions of land were made after 109 A.D., but by then the biggest and best chunks had already been turned into private farms (33).

Perhaps the most important aspect of Han policy was its public works. For agriculture, this meant water control, in which the state was already involved. Before Han, the great Min River irrigation scheme had been constructed under the direction of the Li family of engineers; this monumental project is still in use today. Diking and diversion, however, when practiced by lesser men than the Lis, led to progressive silting and aggrading of the riverbeds followed by inevitable dike-breaching and flooding. Natural fluctuations in rainfall turned into disasters on a far greater scale than before: Hsu counts, during Han (including Hsin), forty-three major droughts and sixty-eight major floods (80). But they were hardly, as Hsu calls them, "natural" disasters. They were man-made as surely as the wars and intrigues of the period, the inevitable costs accompanying the benefits of public works in an age when such projects could not be easily controlled. The lessons have not been fully learned even today: modern China, like most other modern countries including the United States, has had its share of such disasters following from overambitious and poorly planned public water control projects.

The state also helped to disseminate agricultural knowledge, supporting manuals for farmers and instructing officials to propagate useful knowledge. In Former Han (206 B.C.–8 A.D.), Chao Kuo, a government procurement officer, disseminated intensive cultivation techniques as part of his duties (Swann 1950:184–85); Fan Sheng-chih and other writers had state support in producing agricultural manuals (Shih 1974). Some people were resettled in new lands, but Hsu shows that this was usually more strategic then economic; people were settled in the agriculturally unpromising but defensively important northwest, rather than the rich, productive, thinly settled south.

A very significant Han Dynasty act was the restoration of the plowing and silk ceremonies. The conscientious Emperor Wen revived these in 178 B.C., almost as soon as he succeeded to the throne. (After the fall of Empress Lu and her family, he was suddenly elevated from nominal kingship over a happily obscure backwater, and he never forgot his relatively humble background.) The edict restoring the ceremonies said: "Agriculture is the basis of the empire. Let the Field of Tribute be laid out and I in person shall lead the plowing in order to provide offerings of millet for the ancestral temples" (Watson 1967:352). As in the *Li Chi*, Wen's explicit reason for leading the ceremony was to show how seriously the government took agriculture (Dubs 1938–55:1:281–83). Silk culture was similarly led by the empress.

In his long reign of fifty-three years (140–87 B.C.), Emperor Wu expanded the empire and extended its contacts. His famous envoy Chang Ch'ien brought back various useful plants from Central Asia. Accounts differ on just which ones—grapes and alfalfa are the most popular candidates. Chang did not introduce most of the plants later credited to him, a few of which came earlier (e.g., wheat), many later (from carrots to spinach; Laufer 1919). But no doubt the era was a crucial one for the transmission of ideas in science, medicine, and agriculture: the Silk Road flourished as never before.

The farms of Han were most often small and worked by a large but not widely extended family, as was the rule throughout Chinese history. Small landlords with one, two, or several tenants renting land from them were common. But the few large landlords held much of the land and boasted vast numbers of tenants, serfs, and slaves. The Han government had about a hundred thousand slaves, and a very rich private individual might have several thousand. Slaves were primarily war captives or criminals and their descendents, and they were of little significance in society or agriculture (Chao 1986). The poet Wang Pao (or Wang Tzu-yüan, first century B.C.) wrote a bit of doggerel in the form of a slave contract to "upbraid" a slave who protested to his owner, Wang's host. (Wang was actually tactfully criticizing his host for working the slave too hard.) The poem lists every manual task Wang could imagine for a man to do, and the list is a gold mine of information about running a Han farm (Hsu 1980:231–34 contains a translation of the poem).

Productivity in good years seems to have been high, but figures are impossible to interpret because of uncertainty about their reliability and the exact size of Han measures (Hsu 1980; Swann 1950). A typical farm of 70 mu supported a typical family of five. But the Han mu was smaller than the modern one (which is about one-sixth of an acre). The mu changed size from 100 to 240 paces in 87 B.C., and the 70-mu figure refers to the larger 240-pace mu. The pace in question was two strides, standardized as 6 *chih* (feet) of about 9 inches each. This mu, 240 paces long by 1 pace wide, was about one ninth of an acre (Swann 1950).

The typical farm, then, was about 7.7 acres. This is a conservative estimate, but at best 70 mu of land was a tiny holding, incapable of supporting a family of five without intensive land use. Some farms were a good deal smaller than this. Han Chinese were physically small people, which would have kept their calorie requirements low, but they worked hard, so that active household heads would have needed a good diet. Many households had to produce a ton of grain on 7.7 acres (and this after seed was reserved for the next year). Han agriculture was productive by feudal standards

—more productive than medieval European farming, in which yields of 500 pounds per acre were considered high, and as much as a third of the crop had to be saved for seed because of the low-yield grain varieties grown (Slicher von Bath 1963). The Chinese saved much less seed and got better returns. Tables from just after Han show yields of 1:10 for wheat, 66:1,000 for millet, and 266:1,000 for rice (I am anonymously informed; see Bray 1984, Chao 1986). As to yield, 2–4 Han *piculs* per mu was typical. The Han *hu* (picul) was 20 liters, or about 37.4 pounds of grain. Yields were thus roughly 75–150 pounds per mu or 675–1,340 pounds per acre. Ssu-ma Ch'ien says that during Ch'in and Han, the best land, newly irrigated, produced a *ch'ung* (614 hu) per mu—almost 2,500 pounds per acre, the yield of better fields in early twentieth-century North China. The Han Shu (a history of the period; Bray 1984) tells of an experiment in trenching fields that raised yields by 1 hu per mu; and Fan Sheng-chih noted yields of 100 hu per mu in pit cultivation, which seems unbelievably high but may not be (Anderson 1987; Bray 1984; Shih 1974). Of course the farmer not only had to support a family but also had to pay a small but far from insignificant tax. Military draft, forced labor, and so on took people from their homes; because of the labor-intensive nature of agriculture and industry, these people had to be replaced. Thus, then as in more recent times, the Chinese had as many children, especially sons, as possible, at least until they had enough that after the draft and the corvée one son would be left at home to raise food.

Fan Sheng-chih's agricultural manual of the first century B.C. (Hsu 1980:280–94; Shih 1959) survives in extensive fragments quoted in later agricultural works. Some of the most elaborate procedures described in Fan's manual indicate how intensive Han agriculture was:

1. Multiple cropping (winter wheat or barley followed by millet or another summer crop) was common, though not by any means universal.

2. Pretreatment of seed is discussed at length in the manual. Seed was steeped in fertilizer made from cooked bones, manure, or silkworm debris, to which aconite or other plant poisons were added. The seeds were repeatedly covered with coats of this paste; care had to be taken to dry them between thin coatings so they did not rot. (In the West, pretreated seed is considered a modern laboratory miracle, innovated only in the last couple of decades.)

3. Not only was rice irrigated and its paddies leveled, but the circulation of water was changed by rerouting the channels during the year, so the water would be warm in spring but not hot in summer.

4. An elaborate and effective water-trapping system was used on the dry fields of the North: Soil was repeatedly pulverized in summer, creating a dust mulch that held water. In winter, snow was rolled down to keep it from blowing away. Fan notes that this practice also freezes and kills insect eggs that would otherwise survive the winter.

5. Cultivation in pits (which traps moisture) was practiced. Gourds in pits were cut back to keep the fruit large, and straw was put under each gourd so it would not rot from contact with wet soil. Larger, shallower pits were dug for grain; they produced yields of 100 hu per mu.

6. In areas where drainage rather than moisture conservation was a problem, ridge cultivation—the ancestor of the intensive methods used in China today—was practiced.

7. Pot irrigation was practiced on crops that were not canal irrigated.

8. Fen's manual offers exceedingly detailed and precise timing of fertilization, watering, planting, and so on.

9. Everything with any nitrogen content seems to have been carefully saved and used for fertilizer. A whole science of what fertilizer was best for what crop at what stage is embodied in the manual.

10. Knowledge of the soils best suited to each crop was almost as extensive as it is today.

11. Iron tools became common, diverse, and sophisticated, raising productivity.

The crops that Fan Sheng-chih mentions include most importantly the Nine Staples: wheat, barley, millet, glutinous millet, spiked millet, soybeans, rice, hemp, and small beans (*Vigna* spp.; their cultivation technique differs from that for soybeans). The classic Five Staples of Chinese cosmology are not a concern in Fan's manual. In Han the Five Staples were millets (two species, or else glutinous vs. nonglutinous), wheat (understood to include barley), beans, and rice (or hemp in the dry North). Hemp was an important seed crop for food and oil. Another manual, Ts'ui Shih's *Ssu-min Yueh-ling*, discusses similar issues (Hsu 1980:215–28).

Besides the staple seed crops, Fan mentions gourds (apparently the bottle gourd, *Lagenaria*); taro; "water-darnel *Panicum*" (Shih 1959:27; the identification is somewhat tentative but clearly refers to a grain); mulberries (mostly for silkworms); *Artemisia*, primarily a wild-gathered plant to keep insects from grain saved for seed, but also a flavoring herb; melons; scallions (*Allium*); perilla (an oilseed whose leaves are a good potherb); sesame (a newcomer); and elm trees. The elms (*Ulmus* spp.) are not mentioned as a food in Fan's book, but we know from the *Ssu-min Yueh-ling* that they were. The seeds and almost certainly the leaves were eaten, the leaves being made into a sauce, probably fermented much like bean paste (miso). No doubt the trees were often planted, as in more recent centuries. The seeds were gathered in the second month and made into sauce then and/or in the fifth month. This seems strange, since the common Chinese elm (*Ulmus parvifolia*) fruits in the fall. Young elm leaves are excellent food; the seeds are edible but tough and dry.

The *Ssu-min Yueh-ling* adds other crops to Fan's list: mustard greens (or Chinese cabbages), mallow (*Malva* sp.), leeks, large and small green onions, water peppers (aquatic greens similar to watercress), an unidentifiable herb that Hsu (1980:217) mistranslates "thyme," and others. The crops are more or less those of modern North China, except that sorghum and maize have recently entered and have tended to replace millet. Rice was important, as now, in the south and center.

From archeology and other documents we can complete the list of major Han foods (Yu 1977; Wang 1982): horses, sheep, deer and other wild game, ducks, geese, pheasants, pigeons (all possibly kept in captivity), wild birds, turtles and tortoises, various carp including common carp (raised in ponds), many wild fish, lotus (rhizome and seeds), longans and litchis (new, exotic southern discoveries), cinnamon, fagara (*Zanthoxylum* spp., also known as Chinese pepper, Szechuan pepper, and brown pepper), magnolia buds, peonies (in sauce), rush shoots, galangal, daylilies, waxmyrtle fruit (miscalled "strawberries" in some references, the Chinese words being similar), true oranges, grapes, chestnuts, water caltrop (*Trapa bicornis*), bamboo shoots, sugarcane, honey, and assorted wild herbs including goosefoot, sowthistle (*Sonchus*), and a wild ginger. The "small beans" of the texts appear in the archeological record as the adzuki bean or red bean, *Vigna angularis*, in the Ma-wang-tui tombs. Very possibly other *Vigna* species were also used.

Millet was certainly the preferred grain for both eating and brewing; this is amply attested in the sources and in archeological finds. Rice was next. Through most of Han, wheat was definitely considered inferior, beans and barley even more so. Meals of wheat and beans are the Han equivalent of the Chou's meals of plain vegetables, that is, literary tropes for plain fare.

In early Han, food was like that of Chou. Beans were boiled. Boiled soybeans are at best uninspiring; they produce much flatulence and are disliked by almost all who eat them (although a few dedicated health food eaters might disagree). Boiled "small beans" (adzuki beans in Han) are excellent but were a minor crop. Grain was boiled into porridge or steamed over stew. For these purposes, millet is superior to wheat: it cooks into a soft, delicate porridge or a fluffy, tender mass of steamed grain, while wheat remains tough and chewy. Millet's nutlike, almost sweet flavor contrasts with the slightly bitter flavor of boiled whole-grain wheat.

By late Han, the situation had dramatically changed. Pickling and salting were key techniques in Chou foodcraft. Sometime in late Chou, or even as late as very early Han, the art of fermenting soybeans was perfected. Han texts thereafter devote much space to *tou shih* (or *shih*), the *tausi* of modern Cantonese cooking, salt-preserved soybeans. *Chiang*, fermented sauce, was being made of beans as well as elm products and meat. The "minced meat sauce" discussed in the *Ssu-min Yueh-ling* was made of sausage meat, fermented like modern *lachiang* or salami. For these products, the food is first salted, then allowed to ferment.

Fan says, "for soybeans, the rule is: per person, five mu—this is the field's basis!" (Shih 1974). In our ideal farmstead of five people on one hundred mu this would mean a fourth of the land under beans. He notes that soybeans are unfailing, even in years that are bad for grain (true only in areas with good rainfall or some irrigation).

Bean leaves were a popular vegetable and Fan does not fail to warn his readers to leave enough foliage to ensure a good bean crop.

For wheat, the key innovation was noodle technology (Yu 1977). Improved flour-milling technology entered, apparently from Central Asia, and the Chinese took advantage, soon beginning their own innovating. They also used grain, roasted or otherwise cooked and then dried, for instant rations: this, along with jerky (dried meat), was the standard military ration. Ice, perhaps in mobile freezers, was also used to preserve food for campaigns, but drying was paramount.

The other great use of grain was in making ale. In addition to chiu, there was *li*, a white substance, apparently untreated, unaged fermenting mash or liquor strained from it, like the *tapai* or *tapeh* of contemporary Southeast Asia. It could be brewed while the guest waited, if he didn't mind waiting a while. Chiu was more complex to make and more socially important stuff. Herbs were often added, presumably to keep it from going sour and to give it medicinal value as well as to flavor it. (Hops were used in Western beer to keep it from getting cloudy and sour; only later did people learn to like their flavor. Presumably the order of events was the same in China.) In Han, following Chou custom, herbed dark millet ale was the drink of choice. With the grain food and the ale, the commonest dish was still keng (stew), as tomb finds confirm. Roast meat is also well attested: all sorts of game were devoured, with exotica being desired. One powerful official raised rabbits and executed poachers (Ch'u 1972). Overly ostentatious people were criticized by being accused of giving even their slaves ale and meat (the Han trope for fine food), instead of thin soup and bean leaves (the foods of the poor; Ch'u 1972). Conversely, for special celebrations the government granted the leading households oxen and ale.

In general, methods of cooking were similar to those used during the Chou Dynasty, except for the important addition of stir-frying, which is likely to have been another Han innovation. Although it is not directly mentioned in the texts or otherwise, it can be inferred from the great stress on slicing foods thinly and evenly, and the presence of model woks in the archeological record. The Han Chinese had the archeologically invaluable custom of making pottery models of everything the dead might need in the other world: boats, servants, dogs, pigpens, houses, and, of course, stoves. Huge stoves like those of old Chinese farmsteads today, with great stokeholes and apertures for the curved bottoms of pots, are commonly found in modeled miniature; the terra-cotta servants and cooks indicate their scale. Great kettles and stewpots dominate the burial goods, the stewpots strongly shouldered like modern curry pots, but woks are also prominent. These are the world's oldest pans of this shape, to my knowledge. The wok (the name is the Cantonese pronunciation of *kuo*) is a specialized piece of equipment, perfect for stir-frying and not at all the tool of choice for anything else. The presence of wok models on model Han stoves is thus good evidence for the development of the most distinctively Chinese method of cooking.

The existence of woks and stir-frying implies large-scale oil rendering. Doubtless the new milling technology was applied to the new sesame and perilla seeds, thus introducing vegetable oil to China.

Religion continued to affect food consumption enormously via sacrifices and ritual feasts. People even stole food to fulfill ritual obligations. By the 40s B.C., sacrifices to the Imperial ancestors cost 24,455 cash per year and required a staff of 57,546 people, many of them food preparers. After this the court, in desperation, drastically simplified the sacrifices (Ch'u 1972).

Han is also famous for its writings on medicine. The Huai Nan Tzu combines medicine with mysticism (Loewe 1979, 1982). Shunyu Yi wrote a medical book in early Western Han. Chang Chung-Ching is famous for his *Shang-han Lun* (Discourse on fevers; Chang 1981), Hua To for his surgery. *Shen Nung Pen Ts'ao* (Shen Nung's basic herbal) and the Yellow Emperor's Classic of Internal Medicine appeared (Veith 1966). Both seem to have been in recognizable or even final form in the first or second century A.D., and both evidently embody earlier knowledge sifted and combined with newer data. Both are aimed at a sophisticated medical audience and are named after mythical emperors.

Medicine was structured in terms of the Han cosmology, based on Ts'ou's Five Elements theory from Warring States. Tung Chung-shu and others systematized it further during Western Han. All things were classified as yang or yin and as one of the Five Elements. Foods and flavors were also systematized and associated with the major bodily organs. Han thinkers brought systematic rational synthesis to medical thinking as they did to political and moral philosophy (Unschuld 1985). Earlier, sickness had more often been ascribed to punishment by the ancestors for sins or to attacks by demons; naturalistic, rational medicine had been there too, but it did not rise to preeminence until Han. The Han thinkers did not stress the balance, harmony, and holism commonly featured in modern Chinese medicine; perhaps this was because the period was an optimistic, open one in which no controlling paradigm was dominant. With the rise of naturalistic medicine came increased stress on food and nutrition, already the most important of medical considerations (as the *Chou Li* shows us). The major drugs listed in the Shen Nung Herbal became part of the diet, if they were not already. From then on, medicine had much to do with making Chinese diets more varied and nutritious.

Regional differences in diet were discussed (Veith 1966:147–48). The Yellow Emperor's book describes how to make soups and offers much other nutritional lore. It correlates salt eating with circulatory diseases—a standard point in Chinese medical thought and of course quite correct: salt can exacerbate high blood pressure, which in turn makes stroke and other circulatory accidents more likely. The other dietary warnings found in the Yellow Emperor's Classic probably also have some value, though excessive systematization intruded and empirical accuracy was sacrificed to simplicity and order wherever the two conflicted.

During Han and throughout Chinese history, the boundary between medicine and food was so vague as to be nonexistent in practice. Many things were purely medicines, but medicines often became foods if people learned to like them; many foods became merely medicines when people stopped relishing them; and all foods were considered to have medicinal value, positive or negative, with important effects on health. The Shen Nung Herbal classified medicines into three categories. (These, corresponding with Heaven, Man, and Earth in the Confucian system, Ruler, Minister, and Aide on earth, were good categories in their own right, not just another example of systematization gone wild.) In the upper class were tonics and strengthening drugs, such as ginseng, fossil bones, and plantain seed. Now they are considered to have a tonic, mild stimulant, or nutritional value. The middle class consisted of medicines that had both specific value and general nutritional and/or remedial effects. In the lower class were medicines considered valuable to treat specific conditions and nothing more. (With some important exceptions, Han medicine treated particular suites of symptoms rather than trying to infer "diseases" behind them.) Modern people might put wheat germ in the upper class, calcium in the middle, penicillin in the lowest category. What we have of the Shen Nung Herbal (it survives only in sections quoted in later works such as Fan Sheng-chih's book) treats some 365 drugs. A bias in favor of plants is revealed: 246 are plant drugs, 67 animal (including one human product), 42 mineral. Many of the drugs do not, by modern standards, have the value alleged for them. A few do. At worst they could not do much damage, because the authors of the Herbal had the good sense to put only the mildest and safest medicines in the upper class.

By the end of Han, Chinese food, agriculture, and nutritional science were advanced far beyond their basically Neolithic situation at the dawn of Chou. Most of the progress was made between 500 and 100 B.C., helped by specific government action as well as by increasing population, urbanization, and commercialization. Peasants wanted to grow more food to feed their increasing families and to sell to the growing cities. Governments saw in this desire for increase a way to power and thus aided the peasants by economic and technical means. During Han were developed the world's first systematic farm price supports, the first ever-normal granaries, the first standardized weights and measures for peasant agriculture, the first agricultural extension services and manuals, the first official, government-sponsored, controlled experiments in agronomy, the first comprehensive and modern agricultural policy at a national level, and the rationalization of the bureaucracy that allowed all this to function. The observations that independent smallholders were the most productive farmers and that big estates were a threat to both production and the state had become entrenched (though they were sometimes challenged) in the official mind. China's bureaucratic machine—aided by such innovations as the civil service exam and the concept of promotion strictly for merit—continued from this time on, allowing Chinese governments to function even when emperors were incompetent or when disunion created serious problems. Agriculture continued to be one of the first priorities of whatever government was in power.

China's agricultural success in later millennia was due, most of all, to the high level of skill and knowledge among the peasants. This owed a great deal to the public diffusion of knowledge, by governmental extension (as with Fan Sheng-chih's book) and family effort (as with the *Ssu-min Yueh-ling*). No other ancient empire met the challenge of population pressure and commercial agriculture in urban zones so creatively. Hsu (1980) stresses China's need to respond to rising population pressure; Chao (1986), by contrast, sees Han as a period of low population; thus innovations came in labor-saving methods to make better use of the rather limited labor. The truth is, I believe, that the early Ch'in–Han period was one of low population, but population growth (especially in the periurban zones) came to have a significant effect by the middle of Han. To Boserup's dynamic was added the need to feed a huge army and court. Landlords also wanted more than mere subsistence grain. Demand for food grew greatly, and the population grew with it. Seed drills, horsecollars, square-pallet chain pumps and iron tools propagated and made labor more efficient, but the government seems to have been more interested in the labor-intensive, land-sparing methods popularized by Fan Sheng-chih. The fateful transition from labor-saving "mechanical" innovation to land-saving "biological" innovation was well under way.

Also, the rise of an entrenched elite led to increased gourmetship, originally justified by appeal to ritual—specifically, rituals that underlined social differences. Public validation of the social order won out over austerity, and never again would the Chinese entertain seriously the notion that those in power should not enjoy the fruits of success.

Finally, Chinese medicine took a modern shape. From magic and conjuring it developed into a rational, scientific, logical system in which nutrition had explicit pride of place.

China's success in food production, and thus much of her success as an empire, has been due to these factors: government aid—especially information dispersal—in an environment of population growth and commercialization; importance of the smallholding peasant; gourmetship; and preeminence of elaborate nutritional lore in the medical field.

4 Foods from the West: Medieval China

The Period of Disunion

After Han, China was divided for almost four centuries. During this time, agriculture continued to change and progress. Rule by Central Asian peoples in the north led to introduction of crops and ideas from West and South Asia, including new land tenure systems. Local dynastic autonomy in the southeast led to rapid and dramatic growth in the importance of that area; its wealth became proverbial, its agriculture highly developed, especially near the great lower Yangtze cities. Crops and technology from South China—previously an alien realm—became well known and were incorporated into the Chinese system. In spite of disunion and governmental preoccupation with matters other than agricultural policy, the period was one of exciting innovation in agriculture and food. Tea, for instance, seems to have entered Chinese consciousness at this time.

By a process of attrition, certain successful families came to dominate much of Chinese life. They provided stability both by filling mid-level positions in government and local economic and political life and by preserving Chinese culture, philosophy, and world order (Ebrey 1978). They translated the great Han Confucian synthesis into practice, providing administration that was often arbitrary and self-centered but equally often responsible and competent. The two need not be opposed: enlightened self-interest motivated these individuals as well as Confucian responsibility to family and to the governed, or the new Buddhist ideal of compassion. The Han ideals of low land taxes and small, privately held farms roughly equal in size were generally honored in principle, but high taxes and the contrast of wealthy estates with tiny plots were the actual practice most of the time. In the north, the Wei (a Turkic dynasty) introduced Central Asian ideas of common land ownership, blending them with the ancient Chinese practice of dividing fields equally; the result was an attempt at total state control of land and fair distribution to individuals: able-bodied men received more than women and old people. This concept, however, seems to have been caught between the rise of Buddhist and elite estates (usually free of taxes and controls) on the one hand and regional anarchy on the other, and it did little to ensure a fair land share to everyone. Under the Southern courts, great estates were scattered among small estates and many tiny holdings. As usual in Chinese his-

47

tory, most peasants seem to have been de facto owners of their tiny farms, though they were heavily taxed and always subject to legal or illegal dispossession by powerful figures.

The age was marked by an obsessive concern with ale. Rarely in the history of the world has alcoholism been so idealized. No doubt much of this was poetic license; we need not believe that the bards were drunk all the time (as they would have us believe). Alcohol was, however, definitely considered the great social facilitator and a proper part of all social gatherings. On the other hand, in this age of rebellion and escape, use of alcohol for frankly escapist purposes was also common. Many people used hallucinogenic drugs as well: the properties of datura, hemp, and many other plants were well recognized (Hiu-lin Li 1977). Drugs were ostensibly taken for quasi Taoist consciousness expansion, but a deeper escapist motive seems to have underlain their popularity.

Many drinkers were socially prominent men who were at considerable risk of their lives due to court intrigues; some of them cultivated the image of "harmless drunks" for self-protection. Donald Holzmann's (1976) brilliant and thorough biography of Juan Chi exemplifies this. Juan was an ardent and scathing critic of the government and a prominent man of high family. He cultivated the image of a drunken Taoist recluse in part to save him from the deadly consequences of his criticisms—and, indeed, he was eventually executed. He was, however, clearly attracted to such a life, as was his circle of friends, many of whom had no such excuse for their behavior. Some other drunken poets of the era had such high status that they did not need to worry—several emperors, for example, were more adept at drinking and poetizing than at ruling.

Literary documents tell us about the food of the times. T'ao Yüan-ming (365–427), unquestionably the greatest poet of the period and one of the finest in all Chinese history, spent his life as a small farmer in central China under the Wei (Hightower 1970). Devoting much time and money to poetry and ale, he was a marginal farmer, living on the ragged edge of poverty and sometimes forced to ask for charity to survive. He was once prevailed upon to take office, but he resigned, apparently under pressure because of his lackadaisical attitude to ruling. Moral integrity was perhaps less important to him than genuine love of a relaxed, retired life unworried by political operating. His poems leave us a full account of his beloved farm.

T'ao lived in almost Neolithic simplicity. His farm was divided into fields, orchard, and garden. His crops were millet, possibly wheat and soybeans, peach, flowering apricot, mulberry, hemp, mallows, and a few other vegetables. He also grew his beloved pines and chrysanthemums, and perhaps pears, willows and a few other plants. Bamboos completed his husbandry. He singles out mallows—coarse, bitter, fibrous, and glutinous—as his favorite vegetable. Much of his millet was brewed into ale (mistranslated "wine" by most English-writing scholars). He kept chickens and probably a few other animals: a farmer in 3000 B.C. would probably have had

more. T'ao lived on the edge of starvation, in part because of his primitive techniques. Yet he was a brilliant and educated man. The ordinary farmer probably did
not fare any better, even though T'ao clearly devoted much time to poetry and ale
that could have been spent in agricultural swink.

The other major poet of the age, Hsieh Ling-yun, was a rich landlord in the
South. He once appalled a distant neighbor by suddenly appearing on his land after
having his men cut a wide road through solid forest; the neighbor was disconcerted
at the trespass and damage (Frodsham 1967). Hsieh's poetry breathes a spirit of
Thoreau-like detachment that has as little to do with his life as Thoreau's image had
to do with his stormy career. But such ruthless developers helped turn the South into
a huge garden.

In 304, Ch'i Han produced a prose account of the economic botany of South
China, roughly the area of modern Kwangtung (Li 1979). Even his mistakes are the
result of shrewd observation. Thus he notes that rape-turnips become mustard-
greens when planted in the South, having observed that in a land without winter
they do not produce a swollen root, and he compares this with his observation that
the orange turns into the inferior trifoliate-orange when planted in North China.
This bit of lore is evidently based on the fact that tender citrus species are routinely
grafted onto the tougher trifoliate understock, and in a cold, dry climate the scion
wood is often weakened or killed, leaving the trifoliate underwood to proliferate
infuriatingly. Ch'i describes no fewer than eighty plants and refers to sophisticated
raft agriculture in water and other interesting techniques.

In the late 400s and early 500s, T'ao Hung-ching compiled all the herbal, chemical, alchemical, medical, Taoist, and general occult lore of South China. A mountain
recluse who hobnobbed with emperors and a retired meditator whose writings
run into the dozens of volumes, he is one of the truly great men of all time. He
assembled the herbal, dietary, and botanical lore of previous ages, including the *Shen
Nung Pen Ts'ao* of latter Han, and added much of his own, creating many huge
herbal encyclopedias that were the direct ancestors of the later, more famous *Pen-
ts'ao K'ang-mu* of Li Shih-ch'en (ca. 1593). His classifications and exhaustive treatment —including extensive quotes from earlier authorities, tabulated data, and
many special categorizations of the medical qualities of plants—set a standard that is
still with us, lying behind the great compendium *Zhong Yao Da Zi Dian* (Great Dictionary of Chinese Medicine), published in 1979. In T'ao's work we first see foods
classified as "heating" or "cooling," a Western belief that may have entered China
with Buddhism. This humoral theory influenced Chinese eating enormously, as
people tried to maintain a harmonious balance between hot and cold principles in
their bodies, and to some extent between wet and dry energies as well.

These herbals were embedded in a wider tradition that involved the development
of all aspects of medicine, especially the search for longevity or immortality (Schafer
1980; Unschuld 1985; Wong and Wu 1936). The long-term effects of the expansion of
food uses that accompanied this search were considerable. Adepts seeking longevity

abstained from staple foods and meats, often eating very bizarre diets. Alchemy, mineral nutrition, and longevity drugs were subjects of intense study and caused much heavy-metal poisoning (Needham 1976–80). The enormous influence of Buddhism led to the adoption of Buddhist foods and foodways, including medical dietary codes. Buddhist missionaries, like many missionaries since, found that they made more converts by helping the sick than by arguing fine points of theology.

The other great work of the period is the *Ch'i Min Yao Shu* or "ordinary people's needed skills" (the title somewhat ambiguous and subject to other translations) by Chia Ssu-hsieh. Chia was a local governor under the Wei who evidently took his position seriously. He compiled all the agricultural knowledge that he regarded as valuable, using all the older books available to him, peasant experience, his own observations, and considerable experimentation and field work. Shih Sheng-han (1962) recently edited the encyclopedic book and produced a valuable summary and partial translation in English; more accurate translations of portions of the work are provided by Hui-lin Li (1969).

Chia was a superb agronomist. His book is very much a product of the dry north. In this it resembles Fan Sheng-chih's book, which was one of Chia's major sources. In addition to agricultural advice, Chia's book includes a long section on fermentation products. Starters were made from cereal and water. Artemisia (sagebrush, mugwort) leaves were often added, almost certainly for the same reason that hops were added to beer: the strong antiseptic effect keeps bacteria and other problems at bay. Cocklebur leaves were sometimes used, possibly for the same purpose, or perhaps just to add wild yeasts or extra nutrients. Top-fermentation is described: Chia refers to "floating ants" appearing on the surface of the liquid during brewing. (The significance of this term has been missed by other commentators.) Top-fermentation is expected anyway; modern bottom-fermenting beer yeasts are the product of long and careful selection of special strains of *Saccharomyces cerevisiae*, whereas the makers of Chinese ale used wild or semiwild strains of this yeast and many other distantly related fungi. Chia also describes the making of yogurt, cheese, and butter—commodities of some importance in his day. Central Asian rulers and Buddhist travelers had popularized dairy products, especially in the North, where they were a major part of the diet. China's famous avoidance of dairy foods was not to be seen— the opposite was the case in the Northern dynasties. Chia also describes how to dry meat with or without salting. This was, of course, more essential for the armies than for the household; troops carried their meat in the form of jerky. If we leave out a long section on exotic plants that derives from earlier natural histories such as Po Wu Chih and Ch'i Han's book, we find that Chia described roughly sixty economic plants.

From the poems and food manuals of the age, it is evident that the Chinese diet had become sharply differentiated. The North was a land of millet, meat, and dairy products; in the South, where economic activity centered on the lower Yangtze, people ate rice, fish, and water foods. Northerners teased Southerners about eating frogs and snails; Southerners reciprocated with snorts about yogurt and cheese, which must have seemed to them to be nothing but spoiled milk. The South had a greater variety of vegetables and fruits and probably a more elaborate cuisine; it was also the home of the most advanced herbal lore. The Yangtze Valley and even the lands south of it were coming into their own; their economic growth continued in succeeding dynasties. Eventually rice came to dominate wheat and millet economically, demographically, and (to some extent) culinarily. This process was begun, or at least helped, by the long period of disunion.

Reunited and Triumphant: Sui and T'ang

The reunification of China came more suddenly than most would have predicted. It began with a palace coup of the sort typical of the previous hundred years. In 580 A.D., Yang Ch'ien made himself full ruler of a new dynasty (Wright 1978, 1979). Yang was far different from the petty tyrants who ruled the many previous kingdoms. A stern, ruthless, and paranoid man, he rolled over opposition like a whirlwind.

Yang Ch'ien established the equal field (*ch'un t'ien*) system in its Turkicized form as devised during the Northern Wei Dynasty. What was new, indeed revolutionary, about the revival was its uniform extension to everyone in all of China. The system was a form of socialism. Ordinary male householders received 80 mu of land to work during their active lifetime—it reverted to the state when they reached the age of sixty—and 20⅓ mu of land that could be kept for life and passed on to descendants. Of the allotment, 20 mu was for fiber growing (mulberry and hemp land), the remaining one-third mu was for a house and garden. Women received only 40 mu of active-life allotment; almost all women were part of a household headed by a man. Men of servile status got the basic 80 mu, but nothing else except one-fifth of a mu for a house and garden. Men of high status got more: nobles received anywhere from 40 to 10,000 mu of inheritable land, and additional land accompanied government offices, the amount depending on the level of the office. Buddhist temples had their own allotments. In densely populated parts of the Empire, there was probably too little land to go around even at the beginning of Sui, and by 592 there was only one-fourth the reallocation land available as was needed to make the system function. One assumes that as soon as Sui became stable, people flocked to the city outskirts, and there appeared the situation we already encountered in Han, in which the rich periurban districts had exceedingly dense populations even though more remote areas were seeking people to till good land.

Most important, this system firmly established the state as the ultimate owner of the land and made it clear to everyone that land was given only at the pleasure or discretion of the Empire. It also defined a stable social system in which the vast majority of people were equal and part of a collectivity, although many were of strictly defined higher or lower status—again at the pleasure of the court. The Sui government was particularly interested in stimulating grain production, needing to rebuild the national stocks ravaged by decades of war and neglect. They were spectacularly successful, amassing up to ten million (Chinese) bushels of grain in the public granaries (Wright 1979:93–94). These granaries, like those of Han and other dynasties, were used as security reserves and functioned to keep prices level; the government kept prices up in good years by buying large stocks and kept prices down in bad years by selling off some of their surplus. During the Sui Dynasty grain was emphasized over other crops. The hereditary land allotments were supposed to be primarily for fiber crops. Taxes were paid in grain, cloth, and labor—this threefold tax system was another major Sui contribution. Fruit, vegetables, and meat were luxuries, important to the court, rare in the lives of the commoners.

Yang Ch'ien's successor possessed his father's paranoia but not his intensity of concentration and effort. He has become famous in history as the archetype of the Bad Last Emperor, living out everyone's fantasies in under-the-counter novels. The T'ang victory was essentially a replay of Sui's (Bingham 1941; Twitchett 1979). A powerful military aristocrat, Li Yuan, the Duke of T'ang, marched from a northern garrison and took Ch'ang-an in 618.

T'ang rose to brilliance in the 700s but was dogged by cold, dry weather that contributed (along with social factors) to famines and revolts such as An Lu-shan's in 754 (Pulleyblank 1955). After 800, the climate seems to have recovered somewhat, but the regime had already been weakened, and apparently at no time did it enjoy as good a climate as that of Han times.

Many of the late T'ang emperors—five in succession, by one story—died by taking "immortality" drugs. As Michel Strickmann has pointed out (1979), the death of the material body was not taken as evidence of the worthlessness of the drugs, for the immortality was supposed to reside on a higher plane; still, it is perhaps the only case in world history of a suicidal cult influencing a national government for decades. Why the T'ang Chinese took so seriously the idea of immortality, when few other elites have ever been so persuaded, is a question we are only beginning to solve. Some of the emperors may actually have been poisoned by enemies.

The T'ang Dynasty officially ended in 907. The period from 907 to reunification in 960 is known as the Five Dynasties, but there were many more than five if all the essentially independent local strongholds are reckoned. This period was one of constant strife both between and within the kingdoms (Schafer 1954).

As in Sui, during T'ang land was distributed to people as their capacities allowed (Twitchett 1962, 1963, 1979; Twitchett and Wright 1973). The male head of a household got 100 mu, of which 80 was "personal share land" to work while he was active and 20 was tree crop land that could be passed on to his descendants. Other classes of persons got lesser holdings. The 100-mu holding amounted to about six acres. Previous figures put it at thirteen acres, but the T'ang code states clearly that the measurement used was the smaller Han Dynasty mu (Twitchett 1963:124). The code specified that a mu should have fifty mulberry or ten elm trees, which suggests the smaller mu, since the Chinese plant mulberries very close together and prune them into an almost bushlike appearance. Six acres was not exactly a liberal holding, but it was no worse than most Asian peasants have come to expect through history. In 737 there was an attempt to make the whole 100 mu revert to the state at the death of the user. Documents found at Tun-huang Oasis show that the land distribution system was carried out conscientiously, and the system actually functioned, though Tun-huang (small, confined, and on the frontier) may have been a special case (Twitchett 1963).

However, as time went on, the system was bound to fail. It required almost impossibly honest enforcement and registration by the very people who could most easily take advantage of the system and subvert it to their own ends. In the South, land was easily available but it was often worked by slash-and-burn methods involving long fallow periods; the allocation system there can have been little more than an ideal to hope for. Compromises were also made in other special areas: for example, extra land was given when some of the land in an allotment was uncultivable or of very poor quality.

We have followed China through three radical transformations in landholding. The first came when primitive common ownership of land by the community was replaced by classic feudalism: ennoblement and enfeoffment of the supporters and kin of the ruler. This came probably in Shang and certainly by Chou. The second was the rise of private landownership and yeoman farming, a trend that developed in late Chou and was given official standing by Han. (Along with this came the fiction of total state control and experiments in state socialism.) The third was the rise of full-scale redistributive agrarian socialism under Wei and more generally under Sui and T'ang. The fourth transformation was the destruction of this system by An's rebellion, which led to the rise of giant estates owned by politically powerful figures. This situation continued through the Sung. The fifth and final premodern transformation came gradually during later dynasties (Ming and Ch'ing): and the great estates declined in importance and small farmers rose once again.

In monastic landholding, T'ang land tenure and its effect on development was comparable to that of medieval Europe. Buddhist and Taoist establishments acquired huge agricultural holdings, which the state expropriated on occasions when it felt short of cash.

The staple food during T'ang continued to be millet; rice was popular in the rapidly expanding South. From tax figures, I calculate grain yields to have been about 1,300–1,600 pounds per acre (the figures are Denis Twitchett's, recalculated using the correct mu; Twitchett 1963). These figures are similar to good Han yields and to poorish yields for the early twentieth century. There was a tax of 2 shih (then about 140 pounds per shih) per household, so a household with more land was in better shape than one with less. Other taxes affected cloth and so on, and there was the usual tendency to take more than the legal and ordinary tax. The government salt monopoly also reappeared (as in Han and other early reigns), stressing the people by rendering this essential commodity harder to get. Pickling was still a primary mode of preserving vegetables and the like, requiring large quantities of salt. Many of the rebels of late T'ang cut their teeth as salt smugglers.

Near Eastern crops—among them spinach, sugar beet, lettuce, almond, and fig—became known during Tang (Laufer 1919; Schafer 1963). Southern crops became more widespread, but most of them were ones known to Ch'i Han centuries before. Palm sugar (jaggery) and toddy, dates, greater yam (*Dioscorea alata*), cardamom, galangal, and many new varieties of rice, taro, myrobalans, citrus, cassia, banana, *Canarium*, litchi, and similar fruits were among the important crops from the South; litchis and other subtropical fruits were iced and brought to the court by couriers; they were considered great delicacies (Schafer 1967). By far the most important change in Chinese food and agriculture during Tang was adoption of the Southern strategy of double-cropping of rice. Evidently practiced for centuries, if not millennia, by the native peoples of the deep South, it spread widely during and after Tang, set into practice by Chinese farmers who now settled in great numbers in the newly secured lands. The southeast had been Chinese territory off and on since Ch'in, but only during Tang did it receive much settlement; thus the Cantonese call themselves "people of Tang" rather than "people of Han," as the speakers of other Chinese languages call themselves. In the deep South the aborigines' regional diet based on rice and tuber crops was adopted by the Chinese as well. "Yams and taro" became a standard trope for aborigines' coarse, uncouth fare (Schafer 1969). Rice, by contrast, was well on its way to becoming the universal favorite that it is now.

In the North, wheat continued to gain. Crop rotation, allowing both wheat and millet to be grown, continued to spread; new milling methods made wheat's most usable form, flour, generally accessible (Schafer 1977). Wheat was eaten in the forms well known in modern times: dumplings, fried dough strips, and noodles. Ancestors of the modern *shao-ping* ("roast cakes," small breads covered with sesame seeds and baked on the sides of large ovens) were popular and apparently regarded as new. Shao-ping are actually diminutive versions of the standard Persian and Central Asian bread widely known as *nan*, and they were derived from that part of the world; in Tang China they were exotic items baked by Central Asians in the big cities (Schafer 1963, 1977). Wheat-flour cakes of various kinds have been found in Central Asian Tang sites (China Pictorial 1976:36–39).

From the many writings we have from Tang, and especially from the extremely complete diary of the Japanese monk, Ennin, who visited China in the 840s, we learn that millet was the daily staff of life in the north; wheat was considered something of a luxury (Reischauer 1955). Ennin records that wheat cakes and dumplings of various kinds were special fare brought out to greet him and his entourage or eaten as the fancy food at great feasts—taking the place of the meat that non-Buddhists would have eaten at such occasions. Bean curd and wheat-gluten meat imitations were not yet known. Buddhism led to large-scale vegetarianism and the development of a variety of wheat products that substituted for meat and reminded the "Western barbarians" of their home foods; cow's flesh was progressively abandoned as a food. Chinese continued to eat beef, but with a sense of shame, and many older Chinese still regard the cow as unfair game; non-Buddhists and Buddhists alike say it works too hard for humankind to be treated in such an uncaring fashion. Japanese, more influenced by Buddhism, later ceased entirely to eat beef, and only with massive Westernization has it again become a food there. However, cream, yogurt, kumys (fermented mares' milk), cheese, curds, and butter were popular. Since the dynastic family itself was of part-Turkic background, these foods necessarily took on some status. This seems to have been the climax of dairy product consumption in China. Other Central Asian foods, such as grape wine and other wheat products, were also very popular.

Tea may have reached China well before Tang, but it owes its popularity to a craze that developed in that dynasty. Lu Yü's *Book of Tea* (1974, original eighth century) set the seal on a developing conoisseurship; it is still widely read today. Tea, which originated somewhere in the Burma–India border country, was most likely introduced to China by Buddhist monks, although we have no proof of this. In comparison to rice or Chinese cabbages, it is a very recent addition to the Chinese food roster. We now think of tea as quintessentially Chinese, but in Tang it was a new, exotic drink—a major example of the importance of westward influence at the time.

Leaving aside such oddments as the baby macaques mentioned in a poem by Li Ho (Frodsham 1967:201), we find that the ordinary people ate about the same things they had always eaten. Fish abounded, and great fishing expeditions are described. Raw fish was very popular; indeed, it was one of the major luxuries, and several poets describe the thin slices flying like snow from the cleaver of a skilled cutter. The thinnest slices of the freshest fish were considered ideal. Freshwater fish were normally available, since the capital and most major cities were far inland on rivers. Some varieties were preferred over others; sea creatures in general were somewhat unusual to literati. Meat, sliced thin and cooked probably as it is in the northwest today (usually stir-fried with onions, chives or other alliums), was a sign of affluence or luxury. Chickens (and rarely other poultry) were eaten only on special occasions and were a trope for such in poetry. By contrast, there were tropes for simple rusticity, as in a poem by Kao Shih:

Ploughing the land between the mulberry trees,
The land is rich, the vegetables ripen fast,
May I ask how these mallows and beans
Compare with the viands at court? (Chan, 1978:91)

Like other eras, Tang was a period of recurrent famines. The aftereffects of war and civil strife were augmented by the erratic tax systems. Pestilences, apparently more common because of close links with India and the Near East, whence contagion often spread (Twitchett 1979), were exacerbated by famines and led to worse famine in turn, as the able-bodied died off. There is no evidence that they had the effect, as in Europe, of forcing up the price of labor; more likely they had the effect they had in the Middle East, where they killed the well-to-do urbanites, thus reducing demand for labor even more than they reduced the supply, leading to lower wages and economic decline (Dols 1977).

China's first known cookbook and the first nutrition textbook (both now lost) appeared during T'ang. Herbals and agricultural manuals grew on the model set by T'ao Hung-ching and Chia Ssu-hsieh, appearing under court auspices to the improvement of medicine and agriculture (Unschuld 1985). Distillation appeared toward the end of T'ang; it may have been invented in China (Needham 1956, 1976–80).

T'ang was the Golden Age of China, remembered for its incomparable poetry and arts of life. In the evolution of the Chinese food system, however, it does not stand out as especially important. Earlier inventions and creations reached fruition at this time. Borrowings from the west and south were integrated into the system. The experiment with socialist land management failed, never to be revived in China. Tea became important for the first time. T'ang was a period of consolidation, of splendid success built on earlier work.

𝒱𝓏 5 Definitive Shaping of the Food System: Sung and the Conquest Dynasties

The Sung Dynasty

During the Sung Dynasty, China's agriculture and food took definitive shape. Food production became more rational and scientific. By the end of Sung, North China—no longer ruled by the Chinese—was agriculturally mature. Little change took place thereafter until the mid-twentieth century. South China expanded its farming and added new crops in succeeding dynasties, but there too the pattern was set in Sung, and little basic change in technology followed.

China's great cuisine also appears to be a product of Sung. T'ang food was simple, but by late Sung, an elaborate cuisine with regional specialties is well attested. The rise of regional bourgeoisies led to this elaboration; imperial food remained expensive but less innovative than the fare of the merchants and local elites.

Chao K'ua-yin, the founder of Sung, consolidated governmental control under the civilian bureaucracy and did everything possible to weaken the military and to prevent the reappearance of local landlords. Virtual satrapies, like the northeast under late T'ang, did not reappear. Chao centralized tax collection, made governors answerable directly to the state, and rotated officials frequently. Moreover, he showed a truly Chinese grasp of the value of deliberately managed ideology by explicitly and continuously stressing—more than in previous centuries—the moral and cultural superiority of civilian scholar-bureaucrats over military men. The Sung military machine later grew enormous, eventually eating up two-thirds or more of the state revenue and garnering over a million men, but its entire command and funding structure was subordinated to the civilian elite. It was not brilliantly successful even at its primary purpose of suppressing internal dissent, and it was stunningly incompetent at dealing with external challenges.

The serious military problem during Sung was the northern barbarians. During the Five Dynasties, the Khitan, an Altaic people, had conquered China's northeast frontier and established control over much of what is now Manchuria. By the beginning of Sung, the Khitan empire stretched from south of Peking to Korea, and many more Chinese than Khitan were under their control. The Khitan developed Peking as a southern capital of their new Liao Dynasty, the beginning of Peking's career as an imperial capital. Powerful hunters and raiders, able to withdraw into the wintry fastnesses of Manchuria or to mass huge Chinese armies on the plains of Hopei, the Khitan were virtually unbeatable. The Sung Dynasty paid them off instead, using a great deal of money for the purpose, but less (they hoped) than they would have had to spend on military buildup to ensure a conquest.

The idea of Chinese nationalism greatly developed during Sung. The eclectic spirit of half-barbarian T'ang was replaced by a violently nationalistic attitude reflected in, for instance, the patriotic poetry of Lu Yu (1125–1210). However, the Khitan grew in power, eventually giving the West another word for China: the name Khitai (land of the Khitan), anglicized Cathay. Liao succumbed to the easy life, but another and far more menacing group arose on their flank: the Jurchen, a Tungus tribe. The Jurchen conquered Liao in 1125 and moved on against Sung. In 1127 the Sung capital, Pien Ching (now Kaifeng, in the Yellow River valley east of Loyang), fell to them. (For full historical details, see Gernet 1962; Golas 1980; Haeger 1975; Liu and Golas 1969; Rossabi 1983; Shiba 1970; Wittfogel and Feng 1949.) The Sung emperor was captured. However, the Jurchen were unable to follow up on their triumph, and the Sung reconstituted itself under a new emperor in the city of Hangchow. Thus began the Southern Sung (the period before 1117 is called Northern Sung). Huge tribute payments were made to the new rulers of the north, and after 1234 to the Mongols.

Southern Sung kept up a continual but half-hearted harassment of their southern flanks. Under a group of military leaders that included Yüeh Fei, one of the most brilliant generals in Chinese history, they drove hard against the Chin. Yüeh Fei was an idealistic, ambitious, intense man—at best a threat to Sung's traditionally peaceful and antimilitaristic policies, at worst a very real threat to the dynasty itself (Wilhelm 1962). He presented himself as a hero. The Prime Minister Ch'in Kuei, with the obvious if less than public support of the Emperor, eliminated Yüeh Fei by double-dealing and negotiated peace with Chin. Later Chinese show their feelings on this subject by referring to common deep-fried crullers, properly called dough strips, as "oil-fried devils" in honor of Ch'in Kuei and his wife; the crullers as they fry are seen as representing the fate of the pair in hell.

Eventually, after decades of tension, Sung supported the Mongols against the Chin (as they had probably supported the Jurchen against the Liao) on the time-honored principle of using barbarians to control barbarians. The strategy backfired, and by 1278 Sung was in full flight. In 1279 the last boy emperor was run down in a far southern refuge, and the Sung Dynasty was over.

Deterioration of the climate ended and even reversed itself about 900, but a sharp and dramatic downturn may have occurred about the end of Northern Sung (Lamb 1982; Zhang 1982), and another bad period came just before the dynasty fell. Presumably these bad times were not unassociated with the sufferings of the Empire. Between them, the climate rebounded to essentially modern conditions, but at best the period seems to have suffered considerable fluctuation. The conquest dynasties suffered more, for they were in the north where the cooling and drying trends were more serious. But this did not prevent the population of China from rising to new heights. Population during Northern Sung passed the 100 million mark; Chin reached 40 million or more, and Southern Sung at its height was even more populous, so the combined total was at least 110 million (Ho 1970; cf. Golas 1980). Obviously food and agriculture must have developed greatly to feed so many people in the face of ecological deterioration and the loss of China's Central Asian lands. The figures represent a doubling of China's population since early T'ang.

Economic decentralization went so far that some have described Sung as capitalist or proto-capitalist. However, it has also been described as feudal, modern, traditional, and everything else imaginable. In fact Sung was in a class by itself in Chinese history, but it was rather like many medieval Western states in allowing the economy to run without much government interference, but enough to guarantee that nothing like modern capitalism arose. The monopolies on salt, wine, tea, and other commodities were in force for varying times; even the salt trade was relatively free for a while, but the government often relied on the revenues from monopolies. The northern Altaic dynasties never dreamed of doing without substantial government control of trade in basic goods. Liao introduced a style of government influenced by West Asian autocracy, more centralized and authoritarian than Sung or even T'ang. (Wittfogel and Feng [1949] described the system; Wittfogel [1957] drew on it for his model of Oriental despotism, not realizing that it was new in eleventh-century China.) Probably the most important way government influenced economy was through its enormous procurement. Supporting a standing army of a million men obviously required large amounts of grain, weaponry, horses, and so forth. Supporting a capital city of another million—most working directly or indirectly for the government—meant another huge procurement effort. When the capital moved, the people moved with it; former capitals were almost deserted. Obviously the government was in a position to make or ruin any industry or entrepreneur who could supply it. The spectacular growth of sea trade and of porcelain, metal, and printing industries serve as examples of the government's influence. Iron farm tools also proliferated. Robert Hartwell (1961–62) has shown that production (mining and manufacturing) expanded twelvefold and modernized accordingly, so that the Sung produced as much iron as did Europe several hundred years later. (On Sung economy, see also Chou 1974; McKnight 1971.)

The leading intellectuals of Northern Sung—men like Ou-yang Hsiu, Wang An-shih and Su Shih—were to some extent the architects of the famed Sung Chinese fusion of Confucian public morality with Buddhist and Taoist metaphysics (Chu and Lu 1967; Graham 1958; Nivison and Wright 1959). Their ideals are stated over and over in their poems, with explicit references to Buddhism and philosophic Taoism. They were not often active practitioners of these religions, though Wang (among others) became a devout Buddhist and Su Shih dabbled in alchemy (Lin

1947; Clark 1931). In Southern Sung, these questions were further studied and the ethical system of neo-Confucianism elaborated. By far the most famous and important philosopher of the period was Chu Hsi (1130–1200). Translating beliefs about human nature into policy, in the historical context of Sung, involved much more than worrying about the Rites and the meaning of Principle. There was, for instance, the problem of who was going to do what. With the aristocracy gone, the military downplayed and the bureaucracy still relatively small and underpowered, delegation of authority had to be planned. Several new institutions arose, among them the *pao-chia*, a government system in which a group of households are responsible for each other. Local minor officials outside the scholar-bureaucracy took on new importance. Of great long-term import was the rise in importance of the lineage. Aristocrats had always had much power and wealth vested in the lineage, but only beginning in Northern Sung could any lineage be a corporate body with its own rules, lands, rents, educational institutions, and leadership. The first known true lineage estate was established by Fan Chung-yen in 1048 (Ebrey 1981). Estate lands were to be used for mutual aid within the lineage and were initially tax-free. One of their important purposes was generating funds for educating lineage children, thus giving them a chance at the civil service examinations. The corporate lineage also came to serve as a way of delegating authority. Lineages became tiny empires within an empire, regulating their own affairs according to Confucian guidelines, and freeing the state for overarching concerns.

The other group that stepped into the void was the new rich. Trade rose dramatically in Sung, as in previous major dynasties, but there was an important difference: Sung's loss of the north and west. Even at the beginning, the dynasty did not hold the northern marches or Central Asia. This, coupled with the final fruition of the long-obvious trend toward developing the south and east, led to a dramatic and almost total redirection of trade between High T'ang and Sung. T'ang's most flourishing external trade had been with Central Asia and the west, while internally the important flow of goods had been from Szechuan and the Yellow–Yangtze interfluve to the capital. Sung's major external trade, by contrast, was maritime; constant voyages were made to Korea and there was considerable contact with Japan, Southeast Asia, and some enterprises even farther afield. Internally, the trade along the Yangtze and into the deep south became far more important—especially, of course, after the fall of the north. Its capital in the Yangtze delta at Hangchou, the Sung world became an aquatic one; its main street was the Yangtze, its door on the world the China Sea.

This had its effects on the sociology of enterprise. During T'ang, the Central Asia trade (and what little maritime trade T'ang had) had been largely controlled by foreigners and by government enterprise. Trade across the deserts required organization of huge, expensive, slow caravans. In Sung, by contrast, anyone who could afford a sampan could become a trader of consequence. Cuisine was benefited as regional middle classes arose, a bourgeoisie loving its solid comforts.

This brings us to agriculture, via the question of land use and land tenure.[1] The average family—independent peasants or tenants—controlled about 100 mu, a large amount of land, for the mu had reached its modern area of about one-seventh of an acre. However, an average tells us little in this case. Many, perhaps even most, independent peasants had only around 20 mu. The *chuang-yuan* (large estates) controlled much of the empire, especially in the most developed areas. Still, perhaps 60 percent of the peasants were small-scale freeholders. Others worked government land of various designations. Those on the chuang-yuan enjoyed varying degrees of security, autonomy, and control over their land, depending on local circumstances. The great estates were most highly developed in the lower Yangtze region and later in Fukien (Eberhard 1977:216), areas where trade was most active and where the land was most valuable because of its richness and its proximity to markets. These areas were the centers of power and learning as well, and the scholar-bureaucrats and landlords mingled. Inevitably, the landlords found ways to avoid taxation, laying a heavy load on the backs of the smallholders and often driving them to seek tenant status. Perhaps 70 percent of the land was tax exempt (Chou 1974; Golas 1980; McKnight 1971, 1975).

Meanwhile, Liao and Chin were working out a different accommodation. They did not have the option of maintaining a small and relatively unmilitary government. Tribal conquerors, forced to hold down their Chinese subjects while fighting other Altaic peoples, they never questioned the need to maintain a strong and militarized government with a broad financial base. Insofar as they moved away from this, they fell rapidly; softer Chinese ways were adopted by Liao and then by Chin before the conquest of each. The tribes still owned land collectively, for extensive herding, but private property and government landownership were dominant in the agricultural areas. Chin in particular depended heavily on state monopolies, adding iron and a half a dozen other commodities to the salt, wine, and tea already mentioned. Few people were spared: even the tribesmen, the ruling house's people, were taxed, although under Chin, taxes on Chinese were as much as forty-four times greater than taxes on Jurchen (Buell 1982; Jing 1976).

In 1068, a new Sung emperor took office under the title Shen-tsung. An aggressive fighter for public welfare, economic improvement, and centralization of power in his own hands, Shen-tsung called Wang An-shih to become his Prime Minister. Wang, already well known as a militant advocate of reform, embarked on a series of far-reaching changes that alienated his previous backers and eventually most of the rest of the country. The story is too complex to be summarized here (see Liu 1959; Meskill 1963; Williamson 1935–37), but Wang's broad and sweeping reforms had two goals: to strengthen the state and to increase production. His measures included a new and more far-reaching militia act and several other military measures; tax reform and equalization; reorganization of the fiscal system; and reform of the examination system to make specialized training and knowledge of statecraft more important while reducing the stress on purely literary skills. He increased coinage considerably, thus furthering the monetization of the economy. More directly relevant to agriculture was the agricultural loan program and the rebirth of the ever-normal granary system. The latter had been tried many times before in Chinese history, with varying success. The former measure involved loaning money to peasants in the spring (hence it was called the Green Shoots Plan) and receiving repayment in the fall at a rate of interest that, while usurious (up to 40 percent) by modern standards, was far below then current rates in the countryside. Wang also favored land reclamation and water conservancy measures. One of his most important ideas was a survey in which all the lands of China were to be classified according to yield and taxed accordingly. (Land was supposed to be taxed according to its potential, but good data on potential were notably lacking in Wang's time.) He reformed taxes broadly with an eye to easing the burden on ordinary people while increasing state revenues. Thus some previously exempt groups were taxed, and well-to-do people began to pay something like their share. (Large landlords, however, still appear to have gotten off lightly, if they paid anything at all.) Corvée labor was likewise reformed—a cash payment in lieu of service was introduced as a preferred way of discharging this responsibility. In every measure, Wang showed himself the friend of the smaller landlords and merchants of the central areas of China—the class from which he himself came. (He was the scion of a small landowning family in Kiangsi.) More important than class aid, however, was his contribution to the development of the powerful, centralized, technocratically managed bureaucratic state.

Naturally, however, Wang's program attracted criticism from all sides, and it was repealed at his retirement. With it died any hope of major reform in Sung China.

According to Mark Elvin, a revolution took place in farming during the Sung. Indeed, it may be described as China's second Green Revolution, the first being that of the late Warring States, Ch'in, and Han. He describes its elements as follows:

(1) Farmers learned to prepare their soil more effectively as the result of new knowledge, improved or new tools, and the more extensive use of manure, river mud and lime fertilizers. (2) Strains of seed were introduced which either gave heavier yields, or resisted drought better, or else by ripening more rapidly made it possible to grow two crops a year on the same land. (3) A new level of proficiency was reached in hydraulic techniques, and irrigation networks of unprecedented intricacy constructed. (4) Commerce made possible more specialization in crops other than the basic foodgrains, and so a more efficient exploitation of varying resource endowments. (Elvin, 1973:118).

Yet, as we learn from Chou Chin Sheng (1974), "farming techniques did not differ from those of earlier times, but credit and land measures did" (96). How does one reconcile these apparently disparate views? The first point of reconciliation lies in the fact that Elvin's revolution was quantitative, not qualitative. Fertilizing, land preparation, erosion control, double-cropping, water wheels and other irrigation devices including the noria and treadle pump, irrigation management, and commerce were all of long standing in China. What was distinctive about Sung was the increase in all of these. There is not much question as to what led to the increase: the expansion of commerce and markets created a need for high production, and the loss of Central Asia, the cross-Asian trade, and eventually the whole of North China necessitated extreme intensification of agriculture. Facilitating this were the enlightened policies of the government and the rise of printing. The government kept taxes relatively low (especially when one averages in all the exemptions), encouraged trade, engaged in large-scale procurement, opened up new lands and encouraged their colonization (often settling them with landless wanderers), and promulgated new information, technology, and technological-aid policies. Book printing (which was invented in T'ang and became common in Sung) facilitated rapid dissemination of agricultural knowledge. Chia Ssa-hsieh's Ordinary People's Needed Skills, written during the period of disunion, was printed and soon followed by a host of agricultural manuals long and short, updated and adapted to the various conditions of Sung, national and regional. This spate of publication climaxed just after Sung's fall, with the Mongol-sponsored Essentials of Farming and Agriculture and Wang Chen's Book of Agriculture (Bray 1984; Elvin 1973). These embodied most of the agronomic knowledge that the Chinese amassed in traditional times.

Most important of all, and the only really revolutionary innovation in Sung, was the introduction of new crop varieties. The most famous and significant of these was short-growing-season rice from Champa, described by the Sung Buddhist author Shih Wen-ying:

Emperor Chang-tsung (998–1022), being deeply concerned with agriculture, came to know that the Champa rice was drought-resistant and that the green lentils of India were famous for their heavy yield and large seeds. Special envoys, bringing precious things, were dispatched . . . with a view to securing these varieties. From Champa twenty *shih* . . . of . . . seeds were procured, which have since been grown almost everywhere. From central India two *shih* of green lentil seeds were brought back. . . . When the first harvests were reaped in the autumn, [Cheng-tsung] called his intimate ministers to taste them and composed poems for Champa rice and Indian green lentils. (Ho 1956–57:200–18).

The rice was distributed in 1011 and widespread by 1012. Surely only the Chinese would not only have introduced such crops but gone on to write poems in praise of them. The green lentils mentioned in the quotation seem to be a variety of mung bean, the green bean of modern China, and this may also describe the introduction of that very valuable crop into the country. The Champa rice, fast-ripening and tough, permitted an expansion of rice-growing and a vast increase in double-cropping, which slowly became the rule throughout southeastern China. We have less information about the introduction of other crops. Fenugreek came via Arab merchants—the name still used in China is derived from Arabic—from the southern ports (Laufer 1919:446). Watermelons and sorghum reached the northern dynasties and became established there, soon finding their way to the rest of China—although sorghum perhaps did not arrive until Yüan; certainly it was not an important crop until then (Anderson and Buell MS; Hagerty 1940; Laufer 1919). None of these had revolutionary impact, though watermelons and sorghum were to become mainstays of North China's dry landscape and important foods throughout the whole country. Of far greater importance, however, was the spread of cotton, which truly revolutionized Chinese clothing. Cotton was noticed as a new and valuable item by Ch'ang Ch'un in 1221 on his journey through Central Asia to the court of Chinggis Qan (Waley 1931:86). It was probably in China by T'ang, but it must have been rare. By the end of Sung it was uncommon but well known, spreading from the south as well as the northwest (Gernet 1962:130). The chief Chinese method of keeping warm—wadded cotton clothes and coverlets (the cotton traps warm air)—probably did not exist prior to the Sung Dynasty. These were patterned after the time-honored technique of making wadded silk clothes, but cotton democratized warmth and must have allowed incomparable expansion in winter work, not to speak of sheer survival.

There were probably other new crops. Vast amounts of material were brought from South and Southeast Asia by the expanded trade and tributary missions (Hirth and Rockhill 1911; Netolitzky 1977; Wheatley 1959). Sung ships were commonly 100 feet long and 150 tons displacement (Lee 1975–76). Many minor crops must have come along with the Champa rice and Indian green pulses. This is especially true of sugarcane, which became enormously important in Sung China, displacing staple food crops as it does in so many countries today (Elvin 1973:129, Sucheta Mazumdar, pers. comm.).

Innovation was concentrated in the estates of the periurban and other highly commercialized zones, especially in the south and east (Elvin 1973; Gernet 1962). But the spread of watermelons, sorghum, and cotton in the north shows that not only the Sung Dynasty was aware of the benefits of agriculture. As previously, the government actively supported agricultural development by all possible means—and this attitude was facilitated by the connections between big landowners and bureaucrats. A government made up of large and would-be large landlords, who relied heavily on monetized markets to sell their products, would not lean hard on the farming sector. However, owners of large estates in remote regions had no reason to modernize (they were doing quite well already) and one good reason not to: it give too much power to the tenants who were actually learning and implementing the new techniques. If tenants became highly sophisticated, outward-looking, and indispensable, they would be hard to control. Small landlords and relatively rich yeoman farmers, especially if producing for specialized markets and competing with other such commercialized producers, had every incentive to stay abreast of current technology.

Intensification of agriculture, however, led to ecological problems. Soil erosion, for example, worsened flooding and other disasters (Lee 1921), even though the Chin government noted and tried to prevent it (P. Buell, pers. comm.). This fateful decline was greatly accelerated by deforestation. Enclosure of commons by the great estates alienated much forestland from presumably conservation-conscious villagers. The growth of the iron industry, the ceramics industry, the printing industry (pine soot was used for ink), and other economic activities led to a wholly unprecedented demand for wood. Eventually there was a major shift from wood to coal as an energy source, but wood consumption continued high, and much of the damage was already done. It is preeminently to Sung and Chin that we owe the barren, ravaged landscapes of north and central China and of parts of the southeast as well. Contemporary observers were aware of the problem, but seem to have had no idea how to stop it, except for expanding the use of coal. Ecological deterioration had long been part of the Chinese scene, but the Sung period saw a serious increase in the rate of deterioration.

During Sung China the importance of grains underwent a substantial (if unquantifiable) shift. Rice became far more important, at last gaining its modern status as China's chief grain. Wheat, too, continued to gain, thanks to the new techniques introduced midway through T'ang. Sorghum was also spreading, at least in the far west and north outside Sung control. The north, under its Altaic leaders, still relied on the ancient millets to a great extent, though there was some rice, wheat, barley, and other crops. But rice was the miracle crop of Sung. Even before the introduction of Champa rice, varieties were diverse and superior.

Even before the fall of Northern Sung and the restriction of the dynasty to the rice-growing regions of China, rice had become perhaps the preeminent grain. By the end of Sung—with the dynasty confined to the rice areas and intensive cultivation as the rule—there was an incredible variety of rices. Early- and late-ripening, drought-resistant and flood-resistant, hard and soft rices were known. Yellow, pink, and other colors were represented among the grains (Gernet 1962:85). All degrees of stickiness were found; the stickiest were earmarked for brewing (Elvin [1973:121–27] mistakenly ascribes the stickiness to gluten content. Rice does not have gluten; the stickiness is due to a form of the starch amylose). No other grain came in such variety, yielded so much, or responded so well to labor input. Indeed, rice had much to do with the rise of labor-intensive farming in China.

While Sung was becoming increasingly dependent on rice, the northern dynasties continued the age-old dependence on millet (Wittfogel and Feng 1949). The other northern grains were also present in some quantity. Ch'ang Ch'un explicitly noted that buckwheat was absent among the Mongols in Central Asia (Waley 1931:105), so it must have been important in China, no doubt in the dry, cold, montane areas where it flourishes best. The Khitan and Jurchen peoples traditionally lived the northern tribal life of hunting, herding, fishing, and small-scale nonintensive farming. Hunting was considered important to keep fighting men in shape; fishing was a less purposeful act, but even the Liao emperors enjoyed their fishing trips. Game was of trivial import as food, but fish were important anywhere near extensive water. The most important animal foods eaten by these peoples and the Mongols were dairy products, almost always soured or fermented. Yogurt, sour cream, cheese, kumys, and other products were made from the milk of all sorts of animals, but sheep were the most important. These dairy foods were consumed in enormous quantities. Chinese ambassadors from Sung were disconcerted by milk and porridge, and one found it too much when his Liao hosts added cream or butter on top of that (Freeman 1977:170; Wittfogel and Feng 1949:116). Starting from very simple tribal cooking, like that of the historic Mongol and Tungus tribes, the dynasties developed quite elaborate cuisines, based on their own ingredients but involving the complicated processing that had recently come to characterize Chinese culinary art. The Chinese were interested enough in the result to record some recipes, which still survive.[2] This comprises most of our knowledge of food in the northern dynasties. They had fruit trees—apples, mulberries, jujubes—and wild onions and leeks; they had various melons, and in Central Asia they grew the incomparable Persian-style melons ancestral to the Hami melons of today. Such travelers as Ch'ang (Waley 1931) noted these with surprise and delight; the size, sweetness, and flavor were astonishing. The tribal peoples ate as much meat as they could, but their animals were too valuable for dairy products and transport to be slaug. tered for food except on special occasions. Even so, culling of the herds and natural deaths ensured a supply of meat for all but the poorest. Small game such as marmots and birds supplemented the meat diet.

In the Sung realms, which are much better known to us than the northern dynasties, a very different picture emerges (Freeman 1977; Gernet 1962). Kumys was still common and popular in Northern Sung, but it was probably during later Sung that the Chinese indifference to dairy products developed. The Chinese were never deeply fond of milk products, but from Wei through T'ang, powerful Central Asian influences meant that dairy foods were more extensively used. In Sung, during which the dynastic focus was in the southeast (where Central Asian influences had been minimal) and the Altaic dynasties were considered enemies, dairy foods came to be marks of the barbarian and foe. This attitude was reaffirmed under the succeeding Mongol regime, and resurgent Chinese nationalism during the Ming Dynasty reinforced the rejection of dairy foods. Despite this exception, the Sung was a period of great breadth and tolerance in eating patterns. The southern ethnic groups' various tastes influenced Chinese there, and expanding trade, commerce, and specialized agriculture broadened the choices available. Connoisseurship and gourmetship flourished in the thriving cities.

The change in foodways during Sung is reflected in literary tropes. No longer were wheat, beans, and mallows the inevitable poetic phrases characterizing poverty, though they still occurred in archaizing texts. Different grades of rice were commonly mentioned in poetry. Some low-yield varieties that also lost a lot of weight in milling were considered superior food, while the new Champa rice seems to have had the same troubles with consumer acceptance that modern high-yield grains often have; thus it was a poor man's food. The ration for low-level bureaucrats was graphically described by Su Shih as "old rusty rice no better than mud" (Watson 1974a: 217). In addition, pickled vegetables replaced mallows as poetic poverty foods. In the south, yams and taro were starch staples, especially for non-Chinese peoples, and these two tubers thus were used as a trope for the rough fare of the wild margin of civilization; however, they were also eaten all over south and central China (Schafer 1969). Su Shih knew taro in his childhood and in southern stays during his later life (Watson 1965). Conversely, fine white polished rice was a standard of good food. But the most common trope for special fare, universal in the poetry of the age, was fish. Chicken began losing out to fish during T'ang, especially from Hsuan Tsung's time, but during Sung chicken virtually disappeared as a poetic commonplace— proof that the Chinese did not always archaize, at least in some of their poetic stock-phrases. Fish became much more important in the diet not only because of the eco-logical factors involved in the shift to the south, but also because the center of the Chinese world had shifted to an area where fish and indeed all aquatic organisms had always been culturally important and deeply loved. Salt fish was a staple article. Fish were raised as an industry, with special suppliers of living fry to fish farmers, as in modern China. Some of the old rivalry of north and south—teasing over eating frogs, for instance—continued during Sung, but the south was winning increasing acceptance for its ways.

In late Southern Sung, Wu Tzu-mu coined a phrase that became famous: "the things that people cannot do without every day are firewood, rice, oil, salt, soybean sauce, vinegar, and tea" (Freeman 1977:151). Wu Tzu-mu's seven necessities are pro-verbial to this day; Chinese schoolchildren learn them as a kind of jingle. But in Sung the list was a striking novelty. Only recently had rice taken such prominence (and the term really does refer primarily to rice, not just grain). Only in Sung had *chiang* come to refer unequivocally to soy sauce; as late as T'ang it would probably have been understood, at least in literary contexts, to cover various ferments. Vinegar is notably absent from earlier dynasties' ideas of necessities. Tea was a rare luxury in T'ang and uncommon even in Northern Sung. Oil from sesame, perilla, and hemp also became more available during Southern Sung as industry and commerce devel-oped its processing and trade.

Those who were better off had plenty of *hsia-fan* (which literally means "downing the rice," that is, "something to make the rice go down"—(compare the equivalent French remark, "it helps the bread go down"), evidently the Sung equivalent of the modern word *ts'ai* ("vegetables" or "dishes to go on rice") and of the Cantonese word *sung* ("food to eat on rice"). This and soup were made as they are today: the hsia-fan stir-fried or steamed and consisting largely of vegetables, preferably with a bit of meat or fish; the soup was a thin, vegetable-based dish. The better off, how-ever, continued to eat much meat and fish. They also inherited the T'ang fondness for raw foods. Sinoda (1977) describes Sung as "the golden age of Chinese *sushi* making" (490). This sushi was made of rice, vinegar, oil, and any meat available—raw fish was evidently among the choices. Other meat was normally cooked. As always, pork was the main meat eaten, but sheep, goat, and even donkey were common, and all sorts of game and minor domestic animals were also used. Poultry—chickens, ducks, geese, quail, pheasants, and game—was abundant. Beef was also well known but seems to have been losing popularity because of Indian religious influence. Garish stories about eating human flesh, even about shops specializing in it, were common (Gernet 1962:1–35). The most famous is that immortalized in the novel *Shui Hu Chuan*, written in Yüan but set during Sung. Gernet accepts this purely fictional account as an accurate description of the times, but it is certainly not. Apparently, human flesh was eaten only during desperate famines.

Vegetables included cabbages, onions and such relatives as garlic, spinach, turnips and radishes, cucumbers and gourds, eggplants (considered beautiful as well as excellent food), cresses, carrots, and many others, especially domestic and wild greens. Fruit was widespread and as popular as ever—particularly noteworthy were the enormous pears. Marco Polo's claim that the biggest pears "weigh ten pounds a piece" (Freeman 1977:149) may be compared with Lu Yu's observation of giant pears (1981:171). Huge pears were noted as early as the Wei Dynasty. Other common fruits included apples, mulberries, jujubes, litchis, persimmons, Chinese quinces, tangerines and mandarin oranges, apricots and mei, haws, arbutus, peaches, plums, pomegranates, bananas, coconuts and jakfruit (often imported from Southeast Asia). Pine nuts, almonds, chestnuts, walnuts, foxnuts (from *Euryale ferox*, an aquatic plant), and others were also important. Whole books were written on the qualities and cultivation of some of these plants, including jujubes, litchis, and oranges; other books, intended for estate owners, dealt with bamboo shoots and the like. Gourmets delighted also in books on wild mushrooms, crabs, and other wild items (Sinoda 1977:490). Fruit was dried and also candied—using the white sugar that had just become commonly available.

Two other of Wu's necessities need special consideration: salt and tea. Salt was under government control throughout Sung, but the control was rather light and indirect at first; later, the monopoly tightened. Merchants were licensed, under increasingly stringent restrictions, to handle the salt; the government collected much revenue. Salt was produced from sea water allowed to flood fields: the crystals were scraped off the soil when the water evaporated and then purified and boiled down. In one method, ashes from the boiling fires were spread on the fields before flooding, thus capturing the natural salts concentrated in the plants (Worthy 1975). These methods are of great nutritional significance: they would have guaranteed the presence in salt of such trace minerals as potassium, iodine, magnesium, manganese, copper and other ions present in seawater and plant ash. Plant ash in particular is rich in potassium. These methods introduced trace elements into the Chinese diet, and the plant ash method also helped maintain individuals' sodium–potassium balance. The Chinese heavy consumption of salt is less unhealthy than in the West because the

Chinese plant-based diet is so high in potassium; use of plant ash would have improved the situation still further. In west China, however, salt was produced from wells and thus was not rich in trace minerals. Nutritional problems must have been more common there, as they were in recent times.

Tea—also the subject of increasingly monopolistic government control—was still a rather exotic luxury at the start of Sung, and surely no one predicted that it would become a poor household's necessity by the end of the dynasty. The cult of tea, however, developed greatly, along with other refined arts of life. Such poets as Ou-yang Hsiu (Freeman 1977:156) and Lu Yu displayed great concern with the water used to make tea; Lu, during his travels, diligently sought out springs famous for this (Lu 1981). Tea production became intensely commercialized, true agribusiness utterly different from peasant subsistence farming.

Food was still spiced with native condiments, especially ginger, cassia and brown pepper, nutmegs, and various Indian and Near Eastern aromatic fruits and seeds. Sugar was now used for preserving foods and made into all sorts of sweetmeats and candies, including little models of humans, animals, birds, flowers, fruits, and so on (Gernet 1962:95). Bean curd—*tou fu*, Japanese *tofu*—is first mentioned early in Sung, whose texts ascribe its invention to Liu An of the Han Dynasty, but this is preposterous. In fact the commodity was invented in late T'ang or early Sung— possibly by Taoists and/or people from the Huainan region, who then ascribed it, out of a sort of respect, to Liu An, the Taoist prince of Huainan (B. W.-C. Young, pers. comm.). Buddhists quickly took over the food as a good substitute for meat and for the dairy foods so important in Buddhist literature. No doubt it was invented when someone put ordinary sea salt into bean milk, possibly with an eye to preserving it, and found the resulting coagulate a delightful food (Shurtleff and Aoyagi 1983:92). Strong sea brine still makes the best coagulating agent, though gypsum is more generally used; calcium and magnesium ions act as the main agents.

The variety of dishes eaten during Sung completely defies description. At a single banquet there might be over two hundred, ranging from many different ways of serving ordinary rice to "dishes based on fruits and sweetmeats" (Gernet 1962:138). Every sort of soup, pie, dumpling, noodle, and snack that now characterize China seems to have been available in some form or other, often apparently rather close to modern forms. The small pastries now called *tien-hsin* seem to have been particularly diverse, often larger and more substantial than they are now. Many varieties of cakes existed, some called *hu-ping* (Iranian cakes). In the cities, restaurants became famous for particular dishes. (Gernet cites several accounts; 1962:127.) Breakfast in the capital consisted of fried tripe, soups, steamed hot cakes, and fried puff-pastry shreds. Light lunch from food vendors might include sweet congee, *shao-ping*, *man-t'ou* and many other cakes. Blood soup, tripe soup, and other "variety" items abounded. Kaifeng had also had its special restaurants, serving food hot or cold, regional or general.

Regional cuisine was well developed, as was the Chinese tendency to patronize regional restaurants in the capital cities. Sung writers made a primary distinction between northern cuisine, based on meat and using dairy products and dry-grown grains, and southern cuisine, with its rice and aquatic foods. Szechuanese cooking, set apart already by its spiciness and use of mountain products and herbs, was also distinctive. This is ancestral to the modern pattern; only Cantonese cooking was recognized later. The custom of regional restaurants began to serve homesick emigrants and was always maintained mostly by this trade, but even before T'ang there were some who patronized such restaurants out of a spirit of curiosity and adventure, and by Sung variety had become a major appeal of such restaurants. Urbanites in the capitals delighted in trying the minced meat and noodles with fish and shrimps typical of Ch'u-chou, or the spicy food of Szechuan (Gernet 1962:134).

They were less prone to eat, but fascinated to read about, the ethnic foods described in a Sung text summarized by Gernet:

Little frogs in Fukien and Chekiang, large frogs in central China, snake soup in Canton. The islanders of Hainan eat various insects (flies, gnats, earthworms) cooked in pieces of bamboo. The foreigners in Canton, Muslims for the most part, flavour their food with sugar, honey and musk. In Manchuria they eat dairy products flavoured with sour butter. In general, remarks the author of this work, food is salty in the South and acid (seasoned with vinegar) in the North. Non-Chinese people in China and villagers like sweetened food, while those in the plains of the Yellow River and town-dwellers prefer unseasoned food. Another source says "that people in the extreme south eat snakes, but change the name to 'brushwood eels.' Similarly, they eat grasshoppers under the name of 'brushwood shrimps,' and rats under the name of 'household deer.' (Gernet 1962:142)

I assume Gernet knows that snakes are also eaten in his native France, under the name *hedge eels*. For Hainan, Schafer's superb study *Shore of Pearls* (1969) allows us to add sago (palm starch), jaggery (palm sugar), giant bamboo shoots, civet cats, bats, and tropical fruit. The Hainan aborigines practised the custom, almost universal among Southeast Asian hill peoples, of sacrificing bovines at special ceremonial occasions, partly to build merit for the elite. Southerners also ate fermented fish, evidently in sauces like modern shrimp paste and *nuoc mam*.

There inevitably arose cookbooks—the most famous is perhaps the *Chung-k'uei-lu*, lost as a coherent text (Sinoda 1977:490). Recipes were also included in encyclopedias. The connection between health and diet was always stressed by Chinese medicine, not least in Sung, and many a recipe book is of medical inspiration. Indeed, much of the elaboration and variety of Chinese cuisine is owed to medicine. The Chinese word *fang* means both a medical formula and a culinary one, as did the word *recipe* originally (Rx is short for *recipe*).

The concept of life stages, for example, influenced diet. Children were often nursed by wet-nurses in elite families: the poet Yang Wan-li's wife attracted attention by refusing to use a wet-nurse, preferring to feed her children herself (Chaves 1975:6).

A new mother received fruits and sweets and a type of man-t'ou called "share the pain." At the infant's first bath (especially if it was a boy, I assume), jujubes were thrown into the water, and women competed to seize them, on the still universal Chinese notion that the pun on *tsao-tzu* (meaning both "jujube fruit" and "early sons") will magically produce male children at an early date (Freeman 1977:165; Gernet 1962:150). As people matured, they could consult the spectacular new Basic Herbals issued with government support. The Illustrated Basic Herbal of 1061 set new standards for botanical illustration, perhaps never surpassed in China. Hundreds of foods were illustrated and described therein. Printing made medical works and recipe books available to the public. Neo-Confucian scholarship and the high level of biological and other sciences in Sung led to reformulation of medical ideas, which became associated with the metaphysics and cosmology of the school—intellectually challenging but scientifically an unfortunate trend. Meanwhile, Taoists continued to emphasize diet and to abstain from the five grains, meat, and other supposed contaminants. Buddhist avoidance of meat and onions or garlic tastes continued to influence Chinese foodways. Special restaurants and temple cafeterias purveying foods acceptable to these congregations became popular with variety-seeking urbanites. Ordinary lore added its own minor traces of medical belief, religion, or etiquette: "Mint takes away the smell of fish. . . . After eating garlic, chewing a mixture of raw ginger and jujubes will restore the freshness of the breath" (Gernet 1962:230, citing Sung texts). Festivals also involved special foods. And the ordinary people contented themselves as best they could. The poet Lu Chih wrote:

Like Shao P'ing I plant melons on the hillside,
And flowers by the hedge like Yuan-ming
I have just dug a pool for lotus
And set up high the vine trellis,
And when my spirits are low, I boil tea in an earthen pot;
Above mean things, I am greatly content,
I have tethered the heart's monkey and the mind's horse.
(Schlepp 1970:52–53; I have retranslated the last line.)

What are we to make of Sung's place in Chinese food history? Lu Chih's poem, written about the end of Sung, captures something of the spirit: an active curiosity and interest in the world, an intense consciousness of food and agriculture, an innovative pose in arts and observation, but in the end a retreat into otherworldly quietism. China seemed to be hovering on the threshold of capitalism, industry, modern science, modern educational and information systems—all things that Europe developed hundreds of years later. However, modern science was never developed in China. The Sung literati made superb scientific observations, but they invested most of their energies in bureaucratic work and literary affairs (Sivin 1975). Education flourished and expanded greatly, herbal and dietary books were written, but the weakness of the Sung Dynasty and the conservative authoritarianism of the conquest dynasties seem to have discouraged initiative and development of a modern, expanding economy, science, and technology. The stagnant bureaucracy and landlordism seem to have weakened the cities and their active, innovative, entrepreneurial classes. At the same time, neo-Confucian philosophy—essentially static, backward-looking, otherworldly, and anti-process—became the authentic and highly reactionary expression of this stagnancy (Balasz 1964; Lo 1974). Sung seemed poised on the brink of a modernization similar to the European Renaissance; instead, it suffered loss of initiative and ultimate decline. China after Sung never regained the thrust.

The Yüan Dynasty: Mongols and West Asian Foods

From 1279 to 1368, China experienced a unique episode in its history. Other non-Han dynasties ruled China for centuries, but in all these cases the conquerors had been small groups on the Chinese imperial orbit. The Mongols, however, were already rulers of a world empire when they invaded and conquered China. They introduced new skills and new foods, but they remained to some extent the overlords of a conquered and rather autonomous province. The stereotype that China always assimilated its conquerors does not hold true for the Mongols. When rebellion finally dislodged them from rule, they did not die fighting on the city walls; they mounted their horses and rode back to their inner Asian steppes, with (I believe) a sense of relief.

The rise of Chinggis Qan, popularly known as Genghis Khan, set the stage for the conquest of China. Chinggis united Mongolia and consolidated control over all Central Asia, building up not only a world empire but a whole new bureaucracy to run it. Although he did not directly attack the Chinese realm, he planned China's conquest and set the stage for the actual event. Thus his effect on China's history was profound, both through his military activities and through his creation of a political order capable of managing a far-flung domain.

It was after Chinggis' death that China was attacked. According to the classic legend, he was saving China for last (as a child saves his or her favorite chocolate), but he died before he could thus crown his life "work," if work it can be called. The *Secret History of the Mongols* tells us that Chinggis' character was thus summed up by his mother:

You are like the panther that dashes itself against the cliff-side, like the lion that cannot quell its wrath, like the boa-constrictor that swallows its prey alive, like the falcon that flings itself at its own shadow, like the pike that gulps silently, like the randy he-camel that bites the heels of its own young, like the wolf that works havoc under cover of the snowstorm, like the madaqrin-duck that eats the ducklings that cannot keep pace with her, like the jackal guarding its lair, like the tiger that with no second thought pounces on its prey, like the wild *barus* [unidentified] that dashes into things at random! (Waley 1963:228)

(Never mind that there are no boas in Mongolia; the story is apocryphal, but a good one.) Attacks on the Jurchen concluded with their conquest in 1234. The Mongols soon turned their attention south, and Qubilai Qan, Chinggis' grandson, rolled up China like a floormat.

Most of the work of ruling China fell on the traditional Chinese bureaucratic class and on the *se-mu*. The Mongol term is applied to Central Asians, especially Turkic peoples, similar in language and culture to the Mongols, who supplied expertise in technology and administration. The se-mu occupied a middle position in the strict ethnic hierarchy of Yüan below the Mongols and higher than the Chinese. This was a great age for Turkic inner Asians such as the Uighur people. One of the greatest Yüan poets, Kuan Yun-shih, was a Uighur (Lynn 1980). Two Ongut Turks from the northwest Chinese desert, the Nestorian Christians Markos and Bar Sauma, traveled west on a pilgrimage to Jerusalem and found themselves—through a series of inter-esting events—promoted respectively to Patriarch of the entire Nestorian Church and ambassador from the Nestorians to the Roman Catholic world (Budge 1928; Montgomery 1927. See also Dardess 1973; Langlois 1981). Other Turks, as well as Ira-nian speakers of various backgrounds, found themselves occupying high positions in China. One Persian, Sayyid Ajall, ended his days as governor of Yünnan Province in China's far southwest (P. Buell, pers. comm.). At no other time in history have such astonishing changes of place and position brought men back and forth across Cen-tral Asia. Yet even this was not as strange as the saga of Marco Polo, Italian mer-chant's son turned Mongol administrator in China, and the less well-known tales of William of Rubruck, John of Plano Carpini and other Europeans sent as delegates to the Great Qans (Boyle 1977; Yule and Cordier 1903).[3]

Under these circumstances, agriculture did not greatly progress. The slow break-down of the Sung Dynasty and the wars at its fall left China's population at perhaps some sixty million in early Yüan. Population grew at a healthy rate if this figure is correct, for there were about seventy million Yüan citizens by the 1290s. The wars of the decline and fall of Yüan knocked the figure back down to sixty million, reported in the Ming Dynasty's first thorough and reliable census. The main decline vis-à-vis earlier periods was in the north, decimated by unceasing war and the heavy-handed, steppe-oriented early Mongol policies. The lands of Southern Sung fell without much fighting and seem to have lost few people; at any rate, they were back up to their Sung figure of about fifty million people by the 1290s census, while North China had a mere ten to twenty million. Yüan domains in Central Asia added a few million more (Langlois 1981:1–21).

Trade still flourished: Marco Polo's astonishment at its extent and wealth is pro-verbial. Much of the trade was in foodstuffs. For instance, Marco claimed that Hangchow had "ten principal markets" and "a vast number of others." Each of the ten was held three days per week and attracted "40,000 or 50,000 persons"; the meat available included "roebuck, red-deer, fallow, hares, rabbits, partridges, pheasants, francolins, quails, fowls, capons, and of ducks and geese an infinite quantity," as well as "every kind of vegetables and fruits" (Yule and Cordier 1903:2:202–03). The supplies of game indicate vast imports of food by the city from great distances. Marco claimed that "for one shipload of pepper that goes to Alexandria or elsewhere, destined for Christendom, there come a hundred" to Chüanchou, a principal port in Sung and Yüan times in what is now Fukien (2:235). The enormous maritime trade of Sung continued. Tribute relations and other governmental trade flourished. Lavish and bulky presents were exchanged with the court of Muhammad bin Tughluq in India. Agricultural production benefited from the great advances made under Chin and Sung (Raychaudhuri and Habib 1982), and inventions such as the foot-operated endless-chain waterpump wrought great changes in agriculture. The potentials of water wheels and other local water-lifting devices were exploited along with the foot-powered pump (still a feature of the Chinese scene). The Mongols' crowning achievement was taming the Yellow River, a goal not achieved often in Chinese history and perhaps the most spectacular accomplishment of any preindustrial state.

The lords of Yüan quickly learned the Chinese policy mix for agricultural development. The late T'ang twice-yearly tax continued, but it was kept fairly low. Poll taxes were collected, and later property taxes when appropriate (i.e., when there was more property than heads to tax). Trade was taxed at a low rate. The usual monopolies on salt and metals continued, and transiently or locally there were imports on wine, vinegar, bamboos, and all sorts of local products. (Franz Schurmann [1956] ably translated and commented on relevant chapters of the standard Yüan history.) A half-serious suggestion by one crusty old Mongol lord, to the effect that China should be depopulated and turned into grazing land, provided a pretext for Yeh-lü Chu-tsai to present a cogent and sweeping account of the vital importance of agriculture to the Mongol court early in the regime. Yeh-lü, a leading and brilliant statesman, commanded more authority in this position than a Chinese would have done; he was scion of the old Liao ruling family.

But the queer mix of autocracy and anarchy that characterized Yüan China vitiated most efforts at reform. Sung's worst legacy—landlordism and agrarian inequality —was passed on. A powerful rural gentry flourished, regionally based, independent of the government, and threatening to everyone. At first, peasant rebellions were directed against it; but in the end, rebels from the destitute class learned to collaborate with the gentry. Once this collaboration became a fact, the Yüan Dynasty was doomed.

Food during Yüan took on a more Central Asian flavor. The Mongols followed the usual nomadic pattern of dairy food use; kumys, cream, butter, and all manner of milk products were conspicuous among their foods. Mares' milk was of enormous daily and ceremonial importance. The popularity of yogurt in Yünnan, among Chinese as well as other ethnic groups, may well stem from Yüan times, when this province became an important area with many Central Asian colonists (P. Buell, pers. comm.). However, local groups such as the Tibetan peoples have always used milk products, and they surely also had some impact on the present pattern. Game was also a Mongol staple. The *Yin-shan Cheng-yao* (Essentials of Dietetics), presented to the Emperor by the court physician in 1330 A.D., includes entries on antelope, bear, various deer, tiger, leopard, marmot, both whooper and tundra swans, pheasants, cranes, and many other wild animals and birds. Some of these (tiger and leopard, for instance) were of purely medicinal value, but most were considered food. Swans are virtually absent from China and represent the clearest carryover from the steppes. Few fish and shellfish are mentioned, and the fruits and vegetables are typical of the dry interior north. Boiled mutton was probably the most important food after grains (cf. Sinoda 1977:483–97, Unschuld 1985:215).

The book's recipes involve heavy use of the tail fat of the fat-tailed sheep—a mass of fat and connective tissue that overwhelms the buttocks and tail of this animal. Fat-tailed sheep varieties occur in Central Asia, where small carts are sometimes attached to the sheep to support the tail. When cooked, the material is a chewy solid of meatlike texture. The fat in it has a unique flavor, stronger but pleasanter than mutton fat, and it is probably the most beloved food item throughout Central Asia. Nothing could be further from Chinese taste, however, and the emphasis on it in the *Yin-shan Cheng-yao* (both the mass itself and the rendered fat figure largely in the recipes) indicates the Mongol origin and audience of the book. Other recipes in the volume are strongly Arabo-Persian or Turkic in origin. Chinese influence on this book appears largely in its treatment of vegetables. The medical tradition from which it springs (it is a nutrition text, not a cookbook) is found widely in Asia, though the five-element theories it espouses are Chinese. The view of food as medicinally effective, and the concepts of the humoral and "strengthening" properties of foods, must have been accepted by the Mongols before they conquered China. But the elaboration of such theories in the *Yin-shan Cheng-yao* is beyond anything one would expect of nomads and represents strong influence from a widely shared pattern of court cuisines known across West and Central Asia and further (Buell 1987; Sabban 1983a).

A native Chinese counterpart to the text exists in the *Yin-shih Hsu-yao Chih* of Chia Ming. This book was published at the beginning of Ming, but Chia had compiled it earlier, and since Chia's life more than spanned the Yüan Dynasty his work can be taken to reflect Chinese foodways in Yüan (Mote 1977:208). Chia's knowledge is essentially drawn from the herbals of his day, and its extent would put modern Californian health-food addicts to shame. A modern reader must assume that Chia did as modern Chinese do, avoiding possibly dangerous foods when he was at exceptional risk due to sickness or stress. Nourishing aspects of foods—even more specifically tied to humoral and strengthening properties than in the Mongol work—are emphasized, too, so that few foods are without their benefits.

The differences between Chia's work and the Mongol book are predictable. Chia mentions some game animals—tiger, wild horse, and so on—but none of the Central Asian specialties, and these big game animals are buried among detailed accounts of domestic creatures and small birds. Fish receive a great deal of attention in Chia's book, which includes sixty-eight entries on aquatic foods for the *Yin-shan Cheng-*

yao's twenty-two. Vegetables and fruits are similarly richly treated by Chia. Litchis, longans and a possible hybrid—"dragon litchis" (the word made up of the first syllables of the other two words)—are there, along with coconuts, *Canarium* fruit, and other items that the Mongols must have barely known of. The list of vegetables includes such oddments as sweet chrysanthemum shoots.

Wang Chen's great *Nung Shu* (Book of Agriculture), a definitive survey of farming since the Sung Green Revolution, appeared in 1313. The *Chu-chia Pi-yung* (Necessities of Daily Life) and *Shih-lei Kuan-chi* (Wide Descriptions of Everyday Matters), great and long-lasting Yüan encyclopedias, provide much information about food and cooking. Mongol, Muslim, and Manchurian foods are heavily featured in both volumes; dairy products and game appear. Use of vegetables is limited and Near Eastern condiments are important. Sharbat appears under the name *she-li-pai*: boiled water was poured over the flowers, leaves, or straw and used as a drink; in addition, fermented sauce (probably soy sauce) was flavored with the flowers in what seems a rather odd mating of Near and Far Eastern tastes. Tea was imbibed with flavorings or butter as in modern Tibet. Sinoda (1977) quotes an odd Mongol recipe from the *Chu-chia Pi-yung*: "Suck blood and slime out from fresh lung of deer (if there is no deer, hare's or goat's lung may do), pour in water, repeat sucking and pouring until the lung is clear. Crush leek, garlic, and ginger, season with salt, and filter. Fill this garlic sauce in the lung, chill the lung with ice, and serve" (491–92).

The Sung–Yüan period was pivotal for China. China's agriculture and food developed greatly, not to change and improve so dramatically again until the twentieth century. Urbanization, trade, foreign influences, and a relatively open economy all had their share in this. But the circle was closing. Population density increased; resources diminished sharply. Any lingering pressure to save labor rather than land was removed. The Sung–Yüan innovations are primarily of the sort that spare land by lavishing labor on it (Chao 1986; Elvin 1973); this exacerbated the tendency toward extremes of wealth and poverty. The elite and the middle class developed the greatest cuisine the world had ever known; even the poor benefited from many of the changes, but troubles were mounting.

6 Involution: Late Imperial China

The Ming Dynasty: Autocracy and Slowdown

The Ming rulers have been blamed for failing to lead China to capitalism and industry, because the West developed these dubious blessings during the same period. A leading Western authority on Ming agriculture, Evelyn Sakakida Rawski, wrote:

The economic landscape of Ming China is most commonly studied not for itself but as a reference point in larger interpretations of Chinese history. Modern preoccupations, in particular with the "failure" of China to respond as did Japan to Western "impact," have shaped the nature and content of research, so that much of the scholarship on Chinese economic history in the Ming and Ch'ing periods . . . reveals a Europo-centric bias in its focus on why China did not independently sustain an Industrial Revolution. (1972:1)

The Ming sovereigns might have replied that they were having enough trouble trying to be imperial dragons for everyone to blame them for not being savage tigers too. (On Ming history, see Chan 1982, which follows the official histories too faithfully; Farmer 1976; Hartwell 1982; Huang 1974, 1981; Hucker 1961, 1978; Spence and Wills 1979. Historical material in this chapter is synthesised primarily from these sources.)

Incompetence, corruption, and abject failure characterized much of the Ming period and helped prevent China from making major breakthroughs in science and technology. Still, the Ming Dynasty lasted for almost three hundred years, most of which were more peaceful and prosperous by Chinese standards. Population grew more than at any previous time in China's history, there were no significant wars, and external threats were effectively met until the very end.

The strengths and weaknesses of Ming stem from the policy of its founder. Chu Yüan-chang was a phenomenon never seen before in China and rarely in any country: a man from the very lowest orders who took over the country. China had had plebeian rulers before—most notably the founder of Han—but they never had been from the dregs. Chu was a military deserter, a quasi religious figure, petty criminal, and drifter, a member of China's vast lumpenproletariat. Taking advantage of the rebellions at the end of Yüan and of their millennarian religious cast, he parlayed his training and charisma into world power.

Afterward, centralization gave way to imperial sloth. The denouement came in the late sixteenth century, when the Wan-li Emperor went on a sort of imperial strike, refusing for several years to meet or appoint officials or otherwise discharge even minimal functions. Ray Huang (1981) ascribed this, romantically, to frustrated familial love, but others have attributed it to glandular or mental imbalance. Wan-li was followed by young and incompetent successors in the early seventeenth century. The Ming Dynasty could not survive such neglect, and it fell by 1644.

Yet in late Ming, population was perhaps triple what it had been at the start, growing from about 50 million to an estimated 150 million (Ho 1959; Huang 1974; Perkins 1969). To demonstrate the Ming Dynasty's accomplishment, we need only compare Europe, which had perhaps 60 million people by 1500 and 100 million in 1600 (Braudel 1981:39–42, 466), and India, which had about 100 to 150 million in both 1300 and 1800 (Raychaudhuri and Habib 1982).

But before 1500, the inevitable troubles of Chinese dynasties had surfaced. Although the founder of Ming laid down explicit and draconian rules to prevent eunuchs and palace women from getting power, such rules were mere sandbars in a flood. The few thousand powerless eunuchs in 1400 had somehow increased to seventy thousand in the early 1600s (Chan 1982; Huang 1974). The empire was strapped for cash. Its primary source of revenue was the land tax, which with various surcharges and additional imposts amounted to under 5 percent of ordinary peasants' gross. (Of course, corrupt officials took more.) Larger landowners were taxed less than 10 percent of their crops. Other fiscal matters were irregular. One nostalgic Ming writer commented on Sung: "Fiscal administration in those days must have been superior to ours by myriads and millions of times" (Huang 1969:126). The imperial household needed 214,000 piculs of grain a year, and court expenses on food and entertainment reached 260,000 to 400,000 taels annually in late Ming. Enormous quantities of timber were required, which led to deforestation and a shortage of wood for machines and implements. The army was supposed to feed itself by farming but did not (Huang 1974: 38, 256, 282).

Climate compounded the problem. The Ming Dynasty corresponds in time to the worst of the Little Ice Age, a period of extremely cold winters and of summers when the rains were apt to fail or to come in sudden torrents (Harding 1982; Zhang 1982). Disasters and famines struck, agricultural development was inhibited, and the northern base of the empire was sorely stressed. It was not the right time to have few funds for relief. Ming also roughly coincided with the age of the greatest plagues in the West and had its own problems with disease (Chan 1982:236).

For better or for worse, Ming was a dynasty of the upwardly mobile. The royal family was of plebeian origin and never forgot it (Hucker 1978). The eunuchs were all of very low birth, since no one of any standing would subject himself to an operation that was not only demeaning but was fatal half the time. (At least that was the rate reported by medical observers in late Ch'ing; during Ming it is not likely to have been better.) Many scholar-bureaucrats came up through the examinations, not through birth (Ho 1962). The Ming ruling elite was thus a dispersed, heterogeneous, unstable group drawn from the vast and scattered pool of relatively large landowning families, rich merchant households, and low-born eunuchs, which helps explain both its attempts at autocracy and its problems in carrying that out. Insecure and unstable control created a felt need for authority.

Dwight Perkins maintained in an influential book, *Agricultural Development in China, 1368–1968* (1969), that agriculture changed little during this period beyond the extension of cultivated area from 60 million to perhaps 85 million acres. This figure does not match the rate of expansion in population, but the system of registration broke down before Ming's end, and I suspect the true figure is higher. Even the low final figure, however, would mean yields of about nine hundred pounds of grain per person per year, which would have been ample (Perkins 1969:17). More use was made of the high-yield seeds popularized in Sung; further varieties and local strains were developed and made available; relatively new technologies of water control and fertilizing spread; and New World food crops began to enter China (Ho 1955). Rawski (1972) showed that these changes were more important than Perkins thought: spread of high-yield crops and of highly intensive cropping cycles and methods were particularly important.

By the end of Ming, New World foods became well known, at least as famine relief crops in limited areas. Introduced by the Spanish and Portuguese, they spread primarily from Manila with returning Chinese traders. Macau was the other important port of entry. Some plants seem to have come across the mountains from India (and ultimately from the Portuguese at Goa and elsewhere), but this route may not have been active until the Ch'ing (Ho 1955). Sweet potatoes were the most important borrowing almost from the start. They seem to have come to China in the latter half of the sixteenth century and were well known by 1594, when a governor in Fukien propagated them for famine relief. They certainly came from Manila, where they were brought by the Spanish from Mexico; their Nahuatl (Aztec) name, *camotl*, survives in almost all Philippine languages. In China, they were christened *chin-shu* (golden tuber), *pai-yu* (white tuber), or *fan-shu* (southern barbarian tuber), a name by which they are now widely known in the south (although in more polite speech they are called *kan-shu*, "sweet tuber"). They may also have been brought overland from India to Yünnan, for works from that province mention *hung-shu* (red tubers) or *hung-yu* (red taro). But *hung-shu* normally refers to the red yam (*Dioscorea* varieties containing anthocyanin pigments, different from China's native yam, called *shan-yao*), not to the sweet potato.

The peanut is first mentioned around 1538 by two sources from the Suchou area. Maize is first certainly mentioned in 1555, but the source is from Honan; it must originally have been introduced in some other part of China (Ho 1955). Earlier possible mentions, under general names that can apply to various grains, have been cited off and on. Maize definitely came via sea routes, and probably overland as well, from Yünnan. It was not known in China in pre-Columbian times, but it must have been introduced almost as soon as Europeans reached the Far East; the Portuguese found it so much better in tropical conditions than any other crop that they planted it everywhere, often on their first voyage to an area. High-yielding and easy to grow even in hilly and poor soils, it spread rapidly.

Tobacco and probably several minor food crops also entered with the Iberians about this time. Several crops are known in South China by names that combine the adjective *fan* (southern barbarian) with the name of a long-established Chinese crop. (Westerners are sometimes still insulted with the phrase *fan kuei lou*, "barbarian ghost fellow," loosely translated "foreign devil.") Thus the tomato was called *fan* eggplant; guava, *fan* pomegranate; papaya, *fan* quince (although today the *fan* is confusingly left off); jicama or yam-bean, *fan* kudzu. These crops were all introduced from the New World; all are typical of the Latin American plants that the Iberians picked up and spread widely; some are not used by English-speaking peoples. In contrast, standard European crops and late-borrowed New World crops are known by the more complimentary terms *hsi* (western), *yang* (ocean), or *hsi-yang* (western ocean). All the *fan* plants were most likely introduced before the end of Ming. With them must have come the chile pepper, whose enormous popularity throughout most of South and East Asia bespeaks early borrowing and rapid spread. In China it became really popular only in the areas influenced by Hunanese cooking, but it is known and used all over the country.

By the end of the dynasty, New World food crops were already important even in extremely remote parts of China. Hsü Hsia-ko, an inveterate traveler of the late Ming, found the Yao people, of the remote inland mountains in southern China, depending heavily on potatoes and sweet potatoes (Hsü 1974).

Other new crops were few, because China already had most of what the rest of Asia could offer. Cotton growing expanded greatly and the native tallow tree (*Stillingia sebifera*) may have been new in cultivation, since it is not mentioned in sources earlier than Ming (Yuan 1978), but neither of these was a food crop. More important were proportionate changes: rice became even more important, reaching its modern level of significance as China's great staple. At the same time, wheat was spreading in the south, and flour was becoming an important food. Thus Rawski (1972) found the poor in Fukien, unable to afford rice, turning to flour products as a staple. The flour was probably consumed as noodles, still a staple food of rich and poor alike in Fukien.

Sugar underwent a revolution, which had begun in Sung but was consolidated during Ming, when new processing technology led to great growth in sown area. By the end of Ming, China's food was about as it is now. Rice made up approximately 70 percent of the grain, wheat most of the rest (Sung 1966). Sugar, oil, and tea had all reached an importance comparable to—though not equal to—that today. Diversified and specialized farming of fruits, vegetables, and so forth was widespread, but most prevalent in areas with good soil and good communications, especially the Yangtze Valley but increasingly the southward river valleys too. Yields were about 2 piculs per mu in the south, 3–4 on the richest land, about 1,600 to 3,200 pounds per acre.

These crops were cultivated on the tiny, fractionated farms also familiar to observers of the subsequent scene. Huge state farms in reclaimed or early-conquered areas and large estates in the richest and best-placed parts of the country controlled a substantial share of the land; but the vast majority of China's acreage was in smallholdings. Big landlords were few; landless laborers less rare, but by no means prevalent. Holdings of three to four or even ten thousand acres were rarely known; a large landlord normally held three hundred acres or even less (Huang 1974). Local landlords such as the elite of T'ung-ch'eng County, studied by Hilary Beattie (1978), owned acreage that modern American farmers would consider vanishingly small, but in Ming China these holdings guaranteed a stable base from which families could branch out into politics and business. They made money from these pursuits and banked it in land, less easily lost to officials or bandits (Chao 1981).

In the late 1500s the "single whip" tax reform was introduced, in which all the previous taxes and imposts were united into a single payment, theoretically in rice or grain but actually reckoned in silver in many areas. This reform spread slowly and against some resistance, but it may have led to a real reduction in the tax burden, since it provided less opportunity for officials to squeeze and cheat. Like earlier taxes in China, it was collected semiannually, roughly at late spring and autumn harvest times (Huang 1974). Most of the revenue came from the autumn collection.

Toward the end of Ming, a reaction set in against the arid, otherworldly speculation that had come to dominate Chinese philosophy; a utilitarian, practical tradition resurfaced. Among those influenced thereby was one Sung Ying-hsing, who wrote a study of everyday crafts, the *T'ien-kung K'ai-wu*, freely translated as "The Creations of Nature and Man" (Sung 1966). Naturally, agriculture comes first. There is little in this or other Ming agricultural works that would have been new or strange to writers of either previous or subsequent periods; but Sung shows us what the typical farmer actually did. The incredible industriousness of the Ming farmer is matched only by the amount he had to know. Rapeseed makes the best presscake for fertilizing rice, with t'ung next and camphor, tallow, and cotton last; an ox pays only if one has a good deal of land for feed, and a buffalo needs even more care, though it works harder. Beans should be sown in the hollow stems of a previous rice crop, since these fibrous stems trap and hold moisture; plowing for bean crops should be light but thorough; silkworms that hide under leaves are probably sick, but those that spin sloppy cocoons are "merely stupid" (Sung 1966:6, 8, 29, 41). (Actually, the sloppy silkworms were probably parasitized.) Rice was broken free of its stems by rolling in stone rollers, broken free of hulls or husks by hulling mills, then winnowed. The ingenious winnowing machine now found in every traditional Chinese village is well illustrated (85). Hand sieving and winnowing were also found. The rice was pounded in a mortar by a large wooden pestle. Hand-operated pestles were no doubt used in remote areas, as they are still, but usually a foot-treadle pestle or even a water-powered mill with several pestles driven by a shaft was used. Some of these mills ground wheat flour and drew water for irrigation too; "such a machine can only be invented by unusually clever minds," claimed Sung (94). Such equipment could not polish the rice in the way we understand the term today; it produced a grain that was fairly white but that retained at least the inner seed coats; thus it had almost the nutritional value of brown rice.

Wheat flour was milled by horizontal millstones. North of the Yangtze, a good quality fine-grained stone from Anhui was used, worked almost like the Hungarian-type steel rollers of modern commerce; the grain was crushed but not heated, the bran formed large flakes that could be sieved off, and flour of 80 percent or less extraction resulted. It was not as white as today's, as it retained some seed coat and germ, but it was a fine flour. South of the Yangtze, coarse stones heated and pulverized the bran, which mixed in with the flour; a coarse brown flour resulted, and the stones had to be replaced more frequently. In both areas the flour was bolted through silk, and in the north this produced a very fine white flour of low extraction rate. However, there was no way to remove the ground germ, so the flour spoiled quickly (95). It also had more nutritional value than modern white flour.

Other grains were ground or pearled. Sung also described in detail the production of salt and was aware of the physical need for this mineral. He details sugar production and processing, yeast and brewing. By contrast—surprising to a modern reader—he does not bother to discuss pickling or the processing of soybeans into sauce or bean curd, though he briefly mentions them (29). Evidently these were of little commercial importance, however important they may have been to the household; Sung does not deal with activities performed in the home. I infer that—in spite of the detailed discussion of bean curd in other Ming books (which describe a process essentially like that used today in highly traditional areas), bean curd was not produced commercially on any scale at that time.

The Chinese diet must have been overwhelmingly grain-based, using even fewer meat and bean products than are used today. Sung mentions no other foods except beans—soy, mung, broad, dolichos, sword beans, peas, and cowpeas—sesame, and vegetable oils (30–31). These are discussed in a chapter on oil extraction devoted primarily to industrial uses of oils, for example, in candle making. Sung lists the best oils for food as soybean, sesame, turnip, and Chinese cabbage; *Perilla* and rapeseed; then tea-seed (dangerous, as the presscake is poisonous), amaranth, and last hemp (215–16). The official agricultural encyclopedias have more information, but they are less lively and have fewer evidently eyewitness accounts.

Another lively witness was an ordinary Korean, Ch'oe Pu, who came to China by accident. Koreans tended to adulate Ming China, regarding it as *fons et origo* of everything good, but Ch'oe regarded it with an objective eye. He had been caught in a storm in 1488 and driven on the China coast, where he was taken into custody by the government and soon returned to Korea. Meanwhile, he had a good opportunity to see China—a land poorly known and rarely visited by Koreans at that time, in spite of its importance in their culture. His notes on food are usually sparse, but interesting. When he met a regional commander (after long dealings with lesser officials), he was honored with tea and fruit and given good provisions, which he listed as follows:

One plate of pork
Two ducks
Four chickens
Two fish
One beaker of wine
One plate of rice
One plate of walnuts
One plate of vegetables
One plate of bamboo shoots
One plate of wheat noodles
One plate of jujubes
One plate of bean-curd   (Ch'oe 1965:73)

This must have been typical of official gift-giving of the time and must represent what the government believed to be appropriate staples for a not particularly distinguished traveler. In summing up his experiences, Ch'oe contrasts North and South China, using the Yangtze as the division. He thought the food was coarse in both areas, describing eating from common bowls with chopsticks. He found the south more refined and notes—in addition to rice—sorghum, bamboo, longans, litchis, oranges, pomelos, and all the Chinese domestic animals as characteristic foods there. The north he found much less thriving. Jujubes were its fruit.

Another Asian visitor left us an account of a more splendid reception. In 1420, an embassy arrived from Herat in what is now Afghanistan. The painter Ghiyath al-Din Naqqash described it; an English summary is provided by Morris Rossabi (1975). As soon as the embassy reached China, they were given all necessities. Every day they were in Peking they received "flour, a bowl of rice, two large loaves of sweets, a pot of honey, garlic, onion, vinegar, salt, a selection of vegetables, two jugs of beer, and a plate of desserts, and each group of ten secured a sheep, a goose and two fowl" (17).

But the most voluble travelers were the Europeans, who found China much more alien than Ch'oe or Ghiyath did. To them, everything was new except the commonest crops. The variety and cheapness of food in China amazed the "Western ocean folk" (as they were called in China). One of the first accounts is that of Galeote Pereira, a Portuguese who was jailed for smuggling in 1549 (Boxer 1953). The next account, and the first to be published (in Portugal in 1569 or 1570), was that of Friar Gaspar de la Cruz. Like Pereira, he knew only coastal South China, but he heard a good deal about the rest of the country. Cruz noted many of the same things Pereira did: the popularity of pork, the eating of frogs (which were skinned with notable skill), the cheapness of everything, the extreme abundance of aquatic foods. He mentions fruits and vegetables as well: turnips, radishes, cabbage, garlic, onions; peaches, plums, nuts, and chestnuts, oranges, litchis, and the characteristic apple-shaped Chinese pear: "a kind of apples that in the colour and rind are like grey pears, but in smell and taste better than they." He also describes feasts typical of Ming bourgeois eating (Boxer 1953:131, 133, 134). Friar Martin de Rada, who visited Fukien in 1575, records several other food items, including the curious black-fleshed chickens of South China and northern Southeast Asia, and the large stocks of pigeons and doves.

From such accounts as these, Father Juan Gonzalez de Mendoza produced a thorough and systematic account of China, published in Rome in 1585. At one bound, Western knowledge of China increased immeasurably. Mendoza's excellent and broadly accurate account remained the primary source of knowledge about China for decades, known and read by educated people throughout Europe, and is an important source still. By 1588 it had been translated into English, by one Richard Parker, under the snappy title, *The Historie of the Great and Mightie Kingdome of China, and the Situation Thereof; Togither with the Great Riches, Huge Citties, Politike Governement, and Rare Inventions in the Same.* Among the things Mendoza discusses are pine nuts, honey, artificial incubation, tree-crop interplanting with grain (he incidentally notes that one of the grains was maize—a very early reference to this as a Chinese crop), cormorant fishing, and extensive fish farming (Mendoza 1853:15). He notes that duck farmers were paid to run their ducks through infested rice fields near Canton—snails as well as weeds were destroyed thus. Even the ornamental gardeners had fish: "and there is none of them but hath his fish poole furnished, although it bee but small" (150).

But, of course, most of the writings on Chinese food were by the Chinese themselves. Ming writings on food are so extensive that they beggar description. (Frederick Mote's long and thorough essay in *Food in Chinese Culture* [1977] covers this ground well.) Plays, novels, poems and songs of Ming record in loving details everything from the chaff and beans of the poor to the luxuries of the rich.

The court, of course, was the most luxurious. It "operated then as the world's largest grocery store and dining hall. It employed 6,300 cooks in 1425, and toward the end of the dynasty the staff grew larger. . . . From the number of wine jars delivered to this agency and the amount of salt consumed by it, it can be estimated that its kitchen service must have served from 10,000 to 15,000 persons daily. This does not even cover the numerous sacrificial services that were handled by the Court of Imperial Sacrifices" (Huang 1969:90). In 1578 26.6 million piculs of grain or the equivalent were collected in taxes, of which well over 4 million piculs went to supply the court and stock the imperial granaries. The kitchen staff reached 9,462 in the mid-fifteenth century; it had been reduced to 7,874 in the sixteenth century (90). A Ming source noted that in 1468 the Court of Imperial Entertainments required "more than 1,268,000 catties of fruits and nuts" (57). Mote also tells us about the Court of Imperial Sacrifices. Its cooking staff reached 1,750 in 1583. Over 200,000 animals were sacrificed each year, including "160 sacrificial swine; 250 sacrificial sheep; 40 young bullocks of one color; 18,900 fat swine; 17,900 fat sheep; 32,040 geese; 137,900 chickens" (1977:214) that had to be particularly fine, for they were offered whole.

The cooking of the great merchant and landlord households was on a less appallingly huge scale, but probably better. Baking and the making of sweets seem to have been especially well developed; novels take note of the exotic items made from sugar, and Sung Ying-hsing was intrigued enough to immortalize full instructions for making some of them, including hollow sugar animals (Sung 1966). The elaborations were more and more to be found in the great regional trading cities such as Canton, Hangchow, and Changsha and their restaurants and inns, rather than in the vast halls of the court. The complex and sophisticated cuisine reflected in such novels as the anonymously authored *Golden Lotus* (Edgerton 1939) was still confined to the well-to-do pleasure seekers of the most advanced trading cities. In short stories and plays such refinement was virtually a mark of villainy. Only the idle rich could enjoy it—no hardworking, honest official could afford either the time or the money, still less a common person.

At the other end of the social spectrum, the monotonous grain diet of the ordinary people was varied only by rare festivals and all too common famines. The progress of agriculture failed to offset population growth and the harsh, erratic climate that characterized the period. Famines were almost continually raging in one or another part of China. People ate bran, tree leaves, bark, and (at worst) each other. Ming minds developed a morbid fascination with cannibalism, which is a common theme in novels. A good measure of the accuracy of such popular tales can be gleaned from the early and instantly successful story, which persists even today, of Europeans catching and eating Chinese children. It was given official credence in the *Ming History* (compiled in early Ch'ing from Ming documents; Chang 1933). Similarly, Ch'ing government documents duly noted that early hospitals founded by Westerners collected the eyes of their patients for making potions. William Arens shows, in *The Man-Eating Myth* (1982), how wild and exaggerated are most tales of cannibalism. (Arens overstates his case, but for China he is nearer the truth than are the histories.) Chan (1982:231–34), like Gernet before him (1962), is simply too credulous of the tales.

The Ming government did not leave the peasants to starve. Not only did it run the biggest grain storage and relief operation in the world, but it also relieved taxes in afflicted areas and constructed or reconstructed infrastructure to protect the lands (Chan 1982:145, 278). The climax to the famine relief efforts was the Yellow River scheme, a public works project to dike, channel, and control the whole lower river course on a scale that would be daunting even today. Coming late in the Wan-li period, it was expensive enough to drain the country's treasuries, yet it provided only temporary relief. Overcultivation, channel constriction and silting, and the drier, colder climate with more torrential rains conspired to make the Yellow River a worse threat than ever before (Chan 1982:232; Huang 1974).

Perhaps more worthwhile, in the long run, was the compilation of the amazing

Chiu-huang Pen-ts'ao (Famine Herbal), written by Chou Ting-wang and published in 1406 in two volumes. His son Chou Hsien-wang enlarged it, and in 1559 it appeared in four volumes. The government enthusiastically sponsored the encyclopedia; Ming prince Chu Hsiao is given credit for propagating it. Experimental gardens and studies of detoxification of poisonous plants were part of the effort. The book is so good that Bernard Read's thorough summary with modern identifications has been issued and reissued in our own age not just as a historical curiosity, but as a valuable work that has never been superseded (Read 1977; Unschuld 1986). Surely Ming's successful famine control (by grain, dike, and book) helped China's population pass that of Europe and of India.

Agricultural advances increased the quantity and variety of food; court and trade developed great cuisine. One more component of the Chinese food system deserves discussion: the role of nutritional and herbal science. Ming's record must be unique in the premodern world: nowhere else did so much new and important material appear. The Emperor Chu Yüan-chang himself ordered Chia Ming to write down his knowledge (his work is discussed in chapter 5). Cooking and nutrition books continued to issue from governmental presses. Finally, at the other end of the dynasty, Chinese traditional food and medical science climaxed in one of the greatest works in the history of medicine: the *Pen-ts'ao Kang-mu* (Mirror of Basic Herbs) by Li Shih-ch'en, who lived during the sixteenth century (Li 1960; Unschuld 1986). The work has been almost continually available since its first publication, unusual for a book published so early. Li was something of a loner: an indefatigable and highly critical man, operating outside both the governmental structure and the formal and informal bounds of the orthodox medical establishment. He roamed the empire searching for herbs, trying them out on himself, collecting case histories with the acumen and pertinacity of a modern epidemiologist, straightening out local uses and misuses of names, and observing local conditions and their effects on health. A one-man institution of medical science, he raised experimental and epidemiological methods and theories to new heights in China, an accomplishment that may have been even more important than his herbal. Unfortunately, the dying days of Ming were no time for such innovations to catch on; nor was the succeeding dynasty propitious for inquiring minds. A first version of Li's herbal was finished in 1578. Li worked on an expanded version, but it was unfinished at his death in 1593. Some three years later, his sons brought it out. The government remained almost indifferent at first, but eventually—especially under Ch'ing—Li's book was enthusiastically propagated. Ch'ing editions are often huge and illustrated with some of the world's finest botanical plates. The book is still the basic work for Chinese herbal medicine; every East Asian bookstore with a good stock of Chinese materials, from Indonesia to Japan, carries it in one or another of the many cheap new editions. It is the skeleton of the monumental *Chung-yao Ta Tzu-tien* (Great Dictionary of Chinese Medicine) recently issued by the Chinese government (1979). This encyclopedic work is fleshed out with modern biochemical formulas, Latin names, and much else, but it remains true to Li's foundation. He would have loved it.

Among almost two thousand entries in Li's final version are all the common foods of China (the title *herbal* is slightly misleading, for animal, vegetable, and mineral drugs are all covered). Their position on the scale of warming and cooling is given, and their taste and flavor in the fivefold classification system. Then follow their specific medical uses, extracts from earlier medical works, and Li's evaluations. Marijuana "makes one see devils," ephedra relieves what we would now call allergy, datura anesthetizes, sagebrush disinfects and kills parasitic worms; these and thousands of other accurate observations are recorded. A great deal of nonsense or poorly tested material is also included, sometimes without comment, sometimes with sharp doubt. Most of Li's statements have not yet been adequately checked; hundreds of new drugs may await our discovery, in spite of the thousands of hours that contemporary Chinese, Japanese, and other scientists have spent checking Li's claims. Among the claims most in need of testing are statements about the specific nutritive values of various fruits, animal parts, and so on that we regard as no more than sources of a few vitamins, but that may well contain enzymes or similar chemicals that give them special virtues.

Trade flourished in early Ming but was cut back sharply after the early fifteenth century. The great voyages of Cheng Hao, who explored the South China Sea and Indian Ocean in huge vessels, were suddenly stopped. China turned inward. This movement attracted criticism at the time. Chang Han wrote in the sixteenth century: "As to the foreign trade on the northwestern frontier and the foreign sea trade in the Southeast, if we compare their advantages and disadvantages with respect to our nation's wealth and the people's well-being, we will discover that they are as different as black and white." (He meant that the northwestern trade—continued under Ming—was trivial, the sea trade vital.) "But those who are in charge of state economic matters know only the benefits of the Northwest trade, ignoring the benefits of the sea trade. How can they be so blind?" (Chang Han 1981:156). But this and many similar essays failed to sway the court. The move from Nanking to Peking took the court from the lower Yangtze, with its dynamic mercantile economy, to the stagnant, naturally impoverished north and led to the final consolidation of power in the hands of a conservative, landbased aristocracy who were the natural foes of merchants and innovators.

Western observers of China, from late Ming until today, saw the connection between autocracy and stagnation. The thesis was especially developed by Max Weber and Etienne Balasz, and it has been established in more recent years by Victor Lippit (1978) and Qian Wenyuan (1985). Lippit points out that China had been the world leader in technology for centuries; that a huge surplus still existed for investments, as shown by the fantastic amounts of illegal and quasi-legal wealth extracted from the poor over and above the revenues legally derived; and that this wealth was squandered on luxuries for the rich, rather than invested in development. This was related to the fact that in Ming, landlords were often absentees. In earlier dynasties, families had concentrated much effort on developing their lands. Ming landholding families were more apt to concentrate effort on the more profitable pursuit of official position or monopoly trade, neglecting their lands. This was true enough to lead to suppression of technological innovation. Landlords were satisfied with the real but undramatic benefits of introducing cotton, tallow trees, sweet potatoes, and the like onto their lands. At the same time, the new lineage order that evolved during Sung, in which lineages were controlled by powerful organizations of elders, propagated throughout the Chinese elite.

Another theory for China's failure to maintain its technological lead has been provided by Mark Elvin (1973), more or less followed by Francesca Bray (1984, 1986), and closely paralleled by Kang Chao (1986). In China's "high-level equilibrium trap," people worked so hard to make such a small living that their labor was cheaper than machinery or other capital-intensive innovations. Thus China did not utilize new technology and even abandoned what it had. Bray adds that rice agriculture is not amenable to mechanization. Lippit points out that the large surplus in the economy argues against such a point, but Elvin maintains that it was cheaper to hire coolies than to build a machine. Relative prices rather than absolute ability to pay are the real issue. However, Yujiro Hayami and Vernon Ruttan (1971) show that the relatively low price of labor as opposed to resources and capital explains what innovations China did make in later centuries. With abundant cheap labor, a canny estate owner would be encouraged to devise new and more elaborate strategies for using fertilizer, new labor-intensive crops, pest control, and the like, and to utilize surplus labor in production of crafts and maintenance of the infrastructure. Indeed, studies show that a lot of this did go on (Beattie 1978; Rawski 1972). But there was no independent research sector—no government grants, private funding, or even free time for men who might have spent their lives puttering in laboratories. Here, a version of Elvin's theory may inform our position. The "high-level equilibrium trap" may have been a factor at the local level, but it was much more important at the national. The government and its avatars found that wealth could be maximized by forcing more work for less pay, and they saw no great benefit in supporting pure research. So China's modernization failed just as the West's was taking off.

Ming authors pointed to the decline of trade and to fiscal mismanagement and government corruption as the causes of increasing stagnation. After a dynamic start, Ming settled down to a dull, repressive reign. The government, like many others, was effective at stopping individual initiative but was ineffective at taking initiative on its own. Trade, philosophy, science, and innovation slowed down together. The dynamic, intense, fluid society of early Sung and early Ming was giving way to the static, bureaucratized world so familiar to nineteenth-century visitors. Yet missionaries like Mendoza and Matteo Ricci in the fifteenth century were impressed by China's openness, dynamism, and competent rule, and even poor Galeote Pereira noted that Chinese jails (while hell holes) were better than the prisons of his native Portugal.

Lippit's and Qian's argument blaming the autocracy is most convincing, but the dynamic of population growth, resource decline, and substitution of labor for technological advance cannot be denied in explaining China's stagnation. The two are probably related. The burgeoning population was running beyond the administrative capacity of a preindustrial regime. The labor-intensive economy meant that people needed more sons to work the land or otherwise get their living; therefore, population growth proceeded. The government became more centralized in trying to control the rapidly expanding mass, and fear of change set in.

The Ch'ing Dynasty: Manchu Rule and the End of Old China

The early Ch'ing Dynasty was "the age of enlightened despots"; Jacques Gernet (1982) is only the latest to use the phrase. During the early Ch'ing, China added twice the territory of the ancient Eighteen Provinces (Fairbank 1978; Fairbank and Liu 1980; Rossabi 1975; Spence and Wills 1979). Ch'ing was lucky in climate. Shortly after the dynasty commenced, the Little Ice Age began to wane and a warmer, wetter regime followed (Wang and Zhao 1981; Wang, Zhao and Chen 1981; Zhang 1982) that explains much of the economic and demographic expansion of the Ch'ien-lung period. However, wetter weather exacerbated the chronic flood problems, as did deforestation—ever more serious—and the expansion of cultivation in the uplands, over-close diking and the resulting siltation of riverbeds, devegetation of riverbanks (which allowed the banks to wash out), and reclaiming (ironic misnomer) of lakes and marshes that had once been natural reservoirs. Paul Greenough (1982) points out that China was far ahead of India in flood control organization—but India needed less. It had not ravaged its forests, floodplains, and marshes; the British initiated that sort of "progress." The Chinese had no choice; their population, greater than India's, was jammed onto less cultivated and less climatically favored land than India had. (Even Bangladesh has more farmland per capita than China.) The Chinese could not afford to let nature take its course with drainage systems.

This population, moreover, was still expanding fast (Ho 1953). In Ming, China was a bit ahead of Europe and the Indian subcontinent in population. The fall of Ming reduced the population greatly, but by 1662 it had begun to recover, standing at 100 million. In the eighteenth century, population growth began in earnest. Europe had about 144 million people in 1750—almost exactly the same as counted in China's census of 1741, and about the same as India had at the time (Eberhard 1977:284–85). But in 1800, Europe had only about 193 million people; China had 360 million in 1812 and almost 375 million by 1814. Europe's "demographic transition" had begun; China's did not come until after the 1850s. By 1850, China was already more than the "400 million customers" of Carl Crow's famous book title (1937), but rebellions and imperial decline kept the numbers from expanding dramatically after that time. India's population remained steady at 150 million or so.

The Chinese, bitterly familiar with infanticide, abortion, and many other ways of limiting population, knew how to control their birth rate. Any lingering doubts on the effect of such methods in a preindustrial society can be dispelled by examining the record of China's near neighbor, Japan. While during Ch'ing Chinese population was expanding rapidly, Tokugawa Japan's was holding steady, in spite of Japan's even greater peace, prosperity, and stability. The direct cause was population limitation that involved infanticide rates of up to 50 percent on top of all the usual methods of birth control. The ultimate cause was the frozen society of feudal Japan, in which a person could prosper by keeping his place but could not expect to gain much by increasing family labor power beyond a certain point (Smith 1977). By contrast, China had fewer rewards for those who kept population level, more for those who expanded it. There was always room for one more worker or migrant on the road. That one might even make it good. Japan's primogeniture system (common if not universal) guaranteed problems for additional sons; China's partible inheritance, coupled with high infant mortality rates, encouraged families to have as many sons as they could. A Chinese proverb says: "One son is no son, two sons is part of a son; only with three sons can you be sure of a son." (The poor, however, did not always reproduce. Many could not afford to marry; others starved or saw all their children do so.) The result was an inevitable, melancholy, downward sift, as failures from higher classes filled the gap left by the dying poor (Moise 1977). The psychological state this induced can be imagined. Desperate means—crime, corruption, and so on—were felt to be justified as the only way to keep afloat. Even those who remained honest developed a conservative, even reactionary, set of mind. George Foster (1965) described an "image of limited good," characteristic of many peasant societies, in which all good things are seen as fixed in quantity, so that one person's gain is another's inevitable loss. Ch'ing China provides evidence of such a view.

Europe suffered a comparable downward sift effect (Braudel 1982:473), but its economy was expanding, and merchants accumulated not just their neighbor's pittances but also much newly created wealth. Nor did Europe's population expand so fast as Ch'ing China's.

Pressure on the land in China was increased by extreme fractionation; partition of estates led to field patterns that seem preposterous today. Population growth outran land development, and average land per peasant shrank from two acres at the start of Ch'ing to one acre by 1729 (Perkins 1969; Eberhard 1977:285). It was about half that by 1900. A family might own an acre of land divided into ten parcels, one or two of them not much bigger than a room. Boundary zones and liminal dikes took up much of the land, and disputes over encroachment thereon took up much of the peasants' time and attention. Meanwhile, public roads suffered as desperate peasants cultivated more and more of the dirt roadbed, until officials could find no carriage space and repossessed the right-of-way with inevitable brutality. The government supported the trend toward smallholdings (Chao 1981). The Manchus were a tiny band of alien conquerors, and they knew it. They also never forgot that since the Mongols, the Chinese had had no abiding love of foreign lords. The K'ang-hsi Emperor seems quickly to have realized that the right strategy (one as old as Chinese statecraft) was to garner as much support as possible among the common people while preventing concentration of power in the hands of local landholding elites that could serve as a focus for rebellion.

Moreover, the peasants had their own power. Robert Marks (1984) shows that—contrary to almost everyone's previous assumptions—the poor could mass together and demand their own. Particularly in the unsettled days of early Ch'ing, when a rather weak and well-meaning government was trying to get popular support, many peasant revolts were successful. In a world where most families had an acre or less, the owner of three or four acres stood out as a big landlord—and acted it, too, as he desperately tried to keep his family from sinking back into the mass when the estate was divided up. In addition, the richest 1 percent of Chinese comprised (by late Ch'ing) four million people—a large and highly visible pool. But smallholdings were still the rule. Most "landlords" were very small fry indeed, owning a couple of acres. The Ch'ing social order was not sharply divided into elite and mass; there was a complicated gradient. Wealth, government position, and local political power did not always covary. China's "gentry" was not a unitary all-powerful elite, but a dispersed and factionated set who might have wealth without position or position without wealth (Fei 1953). There was a great deal of downward mobility and a fair amount upward (Moise 1977; Ho 1962). The best picture of it is in Wu Ch'ing-tzu's great novel, *The Scholars* (1957), written during early Ch'ing. It depicts the "gentry" scholar often dependent on the charity of lowly but well-to-do butchers and teashop-keepers (Bastid-Bruguière [1980] has a good discussion of the social realities; Braudel [1982] makes comparable remarks about Europe of about the same time).

Three-level tenancy became common. Often an absentee landlord rented out land at a nominal, fixed rate, and his local tenant (a well-to-do landholder with secure tenure and small rent) let it out in turn to peasants. Another system involved renting out "subsoil" rights separately from rights to the surface of the land; in practice these two systems worked the same way. All possible variations on these themes were found somewhere in China. The status of tenants varied about as much as it could; some were secure holders of long leases on huge tracts of land—especially on the frontier, such as Taiwan, where the land could be "rented" from aboriginal chiefs who might not dare try to reclaim it (Meskill 1979). Other tenants were hardly able to rent through harvest a patch of land "barely big enough to stick an awl in" (Zelin 1986). Serfdom and slavery, even, were still to be found. The Manchus had had Chinese slaves in their homeland, and the isolated Nosu Tibeto-Burmans of Szechuan retained enough independence to continue slaveholding; Tibet had a theocratic system in which peasants were often serfs of monasteries. Such conditions were rare in the Eighteen Provinces, but not unknown. We know little about the variety of administrative systems in the marginal parts of the empire (Bastid-Bruguière 1980).

Agrarian taxes fell during Ch'ing to the lowest sustained level in all Chinese history (Gernet 1982:466): in the eighteenth century they were a mere 3–6 percent of the crop—on paper. In practice local officials devised special imposts and outright rip-offs that multiplied the rate by factors up to ten, but even then taxes were less than they were in many agrarian civilizations. Tax dodging was widespread. There was no capitation tax, thus landless laborers were (theoretically) untaxed.

What this meant in terms of food was that people were able to survive, but just barely. Any catastrophe pushed them over the edge into starvation. Wars and rebellions were the worst, but there were also many ecological problems of the sort miscalled "natural disasters" though due to human overuse of the environment.

Susan Naquin (1976) provides cost-of-living figures from the very end of Ch'ing (281–82). Around 1810–20, land in Chihli cost from 300 cash per mu for bad land to 10,000 for good. Chihli is the heart of North China, more or less the modern Hebei Province. It has less choice land than most of China. Honan land, better but farther from big cities, rented at 400 to 1,000 cash (per year, I take it). At this time there were 1,700 cash to a silver tael, worth about 16 1980s U.S. dollars. Thus a decent piece of land could be had for under 100 dollars or rented for under 10 dollars. A laborer earned 70–80 cash per day, 100 in harvest time. A soldier was either paid 1.8 taels a month in addition to his room and board or he drew 150 cash for subsistence. A militia man drew 50, which was surely less than subsistence; he would have been expected to supply some of his own food. One could buy a boy for 1,000 cash or a woman for 10,000, but only the desperate were selling. The 70–80 cash/day figure evidently represents the minimum on which a person could survive; it is probably the price of a worker's daily ration of grain and coarse vegetables. Such a diet would cost about 70 cents in the United States today.

The low price of land is interesting. Land cost several times more in the better parts of the rice regions, but still there were always bits that could be picked up cheaply. However, at a tiny wage that went for subsistence, the ordinary working person could not aspire very high. Good quality land was thus expensive relative to the price of labor, and the prudent landowner worked his labor force hard rather than applying labor-saving technology.

Agricultural and herbal books and encyclopedias reached new heights during late Ch'ing: the successors to the *Ch'i Min Yao Shu* were now huge works occupying many feet of shelf space. Government officials took seriously their tasks of agricultural improvement, introducing new crops, popularizing good strains that appeared in their districts, disseminating technology, organizing flood control and conserving resources. The national grain procurement and storage system was rational and modestly successful (Hinton 1956; Torbert 1977; Zhuan and Kraus 1975). Government monopolies extended to ginseng, the procurement and marketing of which was rigorously controlled (Symons 1981). Famine relief was quick and well organized; of course it could not solve the problem—such a task would have been beyond the capabilities of any preindustrial government—but it had strikingly good effects (Will 1980). Compared to north and west Europe at the time, Ch'ing China appears sluggish and backward in agricultural modernization, but compared to other parts of the world, or Europe of earlier eras, Ch'ing seems successful. Jacques Gernet

(1982) concludes that in the eighteenth century, China's rural masses were richer and better educated than French peasants of the same period, and an even stronger contrast can be made with most of the rest of Europe, since France was by then far ahead of much of that continent (481). The measure of Ch'ing success is thus that rural economic expansion kept up with population. Changes conformed to the late Ming pattern: New World crops, sorghum, and double-cropping spread, selected seed was used, superior crop varieties were disseminated; crops diversified, agriculture was further commercialized. There was no significant mechanization until Western technology began to enter China at the end of Ch'ing.

Agriculture during Ch'ing was highly commercialized. Markets flourished—all the way from the tiny "green produce markets" (at which a few peasants met to exchange produce) to the regional markets in grain and specialty crops that linked all of China and kept the cities supplied with incalculable quantities of foodstuffs and other agricultural products from all parts of the empire. Local markets at every level were large and well organized. Merchants grew rich. Ch'ing literature vividly portrays the enormous wealth of merchant families, and—perhaps even more significant— merchants' nearly universal tendency to buy land and office while landlords and officials diversified into trade. China's greatest novel, *The Story of the Stone* by Cao Xueqin (also titled *A Dream of Red Mansions* or *Dream of the Red Chamber*; the best translation is that by Hawkes and Minford [Cao 1973–86]), portrays a great family in early Ch'ing; their real power derives from official status, but they own extensive farms which provide their subsistence as well as cash crops, and they own pawnshops, trade in cloth, and otherwise assiduously practice portfolio diversification.

The state routinely sold titles both to coopt and control merchants and to raise money. Some people even grew timber as a cash crop—surely some sort of ultimate marker of rural commercialization (Rawski 1972). By the very end of Ch'ing, average cultivated land per capita was a mere half acre (3 mu), surely not enough to feed the population. Starvation and malnutrition were the most common causes of death—operating indirectly by weakening bodies that soon became prey to disease or by creating such desperation that infanticide, banditry, and other forms of violence were invoked by peasants desperate to keep their families eating. Dwight Perkins (1969) calculates that an individual needed 400 catties (533 pounds) of grain per year, which provides about 2,400 calories a day—a reasonable figure, considering China's age structure and the fact that many children did not eat an adult ration (16–19). It is even a comfortable amount; modern Americans, with an older population, consume on the average only about 2,800 calories a day. However, the Chinese were usually working hard (increasing their calorie requirement), and much food was inevitably lost in transport and storage—somewhere between a quarter and a half, if modern Third World countries are any guide. Vegetable and root crops, which produce very heavily per acre, helped the situation somewhat.

In Ch'ing times, an acre of land could be expected to yield two to three thousand pounds of grain, if intensively cropped. Only by using the most intensive methods, and by storing grain carefully, could the peasants eat well. Rents were high (25–70 percent of the crop, but usually less than 50 percent), and special imposts took their share. Victor Lippit (1974, 1978) shows that during late Ch'ing and the twentieth century about a third of Chinese wealth was surplus in the sense that China produced about a third more than was needed to keep its peasant families alive and working. This agrees well with the figures for population and yield. In eighteenth-century China the surplus must have been quite a bit higher, unless much of the land was very poorly cultivated. This may have been the case, for the Macartney Embassy was struck by the desolate and uncultivated appearance of much of the country (Staunton 1797), and even in the mid-nineteenth century Robert Fortune (1847) emphasized the apathetic and desultory nature of cultivation outside the major market areas. Rawski (1972) confirms this distinction, although in milder terms than Fortune's, for early Ch'ing. The inordinate wealth amassed by the eunuch minister Ho-shen in the eighteenth century gives us an idea of how vast the surplus actually was—apparently, few even noticed its loss. But by 1800 people were starving while the court ate well. "Surplus" in the sense of expropriated wealth had become greater than "surplus" in the sense of wealth beyond that needed for subsistence.

For the first time in Chinese history, root crops became important. Sweet potatoes moved from an exotic local famine relief crop to the staple food of tens of millions in the east and elsewhere. White potatoes, virtually unknown in Ming, became abundant, owing much of their spread to French missionary activity in the eighteenth and nineteenth centuries. Maize took over vast stretches of the west and south and began to encroach everywhere. Never before had a crop yielded well in the warmer, wetter mountains of China. Now, suddenly, these areas rivaled other parts of the country for yield. Maize must have contributed to the problem of rebellions in the south and southwest by allowing an increase and immiseration of the populations there. Fortunately, China was spared the full horrors of maize dependence and the pellagra and other nutritional deficiencies that it brings; not only did soybeans and vegetables continue to provide vitamins, but other New World crops that spread along with maize improved the rural nutrition picture. Chile peppers and peanuts were the most valuable, but by the late nineteenth century tomatoes were also becoming known. (Difficult as it is to imagine Chinese food today without the tomato, its spread has been essentially a matter of the last hundred years, though it was locally known long before.)

Commercialization of agriculture had two important effects. First, it allowed a much greater variety in what people raised and ate. Even small towns could call on the resources of the entire empire, or at least of the great marketing regions in which they lived (Rozman 1982; Skinner 1964–1965; Spence 1977). Peasants had access to more kinds of seed and stock and were under more pressure to grow whatever they could. Microenvironments were recognized and sown accordingly: in the early twentieth century, peasants of the North China Plain might grow nothing but cotton, or a mix of cotton and grain, or a variety of grains—the mix, and the grain varieties chosen, depended on differences in soil and water conditions that would seem microscopic even to a modern soil scientist (Huang 1985). China, land of incredible diversity in microenvironments, was rationalizing its agriculture in the direction of ever greater diversity.

Second, there was the more obvious increase in specialty cropping. Nineteenth-century seekers for economic plants, from Robert Fortune (1847, 1857) to Frank King (1911) and Frank Meyer (1911), found China an incredible hunting ground. The almost inexhaustible supply of new species and varieties (in the latter regard, they never got beyond scratching the surface) had been selected and propagated carefully so that they were not only useful but also tough, reliable, highly productive, adaptable, and extremely responsive to fertilizer and care. A disproportionate percentage of major new food, fiber, and ornamental plants entering the West in the last 150 years comes from China or Japan; the Japanese plants are almost all sophistications of Chinese originals. Such mainstays of California agriculture as Oriental persimmon, loquat, kumquat, and almost all our plum varieties share this history. So do dozens of our common dooryard ornamentals; the most dramatically important of these is the tea rose, known in the West for about 200 years but important mainly in the last 150, during which time it has completely transformed rose growing throughout the world. Were it not for the deep-rooted conservatism of occidental farmers and food buyers, we could have borrowed hundreds of varieties more. By contrast, the Chinese (once stereotyped for abject slavery to blind tradition) have borrowed almost everything Western that will grow in their realm.

Chinese techniques of composting, organic fertilizing, and land and water management—based as they are on conservation and recycling—became influential as the organic farming movement arose in the West and as conservation became established. The first great proponent of Chinese agricultural techniques in the West was Frank H. King, whose travels in China, Korea, and Taiwan were published by his wife under the title *Farmers of Forty Centuries* (1911). The book remains a classic in conservation literature.

Yet Robert Fortune, as early as 1847, wrote, "in the knowledge and practice of agriculture, although the Chinese may be in advance of other Eastern nations, they are not for a moment to be compared with the civilised nations of the West" (7). The advance of agriculture in the West beyond that of China was quite recent when Fortune was writing (up to the late eighteenth century, the West had been behind). The most important Western innovations before 1847 were in livestock management and breeding and integration of livestock and crop cycles; China's agriculture, in which livestock played no major part, precluded borrowing any of this. Most other Western developments involved growing of Mediterranean crops, which will not grow in China. China already had most of the Western crops and Chinese grains outproduced Western ones, especially under Chinese conditions; thus it was hard for China to draw on Western technology in the eighteenth century. The West, on the other hand, was rapidly expanding and colonizing new lands like California and

Australia, where Chinese food plants and ornamentals often did better than anything
the West had previously known. Robert Fortune's low opinions of Chinese cultivation, and of much else he saw in China, make us believe him when he admits that
"for a few cash . . . a Chinese can dine in sumptuous manner upon his rice, fish, vegetables, and tea; and I fully believe, that in no country in the world is there less real
misery and want than in China" (121). Later, he writes of the tea-picking laborers:
"The food of these people is of the simplest kind—namely, rice, vegetables, and a
small portion of animal food, such as fish or pork. But the poorest classes in China
seem to understand the art of preparing their food much better than the same classes
at home. With the simple substances I have named, the Chinese labourer contrives
to make a number of very savoury dishes, upon which he breakfasts or dines most
sumptuously. In Scotland, in former days—and I suppose it is much the same
now—the harvest labourer's breakfast consisted of porridge and milk, his dinner of
bread and beer, and porridge and milk again for supper. A Chinaman would starve
upon such food" (Fortune 1857:42–43). Fortune was surprised to find that in
Fuchou beef and milk were widely eaten (1847:60).

In Peking University, a new foundation in the last years of Ch'ing, the students
had "rice at least once a day, with salt turnips and cabbage or other vegetables. They
have corn-meal made into *wo wo t'ou*—a kind of a cake which is slapped on the side
of a pot in which cabbage is cooking. The heat of the fire bakes the cake on the pot
side while the steam of the cabbage steams it on the other side" (Headland 1914:194).
So speaks Isaac Headland, who taught there for many years. The students—fairly
well-off youths—also had shao-ping and millet gruel. A common laborer working
on Headland's house lived on "rice which had fermented in the imperial granaries,
and which he preferred to fresh white rice, a few vegetables, and onions, with perhaps a small dish of beans and soy" (196). Corn on the cob, sweet potatoes, and
mixed innards of animals were available for a few cents from street stands. Haute cuisine was recognizably closer to that of today: birds' nests, sharks' fins, pork cooked in
aromatized rice flour, stir-fried mutton threads, and so on.

At the dawn of Ch'ing, the K'ang-hsi Emperor, a true Manchu hunter at heart,
preferred the simple life, singing the praises of the wild pears, peaches, apples, apricots, and *ulana* plums of his cold and remote homeland. He praised the outdoor life
in tones reminiscent of Theodore Roosevelt: "There is the perfect flavor of bream
and carp from the mountain streams, caught by oneself in the early morning—you
can keep something of that flavor for Peking eating if you enclose the fish in mutton
fat or pickle them in brine before frying them up in sesame oil or lard. There is veni-
son, roasted over an open fire by a tent pitched on the sunny slope of a mountain; or
the liver of a newly killed stag, cooked with one's own hands (even if the rain is falling), and eaten with salt and vinegar. And in the northeast one can have bear's paw,
which the imperial cooks value so highly" (Spence 1974:9).

Elsewhere he cites Lao-tzu on the simple life and says that "peasants make strong
old men because their food is plain; on all my travels I've eaten the local vegetables,

and felt the better for it" (97). He warns of the problems with fruit along the way: people want to offer the first of the crop, not yet ripe. But he enjoyed the dried muskmelons of Central Asia (indeed the world's finest melons), in which empty spaces left by shrinkage might be filled with raisins (161). His descendants retained something of the Manchu love of simplicity. In later years it was recorded of several emperors that they left untasted the fantastic meals served to them—including up to 150 dishes—and ate gruel with simply grilled meat or boiled vegetables. Others indulged more in luxury when they could. *The Story of the Stone*, describing the life of one of the richest families, refers often to delicate and finely prepared food—though it is usually maddeningly unclear on just what is being served. Ts'ao clearly felt that long descriptions of meals merely broke up his close-packed and intense story of human emotions. Occasionally, though, he brought in food and drink to make a point. The most famous example is the recurrent attention paid to the teenage nun Adamantina and her connoisseurship of tea; she could distinguish pure rainwater from melted snow taken from the branches of a flowering *mei* tree. (This isn't as hard as it sounds: *mei* flowers have an intense carnation-like fragrance that pronouncedly flavors snow lying on them.) Elsewhere, again pointing to extreme refinement or snobbism, Ts'ao's character rejects not only noodles but also a lunch of "shrimp-balls in chicken-skin soup, a bowl of duck steamed in wine, a plate of red salted goose-slices, another plate on which were four cream-cheese rolls stuffed with pine-kernels, and a large bowl of delicious, steaming-hot, fragrant green rice" (Cao 1973–86: 3:208). The book's hero thinks these much better than his usual fare and is delighted to relieve the girl of the task of finishing them. In general, Ts'ao and other Ch'ing writers show a special fondness for fruit and seafood, especially local products. Then as now, visitors brought packages of the food specialties from their home areas, and travelers to distant shores were expected to bring back such items to their families. Fine fruits have always been the most popular of such regional delights.

The other great novel of early Ch'ing, *The Scholars*, reflects a more middle-class world and offers a great deal more detail about what the inhabitants of that world devoured (Wu 1957). Spence's magisterial review of Ch'ing food (1977) gives short shrift to this underappreciated novel. Much of the book's action takes place over meals, and it is clear that then as now a feast was an obligatory part of any important deal, agreement, or bargain, as well as of any reunion or affirmation of friendship and alliance. Wu Ch'ing-tzu's world is not one of hypersensitive teenagers. His characters range from rumbustious bravos to withdrawn and ascetic scholars. He gives the former healthy appetites for meat, and the latter—the people he really admires —much more restrained ones. Frequently characters are introduced at feasts, and from how much they take, and how politely they take it, we are to see whether Wu thinks of them as gross beasts or gentlemen.

Wu also has a Frenchman's eye for foibles of the cloth. A monk brings out "tea, sugar wafers, dates, melon seeds, dried beancurd, chestnuts and assorted sweets" —very good Buddhist fare—but then brings in beef noodles (Wu 1957:50–51). Beef, of course, was considered even more sinful than other meats, for the Indian cow cult had influenced China; elsewhere in the book a Chinese Muslim complains that an imperial ban on cow butchering has deprived him of a main meat source. Later, an abbot is offered a ham: "The abbot's mouth watered at these words. . . . Ho told his wife to cook a chicken, slice the ham and heat the wine. The abbot's face glistened as he fell to" (80).

Recipes, menus, and descriptions spice the book. There are walnut wafers of "melon seeds, walnuts, sugar and flour"; "dumplings stuffed with goose fat and sugar"; and duck preserved in wine (112, 169). A poor scholar visiting the West Lake is tortured by the sight and smell of such a duck along with pigs' feet, sea cucumbers, fish, birds' nests, and the like, but he can afford only dried bamboo shoots and such minor snacks as preserved oranges and boiled chestnuts (217–19). A miser "stabbed ducks' breasts with his ear-pick to see how fat they were" and otherwise made himself unpopular bargaining over cheap fare (270). A hawker sells pachyma cakes— small medicinal hot cakes made of the tree fungus *Pachyma cocos*, powdered and mixed with flour (347). After eating a few of these, a character sits down in a restaurant; the waiter spiels off the day's menu: "Joint, duck, fish casserole, mandarin fish in wine, mixed grill, chicken, tripe, fried pork, Peking-style fried pork, sliced pork, meat balls, mackerel, boiled fish head, and cold pork" (347–48). Such descriptions stand out from a continuous obbligato of sausages, frogs' legs, jellyfish, pigs' feet, duck, goose, goose fat, dumplings, cakes of all sorts, vegetables, noodles, crabs, fish, and what not, all protein. The most commonly mentioned food in the book, though, is surely wine. One character describes a jarful of liquor as "made of two pecks of glutinous rice and twenty catties of fermented rice. Twenty catties of alcohol went into it too, but not a drop of water. It was buried nine years and seven months ago, so it must be strong enough now to blow your head off." The jar is dug up and proves to be "as thick as gruel" with "a rich bouquet" (426).

Last, we cannot fail to mention Yüan Mei, the great eighteenth-century poet, litterateur, and hedonist, who delighted in beautiful young people of both sexes as well as in food and drink. His book, *Sui-yuan Shih-tan* (Recipes from Sui Garden), is the Chinese counterpart of Brillat-Savarin. (Sui Garden, where Yüan lived, became his pen name; he thought, wrongly, that it was the garden immortalized in *The Story of the Stone*.) Yüan Mei prefers good ingredients and good cooking to conspicuous display and reports, "I always say that chicken, pork, fish and duck are the original geniuses of the board, each with a flavour of its own, each with its distinctive style; whereas sea-slug and swallows-nest (despite their costliness) are commonplace fellows, with no character—in fact, mere hangers-on. I was once asked to a party given by a certain Governor, who gave us plain boiled swallows-nest, served in enormous vases, like flower-pots. It had no taste at all" (Waley 1957:196).

Food as medicine continued to flourish. Beautiful editions of the *Pen-ts'ao Kang-mu* were printed. Dietary manuals appeared. Doctors saw primarily elite patients (*The Story of the Stone* has some excellent accounts), but pharmacists in cities and small towns spread medical knowledge widely, serving as a bridge from the elite,

literate tradition to the ordinary people. In China and the New Territories a generation ago, this essentially traditional system was still in place, a major conduit for
transmission of knowledge, preventing any watertight separation of "great" from
"little" traditions. Even the specialized realms of gynecology and pediatrics were not
forgotten. Charlotte Furth (1987), who explored this otherwise almost unknown
realm with the help of modern Chinese practitioners, writes of the Ch'ing:

> Like their counterparts in preindustrial Europe, Chinese doctors fussed
> that their genteel patients were too delicate and romanticized the hardy
> peasant wife who, according to stereotype, delivered easily. Their advice
> was also in keeping with the Chinese emphasis on diet as a foundation of
> health and on harmonizing food in accordance with the body's need for a
> balance of "hot" and "cold." Each medical handbook had its own food lists
> for the expectant mother, but all disliked an overly "heating" diet—strong
> meats, heavy spices, oil, and fat. They also frowned on alcohol and the cat-
> egory of "cooling and raw" foods, thought to be indigestible. A highly
> anxious person could find among the available literature elaborate cata-
> logues of taboo foods, based on sympathetic magic ("Eat raw ginger and
> the child will be born with extra toes and fingers . . ." "Eat bird meat and
> the child will be lustful"). A more easygoing woman could be reassured by
> advice to continue eating normally, with prudence." (14).

We encountered this continuum from anxious taboos to looser suggestions in the
Yüan–Ming period, and it is still true today.

With all it had going for it, why didn't Ch'ing China modernize? Why did it fail to
respond the way Japan did, flourishing in traditional times and rapidly catching up
to the West when finally opened to foreign trade? The West was surely part of the
problem. Even in the seventeenth century its impact was felt; its sea trade destroyed
the caravan trade and ruined Central Asia; it preempted the sea lanes and expanded
rapidly into Ch'ing lands. But it also brought trade, paying in good Mexican silver
for even the cheapest and poorest of teas, medicines, and silks. Some of Ch'ing China's early wealth can be attributed to this. Not until the mid-nineteenth century
when opium, gunboats, and unequal treaties became the order of the day, was the
West's effect truly pernicious. Even then, China could have risen to the challenge, as
Japan and Thailand did. And why did the early Ch'ing rulers, so well supplied with
cooperative Jesuits in their courts, never seriously try to learn new techniques?
Clearly Western input by itself explains little. (Moulder [1977] argues the case for a
devastating Western impact on China, but Lippit [1978] refutes this position convincingly.) The classic European explanation was that China was innately a stagnant,
tradition-bound civilization that sat in immemorial indifference to innovation. Confucian ideology is often blamed for this. But this stereotype is contradicted by everything else we know. Even in Ming and Ch'ing, let alone in earlier epochs, there was
much adaptation.

Ch'ing's pattern was one for which Clifford Geertz (1963) coined the term *agricultural involution*. Involution—otherwise known as "growth without development"—occurs when a traditional system is driven harder and harder, becomes more and more complicated, and feeds more and more people—but without any basic change. Inevitably, such a system fails to keep up with population growth, so involution by definition implies immiseration of the majority. Geertz describes this syndrome in colonial Java under the Dutch, showing it to be the effect of colonial policy. The Dutch developed cash-cropping (for the benefit of the homeland) on the best land, adopted policies that led to runaway population growth, restricted the peasants to marginal land, and kept the country under rigid control, seeing all innovation as a threat. The peasants had to work harder and harder at their traditional agriculture to feed themselves. They adopted new ideas, but only those that would fit with their labor-intensive, impoverished, village world. Even if tractors had been available, they would not have used them. With labor so cheap—both because it was so numerous and because the Dutch brutally suppressed all attempts by the workers to raise their wages—there was no incentive to replace workers with machines. Rather (and here Geertz anticipates Mark Elvin's "high-level equilibrium trap"), it was always easier to wring a bit more work out of the peasants than to invest the same effort in replacing labor with land or capital, though only by doing so could true development take place. In the cash-crop sector, modernization ran on apace, for the Dutch wanted to maximize production of sugar, quinine, and so forth; but who cared about peasant agriculture?

East Asian farming is particularly susceptible to involution. The "biological technology" of East Asia is land-saving and labor-intensive. Changes normally involve pouring even more labor into intensive cultivation of tiny plots. Rice and Asian vegetables respond well to such a system, always somehow managing to produce just enough to feed one more hand. Such a system does not preclude true development (defined as more product per capita), but it does allow "growth without development" to establish itself: a vicious cycle in which peasants need more children to work the land, so that labor supply keeps rising faster than food supply. Agricultural intensification takes place, as Boserup (1965) predicts, but the peasants end up even worse off. (Chao [1986] gives the latest and best account of the process.) Only a continuous flow of biological innovations—new crops, new high-yield strains, new fertilizers, new methods—can prevent this. Throughout Chinese history before Ch'ing, population had grown rather slowly, and biological innovations had come often. In Ch'ing the reverse was true. Imperial authoritarianism is a major part of the cause.

So ends the story of the historical development of Chinese food. The contemporary scene of the twentieth century occupies the rest of the book. The modern history of Chinese agriculture is an amazing, complex and instructive story, but it is beyond my scope. China's foodways were established by late Ch'ing; what follows belongs to modern world history.

7 The Climax of Traditional Agriculture

At the beginning of the twentieth century, by far the most productive lands in the world were those of East Asia. Japan was probably the most intensively farmed, due to spectacular development during the whole Tokugawa period as well as the Meiji era (Smith 1959); but Japan was using an almost purely Chinese technology. Java may have been ahead of China too. But at least some parts of China—especially the Yangtze and Pearl deltas and the Red Basin of Szechuan—were well into the competition. And the truly intensive measures used in other realms were primarily originated in China.

Intensive farms were producing two to three thousand pounds of grain per acre; other crops yielded in proportion. Root crops and vegetables yielded higher tonnages, but no more calories per acre. Since the southeast was routinely double-cropping by this time, as was much of the center and even the north, the richer parts of the nation were producing about five thousand pounds per acre. The southeastern fringe even triple-cropped. Since a person requires about four hundred pounds of grain a year—five hundred allowing for storage losses, seed, and an extra reserve for hard work—an acre could easily feed ten or fifteen persons. In fact, population densities in many rural areas reached twenty per acre, suggesting yields of ten thousand pounds per acre per year.

These yields were far ahead of anything found in the West at that time, and indeed very few areas in the Western world produce anything like that now. Those that do tend to grow rice, borrowing Chinese technology. Before 1900, few Western farms could boast yields of even two thousand pounds per year. Eastern Europe was still at a virtually Neolithic level of agricultural development, and parts of Russia were barely into the Neolithic (Warriner 1939; Wallace 1881). Wild wheat yielded better than did the wheat on many European farms of that time. Returns to seed of four or five to one were still common in Europe; Chinese returns were far higher. And China was producing not only calories, but sufficient supplies of vitamin A, vitamin C, and other nutrients. The Chinese managed to produce vast quantities of vegetables, beans, and fish, pigs and chickens—enough to provide a basic living for all but the poorest—in spite of the necessity of committing most farmland to grain. Intensive agriculture did not mean providing calories alone; it meant providing a whole balanced diet. Thus it was, of necessity, diversified—in many areas, highly so. That the average peasant lived on the margin of starvation had more to do with rapacious officials, soldiers, and bandits than with agricultural inadequacies. Victor Lippit (1974) shows that large surpluses—that would have provided decent food for all, at least in a year without undue misfortunes—were being diverted to the elite.

If there was one key to the system, it was recycling. No nutrient was lost that could possibly be conserved. The most efficient possible use was made of each "waste" product. Human manure, for example, was fed to dogs and pigs, which are more efficient digesters than humans and can use as food up to half of what we excrete. Weeds and straw were not composted directly but fed to pigs and cattle. Animal dung, as well as human wastes in excess of the needs of the pigs, was the major fertilizer, along with all vegetable substances that were not choice animal food. Ashes, worn-out sandals, pulverized bricks and adobe, algal blooms from ponds, and above all the mud scooped from canal and stream bottoms were all critically important not only for supplying nutrients but also for maintaining the structure and texture of the soil (King 1911). Many wastes also wound up as fish food and pond fertilizer. Coarse grass growing on dikes was eaten by grass carp, and the residue of oil-pressing made ideal pond fertilizer and feed. Other wastes were typically composted. Manure and night soil, for instance, were left in pits to cure for a few weeks or months—this process incidentally destroyed, through the heat of decomposition, the eggs and larvae of parasites. (Of course, desperate peasants often cut the time short, with disastrous results.) Since water was boiled before use, and food almost always cooked (although not always enough), parasite transmission was far less than it might have been; it may have occurred more often from direct skin contact and dirty washing water than from food or fertilizer.

It was almost impossible for a nutrient to escape this cycle. Meanwhile, nutrients were constantly entering the cycle, at least in the irrigated lowlands. Chronic burning and erosion of hills and slopes were ecologically disastrous in the long run, but they did steadily enrich the lowlands that received the runoff, as many farmers were well aware. The burning kept the hill vegetation in an early stage of succession, characterized by a high proportion of nitrogen-fixing plants; and minerals weathered out from the underlying rock as erosion progressed. Not only did China's farmland area increase as deltas built seaward, but its fertility increased or was maintained by floods and irrigation.

Consider the history of a hypothetical atom of nitrogen. From the air over a southern Chinese mountainside, it finds itself fixed by root-nodule bacteria on a wild legume. The hill is burned. All too much nitrogen goes up in smoke, but this particular atom is trapped in the ash and washes downstream. The stream is diverted into a high field, where it waters vegetables. The atom is eaten by a human. Eventually excreted, it cycles through a pig, is eaten by a human again, and—let us say—goes once more through a pig, then escaping in pig dung, which fertilizes the vegetable patch. This time, the atom happens to be consumed by an insect nibbling on a vegetable leaf. But it is not lost as human food. The farmer turns his chickens and ducks into the field once the vegetables are big enough not to be eaten by the poultry. The birds eat the insects and weeds. So the atom goes again through the human gut.

Perhaps the atom escapes downstream. Here it falls into a rice paddy, and the whole cycle starts again. If it becomes part of a seed, it is human food; if straw, it is buffalo food; if roots, it may be used as fuel and returned to the field as ash; if it escapes into an insect or weed, the ducks eat it. Duck farmers in South China routinely rented their flocks to rice growers or, depending on the local price ratio, paid a slight fee to run their ducks through the fields. The atom escapes the rice field cycle eventually. But below them, on ground that floods too deeply or constantly for rice, are duck pens, water buffalo pastures, and water farms that raise watercress, lotus, *k'ung-hsin ts'ai* (*Ipomoea aquatica*, a leaf vegetable), and other aquatic foods. Then there are the fish ponds, and beyond them the marshes where wild fish and shrimps are trapped and thatching reeds cut. (The thatch is composted when worn out.) Even the nutrients that escape to the sea are not lost, for the marine fishery sweeps up everything: oysters are farmed, and everything that swims, burrows, or crawls in the ocean is taken for food.

The only real escape for a nitrogen atom is into the air. When plants are burned in an open fire, most of the nitrogen is lost. But in rural China, burning was done in the fire hole of the great kitchen stove, that holy shrine (the kitchen god's home) and center of the household. Woks and stewpots neatly covered the holes in the stove top. In the cold north, flues ran from the stove under the floor, heating it; thus the kitchen became the winter home of the whole family. A minimum of fuel was used to maximum effect; a handful of straw accomplished as much as a good-sized bonfire in an open hearth. Not only the absolute shortage of fuel but the cost of using valuable feed and compost as fuel determined this extreme economy. (For full accounts of Chinese farms, see Anderson and Anderson 1973; Buck 1937; King 1911.)

Nitrogen was lost in smoke, and when plants decayed, but composting was done in pits or closed places to avoid nutrient loss. What was lost could easily be made up. Beans and peas were universal crops. In the rice paddies grew blue-green algae that fix nitrogen. Many of these live symbiotically on small floating water-ferns of the genus *Azolla*. In Vietnam, there were actually selected varieties of *Azolla*, propagated by peasants who knew their fertilizing gifts; I assume the Chinese were not less aware. The value of algal and fern pond scum was discovered by Western scientists in the Philippines, where the local people told them that rice grew better in the downwind end of the fields because the wind blew the pond scum there. The scientists dismissed this as superstition until someone actually took a look (Copeland 1924; see also Grist 1975; Hill 1976, 1977).

Other nutrients followed the same path. Minerals like calcium and potassium were less limiting and common enough in the various fertilizing agencies. The Chinese never had a god of manure, as the Romans did, but they were certainly the world's most intensive fertilizers, until the rise of artificial fertilizers in the Western world in the last half century.

The Chinese were far ahead of even the most intensive and self-conscious of modern organic farmers. Not even the most devoted organic farmer in the United States pulverizes old bricks or composts old shoes (straw sandals are better compost than leather, let alone plastic). Even the most dedicated opponents of pesticides do not specialize in developing pest controls they can eat. The Chinese not only used chickens and ducks, they hunted and ate the wild birds and frogs ("paddy chickens") that controlled insects.

Exquisite care in choice of cultivation site was practiced. High, well-drained sites were used for vegetables; mid-level sites that could be flooded or drained were used for rice, which must be irrigated when young and dried off when ripening; lower sites, usually flooded, were used for water crops; still lower ones for fish. In areas where rice did not grow, the same careful siting was found.

Siting was governed by the folk science of *feng-shui*. Usually (and badly) translated "geomancy" and regarded as magic or superstition, this unique belief system was actually based on empirical fact. Feng-shui (wind and water) refers to the science of siting human constructions to maximize the benefits to the users. In its developed form, this science has indeed taken on a vast burden of magic and religion. Graves beam good luck to the descendants of those buried there; room arrangements can bring blessings or curses upon the occupants. (Anderson and Anderson 1973; Feuchtwang 1974; Rossbach 1983; Yoon 1976.) Bizarre feng-shui wars have erupted when rival families desecrate each other's graves to harm each other's luck (Baker 1979:219–25). But in the folk form found in the villages, feng-shui is mostly good sense. Groves of trees are left around villages and streams, where they create good luck—and also the very real blessings of firewood, fruit, erosion control, and shade. Villages must be sited off farmland if possible, and above floodland. I first realized how sensible feng-shui was in the great June floods of 1966 in Hong Kong—all the traditionally sited villages in the western New Territories were unharmed and all the modern ones were flooded. Houses face south, toward the winter sun, and are tightly bunched to minimize the area they occupy and prevent sprawl into the fields. Villages and houses are situated on the leeside of hills and have good views. Paths and roads are not made straight or easy to follow, since bad influences—not only magical but real ones, such as soldiers and bandits—travel in straight lines. Cutting deeply into slopes is outlawed, for it "cuts the pulse of the dragon" that lives in every hill. Peasants point to the terrible washing and landsliding that followed from modern construction cuts as proof of this. Although not every reader may accept the existence of the dragon, every reader should see from this the wisdom and the hardheaded empirical basis of the custom.

The next issue is the maximization of efficiency reflected in the choice of major crops. Rice, maize, sorghum, and millet produce far more under most conditions than do wheat and barley. Naturally, the most productive grains were grown. It is the phenomenal productivity of irrigated rice, which stands alone among grains, that explains more than any other factor the steady shift to the southeast of China's wealth and population after the Han Dynasty (Hartwell 1982). The Chinese diet was primarily grain based; not only calories but protein and several minerals were obtained therefrom. But other crops were essential too, and here again the Chinese were lucky or wise. The chief protein source after grains was beans, especially the soybean, which yields more protein per acre than any other bean. The vegetables most grown were those that yielded most per acre and also had high nutrient density—that is, a high ratio of nutrients to calories. Among common Western crops, the highest nutrient densities are found in turnip greens, parsley and coriander greens, bell and chili peppers, spinach, collards, broccoli, and carrots—in that order (Basic and Traditional Foods Association 1979). Chinese cabbages are comparable to collards and broccoli. The other crops were grown in China, especially spinach (and amaranth greens, similar if not higher in value) and carrots. A number of other leaf crops indigenous to East Asia were grown too and have similar values; some, such as purslane and mallow, are minor now but were once famine staples; they are comparable to turnip greens and parsley. The only other major vegetable crop, the radish, is also exceedingly high in nutrient value—not far behind carrots—especially because of its high vitamin C content. Other vegetables of significance, such as eggplants and tomatoes, are also nutritionally superior to most foods.

So the traditional Chinese diet of grain pieced out with soybeans and leaf and fruit and vegetables was perfectly adapted to the intensive agricultural system. Meat was barely significant in the diet, but even here the Chinese were efficient. The major domesticated animals were pigs and chickens—excellent converters of cheap, inferior food into meat. Unlike cattle and sheep, they did not need grazing or special feed. Moreover, they put on about twice the weight of those ruminants for the same weight of feed, and of course chickens give eggs, too. The pond fish have even better conversion ratios and were picked to maximize use of food in the pond (see chapter 8). All these animals are vegetarian, living low on the food chain.

Readers of some modern books advocating vegetarianism may wonder why the Chinese ate animals at all. Why not stay low on the food chain themselves? Why waste space or food on animals? The answer is that people can't eat everything. In the best-managed system, there are always things inedible to humans—most obviously human excrement. Chinese stock was fed exclusively on such by-products: dung, tough stalks, bones (for dogs), roots, straw, rotted or burned food, and the like. Nothing humanly edible was given to animals, nor was land diverted from growing human food to growing animal fodder. What little grazing was available was on steep slopes, flood-prone ground, dike banks, and other unfarmable spots. A major reason for the nonuse of dairy products was lack of space to pasture cows. Cattle were raised for traction, but they needed what little milk they could give to feed their calves.

Chinese agriculture represents the culmination of the labor- and land-intensive, hyper-efficient "biological" option in farming (Bray 1986; Hayami and Ruttan 1971). Modern American agriculture represents another pole: the "mechanical" option, characterized by enormous use of energy (mostly from petroleum) and an extremely wasteful approach to land. Not only is land used at far less than its potential, it is allowed to erode. China has suffered dreadful erosion over the millenia, but if it had been eroded at American rates, it would have ceased to produce food many centuries ago (Brown 1981).

It is now obvious that American farmers must eventually move toward a more efficient agriculture similar to that of East Asia. A particularly pertinent and persuasive documentation is in the books of William Shurtleff and Akiko Aoyagi (1976, 1979, 1983). David Pimentel and his collaborators calculated how wasteful of energy our system is and how soon it must change (Pimentel and Pimentel 1979). Fossil fuels, topsoil, clean air and water are running out; above all, the planet's capacity to absorb pollution from crop wastes, pesticides, artificial fertilizers, and wasted fuel and petrochemicals is being stretched beyond its limit. Many lakes and rivers have died already, and the oceans may not be far behind.

The Chinese option is waiting, but the barriers to adopting it are twofold: economic and psychological. Petroleum and petrochemicals are still cheaper than the cost of the labor necessary to perform Chinese intensive farming. Chinese peasants were distinguished by their high level of effort and of skill. They learned elaborate routines and did not take long siestas or spend much time idling, either daily or seasonally; they worked efficiently, without wasted motions. Working alongside Chinese fishermen and peasants, I found that I got tired sooner than they did, until I learned to move as smoothly and evenly, in routines as formalized as t'ai chi.

Gourmetship among the rich, and necessity among the peasants, led the Chinese to try a wide range of foods and learn to make them edible. No puritanical scorn interfered. Most people outside East Asia waste or underutilize a tremendous percentage of the world's resources by refusing to eat insects, dogs, cats, many game animals, almost all vegetable foods except the very blandest, and even such superb food as internal organs, fish, and shellfish (Schwabe 1979). Much of the diversity in the Chinese diet is maintained because of traditional medical beliefs, and many of the foods eaten for primarily medical reasons are exceptionally high in nutritional value. The main medical problems treated with these foods are deficiencies of vitamins, proteins, and minerals (or syndromes in which such deficiencies are components).

The main conclusion that emerges from some four thousand years of change is that agricultural development more or less tracked government policy. When the government was strong, open, and responsive, it both encouraged agriculture and allowed private farmers to prosper and innovate. When the government was autocratic and authoritarian or imcompetent, agriculture stagnated or backslid. Private ownership on the whole was better than state control of land, but general smallholding did not prove particularly innovative; periods in which great landlords had power were sometimes exciting for agriculture.

There were three important and innovative eras in China's history of food:

1. *The Warring States and the Ch'in and Han dynasties.* Iron tools came into use, flour milling reached China, great irrigation systems were devel-

oped, Western crops began to be used, and above all a widespread comprehensive strategy for managing agriculture was introduced. Gourmet food
became ritually sanctioned, and medicine gave nutrition a central role.

2. *The period of disunion following Han, particularly the Wei Dynasty.* Buddhism and West Asian crops and foodways came to influence China
greatly, and the great agricultural and herbal encyclopedias took more or
less modern form and size. During this period, too, South China became
an important region, with its own agriculture and food, and began the
climb to its modern position as the wealthiest and most dynamic part of
China. Many or most of the West Asian innovations credited to T'ang
were probably introduced in this earlier period.

3. *The Sung Dynasty.* Chinese agriculture, land use, and cooking developed very rapidly and took essentially modern form, and China's knowledge systems—ideological as well as agricultural and scientific—were
more or less definitively established. After Sung there was a great deal of
elaboration on the basic pattern, but the pattern itself did not change.

The most obvious pattern that emerges is the correlation of advance with periods
of disunity. The dynamic of a world of rival states is very different from a period of
union. In rival states, the wiser rulers bid for experts and give them a free hand to increase their states' competitive advantages. In times of union, rulers are tempted (or
forced) to impose rigid, dictatorial control that inevitably stifles inquiry and innovation. The two exceptions—early Former Han and all of Sung, especially Northern
Sung—are thus to me the most intriguing periods in Chinese history. They are also,
arguably, the most important from the point of view of basic agricultural change.
Their distinctive characteristic is tremendous social openness: relatively low taxes,
low corruption (at first), upward mobility, considerable freedom of speech, and
above all a willingness to support eclecticism. New ideas were tried and old ones
combined in new ways.

During the long intervening periods, agricultural change of an involutional order
continued. People worked harder on smaller plots, faced larger exactions, produced
no more per capita, and had to manage by using every trick in the book. But at least
they had the tricks and could intensify. This is what differentiates China from premodern India, Europe, the Near East, and elsewhere. Widely diffused knowledge of
farming and a government that never quite lost the vision of agricultural development that Han had set allowed China's population and output to expand while that
of other countries stagnated.

Eventual stagnation of agriculture even in China was part of a general stagnation
of science. Development in a food system often must await development in other
realms. China, by Ming, had gone about as far as possible without microscopes, mi-
crotomes, and laboratory science. Above all, the conceptual framework of modern
science was lacking: the ideal of free and general publication; the search for basic
truth, as opposed to applied lore; the centrality of the controlled observation and ex-

periment. Experiments were most certainly performed, but often without systematic observation and records. These bits of "intellectual infrastructure" cannot survive in an authoritarian regime.

Even so, China did astonishingly well. In the tradition of devotion to useful knowledge, lone scientists produced brilliant, innovative work even in the most unpromising times. The most spectacular example is probably Li Shih-ch'en's *Pen-ts'ao Kang-mu*, not only the most thorough herbal compiled anywhere in the world up to that time, but also the fruit of a lifetime of independent research on the names and properties of the plants. Yet the book was written during some of the most dismal days of terminal Ming. To explain Li and others less illustrious but similarly pragmatic and inquiring, we must have recourse to ideology. These men were driven by the vision—best articulated by Mencius—of good people in a good world, developing the potential of both. Their holy crusade was not killing infidels, but helping humanity—by helping us live in harmony with nature.

This vision had its limits. It was not conducive, first of all, to the development of pure science. However, it was a far cry from the Western stereotypes of Asians as otherworldly and religious or changeless and tradition-bound. China's leaders were more worldly than, say, those of India. The peasants of both realms were necessarily practical—they would starve otherwise—but the peasants of China were served by more pragmatic literati.

Ideology does not develop in a vacuum, so it is important to see why the ruling class propagated common sense in China. The apotheosis of practical reason took place in the late Warring States, when contending schools and kingdoms had to succeed in the real world. The early Han sovereigns completed the integration of practicality and national rule. The rise of central authority brought with it the mystification and obscurantism that seems necessary and inevitable in authoritarian governments, especially when they feel insecure, but even when the rulers flew off into lunacy, the Chinese literati never lost the Confucian vision. Since many of them were or aspired to be landlords, they wanted good agricultural books—ones that would help them farm not for subsistence alone, but also for market sale.

It is instructive to consider Li Shih-ch'en in contrast to his rough contemporary Francis Bacon and the slightly earlier Indian writer Kabir. All three were rebels in their time but revered by future generations. Kabir was one of the most brilliant, original, agonizingly self-searching, and deeply insightful of mystics—a climax of Indian religious experience. Li Shih-ch'en was the climax of China's long and passionate search for the useful; his lifework, based on a Confucian commitment to benefit humanity, is as powerfully religious, in its way, as Kabir's. Francis Bacon, with his insightfully mordant comments on human psychology, insisted on free inquiry and experimental test. Michel Foucault and others show clearly that the West's dedication to science is an ideology often as mystifying as any Brahmanical vision of the gods. The real-world consequences are somewhat different, however. Kabir gave India spiritual insight but had little effect on its poverty. Li vastly advanced herbal and nutritional science; thanks largely to him, China led in those fields until perhaps as late as 1900. But it was Bacon whose ideas opened the door of the future, for good or ill. It is now time to combine Baconian science, which has given us nuclear energy and chemical poisons but not the understanding to use them correctly, with the ethics of Kabir and the moral vision of Li.

The role of transportation in the development of the Chinese food system is also highly important. In early times, and indeed throughout much of Chinese history, transportation was difficult and relatively expensive. This served as a powerful spur to intensification—perhaps as powerful as high land prices relative to labor. Skinner's theory of regions and marketing ultimately depends entirely on relative transportation costs, and its predictive value is demonstrated (1964–65). Critiques, such as Rozman's (1982), do not challenge the importance of marketing regions and of transportation costs in defining them.

As China's network of canals and river traffic developed—largely due to conscious attempts to lower these costs, which threatened development and stability—agricultural intensification spread out along canals and major rivers. Intensive cash-cropping and specialty cropping could be practiced far from cities but not far from good ports or cartage stations. Intensive agriculture developed in these areas, above all in the periurban fringes, and spread to the more remote areas. Two alternative models of Chinese agricultural dynamics have developed. In one, relative factor prices of land, labor, and capital are all-important (Bray 1984; Chao 1986; Hayami and Ruttan 1971). In the other, transportation costs are crucial drivers (Skinner 1964–65). From the data we have for the early dynasties, it seems that both are correct. Even when land was cheap or free for the taking, farmers clustered and farmed intensively as near to markets as they could get. (*Near* means, of course, economically near—a mile over mountain roads, ten miles over flat ground, fifty miles by good canal. It is no accident that a *li* was traditionally not a measure of distance but of travel time.)

What about the dark side? Obviously China had famines (Mallory 1926). Then as now, it was threatened by erosion, deforestation, destruction of game and wildlife, and shortages (Smil 1984). Most of these resulted from misuse of the landscape—in Chinese terms as well as Western. The peasants knew when they were overhunting or cultivating too intensively on a steep, unstable slope, but often they were reduced by desperation to acting against their well-known long-term interests. This led to, for example, an indifference to trees. Peter Goullart (1959), wandering in southwest China on the frontiers between Han Chinese and local minority groups, chronicled in detail the almost instant destruction of virgin forests whenever the Chinese entered an area. All the minority groups had preserved at least a reasonable proportion of the tree cover; the Chinese almost invariably destroyed it. As recently as the "grain as the key link" campaign of the early 1970s, Chinese eliminated forests wholesale, even on steep slopes and other areas unsuitable for grain. Apparently, they were quite unable to see any possible benefit of trees.

This neglect extends to tree crops. Fruit has never been of much significance in the Chinese diet. First, it has always been expensive; fruit trees require an inordinate amount of care, and thus superior varieties and superior skills are lacking or narrowly disseminated. Much attention was paid to tree crops as early as Han, Ch'i, and T'ang, but they never caught on. I believe the reason was the relative nutritional inferiority of fruits to vegetables and other foods. The exceptions—the citrus fruits, especially the orange, and to an extent the jujube—*were* cultivated industriously, if not as industriously as vegetables. Another reason is the slow and uncertain return on fruit and nut trees. Some species are called "grandfather–grandson trees" because a man plants them not for himself but for his grandson! A long history of scorched-earth warfare is also relevant; trees take much longer to recover than annuals. The indifference to most tree crops is strikingly highlighted by the extreme success Chinese had in cultivating, developing, and breeding mulberries and tea. Both are better called bush than tree crops as they are usually grown in China, although they are trees in their natural state. They are cultivated as intensively, and with as much skill, as any vegetable. But the one is valued for its role in producing silk, the other for its ability to keep people awake and functioning in spite of fatigue and difficult hours.

It is highly significant that the many utopian schemes for agricultural improvement in the modern world, such as Bill Mollison's (1978) polyculture concept, have drawn on Chinese agriculture in the main but have added Southeast Asian–style intensive tree-cropping to the system. Today, forest protection, massive reforestation, shade and windbreak plantings, and expansion of tree-cropping are transforming the Chinese rural landscape. Diet changes to avoid salts and pickles, which may cause cancer, are also at hand (Anderson, Anderson, and Ho 1978; de-The and Ito 1978; Kaplan and Tsuchitani 1978).

Imitation of the West, often in unsuitable situations, is leading to a worldwide loss of crops and crop varieties that is nothing short of catastrophic (see e.g. Hawkes 1983). The loss of traditional knowledge—of skills, facts, and systematic views fitting them together—is probably even worse than the loss of crops. The knowledge of Philippine cultivators and Micronesian fishermen, for example, has been of value to biologists; think of the value to agricultural science of the traditional Chinese peasant lore (Conklin 1957; Johannes 1981).

In the early dynasties, China still had a reasonable amount of land per person, except around the cities. Thus innovation was often labor-sparing. By the later middle ages, China had filled with people, and innovations were largely in the line of more productive crops and more intensive farming (Chao 1986).

The food of China has always been based on grain, except in a few areas in the latest centuries, where white or sweet potatoes proved more successful. (Potatoes are considered grain in modern Chinese statistics.) These starch staples comprised 90 percent or more of the average diet. The rest consisted of vitamin-rich vegetables—otherwise, no one could have survived on such a diet (Anderson MS). The greatest changes to the system have been the steady additions of new crops and animals, new processing techniques, and new foods. The rise of great cuisine was less steady; it can be traced largely to two periods, the Chou Dynasty—especially the Warring States period—and the Sung Dynasty. These were times when China's social order was differentiating, becoming more complex, and regional and imperial elites were arising. They were also times of private enterprise, open economy with much trade, and a relatively open society. A flexible social order, with much upward mobility and few controls on experimentation in thought, technology, or eating, clearly helped the process. Periods of markedly autocratic control were less innovative by every measure.

China's foodways developed, then, in a country of tremendous ecological diversity, inhabited by a dense population that found it necessary to use every resource, and blessed or cursed with a social order characterized by great differentiation and in key periods by considerable openness and social mobility. My impression is that the same is true of other great culinary regions of the world, but further investigation is needed to establish this. Certainly no country did more with its resources than did China.

8 Chinese Foodstuffs Today

The Chinese are united by an interest in and commitment to good cooking and good food. People discuss food for hours, and almost everyone from the richest to the poorest, from scholar to laborer, from northerner to southerner, is concerned with the best and can tell the observer how to find it.

The basis of the diet is boiled grain, which usually provides most of the calories. A few of the poor in marginal or soil-poor areas subsist on root crops and the like, but people in such situations regard themselves as exceptional and unfortunate and escape as fast as they can. Baked grain products such as bread are minor or absent except in some western montane areas. Whole grain, boiled soft and dry (as rice usually is) or made into thick porridge, is the usual fare, but boiled flour products—soup and noodles, for instance—are also often important. In the north, steamed flour products (man-t'ou, like loaves of bread, and various smaller dumplings) are important.

The basic diet includes several grains and tubers. There is rarely the utter dependence on rice found in Southeast Asia. Rice, wheat, millet, and other grains all cooccur—at least two in each region. The rest of the diet consists primarily of soybean products and vegetables, especially those of the mustard and cabbage family (Brassicaceae). Even cooking oil is derived primarily from these plants, or it was before the peanut entered from South America in late Ming times. Meat is rare (except among the rich) and eaten only in small quantities. Fish (locally) and eggs provide some animal protein, but the great protein sources everywhere are grain and soybeans.

Many of the beans and vegetables—and even meats and fish—are pickled or fermented, and these products are recognizably different from their many imitations and fellows in the rest of the world. Greens, for instance, are often half-dried before pickling; the product is less crisp but more fresh-tasting than most pickled greens (e.g., sauerkraut, kimchi), because bacteria can work less on the sun-cured product. The connoisseur of pickles can easily distinguish Chinese from others.

Foods are usually boiled, steamed, or stir-fried. Boiling is most important, not only because it is the usual method of preparing grain, but also because soup (from thin clear soup to thin stew) is universal, a key part of virtually every meal and even of snacks. Soup noodles are the most popular snack throughout China, but by no means the only soupy snack—even sweets are often soupy. Cooking in covered slatted steamers over a water-filled vessel is perhaps the next most common method. The most famous Chinese method, however, is *ch'ao* (stir-frying). Ingredients are made or cut small and thin and stirred rapidly in very hot oil, searing them quickly. Often the ingredients are briefly blanched first. Sometimes they are stir-fried first, then water is added to the pan and the cooking is finished by boiling.

Chinese cooking strategies differ from others in interesting ways. Chinese fried rice, for instance, is boiled, cooled, then stir-fried. Pilaf (and its many descendants, such as Mexican *sopa seca*) is made the other way round; the rice is first stir-fried, then boiled. Boiled rice is a staple; fried-then-boiled rice is a luxury or special commodity. Monsoon Asia boils its rice; in the Near East and Mediterranean rice is usually fried first—a more special, elaborate way of cooking. Stir-frying demands care and good oil (not always cheap), thus tends to be the method used for fancier food. At a typical Chinese meal, the simplest and most basic items will be boiled, the next simplest steamed, and the richest, most special items more often stir-fried. Other processes—deep-fat frying and sautéing, eating foods raw, and stewing in thick gravy—are all quite rare.

Seasoning is light but almost always present and emphatic. It is usually a matter of a few strong flavors, among which the most universal are fermented soy products, ginger, and garlic and onions. There is little of the subtle compounding of many spice flavors that characterizes South and Southeast Asian food, but Chinese foods are more spiced than are foods farther north in Japan or farther west in Central Asia (Rozin 1973).

These points serve to identify Chinese food, but they are not those a Chinese would list. Interviewees—mostly Hong Kong Chinese and thus not a representative sample, but probably not atypical—usually started by saying with pardonable pride that Chinese food was better than anyone else's. Asked to be specific, they would almost invariably begin by saying that the food was fresher ("you Westerners eat only canned or frozen food"). They would also say that Indian food was too spicy, while other cuisines were not spicy enough: "Our food has more taste to it—Western and Japanese foods are tasteless." A concept of balance runs through these comments; Chinese food is said to steer the middle course between the food to the south, "where flavors are drowned in spice," and the overly bland food of the west and north, where flavors are cooked out of the food. This emphasis on balance at the center is typical of China, the "Middle Country."

The comments on freshness and on natural food flavors are the keys to the most central ideas about food in Chinese society, those that unite food, health, and ethics. The underlying principle is that clarity and purity should be evident in all things—men and women should be honorable and trustworthy, food should be pure and fresh. The former is necessary for a healthy and harmonious society, the latter for individual health. But food is not singled out; the same set of ideals governs many other aspects of relationship with both human beings and the natural world. Food is part of a system of belief in which quality, freshness, purity, and high standards are matters of necessity, if one is to remain in any way truly human.

Plant Foods

The food most associated in everyone's mind with China is, of course, rice. In South China as in much of East Asia, the phrase *chih fan* (to eat rice) also means simply "to eat," and the word *fan* (cooked rice, cooked grain) also means simply "food." A southerner who has not eaten rice all day will deny having eaten at all, although he or she may have consumed a large quantity of snacks. A meal without rice just isn't a meal. "Even a clever wife can't cook without rice," claims a common proverb, and although the people who quote it are quite aware that many people in the world do cook without rice, they find this fact quite irrelevant to their own state of satisfaction and their own definition of food. An ordinary meal is made up of cooked rice and *sung* (*fan*), a Cantonese word that may best be translated as "topping for rice" or "dishes to put on the rice." Sung includes everything else, all combined into dishes that are, indeed, put on the rice (and in a poor-to-ordinary home are little more than flavorings for it). When the sung is broken down into its component dishes, they are referred to separately as *ts'ai* (greens), even though they sometimes include meat. In part this is a matter of modesty—the host calls the dish plain vegetables just as he describes his house as a humble cottage. But greens are indeed the standard sung. In Mandarin, there is no equivalent word for sung: a meal is based on the complementarity of grain and ts'ai. Local ideology actually overstates the importance of rice; even in the far south, much of the diet consists of wheat products, maize, or root crops.

Rice is the most useful plant known to the human race. Staple food of almost half the world's people, it is also a source of fodder for animals and of a straw that is superior for thatch, sandal making, fuel, and other industrial uses. (In some areas different varieties of rice are grown partly because of the different qualities of their straws.) As a food, it is normally eaten boiled—despite the myth, propagated by many a menu in Chinese restaurants, that it is steamed. The standard way to cook rice is simply to boil it in about twice its weight in water (depending on the dryness and variety of the rice) until the water is absorbed and the rice is fluffy. This produces the usual substrate for other foods throughout monsoon Asia. By cooking the rice longer in somewhat more water, "soft rice" or, more graphically, "spoiled rice" (*lan fan*) is produced; this is "spoiled" as adult food by being too soft, but it is the standard baby food of China's rice-eating areas. Still more water and often still longer cooking produces the porridge (*chu*) known in English by a South Indian name, congee (*kanji*). Most dilute of all is the water drained off boiled rice. Since normally the water is all absorbed by the rice, special provision must be made to use excess water and drain it off. It is used as a cooling drink, both for thirst quenching and in folk medicine. Rice flour is used in noodles, cakes, and confections, as well as for makeup, paper sizing and the like, but it is not a significant end product of rice milling; almost all rice is left whole grain.

The rice kernel has a center of almost pure starch and several seed coats, the inner ones white, the outer ones brownish; all these thin coats are between the true bran and the inner kernel. Milling takes off the coats. Traditional milling removed only the outermost, brownest, and loosest, without too much damage to the nutrient value of the grain. In the nineteenth century, machinery was developed to mill off the inner coats as well; thus was born the infamous polished rice. Some of the protein and vitamins in rice, and about half the thiamine (vitamin B1), are in the seed coats: unenriched polished rice thus lacks much natural nutrient value. Its rise led to an enormous increase in the incidence of beriberi (thiamine deficiency). Beriberi has been perhaps less of a problem in China than in areas farther south, but it has still been a terrible curse, recognized and described in the Han Dynasty. The problem is that Chinese (like most peoples) prefer their rice very starchy and very highly milled.

Rice comes in several varieties, loosely classed into *indica, japonica,* and glutinous rices. (Crop scientists are not very happy with this ad hoc classification.) Indica rices are the familiar long-grain rices and their relatives. Japonica rices have short, round-ish grains, more protein, and usually relatively less starch, and they cook to a more sticky and chewy preparation because of the chemistry of the starch. Much of the carbohydrate in glutinous rices is in the form of amylose; these rices cook to a sticky, sweet, pasty consistency. Intermediates between indica and japonica rices have long been dominant in Taiwan. When the Japanese occupied Taiwan, they bred these already excellent strains (nutritious, fairly pest resistant, and high yielding) into higher-yielding, tougher ones, and the International Rice Research Institute in the Philippines founded upon them its series of "miracle rices," developed by crossing the Taiwanese intermediates out to various indicas and japonicas. Chinese usually prefer indicas to japonicas. Glutinous rice is used for confections and special festive dumplings but is a staple in China only among the Tai people of south Yünnan and nearby areas; they, and their southern cousins in Laos and northeast Thailand, are the only people in the world who use glutinous rice as their staple. Worldwide, indicas are preferred except in Japan and areas near it, where the shorter growing season of the japonicas has made them the only practicable rices and thus those to which everyone has become accustomed.

Starchy, overmilled grains are preferred because when one eats rice three times a day, every day, and gets most of one's calories from it, one wants it to have as little flavor and texture as possible. Variety in the diet is provided by the sung. The marked flavors of, say, Indian *basmati* rice or the unirrigated and protein-rich hill rices (grown in mountains where monsoon rainfall is adequate for watering) are not popular in most areas that depend wholly on rice. There are a few "fragrant" rices in China, however (Lou 1983), and Hong Kong grew an excellent type of flavorful rice within my memory.

Milling costs money, so white rice is more expensive than brown, or it was in earlier days. Being dearer, it became prestigious. A more practical consideration is that polished rice is so unnutritious that even insects, except for a few weevils, cannot thrive in it; thus it stores better than brown. Today, since storage has become more expensive than milling, it is often cheaper than brown.

In China until recently, the ordinary rice ration—the extremely cheap rice made available in the rice-eating areas—was lightly milled, of pale grayish-tan color and pronounced grain flavor—almost a brown rice. It was more nutritious than white rice and to the Western taste very good indeed, but its consumers regarded it with sadness and anger. Outside China and in Taiwan, Chinese everywhere eat polished rice almost exclusively. Parboiling of the raw grain before milling—an old practice in south India—has never caught on in China because it gives the rice a pronounced flavor as well as a brownish color; yet it saves much of the rice's nutritional value. Parboiling is widely recommended, but nutritionally it seems similar to undermilled rice, and it costs more—why not simply advocate using China's ration-grade rice?

It is not true that people's tastes in rice are so conservative and irrational that they are beyond the realm of serious discourse. Polished rice was accepted immediately everywhere; so much for conservatism. Westerners will recognize a parallel with the evolution of bread, except that Chinese have yet to return to preferring the under-milled product when the starch staple has so little value that one eats it for taste, as a treat, rather than for "daily bread."

The importance of rice in the thinking and social life of South China is well known. It is usually the most highly regarded grain, often believed to be a perfect food or even the only important food (other foods being only to flavor it). Thus I was told by a Western-style but very Chinese doctor in Hong Kong: "Chinese babies don't need vitamins! They eat rice." (His small patient was eating rice and very little else and quickly died of malnutrition; the doctor's comment was an answer to my diffident suggestion that vitamins might be useful.) Varieties of rice are assigned different social roles; indica is the staple, while glutinous rice is used only for confections but is obligatory for certain ceremonies.

Yet only in a few very fertile alluvial plains of southeast China is rice the only staple, and only in the alluvial valleys of south and central China is it a staple at all. Most of China's people live here, but much of the land is too high, rough, cold, and/or dry to grow rice. Millions of Chinese in olden days never tasted it. It provides only 40 percent of China's starch staple food today (Wen and Pimentel 1986a), the effect of a recent shift toward wheat, potatoes, and maize. But even now rice is the primary grain for half to two-thirds of China's population.

In addition to its use as whole grain, rice is made into flour, noodles, cakes, and many ferments. Most vinegar has a rice base, though any grain will do. (Chinese vinegars range from red to yellow to white to black, strong to mild. The famous Chinchiang vinegar resembles Italian *balsamico*.) Rice is also used for sweets, cosmetics, absorbent powder, and so on. Boiled rice is left to ferment into *t'ien chiu niang* (sweet ferment), a slightly alcoholic food. Lees from brewing rice ale are used to flavor food. In Fukien, rice is inoculated with fungus that develops a brilliant wine-red color and a slight sweetly pungent flavor. It is a distinctive marker of Fukienese cuisine. (For a discussion of rice, see Bray 1986.)

Wheat is grown primarily in north, central, and west China. Very little has been written on wheat varieties in China, and we are at a loss to chronicle the distribution of hard red, soft white, and other wheats. Durum is not often grown and the more primitive wheats (spelt, Polish wheat, and so on) are virtually absent except in Central Asian Sinkiang, but a highly complex, little understood pattern of varieties and forms occurs in China. The obvious fact that spring wheat is grown in the north and winter wheat in the south (as everywhere else in the world) tells us little about food value, though the spring wheats tend to be hard red wheats, which are more nutritious than the soft white ones. Nutritional analyses of varieties of Chinese wheat from all parts of the country should be undertaken before the old peasant varieties are completely replaced by modern high-yield hybrids.

Technologies for using wheat as a whole or cracked grain (e.g., bulgur) have never spread, in the ten or twelve thousand years that wheat has been cultivated, much beyond the home of wild wheat in the Near East. In most of the world, wheat is used as flour. In China, only the Iranian and Turkic peoples of Sinkiang use wheat primarily in the form of bread. These groups, the Uighur and their neighbors, are part of the Persian food world. They make true bread, sticking the dough in large folded sheets to the inside walls of a sunken oven. (The bread is usually leavened by local yeast or sourdough starter in neighboring parts of Afghanistan and probably in Sinkiang as well.) This process produces huge sheets—up to two feet square and an inch thick—of beautifully fluffy bread, known almost everywhere by the Persian word *nan*. Loaves are sometimes scattered with sesame seeds. The word *nan* has been borrowed, via Turkic *pan*, as a Chinese word, *p'an*, for a flat cake (Buell 1987).

The Chinese adopted this practice, but they or their Central Asian teachers miniaturized it; the small, thin roll is called *shao-ping* (roast cake). It is about six inches square, puffed up in the center but with very thin walls, and almost always scattered with sesame. This is a purely ancillary foodstuff, often used to hold meat, which is fitted into the hollow center; the whole is eaten like the pocket breads (e.g., *pita*) of the Near East, to which shao-ping is related. Some other baked breadstuffs occur in China, but they are even less significant. Wheat flour is more commonly made into steamed dumplings or noodles.

Steamed wheat flour dumplings are the standard food of much of North China and abound almost everywhere else in the country. At their simplest they are much like bread loaves, but soft and white, since they are steamed rather than baked. The man-t'ou of North China vary in size from a bun to a full loaf. A vast number of filled or unfilled *pao-tzu* are bun size or smaller. These, if filled, have a soft fluffy skin about one-fourth to one-half inch thick around a filling that may be meat, a sweet, or virtually anything else. Best known in South China are *ch'a shao pao*, the Cantonese *ch'a siu paau*, (fork-roasted-pork dumplings), which include chopped-up bits of pork, roasted hanging from a fork in a special oven, in a sweetish spicy sauce. Wheat flour is also the commonest flour (rice is second) used for making the much thinner skins of smaller dumplings such as *chiao-tzu*, of a type found all over Central Asia that more recently spread west; the *ashak* of Afghanistan, *mo-mo* of Tibet, *pelmeni* of Russia, Jewish *kreplachs*, *samusa* of Arabia and South Asia, and Italian *ravioli* are all versions. They are a West Asian invention. (Legend has it that Marco Polo introduced them from China to Italy where they became ravioli; this is absurd.)

The other great use of wheat flour in China is in noodles, *mien*. Noodles are usually hand-cut, but often they are made by forcing a flat sheet of dough through the holes in a colander-like device into boiling water (Franck 1925; Hommel 1937; Hosie 1910, 1922). Special noodles are made by holding the dough in both hands and swinging it around so that it stretches in the air. Another common noodle type, *fen-su*, is made by similar "colander" methods from corn, buckwheat, and bean or pea flours. As with ravioli, noodles are usually said to be of Chinese origin, carried back to the Western world by Marco Polo. This is not true (see Root 1971:78), though the Chinese may have invented egg noodles.

Wheat gluten has long been separated from the starch and made into imitation meats for vegetarian cookery (Buddhist-inspired). Some of the imitations are close to the original; others stretch one's imagination. New uses of wheat flour have entered China in the last century. As in Japan, though not as extensively, oven-baked bread and similar goods have been increasing rapidly in consumption, especially in Hong Kong and other relatively highly Westernized Chinese communities. In Hong Kong bread was the first Western food to be widely accepted and has proved the most popular item of Western diet. Then came an ever-increasing range of baked goods, borrowed from British, Portuguese (via Macau), Russian (via the White Russian refugees from the USSR), and other European sources. These have been integrated into Cantonese life and cooking.

Wheat in old China was usually milled to a white flour, but before the advent of European bleaching, steel rollers, and related machinery (developed in the Western world in the nineteenth century), the flours could not have been the low-extraction, highly refined, nutritionally poor flours we know today. (Extraction refers to the percentage of the wheat berry used. Stoneground wholemeal uses almost 100 percent; modern white flour around 70 percent.) Whole wheat flour was also fairly common. By the time highly refined flours became significant in Chinese diet, many were coming from Australia and North America already enriched. Even so, modern food technology has not been good for the diet of those Chinese who must still depend mostly on starch.

The third most important grain in China is now maize, but until recently it was sorghum. Usually the sorghum in question was kaoliang. The word is Chinese for "tall millet" (*kao liang*) and has been borrowed into English. This sorghum grows to ten feet or more and is valuable for its stalks, sources of sugar, firewood, and even building materials, as well as for its grain. Sorghum can vary from a few inches to twelve feet in height; since the stalks are minimally useful in the United States, extremely short-stalked varieties are grown, so that little fertilizer or water is "wasted" in growing stalk. The Chinese, on the other hand, want a great deal of stalk, especially in the treeless plains and loess hills of northwest China, where nothing else can supply fuel and wattlelike construction materials.

Contrary to some claims, sorghum is not a native of China or of Asia. It was domesticated in Africa and spread from there (probably via south Arabia) to India by 1500 B.C. and to China before (perhaps long before) 1000 A.D. Resistant to drought and heat but able to tolerate a very short growing season (some varieties), sorghum is grown in primarily the driest agricultural areas of China and in those with the shortest summer. In these it is often the staple food, but always a poverty food, disliked and if possible avoided. In wheat and mixed-grain areas—most of its range—it is used primarily in porridge. Many, however, pearl it and cook it like rice, which is said to be a tastier way of using it, though more difficult to make and less nutritious. (As with other grains, the pearled-off outer coat has a disproportionate share of the nutritional value.) This process is found primarily in Manchuria (Hosie 1910), where settlers came from the central China coast and Shantung. Kaoliang is also a major source of distilled liquor.

Sorghum is rapidly being replaced in much of China by maize. This replacement has long been developing in warmer, wetter areas—maize needs summer rain—and new, hybrid maizes have recently been spreading rapidly to drier areas with shorter growing seasons. Maize was introduced to China by the Portuguese via Macau and other points of contact in the early 1500s. It has continued to spread, especially since the unification and liberation of China in 1949 allowed rapid dissemination of hybrid strains and development of necessary agricultural improvements. Corn is used primarily in corn meal cakes, large and thick, steamed or baked; it is also used in corn meal mush. Ears of sweet corn or immature flour corn are commonly steamed, even in areas where corn is not used for anything else, such as the rice-growing southeast. Like sorghum, it also has a role in the production of alcohol.

Corn is used for noodles, although corn flour does not stick together well because of its low gluten content. It is also sometimes cracked and mixed with rice. Corn is the staple food of many of the warmer mountainous areas of China, such as the lower mountains of the west and south, and is becoming something close to a staple in much of the central north. The Chinese have not, however, adopted the diverse corn technology of the New World, including lime treatments and other devices that make the corn more nutritious. The lime combines with phytic acid that would otherwise combine with calcium and other minerals to make them less available (Katz, Hediger, and Valleroy 1974). In China the phytic acid and other problems associated with corn remain, and the corn products tend to be heavy, stodgy, and inferior to American Indian corn products in both nutritional and gustatory quality. The inferior nutritional value of China's corn products poses serious danger.

In areas too cold for any other crops, barley and buckwheat are the staples; they are frequently grown in rotation, barley as a winter or spring crop, buckwheat in summer. Barley, a Near Eastern crop, entered China in the early Neolithic and has been important in the crop roster since the dawn of Chinese agriculture. Various barleys of the class known as "Himalayan" or "six-rowed" were developed in Tibet or near it (perhaps in North India or Central Asia) and are important in many high mountain areas. Buckwheat seems to be a Central Asian native crop developed from a weed in barley or a plant growing near it and used as a second staple. The species *Fagopyrum esculentum* was first domesticated, then *F. tataricum* for the higher altitudes in the mountains of Tibet and nearby areas; it may have been a weed in fields of *esculentum*, later made into a crop to extend the cultivated area (Harlan 1975), although it is possible that both were domesticated together.

Buckwheat is now a staple (but not the only staple) in all the cold and/or mountainous parts of China. It is most important to non-Chinese peoples, although the Chinese do not neglect it, eaten as coarse cakes, thicker than American buckwheat pancakes. Buckwheat noodles are locally common, although less important than in Korea and Japan. Barley is more versatile. Roasted and ground to flour, it makes the famous tsamba that is the staple food of most of Tibet, mixed with tea and yak butter into a paste. Pearled barley is apparently of recent introduction; in South China it is called by a name formerly used for Job's tears (*yi mi*) and has replaced that grain as a medicinal broth. It is not used for any other purpose—nor are Job's tears now eaten at all, except occasionally by those knowledgeable in medicine.

Millet is a catchall term for any small-seeded grain, often even including sorghum. In the literature on China, the word millet without qualification most often means *Setaria italica*, foxtail millet, an excellent grain widespread in the north and occasional elsewhere. It is usually eaten as a delicious nutlike porridge, enjoyed as a snack even where millet is a rare food (e.g., in Taiwan, where mainlanders from the north are especially good customers of millet-congee stands). Panic millet (*Panicum miliaceum*; some recognize other *Panicum* spp.), possibly also native to China, has both grain and glutinous varieties, important sources of alcoholic drinks. Brewing is the main reason for maintaining the otherwise lowly panic millets.

The alcoholic drinks of China, *chiu*, are usually lumped under the term rice wine, but they are neither wine (i.e., undistilled, fermented fruit drinks) nor always made from rice. Grape wine is made in China in very small quantities, and recently some of fair quality has been exported. But true Chinese alcoholic drinks are made from grain. The undistilled drinks (i.e., ales or beers) are strong and not carbonated or hop-flavored; they taste something like sherry. The distilled liquors are technically vodkas, that is, liquors distilled from fermented starch. (Many in the Western world believe that vodka is made from potatoes, but in fact it is usually made from grain and is nothing more nor less than unaged whiskey.) The Chinese make chiu, distilled and undistilled, from a great many things, including sweet potatoes, rice, and so on. Occasionally they make fruit brandies. But the standard sources of chiu are kaoliang, glutinous millets, and more recently corn. They are malted and then made into mash, which can be distilled to yield a product identical to the white lightning of Appalachian bootleggers, often strong enough to sterilize surgical instruments (Crook and Crook 1966). Sometimes it is distilled eight to twelve times to achieve this potency. The most favored kind is known as Maotai, after the city by that name in Kweichow in the mountainous south. Made from sorghum and wheat, it is eight times fermented and seven times distilled (Zheng 1987) and over 100 proof.

Many things are steeped in chiu, occasionally just to flavor the liquor (sometimes it is made with plums or other common fruits) but usually for medicinal reasons. Anything of medicinal value is apt to be used in this tincture-making; snake chiu, ginseng chiu, mutton chiu, and thousands of herbal preparations are common. Tinctures are held to have different values from water infusions. The technology of chiu making spread from China to neighboring areas; Korean millet vodkas and the sweet-potato vodka (*awamori*) of Okinawa and other areas sometimes outdo Chinese products in potency, and Japanese sake (usually a rice ale) has become a gourmet drink of great variety and subtlety.

In spite of all this chiu, the Chinese have perhaps the lowest alcoholism rate of any alcohol-using culture. Drinking is done with meals, and slowly; young persons must be very moderate; drunkenness at any age means loss of face. The classic poets loved to speak of themselves as *ts'ui*, translated as "drunk," but the word usually means, at most, rather tipsy (T. C. Lai, pers. comm.). However, many poets did have real drinking problems, and they are sometimes invoked today as sad examples to the young. China's tolerant culture, allowing much but counseling balance, is important in maintaining these attitudes (Maghbouleh 1979). As the old social rules break down in America, Chinese Americans drink more. Most Chinese, and most other East Asians and Native Americans, have an isozyme of alcohol dehydrogenase that makes them react strongly to alcohol; among other things, they flush bright red, so that a common idiom for "tipsy" is "red-faced" (National Institute on Alcohol Abuse and Alcoholism 1978). But this enzyme has nothing to do with low alcoholism rates; several other cultural groups with the same enzyme have exceedingly high rates.

A few other millets and minor grains are grown in China. Millets of the genera *Echinochloa, Digitaria*, and so on, important in various nearby areas, are apparently locally found but insignificant as human food.

The Chinese today class white and sweet potatoes as grains for statistical purposes. (They are counted not by full weight, but by weight divided by four, called *grain equivalent*, because grains have about four times as many calories per pound as sweet potatoes and five times as many as white.) Potatoes are nowhere the sole staple in China, but they are important locally. White potatoes—*ho lan shu* or *hsiao shu* (Dutch tuber or little tuber) or *ma ling shu* (horse hoof tuber)—were introduced primarily by French Catholic missionaries in the eighteenth and nineteenth centuries and are important in areas where the missionaries were most active and where the climate is best for white potatoes—specifically in the China–Tibet borderland and other moderate to high elevations of Szechuan and neighboring provinces. They are grown almost everywhere else as well and are increasing in importance, but they are not much more than one among many vegetables except in west China. They are eaten boiled, often with the skins, or stirred into mixed dishes. Sweet potatoes are known as *kan shu* (sweet tuber), *chin shu* (golden tuber); white ones are *pai shu* (white tuber) or *fan shu* (barbarian tuber). The sweet potato proved a tremendous boon to southern and eastern China's sandy coastlands, since it can grow in very sterile, poor-quality, sandy soil. Sweet potato stems and leaves are good pig feed and can even be eaten by humans as a famine food. The sweet potato provides vitamin A, rare in many Chinese diets, and may have saved many million pairs of eyes in the four hundred or so years since its introduction. Unfortunately, Chinese prefer whiter varieties with little of the vitamin. Sweet potatoes have never become popular in China; they are regarded as the worst of all foods almost everywhere they grow. They are eaten only in desperation; prosperous families feed their sweet potatoes to pigs. Thus a family's income in sweet-potato areas could be judged by the percentage of sweet potatoes in the diet. In spite of this, the sweet potato has been spreading and increasing, recently invading inland areas where it never grew a generation ago. It is usually eaten plain, boiled or steamed, or sliced and dried; the dried slices are steamed and mixed with grain if possible. A conscious effort to improve this dull regime was made in one commune after the peasants made it clear to their canteen that one of the major practical applications of Marxism-Leninism-Maoism was that the food should be good, not wretched (Crook and Crook 1966). This very Chinese attitude produced immediate results.

Other root crops have been displaced by these New World introductions, and to a much lesser extent in the extreme south (especially Hainan Island) by manioc (*Manihot utilissima*), still insignificant in the Chinese diet. The native root crops of China were yams (*Dioscorea* spp.), called *shu yü* or *shan yü*. Beet-red ones exist as well as white. A number of species occur, used both for their starchy roots and their medicinal value, but they have declined in importance to virtual insignificance. They are still common in South China's warmer areas as minor vegetable crops. Taro (*Colocasia antiquorum; yü*), a marsh plant of the tropics and subtropics, has probably never been more than one among the many vegetable crops of China, as it is today in all warm, wet areas. South of China, yams and taro (with its relatives) are still staple crops of many areas, but they may never have been staples in China. Minor roots include Chinese arrowroot (*Sagittaria sagittifolia; fu*) and "Chinese artichokes" (*Stachys sieboldi*, the tuber of a mint). Sago (palm pith) is used as a starch in the south. Its name there, as in English, is borrowed from the Malay *sagu*. In Chinese it is *hsi ku* (Cantonese *sai kou*).

China's famous pulse crop is the soybean (*Glycine max*). The soybean is protected from pests by a number of chemicals that range from unpleasant to fairly poisonous and is thus more or less inedible raw. Nor is it good food if roasted or otherwise cooked in high, dry heat, for the proteins and other compounds bind into indigestible complexes. The Chinese process the seeds in many ways. The simplest and least often used is simply to boil the seeds a very long time until soft or reduced to porridge. The next simplest is to grind the dry bean with water in a small mill with a center-hole feed; the resulting slurry of water and bean flour is boiled. This develops a skin, as when milk is boiled. The soybean skin is removed and dried; it is easy to store, high in protein, and used in vegetarian dishes and snacks. The remaining mix is usually coagulated with gypsum or similar chemicals so that the protein (with some starch and a lot of water) separates as a soft, solid curd—the famous bean curd, *tou fu* (Shurtleff and Aoyagi 1983). The bean curd is drained or pressed in a wood frame between cheesecloth (or similar) sheets. The unpressed fresh curd is custardlike and often eaten sweetened. It can be further pressed and dried or even heat-dried to produce various harder, drier products, generally known as *kan tou fu* (dry bean curd). Bean curd is sliced, chunked, or crumbled and cooked with other foods in soup or stir-fried and used over rice; it is rarely eaten any other way, although kan tou is sliced and eaten with a sauce as a snack. Bean curd is preserved by frying and drying (even freeze-drying). Cubes of fresh or dried bean curd are stuffed, often with minced fish paste. When soybeans are spoken of in contrast to other beans, the general term is usually *ta tou* (large bean). However, a range of varietal names, the best known based on color, are often used in this contrast. The commonest color for soybeans in China is probably yellow, thus they are sometimes called *huang tou* (yellow bean), but black, white, and other colors also occur. (However, "green beans" and "red beans" are of other species.)

The soybean's chief use is in fermented products. Supreme is soy sauce (*tou chiang* or *tou yu*), made by fermenting a mixture of boiled soybeans, wheat flour, salt brine and a complex inoculum involving *Aspergillus*, *Rhizopus*, and other fungi. Local soy sauces are distinctive, using their own strains of fungi. Soy sauce varies from a very thin, highly salty form through rich medium grades to a solid black paste with less water and salt. Lower-sodium soy sauces are now being made for those who suffer from high blood pressure when they eat too much salt—a genetic misfortune very common in East Asia. In traditional Chinese cooking, free salt was almost never used; saltiness came from the soy sauce and other fermented products. A number of other ferments are thick pastes that usually go under the name *tou chiang* (thus the more liquid soy sauce is normally referred to as *tou yu*, bean oil). Many are highly spiced.

One odd soybean item is made even odder by its Chinese name; *sha ch'a chiang*, literally "sand tea sauce." The name is more comprehensible if we read *sha ch'a* in Hokkien Chinese: *sa te*. It is, in fact, the *saté* sauce of Indonesia and Malaysia, borrowed by the Hokkien, who have been trading and exchanging recipes in those lands for over a thousand years. It has been thoroughly Sinicized, however. In Indonesia it is a mix of peanut butter, chile, shrimp paste, and spices (including lesser galangal). In China, it is usually a flour–soybean paste with chile, Chinese spices, and fermented rice. The original fermented bean product was *tou shih*, boiled soybeans salted and fermented to a black color with *Rhizopus* and other fungi. This preparation, made into pastes and sauces, abounds in the Cantonese food region, giving a distinctive flavor to that cuisine. Soybean curd is also fermented; the white or yellow squares are packed in brine for sale. They constitute a Chinese equivalent of cheese and are apt to be overpowering, reminiscent of strong German hand cheese. They are graphically known as *ch'ou tou fu* (stinking bean curd). Only the very stoutest of heart eat them, and then only in small quantities. Soybean products, wheat gluten, and seaweed and other lower plants are basic to the vegetarian Buddhist temples. They supply critical protein, vitamin B12 (found in fermenting yeasts), and trace elements.

The soybean is the primary bean of China and often counted as one of the Five Staples of classical terminology, but its importance is often overrated at the expense of the broad bean (*Vicia faba*), called *ch'an tou* (silkworm bean) because of the bean's vague resemblance to a silkworm. It was introduced to China from the Near East (as an old name, *hu tou* or "Iranian bean," indicates) relatively recently, perhaps under the Mongols if not later (Laufer 1919). In subsequent years it has taken precedence over the soybean in many mountainous, remote, or rainy parts of China; the soybean prefers warm plains with rich soil. The broad bean is commonest in the west, near its home, and thus is little known or quite unknown to most Chinese in the areas best known to the outside world. Accounts indicate that it is eaten green as well as boiled as a dry bean and made into bean curd; it is commonly available in dry-foods shops, but little used. The form usually seen is the classic broad or fava bean; the smaller horse bean also occurs. In Szechuan it is made into fermented paste, often with chile peppers (*la tou chiang*, hot bean paste). Sometimes it is roasted as a snack.

Other common legumes came from the Near East, achieved wide importance, and were once known as *hu tou*, peas, or *wan tou*. They are the field pea (*Pisum arvensis*) and the common pea (*P. sativum*). These are also plants of the interior, more rarely seen in Hong Kong, Taiwan, and the urbanized regions of China than the broad bean (let alone the soybean), yet perhaps commoner than the broad bean. These are boiled, made into pea curd, and evidently made into noodles as well.

The mung bean is apparently of Indian or Southeast Asian origin. Usually a golden-green in color, it is known as *lu tou* (green bean) in Chinese (*Vigna mungo* var. *radiata*). When Linnaeus named these closely related beans, he applied the Indian vernacular name, *mung* or *mungo*, to the wrong bean—the black gram. But the two are now considered one species, so his mistake is corrected. The mung bean is boiled and made into curd; its starch is important in making the thin transparent noodles known as beanstarch or peastarch noodles (*fen-su*), but its great fame is in the form of sprouts, for which it is the bean of choice. The soybean is the other bean normally sprouted, its sprouts being considered coarser. The two are sometimes rather misleadingly distinguished in English as "pea sprouts" and "bean sprouts." Mung beans are grown everywhere in China except in cold or very dry areas.

The peanut (*Arachis hypogaea*) is correctly regarded as a bean rather than a nut by many Chinese. It is called *lo hua sheng*, which means "dropping flower gives birth," referring to the fact that the flower produces a pod that plants itself by growing into the soil. The phrase is confusingly shortened to *hua sheng* in ordinary speech. Peanuts, native to South America, were introduced by the Portuguese and other early European visitors in the sixteenth century. In China they provided a new and superb source of protein and oil that grew best in sandy, warm regions on lands previously almost worthless but made valuable by the peanut and other New World crops (such as the sweet potato). Peanut oil is now more important than any other vegetable oil in these parts of China, especially the central and south coasts (rapeseed oil remains China's most important oil, but is primarily restricted now to the north and interior). The peanut is eaten in every possible way—the plain nut is boiled, roasted, or (rarely) eaten raw; peanut presscakes are usually an animal feed but eaten by humans in hungry times. Ground or broken peanuts abound in pastries, candy, and sweets, and when a new sweet is borrowed from the West, a large dose of peanuts is often a step in making the borrowing into a true Chinese product. A mixture of ground peanuts and sugar is commonly used as a filling for sweets and may be made into sweet soup (as are mung and many other beans).

The red bean (*tou*) is usually the adzuki (*Vigna angularis*), but a small red kidney bean (a variety of the New World species *Phaseolous vulgaris*) goes by the same name, as do red forms of the south's rice bean (*Vigna calcarata*). Red beans, like mung beans, are used for sweetened bean porridge or *t'ang shui* (sugar water), the commonest dessert or sweet in many Chinese households and a standard sweet snack for children at street stalls. It is an important regulator of bodily humors in the traditional medical system; red bean sweet soup is heating. Mung bean is cooling, and mung bean sweet soup is one of the commonest methods of restoring equilibrium in people who feel they are overheated.

Several species of beans are grown primarily or entirely for use as fresh "green" beans. Best known and most widespread of these is the yard-long bean (*V. unguiculata* var. *sinensis*). Round and thin, it resembles string beans except in its striking length; it is rarely a yard long, but I measured one at 39 inches and another at 37½. It is normally cut in sections and stir-fried with other vegetables in mixed dishes. Other green beans, much less frequently used, include the sword bean (*Canavalia ensiformis; tao tou*), and the dolichos bean (*Dolichos lablab; pien tou* or "sided bean," because the pod is flat, not cylindrical). The dolichos bean is often mentioned in ancient Chinese literature but is now a minor food, green or dried.

The yam bean (*Pachyrrizus erosus; sha k'o*) is grown for its root rather than for its seeds or pods. This is the jicama of Mexico, probably a New World introduction of Spanish vintage. The root resembles a large, flattened turnip; it has a very slight, rather sweetish flavor and is quite crisp. Slices are eaten raw as snacks, often with pungent chili sauce as in Mexico, all over Southeast Asia and South China; they are appreciated for their refreshing crispness.

The Chinese have no word or category corresponding to *vegetable*. (Of course, vegetable really means simply "plant." English has never had a word specifically for edible vegetables. Perhaps no language does; after all, the boundary between the edible and the inedible is a very vague one.) The closest word is *ts'ai*, which means "greens" (i.e., leaf-and-stem vegetables) but is generalized to include any dish. A wide range of other categories refer to edible, soft parts of plants. I have already mentioned words for root crops and beans. There are also words for fruits used as vegetables (the Chinese have the same problems as English-speakers in thinking of squash and tomatoes as fruits). *Kua* includes all the fruits of the family Cucurbitaceae— squashes, melons (sweet and nonsweet), and cucumbers as well as the superficially squashlike eggplant. But eggplants are sometimes included in the category *chieh*, fruits of the Solanaceae family (tomatoes, eggplants, and relatives). The latter classification has more traditional as well as botanical sanction, but *ai kua* ("dwarf gourd," because the bush is small) has displaced it in the marketplace in referring to eggplants. There are no terms between the level of kingdom and that of genus—no families or natural orders of edible things. Such simplicity is typical of folk classification systems.

The category *ts'ai* takes a certain precedence because it includes the vegetables that make up the bulk of the Chinese diet apart from starch staples. At the top of the list stand cabbages, which, with grains and soybeans, are the most characteristic Chinese foods and the most universally and abundantly used. Rich in vitamins, minerals, and fiber, low in calories, they make an enormous nutritional contribution for very little extra energy intake (their production of calories per acre, however, is quite high). They are considerably more nutritious than Western cabbages, comparable to broccoli. The main forms are *Brassica pekinensis* (primarily grown in the north) and *B. chinensis* (south), both called *po ts'ai* (which also refers to another southern winter crop) and distinguished where found by local names. Both may be forms of *Brassica rapa*. In Hong Kong, *chinensis* is the *paak ch'oi* proper (and is thus the cabbage known to Westerners as bok choy), while *pekinensis* is qualified by adjectives. Westerners call them Peking cabbage and Chinese cabbage, as the scientific names imply; Peking is also called celery cabbage, Michihli cabbage (one variety), and, confusingly, Chinese cabbage. In appearance and qualities they are quite different. Their taste is milder than that of Western cabbages; Peking has almost no taste at all, but a pleasantly crisp texture. (Its crisp, fibrous leaves are responsible for the quite descriptive name "celery cabbage.") The ruling vegetable of old North China, it is now losing its dominance as other produce becomes available. The third of the three great *ts'ai* is mustard greens (*Brassica parachinensis*), *ts'ai hsin* or "greens heart," because the heart of the plant—the stem, buds, and young leaves—is eaten. The mustard greens of the American South are a different species.

Other Brassicas are eaten in China, especially the many varieties of *B. juncea* (*chieh ts'ai*) and *B. alboglabra* (*chieh lan ts'ai*). *Chieh* means mustard. *Lan* means orchid, referring somewhat hyperbolically to the rather pretty white flowers of *alboglabra*. These are Chinese counterparts of kale and collards; *alboglabra* in particular is very similar to collards in taste and cooking qualities, though it is tenderer and pleasanter. Both are used primarily in soup. They are quite important especially in the hot season when little else grows in the south (again similar to collards). Western cabbage, *B. oleracea*, is well known and becoming increasingly popular as high-yielding strains become available, but it is not liked as well as the native cabbages. Cabbages are favored for pickling; the product is usually crisper than sauerkraut but not so crisp as kimchi. Every major region has its distinctive pickles, usually including garlic, chiles, and ginger.

Spinach (*Spinacia oleracea*), introduced about 700 A.D. from the Middle East, is popular in China. Western-style spinach with blunt-ended leaves is less popular than the Chinese variety, whose sharper-tipped leaves fan out like arrowhead barbs; it is more delicate, less fibrous, more flavorful, and picks up less sand. Spinach is primarily used in clear soups with strips of meat, bean curd, or other protein sources. More popular than spinach in the warm parts of China is the amaranth or red spinach (*Amaranthus gangeticus*, also known as *A. mangostanus* or *A. tricolor*), which has a reddish color and a more succulent taste and texture. It is known as *hsien ts'ai*. Purslane (*Portulaca oleracea*) is very different from amaranth. It is known as *ma chih hsien* (*ts'ai*) or *pa hsi hsien ts'ai* (horsetooth *hsien* or Persian *hsien*—though *pa hsi* may not really mean Persian in this case). It is a common garden vegetable, often grown primarily for its supposed medicinal value rather than for food. A native South Chinese relative of sweet potato, *Ipomoea aquatica*, is grown for its leaves and stems (it has no tubers) where water is too deep for rice but too shallow for lotus or in any odd wet corner where water is hard to control. It is known as *k'ung-hsin ts'ai* (empty-hearted greens) from its hollow stem, or as *weng ts'ai*. It is rather tasteless, but its crisp texture makes it the favorite vegetable of many Taiwanese. Like many aquatic plants of South China, it frequently carries water-borne intestinal parasites, including schistosomiasis (Herklots 1972:148), but stir-frying is hot enough to kill the flukes. In general, Chinese cooking calls for brief but intense heat, which kills ordinary parasites; soups are simmered, but for a longer time, producing the same result. Experience has taught an accommodation between the needs to save fuel and flavor and the need to avoid waterborne pathogens.

Lettuce (*Lactuca sativa*) is known as *sheng ts'ai* (raw vegetable) because it can be eaten raw. Leafy varieties similar to the Oak Leaf lettuce of the West are those usually seen; head lettuce is unpopular because of its wateriness and bitter taste, though a recently introduced Western pattern is to use it as garnish. Lettuce is usually eaten in soup—green salads are unknown in traditional China and generally unsafe in the Orient. Lettuce's book name is *wo chu*, but this name really applies only to the bizarre celtuce or asparagus lettuce, the native Chinese thick-stemmed lettuce. Its stalk, sliced and stir-fried or cooked in soup, is excellent.

Other originally Western vegetables grown and used in China are parsley (*ch'in ts'ai*) and celery (*hsi ch'in* or "western parsley," since it is a very recent introduction). This can be confusing, since *ch'in* originally referred to a native Chinese herb *Oeranthe stolonifera*, and *hsi ch'in* meant parsley. Neither is used much in Chinese cooking, though in American Chinese (and many other) restaurants celery's cheapness means it is often used to stretch more expensive ingredients in mixed dishes. Traditional Chinese gourmets do not like the result.

Watercress (*Rorippa nasturtium-aquaticum*) may also be an introduction from the West, judging by its Chinese name, *hsi yang ts'ai* (western ocean vegetable). It is used very commonly in soup but is not eaten raw. It is a great tonic, believed to be one of the best remedies for overheating (in terms of humoral medicine). The soups are often combined with such strength-producing items as certain fish and internal organs like duck gizzards. Liking shallow water, watercress competes directly with rice in many areas but is a higher-priced crop.

Other common soup vegetables include the matrimony vine or Chinese wolfthorn (*Lycium chinensis; kou ch'i ts'ai*) and the garland chrysanthemum (*Chrysanthemum coronarium; t'ung hao ts'ai*, in Japanese *shungiku*). Mallow (*Malva* spp.; *k'uei ts'ai*) was once the most important Chinese vegetable but fell from grace and has almost ceased to be used. Malabar nightshade or spinach (*Basella alba, lo k'uei* or "falling mallow") has recently entered from South Asia. Dried buds of daylily (*Hemerocallis* spp.— many cultivars are complex hybrids), with their superb, distinctive, musky flavor, are known as *chin chen ts'ai* (golden needle vegetable); they spread from the Chinese vegetable garden to the Occidental flower garden due to the efforts of plant hunters in the nineteenth century. Lotus leaves are used to wrap food, and occasionally eaten with it, under the name of *ho ts'ai* (lotus greens). A vast range of minor green vegetables exists as well, and any trip through a large market will turn up several more.

One leaf crop, alfalfa, is normally called not *ts'ai*, but *mu hsü* (not the same word as in "mu hsü pork"). This Iranian-derived name has spread to clover. King (1911) noted that clover was sold as food in Shanghai and was a common food in parts of North China; tender young growing tips and the young sprouts of alfalfa and clover are used, as in American health-food diets.

The commonest and most important nonleaf vegetables are the root crops. Of the nonstarchy ones, by far the most important is the white radish (*Raphanus sativus; luo po*), which comes in a range of Chinese varieties. The Oriental white radishes range from large (6–8 inches long and 2–3 inches thick) to very large (2–3 feet long), are watery and crisp, and are turniplike in taste and quality, though without the cabbage undertone. (Thus they are often translated "turnip." Most mentions of turnips in Western literature on China actually refer to white radishes.) White radishes are sliced or diced and pickled as cabbages are, usually dried first; often garlic and sometimes fermented soybean products or chili pepper powder are added. The Koreans perfected this spiced pickling. Green radishes are called *ch'ing luo po*. (If they must be distinguished from the white ones, the whites are called *po luo po*, but normally *luo po* by itself is understood to mean the white ones.) The green are not thought as tasty as the white varieties and are rarely used except as medicine—they cool down the body—and occasionally in soup. Western radishes—the small red ones—have been introduced into Westernized parts of China, where they are known by such neo-nyms as *luo po tzu* (little radishes). Some black-skinned radishes exist in China and are naturally enough known as *hei luo po* (black radishes). Other colors occur here and there, with predictably descriptive names.

The carrot is called *hung luo po* (red radish). It was introduced to China via Central Asia at around the time of the Yüan Dynasty (Laufer 1919); first it was called *hu luo po* (Iranian radish). Carrots, far more than green radishes, are used to cool the body, to improve the eyes (this virtue of the carrot was evidently determined in China long before carotene was known to science), to help the throat, and for other medicinal purposes. Carrots can be stored to provide a source of carotene even in winter, a vitamin-poor season in North China and often in the south as well. Carrots are normally used in soup, but they have been steadily increasing in stir-fried dishes, and they are commonly cut into ornamental garnishes.

A number of other roots are eaten occasionally, as well as tubers, bulbs, corms, and so on. Best known of such minor "root" crops is the corm of a bulrush, the water chestnut (*Eleocharis dulcis* or *Scirpus tuberosus*), *ma t'i* (horse hoof) in colloquial speech, more classically *pi ch'i*. This must be carefully distinguished from the water caltrop (*Trapa bicornis; ling chüeh* or "water-caltrop horns"), actually a fruit. The latter is frequently called "water chestnut" in English and is indeed closely related to European water chestnuts (*T. natans*). The "horse-hoof" water chestnut is related to the bulrushes, sedges, and tules, whose corms have often supplied foods in other lands—they were used, for example, by the Indians of California. It is this kind that is so common in foods, with a delicate, sweetish taste and marvelously crisp texture. The water caltrop, a rather tasteless fruit, is roasted or boiled as a snack. It often harbors the snails that carry schistosomes and if undercooked can transmit these parasites to humans.

The shoots of many plants are eaten; seedlings with small leaves are called *ya*; leafless thick shoots such as bamboo shoots are *sun*. Commonest among the *ya* are bean sprouts; among the *sun* bamboo shoots. Bamboo shoots come from species of *Phyllostachys* (smaller) and *Sinocalamus* (larger). Other bamboos are locally pressed into service. The general term is *chu sun*, *chu* meaning bamboo. Bamboo shoots are traditionally best in winter and considered a great delicacy. Asparagus, a very recent introduction to China, is known as *lu sun* (rush shoots) or *chiao sun*. This name once applied to wild rice (*Zizania aquatica*), raised in China not for its seeds (considered a lowly famine food) but for its shoots. These are allowed to become infected with a *Gibberella* fungus that makes the stem grow thick, soft, and asparagus-like, and eaten as a delicacy.

Consideration of roots and shoots naturally leads to *Allium*, the onion genus, whose bulbs and leaves are important everywhere, but nowhere more important than in China. In North China especially, enormous quantities of them are eaten, and they are a vital resource; onions and garlic sometimes provide almost the only source of vitamins in winter. The dominant allium in China is not garlic, however, but *ts'ung* (*Allium fistulosum*, the Welsh or bunching onion. It has nothing to do with Wales; "Welsh" is from the German *welsch* or "foreign," applied after it was introduced from the Orient). This is the "scallion" of Chinese cookbooks. (Scallion actually means any young onion.) Very mild in flavor and bite, it is used widely as a garnish or minor ingredient, but often—especially in the north—it is the main vegetable of a vegetable–meat dish, especially with mutton or an organ meat. Dumplings filled with a mixture of *ts'ung* and chopped meat abound in various forms and are among the best and most widely loved of Chinese snacks; again, this is especially true in the north, where alliums are successful and other vegetables (except the Peking cabbage) rare. Western onions (*A. cepa*) are evidently a recent addition, since their name is *yang ts'ung* (foreign onions). They are used dry, cut up and stir-fried in mixed dishes, and have become ever more popular.

Garlic (*A. sativum*) is also an introduction, but of much longer standing—probably several millennia. It has been part of Chinese culture throughout historic time and has its own name, *suan* (a head of garlic is called *suan t'ou*). It is used most commonly in stir-fried dishes and dumpling fillings. Elephant garlic, actually a variety of leek, is grown occasionally under the name *ta suan* (big garlic). Shallots (*A. cepa* var. *aggregatum*—not *A. ascalonicum* as in older literature) occur fairly commonly in parts of South China but are little integrated into Chinese cooking and seem to be grown primarily for Westerners, in interesting contrast to the extreme importance of these *bawang merah* (red onions) in Malaysia. In China there seems to be no agreed-on name for them. Leeks (*A. ampeloprasum* = *A. porrum*; *chiu ts'ung*) are rare. Much more common are the native Chinese chives (not the Western chive, but *A. tuberosum*), flat-leaved and garlic-flavored, hence called "garlic chives" in the West. Regarded as more or less a leafy form of leek, they are called *chiu ts'ai* and are very widely used, chopped up and used like *ts'ung* when a more delicate flavor is wanted. Last and perhaps most interesting is the *chiao* (*A. chinense*; *chiao t'ou*). Extremely popular primarily as a pickle similar to pickled onions, this plant is so truly Chinese that it has no Western name. It is often known in the West by its Japanese name, *rakkyo* (*kyo* is the Japanese pronunciation of *chiao*) or as "Chinese leek." It is almost always eaten as a pickled snack, but occasionally the pickled bulbs are used in cooking, especially in strong-flavored dishes such as sweet-and-sour pork. Usually it is eaten by children and pregnant women (Chinese tradition, like Western, attributes fondness for pickles to pregnant women). The greatest Cantonese artist, Su Jen-Shan (nineteenth century), was also famous for his addiction to the pickled bulbs.

Solanaceous fruits are in part a natural group in Chinese. Eggplant (*Solanum melongena*) has the most respectable antiquity, introduced from India at some obscure time in the past. Its first Chinese name was *ch'ieh*, an unanalyzable old name. It is little used. Tomatoes (*Lycopersicon esculentum*) were introduced from the West in the 1500s and promptly named *fan chieh* (barbarian eggplant), their similarity to eggplants noted from the start. At first tomatoes were grown only for Westerners near the coastal enclaves where they stayed, but its taste and ease of growth achieved popularity for the tomato eventually, and it continues to spread and become more widely accepted in cooking. At present, however, it is still primarily a part of urbanized Cantonese cuisine—the area that has been longest and most intimately in contact with foreigners. *K'e tsap* means "tomato sauce" in Cantonese; this is sometimes thought to be the origin of the English word *ketchup* or *catsup*, but such is not the case. "Catsup" is cognate with French *escaveche* and Spanish *escabeche*, meaning food in sauce, and was used long before the Cantonese had tomato sauce (David 1986). (The Indonesian word *ketjap* or "soy sauce" is equally unlikely as a source of the English term.)

Among the Solanaceae is the New World's gift to mankind, the chili pepper (*Capsicum frutescens* and *C. annuum*). Brought to the Orient by the Portuguese in the 1500s, these plants did not remain a minor and local part of the diet, as did tomatoes and eggplants, but swept through the Far East with epochal effect. Perhaps no culinary advance since the invention of distilling has had more effect than the propagation of chili peppers in the Old World. The main one is *C. annuum*. Not only did it incalculably benefit the cuisine of all those peoples civilized enough to accept it, it also is high in vitamins A and C, iron, calcium, and other minerals; is eminently storable and usable in pickles; can be grown anywhere under any conditions as long as the growing season is long and warm; and thus is now the world's most ubiquitous high-vitamin supplement to grains and other staples, providing what they lack in both taste and nutritional qualities. In China, the existence of the Chinese cabbages (nutritionally equivalent) and the concurrent spread of the sweet potato (high in vitamin A) made the chili less dramatically important than it is elsewhere, but it caught on fast, especially in remote and mountainous regions where other high-vitamin foods could not grow well. Thus its center of abundance today is in the warmer mountain regions of China—the southwestern part of the country—where among both Chinese and minority groups it is vital to life. It appears to have spread from Macau, and perhaps other Portuguese touchpoints, through the mountains of the south, until it found a true home in Hunan and probably Kweichow. From here it spread rapidly to Szechuan and thence to Yünnan. The near depopulation of Szechuan in the wars at the fall of Ming led to an inflow of Hunanese migrants, who brought their cuisine with them, and a similar flow later went from Szechuan to Yünnan, especially after the great Muslim rebellion that decimated the main cities in that province. Travelers in Yünnan afterward note that the cooks were almost all Szechuanese. Only in these western provinces did chilis achieve the importance they have enjoyed in Korea, Southeast Asia, and India. The chilis used are mostly of the hot annual varieties. The very hot perennial chilis (*C. frutescens*, the bird or tabasco chilis) are grown rarely. Sweet peppers—recent varieties of annual chilis, bred for mildness and size—are very rare except in the immediate environs of Hong Kong and other highly Westernized places. Nowhere have they penetrated into ordinary cuisine. Chilis are called *la chiao* (hot pepper)—they are classified with the peppers, as in English, not with their true relatives, tomatoes and eggplants. Probably this is due to straight translation from Western languages.

The largest class of fruits used as vegetables, including many eaten purely as sweets, is that of *kua* (cucurbits or pepos). These are large fruits with a rind surrounding a central cavity full of flat seeds attached by pith—melons, squash, pumpkin, cucumbers, and so on. Plants with such fruits comprise the family Cucurbitaceae. The Chinese have many and love them deeply. They also include as *kua* a few plants with similar fruits that are not of the family Cucurbitaceae.

The most widely grown is a native Chinese species, *Benincasa hispida*, the wax or hair gourd. It is eaten in two very different forms, derived from different varieties of the plant: the *tung kua* (winter melon) and the *mao kua* (hair gourd) or *chi kua* (jointed gourd). The former is grown to ripeness, at which time it superficially resembles a large watermelon, except for the waxy coating that covers and whitens it. Its watery, slightly spicy flesh is used in soup; often it is steamed in a metal pot with the soup inside the melon, which is often carved. This is the famous *tung kua chung* (winter melon pond). The hair gourd is eaten when small and unripe, similar to a pale, rather fuzzy zucchini squash. The differences correspond closely to those between pumpkin and summer squash (varieties of *Cucurbita pepo*)—particularly when one remembers that in South America the pumpkin is chiefly used as a partially edible stewpot very much like a tung kua chung.

In addition to the hair gourd there is a vast range of minor gourds. Important are the bitter melon (*Momordica charantia*), *fu kua* or "bitter gourd"; cucumber (*Cucumis sativus*), *huang kua* or "yellow gourd" (many Chinese varieties are yellow or brownish and are considered more Chinese than the green ones); and watermelon, *hsi kua* or "western gourd" (it spread from Africa via Central Asia), some varieties of which are grown only for their large seeds, which almost completely replace the meat. Melon seeds are a great Chinese delicacy, the commonest snack. True melons of many varieties are known mostly by name of origin; notable is the famous (*C. melo*) *Ha-mi kua* or "Hami melon" from Hami in Sinkiang. It is often said to be the best melon in the world (it is certainly the best I have eaten). The New World cucurbits have taken some hold in China but are not well liked. Chayote (*Sechium edule*), in spite of its Chinese name, *fo shou kua* (Buddha's hand melon—its shape is reminiscent of Buddha's Hand citron), is considered uninteresting. Winter squash (*Cucurbita* spp.—usually *C. moschata* in the markets) is considered coarse and plebian, a poverty food. Its Western origin and early introduction are betrayed by its name, *fan kua*, "barbarian gourd." (This name applies most usually to *moschata*. *C. Maxima* is sometimes called *nan kua*, "southern gourd"). Unfortunately, the Chinese have not assimilated good ways of cooking these fruits.

Kua also includes the quince (*Cydonia oblonga* and *Chaenomeles* spp.). The papaya

(*Carica papaya; mu kua* or "tree melons") was originally termed *fan mu kua* (barbarian tree melon) when first introduced from the Americas. At present there is no way of telling which fruit is referred to, except by context. Locality of origin is helpful, since the papaya only grows in more or less tropical areas too warm for the quince. (*Chaenomeles* quinces are native to China; *Cydonia* is rare but of long establishment there.) There is a vast confusion in Chinese on this distinction.

Last come the lower plants. Many seaweeds are eaten, among them *tzu ts'ai* (purple vegetable), a flat seaweed used in soup; *fa ts'ai* (hair vegetable), a hairlike black alga from Mongolian desert springs, used especially in Buddhist vegetarian cooking; *yang ts'ai* (ocean vegetable), the agar-agar seaweed; and others. Mushrooms are collectively known as *ku*; the common one seen is *Lentinus edodes*, called *tung ku* (winter mushroom)—the shiitake of Japan. Increasingly common is the padi-straw mushroom, *Volvariella volvacea*, called *ts'ao ku* (grass mushroom). The *tung ku* is usually used dried, the padi-straw fresh. The Western mushroom has become a common cash crop in Taiwan, where it is canned and exported; it is known as *mo ku*. Many other mushrooms are eaten, among them one known as *hsiang ku* (fragrant mushroom). Bracket fungi of trees are given the generic term *erh* (ears) and are used dried; they are popular and common in mixed dishes, where they bring out flavors subtly without adding much of their own, like truffles. Like mushrooms, they are too expensive for any but festal fare, in which they are almost obligatory. The common ones are *mu erh* (wood ears; *Auricularia* spp.) and *yün erh* (cloud ears; *Tremella* spp.). Various species of both exist. *Hsüeh erh* (snow ears) are common in medicinal brews because of their alleged soothing and harmonizing characteristics as well as their nutritional value, but they are not used as food. Several other types occur. One bracket fungus not called an ear is *Ganoderma lucidum*, the *ling chih* ("magical power fungus" or, more loosely, "fungus of immortality"). Traditionally the food of Immortals and a divine plant giving longevity and wisdom, this plant is now used widely in Chinese medicine. It has many alleged values as a tonic, which have not been fully explored.

The Chinese call all fruits *kuo*, including those that are valued only for their kernels (i.e., nuts). The term *kuo* covers both the fruit as a whole and the fleshy part of it. Seeds are *tzu*, particularly if small; *tzu* also means "son," but the extension to "seed" must have been very early—perhaps it always meant both. The kernel of the seed or nut is the *jen*, which also means "honesty"; here the extension may be that truth is the "kernel" of a person's words or intent.

Since some fruits are valued for flesh and kernel both, it is best to discuss this class in correct Chinese style, as one. In general, the Chinese like fruit but eat rather little. Fruit is preferred sour, thus usually eaten green or salted and pickled, unless it is naturally a very sour fruit. The habit of eating green fruit—noted with (usually unpleasant) surprise by a great many travelers in China—no doubt arose from the need to harvest the fruit before birds, rats, or thieves did. "Never adjust your hat in a peach orchard, or your shoes in a melon field" is an old Chinese proverb counseling the hearer to do nothing that might arouse suspicion. Fruit's low nutrient value and vulnerability to theft has kept it a very minor part of the Chinese scene. Fruit culture is expanding now, very rapidly in Hong Kong and Taiwan, where money is available for such well-liked luxuries, but fruit is still a minor item of the diet.

Most widely distributed of all Chinese fruits is probably the *mei* (*Prunus mume*, Japanese *ume* or *mume*). Usually translated "plum" in books about China, it is not a plum; the plum (*Prunus salicina*) is called *li* and is less widely eaten and much less widely painted and written about. The mei is actually closer to the apricot (*P. armeniaca, hsing*); indeed, it is a sort of Chinese counterpart thereof and is often called "Oriental flowering apricot." The fruit resembles a small sour apricot and is usually eaten pickled as a snack. The flowers, which bloom in January or February, are spectacularly beautiful, and their anarchistic tendency to glory in even the worst weather has made them a symbol of Taoism and of the independent recluse as well as making the tree traditional in gardens. The mei has an honored place in Chinese consciousness. There is an entire genre of mei paintings, literally millions of poems about mei trees in flower, reams of descriptions and allusions to the mei. It is a symbol of the Chinese world from its most exalted to its very lowest, from philosophic Taoism to venereal disease. (Mei trees ornamented entertainers' quarters and thus came to refer to the diseases one brings back therefrom. Or—another theory—the lesions look like mei flowers. Mei trees and flowers, like peaches, were probably a symbol of sex and sexual potency in ancient times.) Usually eaten salted and often dried, the mei is also made into a sauce. A number of terms cover the various salted forms, which may be flavored with licorice or other things.

The peach (*Prunus persica, t'ao*) originated in China. The overgrazed, deforested hills of North China are often covered with wild peach scrub; the tree appears to thrive on the conditions of erosion and misuse that make other tree growth impossible there. Peaches are eaten commonly (rather green) in northern and mountainous western lowland China, but in the south, where they do not grow (except flowering varieties and a few scattered fruiting trees), they are usually seen only as rare snacks in dried or pickled form. Even this minor use is a great increase over the recent past, when peach fruit was known primarily through pictures. The flowering varieties, however, are grown everywhere in China, especially for New Year decoration. In Hong Kong a vast flowering peach industry has grown up to supply this market, and fortunes turn on the weather two or three weeks before New Year. Chinese New Year, varying from January to late February, can come so early that the flowers are found only in the warmest areas (and can all be destroyed by a late freeze) or so late that the trees have already flowered out in warmer parts of the colony. At least this problem is somewhat self-adjusting in that the warm areas are well off in the cold years, the cold areas in the warm years. The prudent orchardier tries to plant his orchard on a slope, so that some trees are in warm pockets and some in cold. The value of the peach in China is more symbolic than nutritional. An ancient symbol of fertility, perhaps because of its resemblance to the external female genitalia (not exactly striking; perhaps the pink color of flowers and fruit was more important), the peach took on magical attributes. (On mei and peach in symbol, see Sowerby 1940.) The peach brings luck, abundance, and protection. Peach wood is made into amulets to drive off demons; a good display of peach flowers at New Year gives good fortune through the year; the Spirit of the Locality or Earth God carries—or has boys around him who carry—the Peaches of Immortality, which make the eater an Immortal. The most famous use of peaches in literature is, of course, in T'ao Yuanming's many-layered and complex essay, "The Peach-Flower Stream." One layer of T'ao's symbolism is sexual, and the sexual symbolism of the peach is still important in China (Groot 1892–1910; Schafer 1963).

A subtropical fruit shaped like a long, thin peach and bearing a single seed is known as "fairy peach" or "heavenly peach." The flesh is yellow-orange and tastes vaguely like a not-too-fresh sweet potato, and despite the hyperbolic name the fruit is not well regarded. It is clearly not related to the peach; it appears to be an American introduction of the genus *Pouteria*.

Other rosaceous fruits include Asian natives and many Chinese equivalents of more widely known fruits. The true apricot (*Prunus armeniaca*) is known as *hsing*; the apple (*Pyrus malus*) is *ping kuo*; both are introductions from West or Central Asia. Many native crab apples are grown for fruit, and some for their leaves, which make an excellent tea; the best known is *P. baccata*, the "tea crab." The cherry apple (*P. spectabilis* or *P. prunifolia*), *hai tang*, is also common, especially candied, and looks and tastes like a sweet crab apple. The Chinese pears are also independent of Western pears; they are of several species (*Pyrus sinensis, P. kawakamii*, and so on). Those with silica granules in the flesh are *sha li* (sand pears); crisp, white-fleshed ones are *hsueh li* (snow pears). All are crisp and round, like apples, rather than soft and pear-shaped like the Western world's *P. communis*. The Chinese cherry is also a different species from the Western (*Prunus pseudocerasus* as opposed to *P. avium = P. cerasus*). Some of the many species of flowering cherries also produce edible fruit. There are also the native hawthorns (*Crataegus* spp.), grown for candied fruit; the fruit is also gathered wild. Last and most distinctive of Chinese rosaceous fruits is the loquat, *Eriobotrya japonica*, known by a strange name that may be a loanword from some other language—*p'i p'a*. The lute is also called *p'i p'a*, from its shape, resembling loquat leaves. The loquat's fruit is orange, superbly flavorful, sweet yet sharp; good varieties are among the finest of all fruit and deserve to be better known and more widely grown (they are easy to grow in warm or subtropical climates). Their nearest European equivalent is the medlar, *Mespilus germanica*, which must be eaten rotten and is said to be at best an acquired taste (and at worst reminiscent of raw sewage). The loquat is known in French and some other European languages as the Japanese medlar.

Along with the rosaceous fruits, the main fruit of China's "core" area is the jujube or Chinese date (*Zizyphus jujuba* and *Z. sinensis*). A thorny bush or small tree of the dry parts of North China, this buckthorn takes over railroad embankments, city yards, factory dumps, loess cliff breaks—anywhere too poor and dry for anything else to grow. A favorite yard tree, it bears fruits that look and taste so much like dates that the Western term "Chinese date" is matched by the Chinese term "foreign jujube" for the true date (_Phoenix dactylifera_), known in China as an import since the early Middle Ages. Jujubes are brown or black. Believed to be powerfully strengthening and health-giving, (they bear large amounts of vitamin C and iron), these fruits are fed to infants and used as nutritional aids. Red ones are believed particularly good for the blood (because of their color), black ones for the body in general. A delightful paste of walnuts and jujubes is often eaten for health—the brain-shaped walnut kernels strengthen the brain. (This claim is deleted from packages for sale in the Unites States, due to truth-in-advertising laws.)

An odd "fruit" known since ancient days is _Hovenia dulcis_, the raisintree. What is eaten is not the small fruit, but the stalk that holds the fruit cluster; swollen and sweet, it tastes like a particularly fine raisin.

A great range of minor fruits fills out the list. Several of these are, or once were, exotic. From China's central and southern mountains come plants such as the "sheep peach" (_yang tao_, the kiwi fruit _Actidinia sinensis_) and the "foreign flowering apricot" (_yang mei_), a term used for both strawberries (_Fragaria_ spp.) and ericaceous fruits from the waxmyrtle (_Myrica_) and arbutus. Strawberries are more often called _ts'ao mei_ (herb mei). Other berries are rare in China. Further south, in the tropics, the Chinese encountered the coconut, litchis, longans, and bananas. There was also the _Canarium album_ tree with its olivelike fruit (called Chinese olives when salt-preserved) and superb, almondlike seed kernel. Southeast Asian or tropical Chinese fruits like the starfruit or carambola (_Averrhoa carambola_) and the sour, poor-quality fruits of _Dracontomelon sinensis_ were considered less attractive.

Far more important were the citrus fruits. The sweet orange (_Citrus sinensis_), mandarin orange and tangerine (_C. reticulata_), pomelo (_C. grandis_), wampee (_Clausena wampi_), and kumquat (_Fortunella_ spp.) are the major natives; lemon and lime were introduced early from the West, the lemon becoming well known under the loan name _ling men_ (from Persian _laymun_, directly or via Arabic or some other language). Hybrids of tangerine and orange were known and loved early and given the name of "sweeties" (_kan_—the character combines the graph "tree" and the word for "sweet"). The hybrid of pomelo and orange, however, did not occur; only in the eighteenth-century West Indies did these finally mix, producing the grapefruit. Of all the citrus, the most culturally important was the mandarin orange (the term generally covers both the tangerine species and the tang-or hybrids).

The citrus fruits retained a magical and religious aura, probably attached to them by non-Chinese peoples in what is now South China. Pomeloes, oranges, and mandarins continue to be the commonest fruits at sacrifices. The bizarre "Buddha's hand" (a contorted form of the citron _C. medica_, borrowing from the Western world) is often seen in temples. Water in which pomelo skins or leaves have been soaked is commonly used to drive away ghosts and evil spirits. Small mandarin-orange trees are found in houses at Chinese New Year. The popular name of *C. reticulata*—properly *chü*—is *chieh*, "lucky one."

The European grape (*Vitis vinifera*) was introduced to China by Chang Chien, an envoy sent by the Han emperor Wu Ti to the Western world in the second century B.C. Grape wine followed eventually, introduced via the Turkic-speaking peoples of Sinliang. Popular in the Tang Dynasty, it lost out again later to Chinese grain *chiu*. Pomegranates (*Punica granatum; shih liu*) came soon after, and eventually all the West and South Asian common fruits became known in China. Watermelons came from Africa and became as popular for their seed kernels as for their fruit; they are the favorite fruit of most of North China. Last of all, the New World fruits have become enormously popular in port cities, especially the tropical ones such as papaya and lemon guava (*Psidium guajava*, called *fan shi liu* or "foreign pomegranate," and sometimes nicknamed "women's dog meat" because women eat it to get warm in winter, as men eat dog meat, which is often disliked by women). The avocado has recently appeared and is called "butter fruit." Cherimoyas and soursops, pineapples and sapotes now appear on fruit stalls and in southern orchards.

Nuts play a minor part in Chinese food. In addition to walnuts (the best are Persian, *Juglans regia*, known since the Middle Ages in China), chestnuts (the native *Castanea mollissima*), hazelnuts (*Corylus*), acorns, and so on, fruit kernels are widely used. Most are the kernels of apricots (*Prunus armeniaca*). Special varieties with uninteresting fruit are grown solely for their large, sweet, nontoxic seeds, which are used as almonds are used in the West. A mixture of apricot-kernel powder and congee or milk is used to relieve the distress of colds and sore throats (I can testify to its effectiveness). True almonds are barely known and not normally used. The aforementioned kernels of the *Canarium* tree are popular in South Chinese cooking. Pine nuts—usually the seeds of *Pinus koraiensis*, but other pines will do—are very popular and believed to convey long life, especially if they are one's staple food. (Pines live, evergreen, for centuries.) Other evergreens supply more exotic nuts: ginkgo nuts (*Ginkgo biloba*; usually called "white nuts" but sometimes "silver nuts," of which the word *ginkgo* is a Japanese-English corruption) and nutmeg-yew kernels (*Torreya grandis*). Both of these are roasted. They are bitter and astringent and thus often eaten to relieve swollen and sore membranes in the throat.

Chinese food uses less herbal and spice flavoring than do the cuisines of most of Asia, but the spice list is not small. Most of the classic herbs and spices of the Near East and India have reached China: basil, fenugreek, and so on. They need no special mention here. China's native spices deserve a few words. Perhaps the most characteristic, the most familiar from many dishes, is star anise (*Illicium* spp.) Its large star-shaped fruits have a powerful anise or licorice flavor, though it is not related to either of those two plants. Several species of brown pepper (*Zanthoxylum*) are used in different parts of China, especially in the west and southwest. Once again, the plant bears no resemblance to its English-language namesake. It is, in fact, a form of prickly-ash or fagara, growing on a small thorny bush or sprawling vinelike little tree. The flavor of the small brown fruits is intense and distinctive, with vague citrus echoes. In large quantities, the fruits can produce a numbing effect on the mouth and tongue, apparently harmless.

China is also the native home of cassia (*Cinnamomum cassia*, Mandarin *kuei*). Both the bark of young twigs and the dried flowers are used, but the former is the usual spice. Usually *kuei* is translated "cinnamon," but cinnamon is a different though closely related product (*C. zeylanicum*, from South Asia). The two tend to be used interchangeably in modern Chinese cooking.

Clove, nutmeg, and other Southeast Asian spices have long been used. Various herbs—smartweed, cresses, mints, and the peppery water-lily *Brasenia* spp., for example—are used locally and rather sparingly. Few have any wide usage, and none competes with soybean ferments and garlic in importance as flavoring.

Coffee, chocolate, and opium reached China, of course. Coffee is *chia fei*, from Cantonese *kafei*, which—like almost all other words in the world for the berry of *Coffea* spp.—is derived from the old Ethiopian word immortalized in Kahve (or Kaffe) Province, southern Ethiopia, whence *C. arabica* comes. Opium came early but was not much used until the British aggressively merchandised it in the nineteenth century. The other indulgent of worldwide name, cola (from West Africa's *Cola nitida* and *C. acuminata*), has now reached China too. Much earlier was betel: the quid of *Piper betle* leaf eaten with lime and the nut of the areca palm (*Areca catechu*). This "betel" nut, whose stimulant alkaloids are released by the lime and the chemicals in the betel leaf, was already known as a southern product in the early fourth century A.D. Then as now, it was called by its Malay name, *pinang* (*binlang* in modern Mandarin, but presumably borrowed via one of the south-coast Chinese languages; it is still *pinnang* in some dialects of Southern Min).

It is probably significant that the most widespread words in the world—borrowed into virtually every language—are the names of the four great caffein plants: coffee, cacao, cola, and tea. (Cacao's drug is really theobromine, and tea has theophylline as well as caffeine, but these alkaloids all form one closely related chemical group, the methylxanthines.) Tea is the great Chinese contribution. From Mandarin *cha* comes the Persian/Iranian *chai*, borrowed directly into Mongol, Russian, and East European languages, as well as Japanese *ocha* and many other variants. From southern Min (Hokkien) *te* come all the West European words. *Tea* was originally pronounced closer to the Min form; "tay" gave way to "tee" in the eighteenth century, except in conservative dialects like those of Ireland.

Tea, however, was not known to ancient China. The word then meant any infusion of leaves. (The evolution of the word in English has been the exact reverse —from a term for a specific plant to a catchall.) Some other sources of early Chinese brews are remembered in our words "tea rose" and "tea crab apple"; chrysanthemum flowers and herbal medicines are commonly used in China as tea stock, and anything cooling (from cold sweet bean porridge to beer) is called "cooling tea" (*liang cha*) to this day. It was not until the T'ang Dynasty that the name came to refer preeminently to the infusion of *Camellia sinensis*. This bush—an exquisitely beautiful one, similar to other white-flowered camellias—comes from the China–India–Burma border country; no one is exactly sure where, since unequivocally wild tea has never been found. In this area the hill people chew pickled tea leaves (a sort of tea sauerkraut), called *miang* in Burmese and thought to be a very ancient preparation. Tea may have been established as an aboriginal brew in what is now South China. The classic story of its introduction to Chinese civilization is that the monk Bodhidharma, who introduced Zen to China, meditated before a wall and fell asleep; in fury he cut off his eyelids, which fell to the ground and grew into tea bushes. Shorn of the humorous fiction, this story tells us that tea came from India in about the fifth century A.D., accompanying Buddhists, who used it to keep awake during meditation; if this is not the whole story, it is at least believable. But tea's real popularity is due to a single book, *The Classic of Tea* by Lu Yü (1974). This work of the late T'ang (eighth century) launched the hyperaesthetic and ritualized devotion of tea that lasts to this day in East Asia, climaxing in the Japanese tea ceremony, so well (and ironically) described in Yasunari Kawabata's novel, *Thousand Cranes*. Lu Yü was a purist, describing such things as spiced tea as no more than "the swill of gutters and ditches." (I wonder what he would have said of flavored teas and coffees.) Others were already drinking tea with flowers as well as spices; jasmine tea is the most popular drink in North China today. (The true jasmine, a Near Eastern or Indian plant, had been recorded as an exotic from the south by Chi Han in the fourth century.) Unlike the vast majority of T'ang exotics, tea survived the fall of T'ang and the more nativistic periods that followed, no doubt because it had both stimulant value and fine taste.

Tea is currently prepared in three ways: green, lightly fermented (oolong and the like), and black. Green tea is dried by a rather complex process, without fermentation. Black tea is fermented for a considerable time under controlled conditions. The Chinese call it "red tea" (*hung ch'a*), attending to the reddish color of the brew rather than the blackish color of the dry leaves. Green tea is green in all languages; the Chinese is *ch'ing ch'a*.

The primary tea-raising areas of china are in and around Fujian Province (where the Min languages are spoken, hence the widespread borrowing of the word *te*), including the island of Taiwan, which is off Fujian and primarily Min-speaking. The finest teas are generally considered to be the Lung Ch'ing teas of Fujian and the oolongs of northern Taiwan, but there are multitudes of local patriots who swear by their home brews. Black tea is not liked or much used in China, and though excellent black teas do come from Yunnan and elsewhere, the best are still those of India, such as Darjeeling. (Yünnan also grows coffee, less distinguished than its tea.) In Tibet and neighboring areas, tea is drunk with milk or butter mixed in. The Tibetan national food is buttered tea mixed with tsamba (parched barley). In the T'ang Dynasty, Chinese drank tea with milk and butter, too.

Opium and tobacco are smokes, not foods, but the Chinese idiom is "to eat smoke," so they deserve a mention here. Opium came from the Near East at an early date but was not popular or widely used until the British forced it on China in the 1800s; tobacco is a New World crop, introduced in the 1500s and spreading since. Opium addiction is virtually extinct on the mainland and rare in Taiwan, but it still flourishes in Hong Kong, where the stronger opium derivatives—morphine, codeine, heroin, and so on—have mostly replaced the raw drug. The resinous flavor of opium smoke was until recently a common scent in certain parts of Hong Kong but now is rather rare. Tobacco is now overwhelmingly the drug of choice among Chinese. Almost all men and a large percentage of women are smokers; cigarettes are virtually the only form of tobacco used, though one occasionally still sees pipes, including beautiful old water pipes made from large joints of bamboo. China has made some attempts to combat smoking, but Hong Kong and Taiwan do little, and smoking is rampant among overseas Chinese as well. Lung cancer has predictably become a major cause of death and continues to increase, while other health consequences of smoking (from coughs to heart disease) also grow more common.

The Chinese have always been given to depressant drugs rather than to hallucinogens. Alcohol, tobacco, and opium dominate. Even the stimulant tea is drunk weak in most areas. In spite of widespread and ancient knowledge of a whole host of hallucinogenic plants—marijuana, aconite, henbane, various mushrooms including the fly agaric (at least in the northeast), and many more—the Chinese have never used these to any extent. The Taoist alchemists and immortality seekers of the medieval period swallowed quantities of these drugs, as of almost everything else imaginable, but they were a small and usually elite group. The folk counterpart was self-induced hypnotic trance. I and other anthropologists have witnessed many such trances, considered spirit possessions; drugs are unused or very sparingly used (people may smoke, drink, or even take a bit of opium at such events). In general, throughout East Asia from China south, avoidance of hallucinogens and reliance on self-induced trance is prevalent. Expense and the possibility of physical damage are probably at the root of this; the Taoist alchemy simply could not trickle down the class hierarchy, or survive the difficult days of the late medieval period, because it was so expensive in both financial and human terms. Confucian morality opposed it for these reasons, but ultimately it fell because it led to quick death rather than to longer life; and with its rejection went any tendencies toward violent drug-induced stimulation in Chinese culture. Chinese communities today reject marijuana and the like with horror, viewing them as both alien and dangerous. (This is rather ironic given the universal acceptance of tobacco.)

Animal Foods

Throughout the world, more kinds of water animals are eaten than land animals. The Chinese avoid very few animals, and it follows that essentially anything aquatic is fair game. Jellyfish, sea cucumbers, sea slugs, limpets, barnacles, sea snakes, gulls, and every other marine and freshwater being big enough to gather is eaten somewhere. Avoidances exist, but are local. Fishermen I knew in Hong Kong believed petty creatures like barnacles were too small to bother with (except in famine) and avoided sawfish, sturgeons, whales and porpoises because these were "divine fish," tabooed by the gods. But elsewhere in China all of these have been used.

The traditional Chinese favorites among aquatic foods make an odd group, including sea cucumber, shark fins, shrimp, crab, carp, groupers (rockfish), pomfret, oysters, and some other bivalves. The Chinese were originally an inland, riverine people whose main fish resources were bream and carp. Several species of the latter were domesticated early, caught and pond-reared in the Chou Dynasty and bred selectively in captivity well before its end. In addition to the common carp (*Cyprinus carpio*), domesticated in China but spread worldwide in the Middle Ages, there are the crucian carp (*Carassius auratus*—goldfish are selectively bred ornamental forms of this species), the grass carp or ide (*Ctenopharyngodon idellus*), the black, bighead, or noble carp (*Aristichthys nobilis*), and the silver carp (*Hypophalmichthys molitrix*) (Ling 1977). The first two of these are the most truly domesticated; many ancient cultivated forms exist. Mullet (*Mugil cephalus*), eels (*Anguilla* spp.), and sometimes other fish are caught as wild fingerlings or fry and raised to maturity in ponds. These freshwater fish, with their firm, white flesh and delicate taste, set the standards of fish quality. They are not muddly-flavored when raised properly; the muddy flavor we associate with carp is caused by dirty feeding and by the ingestion of geosmin, produced by certain algae in stagnant water. Chinese ponds are kept fresh; feeding and fertilizing is done carefully; ponds are drained for harvest and dried off. Well-raised fish thus pick up little off-flavor.

Marine fish with similar qualities—white, delicate-flavored flesh that is firm but not chewy—are naturally preferred. Softer-fleshed marine fish are acceptable, especially for fish balls and other lowly uses, but the fish favored in Japan and most of the West—strong, rank, tough, oily fish like mackerel, salmon, tuna, and swordfish —are despised in China. I heard a tuna-canning plant described as a good way to rip off the Western world by selling trash fish that would otherwise be fertilizer. My explanation that Westerners liked tuna was met with incredulity.

Shrimp and crab are preferred to lobster (Chinese lobsters are of the "spiny" variety, i.e., various species of *Panulirus*), but all crustaceans are well regarded, even the lowly mantis shrimp, which can be quite good when boiled, and the mud-lobster. Among mollusks, bivalves rank higher than snails, the oyster and pen-shell considered very choice. Small clams (including scallops) and snails are not for gourmets, with the noted exception of the large whelks, which are delicious, and the abalone (*Haliotis* spp.). These huge snails are chunked and cooked in many ways and are among the most highly regarded of foods. China's native abs are now depleted; they have been imported from California and Baja California since early in this century. Whelk and abalone are chewy and strong-flavored; I suppose the taste for them was borrowed from some nameless, long-lost coast-dwelling people. Sea cucumbers —technically *Holothuria* of many genera—are sold dried; stewed, they become gelatinous, chewy, and faintly fish-flavored. Their principal virtue is one common in Chinese cuisine and deeply loved: they absorb and heighten the flavors of other foods cooked with them and provide a chewy, soft, high-protein, easily digested morsel as a vehicle for these flavors. Shark fins are liked for the same reason (as are many of the mushrooms and lichens, edible birds' nests, beef sinews, and several other very high-priced items of cuisine that non-Chinese find bizarre). They have a more pronounced taste, clearly reminiscent of good marine fish, and are also sold dried for long boiling; a dish of shark fins is somewhere between a thick soup and a thin stew and is traditional—virtually obligatory among the affluent—at wedding feasts and other major life events.

Fish swim-bladders (fish maws) are somewhat behind these but also popular. Finally, perhaps the best among fish products are dried roes, sometimes lightly salted; they are at least as good as caviar, though dry and chewy rather than wet. They are sliced and fried or steamed. Some of the best come from the sea perch (*Lates*). Magical beliefs attach to certain fish products; the swim-bladder and some other parts of the giant grouper are supposed to give the eater some of this mammoth fish's power, while parasites from its gills are even more effective. Indeed, a complex medical lore spins around seafoods; some crabs are cooling, others heating. Some shrimps and other shellfish exacerbate venereal disease, leading to much low wit if a man refuses them at an all-male gathering.

Fresh seafood should be *fresh*. Fish is rarely eaten raw as in Japan, partly because of awareness of parasites; in T'ang China and more recently in the south, raw fish was popular. But fish is not overcooked, nor is it tolerated when long out of water. In the old days, and often today, restaurants would keep fish alive in tanks. Shore inns would have well-smacks: old boats with the bottoms replaced by wire mesh, in which fish and shellfish were kept in their native element. Many fishermen turned to running live-fish operations. Living on a houseboat surrounded by well-smacks, these people lived by buying live fish from boats and selling them to gourmets, who would run (not walk) with them to the nearest restaurant. Water pollution in the more affluent cities has ended this practice, to the eternal sorrow of gourmets, for the difference between a fish kept thus and a tank fish—let alone a dead fish—is really quite pronounced. (I spent some of the happiest months of my life living in a small houseboat on Castle Peak Bay, Hong Kong, tied to the well-smack fleet of Kwok Wai-tak and his family, some of the finest people I have ever known. I would buy seafood and run with it to the excellent restaurant of ex-fisherman Tam Muk Choi. I ate the best I ever have or ever will. The bay's waters are too dirty now, and fish are kept in tanks; it's not the same.)

Good seafood cooking is kept simple. Fish is typically steamed with the classic "fish flavors"—oil, garlic and/or green onions, and ginger, often with wine, soy sauce, dried tangerine peel, tree fungus, or a coriander leaf or two added somewhere in the process. ("Eggplant with fish flavors" on a menu means not an eggplant that tastes like a fish but eggplant flavored with these things.) In Hong Kong, shrimps are best liked when simply boiled; they are often eaten with a soy sauce and chile pepper dip. Crabs are cooked as simply as possible and dipped in red vinegar. Of course fish cookery can be very complex, but such methods tend to be reserved for inferior fish.

In old China, lack of refrigeration and hot, humid climate guaranteed that fish salting would be important. Lightly salted fish spoils fairly easily, making it at best no treat and at worst downright dangerous. Not only food poisoning but cancer from nitrosamines created by bacterial breakdown of flesh are risks. Well-salted fish, however, can be a true gourmet delight. Fish with thin bodies and firm flesh are best; the salt penetrates them thoroughly and doesn't reduce them to mush. Pomfret and white croaker are typical species used. They are often "salt-hidden"—buried in salt for a thorough job, rather than merely being rubbed with salt. They are then sometimes chunked and packed in vegetable oil. Smaller fish are simply dried, as are small shrimp. The latter, known as "shrimp seeds" or "shrimp children," are a common flavoring; they are, for instance, often stir-fried with cabbage. Small shrimp are also made into shrimp paste. Packed alive in barrels with enough salt to eliminate microbial action, the shrimp digest themselves, producing a fine, purple, highly nutritious, predigested food product of rather strong but interesting flavor. Essentially the same thing is known as *belachan* in the Malay world. Similar products made from fish instead of shrimp are typical of cooking throughout Southeast Asia: *bagung* and *patis* in the Philippines, *nuoc mam* (fish water) in Vietnam, and so on. *Patis* and *nuoc mam* are liquids drained off from the autolytic brew: *bagung*, *belachan* and Chinese shrimp paste are solids. The Chinese evidently learned this art from Southeast Asian peoples and have not really taken to shrimp paste; it is made fairly widely in the deep south but not much used except by Chinese with some Southeast Asian experience. Westerners who are repelled by it should remember that anchovy paste (a descendant of Roman *garum*) is the same sort of thing and tastes a lot stronger. Such products are not rotten or fermented (contrary to frequent mistaken claims in the popular literature), simply predigested.

Near water, most animal protein came from that source, and the choicest foods of all East Asia are aquatic. The greatest potential for increasing world food production lies in farming the sea; only the Chinese and Japanese have seriously developed its potential. Their tastes condition their development strategy and guide it in much more promising ways than orthodox Western agriculture holds. Aquatic farming is naturally coupled with wet-rice agriculture. Here, even more than elsewhere in Chinese food ecology, we see the mutual feedback and mutually beneficial relationship between taste and ecology. The Chinese fondness for aquatic foods can be traced right back to the earliest literary documents, and even to the earliest art, since the designs painted on Pan-p'o pottery emphasize fish and the bones in the site confirm that river fish were a major food.

By 5000 B.C., the Neolithic villagers' main meat animals were pigs and chickens, as they are in China today. The villagers also grew and ate sheep and dogs, as do the Chinese now. It was not long before the cow, water buffalo, and duck were added and the Chinese meat roster was essentially complete. The pig, sheep, and water buffalo were apparently independently domesticated in China at about the same time that they were domesticated in the Near East, or, in the water buffalo's case, India. The duck (mallard, *Anas platyrhynchos*) was probably domesticated in China and spread to the West, like the carp. The Chinese goose is a different species from the tame goose of Europe (*Anser cygnoides* vs. *Anser anser*), so there is no question of anything but independent domestication here; the water buffalo too was originally a different form from that tamed in India. For the dog, cow, and goat—the last appearing by about 3000 B.C.—China drew on the Near East. With the exception of a few very minor creatures (rabbit, pigeon, guinea fowl, and a few newcomers like the American turkey and muscovy duck), these constitute China's domesticated animals. Horses are known and widely used but not much eaten, due simply to lack of availability; they were a delicacy in ancient China, though the liver was avoided because it was thought to be poisonous. (The early texts speak of this so matter-of-factly that I suspect the horses really were concentrating toxins from some food in their livers.) Cats, rats, mice, and other oddments have been eaten in China, but only rarely, contrary to certain stereotypes current in the West. Every wild animal that can be found has been eaten somewhere by someone, and early Chinese lived on game to a great extent; as civilization advanced, game grew rarer, but it remains very popular today. Snakes, frogs (called "paddy chickens" when used as food), grasshoppers, and other small game are as popular as big game, often for reasons rooted in folk medicine.

I begin with "the gentleman that pays the rent": the Chinese might well borrow this Irish name for swine. The pig is overwhelmingly the chief meat source in China, outranking all other land animals combined. Daily meat for the rich, festival fare for the poor, source of oil and industrial products, and a constant feature of the scene, it is so common that the vast majority of the world's pigs are on Chinese farms. The traditional porker is lean, rather slow-growing, but exceedingly fertile, tough, resistant to disease, and of excellent quality as a meat and lard animal. Modern outcrossing has produced a faster-growing but otherwise inferior animal, and Chinese pork has deteriorated depressingly; some attempt to correct the situation is now underway. Traditionally, pigs did not get fat enough to be a major source of cooking oil, but in a few areas—especially Fukien and Yunnan provinces and some montane parts of the central south—they filled this role. As for cooking the pig, suffice it to say that another book as long as this one would be needed to provide even an introduction, and that every part of the pig is used (even the bristles, for toothpicks, skewers, and food-cleaning brushes) in every conceivable way. Its blood is coagulated and fried, especially in Fukien. Superb sausages and hams are made; the hams from Yunnan Plateau are among the finest in the world. Sausages are often fermented with *Lactobacillus*, like salami, and high-proof spirits are often part of the preservative.

Among mammal meats, mutton probably ranks a very long second. It is indifferently from sheep and young goats and is eaten primarily in the west, especially among Muslims and minority peoples. Beef is rarely eaten, avoided by traditional Chinese because of an Indian-derived respect for the cow that entered with Buddhism. It tends now to take the form that the cow is too useful to be treated with such disrespect. Perhaps more cogent is the fact that Chinese beef—which traditionally comes from animals that die after long careers of pulling the plow—is no delicacy. Indeed, by comparison, shoe leather is definitely appealing. But the spinal cord is good when sliced and stir-fried with vegetables.

As is well known, East Asian peoples make little use of dairy products. Milk is considered food for babies that comes from human females. The Chinese and most minorities in China avoid all dairy foods. The great exception is the band of nomadic or nomad-influenced peoples occupying China's west. Not only the Mongols, nomadic Turkic groups (not so much the settled ones), and Tibetans, but also the western Chinese eat yogurt, cheese, kumys (which tastes like spiked thin buttermilk), and other fermented products.

Most Asian peoples (and the majority of the world's peoples) cease to produce the enzyme lactase at the age of six or a bit older. Thus they cannot digest lactose, and large amounts of fresh milk give them bad indigestion. But *Lactobacillus* spp. break down lactose, producing lactic acid, which helps to preserve the resulting yogurt. The yeasts that create kumys also break down lactose, but they work only on mare's milk; other milks have too little sugar and phosphorus to feed them. Rudimentary cheese-making occurs among nomadic groups. Butter is the principal cooking oil among these peoples, as well as the universal unguent; fermented to allow storage— and thus tasting slightly cheeselike—it is the favored food of Tibetan nomads. (With good care in their cool climate it does not spoil but ripens; why Westerners who eat cheese refer to this butter as rancid is unclear.)

Much effort has gone into explaining the East Asian abstinence from dairy products. The failure of Central Asian influence to spread dairy foods in China, even though Chinese in Yunnan and the Central Asian borders (many probably sinicized Mongols and Tibetans by ancestry) have taken to yogurt, is as strange as the failure of Indian influence in Southeast Asia. The conversion of that region to Hinduism and Buddhism in the Middle Ages went with an increase in the use of milk products, as did the rise in Indian influence in China in the T'ang Dynasty. But the use of milk products waned, and not wholly due to the decline of Indian religions, since Burma and Thailand are still thoroughly Buddhist and resist dairy products almost totally. Yogurt maintains an amazing, precarious foothold in Sumatra, among the Batak and Minangkabau peoples, isolated until fairly recently. There it is a rare delicacy—I believe one of many vestiges of the great period of Indianization in 600–1200 A.D.

Recently, the lack of lactase in adult East Asians has been adduced to explain this avoidance, but it does not stop the Indians and Central Asians from depending on dairy foods for most of their animal protein. The classic Chinese explanation is surely in part correct: prejudice against Central Asians and desire to avoid economic dependence on them. Since China is not good pastureland, the Chinese would have had to import most of their dairy foods. They traditionally imported horses and thus were perpetually dependent on Central Asia for animal power. Doubtless another dependence would have been too costly and too humiliating. Yet this does not explain the equally pronounced rejection of dairy foods in Southeast Asia. One can only propose that given the environment, which is not only bad for raising cattle but also for keeping milk even when preserved as yogurt or cheese, milk processing was too difficult, expensive, and dangerous. Cattle and buffaloes are kept in great quantities but are used as work animals, able to feed only their own offspring. Around the world, hot, humid areas are poor for traditional strains of cattle, although in India strains and techniques were developed due to religion and in the teeth of opposition from the environment. Chinese and Southeast Asians more sensibly invested in beans and fish for their protein. (Soybeans now provide equivalents to all dairy products, including yogurt and cheese.) The rise in popularity today of canned milk and other milk products shows that the avoidance is due neither to intrinsic dislike nor to any deep-seated opposition or taboo. Indeed, some South Chinese dishes now incorporate evaporated milk in a "cream sauce" derived from European influence; it has been thoroughly Sinicized. Cheese, however, is usually too much for Chinese to swallow—I have heard it described, to translate roughly, as "the mucous discharge of some old cow's guts, allowed to putrefy." Even Chinese who have learned to eat this product usually confine their attentions to the mildest of "American cheese"-type products.

Among minor animals, the dog may be preeminent. A delicacy throughout China in ancient days, this so-called "fragrant meat" is now eaten only in the south; Islamic and perhaps Buddhist influence ended its popularity in the north, in spite of its high status in classical texts such as *Mencius* and the *Li Chi*. In the south it is eaten primarily for winter warmth, for it is fatty. Tender young puppies can be good, but dog meat is generally tough and rank, no delicacy by anyone's standards. Cats are very rarely eaten, but a dish called "dragon, tiger, and phoenix" is made from snake, cat, and chicken. I suppose it is one of the most hyperbolically named dishes in the world.[4] It, too, is eaten more for medicinal than for gustatory reasons.

Poultry are festival fare, traditional for all special occasions from sacrifices to the gods to visits by relatives, but not much eaten otherwise; they were expensive until recently. Much care is devoted to raising and feeding them properly. The best are those raised in the backyard of a home run by a good cook. Eating the table scraps of the world's finest cuisine all their lives, they become unbelievably good, especially the pigeons (*Columba livia*, a borrowing from the Middle East, perhaps in medieval times), which are equalled only by chickens fed exclusively on sesame seeds. Such chickens, killed at a tender age, are the proper raw material for the Hainan Island national dish of chicken rice. The chikens are boiled, the rice is boiled in the stock, some more of the stock becomes a soup, and the three-course meal is served with various sauces and garnishes. A good meal of chicken rice is better than any fare I have had in fancy Chinese restaurants; but the chickens must be fed right. Peking duck, too, is so dependent for quality on its feeding that the recipe given in one authoritative cookbook in China begins with the duck egg and tells the prospective cook how to incubate, hatch, and raise the bird, so that not one second of its life is left to chance. The duck doesn't get to the kitchen for several dozen pages.

Poultry is almost as versatile as pork, though no one has yet figured out how to eat the feathers, and no one makes sausages or preserved meat out of chicken (it's too valuable fresh). Duck is preserved, however, especially in the flattened and dried *la ya*. Blood, tongues, and brains are choice. "Beggars' chicken" is a specialty of Shanghai. Chickens are stuffed and enclosed in a thick ball of mud, which is put in the fire (or oven) and baked. This dish originated among beggars who were reduced by desperation to "borrowing" a chicken or two; the mud ball supposedly served as camouflage. ("Chicken? What chicken? You're free to look all you want." Likewise, the "bandit's lamb" of Mediterranean countries is wrapped and buried in the ashes.) The mud ball also seals in the flavors so that the cooked meat is meltingly delicate. Leaves such as lotus, with their own good flavor to add, enfold the chicken before the mud is put over all.

Snake meat, believed to be tonic and heating, is eaten primarily as a medicine. The more poisonous the snake, the higher the medicinal value. Snake meat as normally cooked is virtually indistinguishable from the white meat of chicken. Like dogs, snakes are now avoided in the north, but, again, this is a recent and foreign idea. Snake is expensive and eaten primarily in winter. Frogs are popular; as in France, it is the legs that are relished, because they have the big pieces of meat. Grasshoppers, caterpillars, and other insects have been famine food for thousands of years, and fried grasshoppers are relished as a rustic snack in some areas (they are not very good but no worse than most American cocktail snacks). Any and all wild animals are eaten, at least during famines, but the only ones worthy of note are those with traditional medical values ascribed to them. Animals that are very tenacious of life, or very unusual-looking and -acting, are regarded as having special power; they are *pu* (supplementing). Notable pu foods are pangolins, raccoon dogs, soft-shelled turtles, tortoises, snakehead fish (some say), birds of prey, wild ducks, and similar wildfowl, and several larger game animals. (Tortoises, because of their phallic-looking heads, are of obscene significance in folklore. They are believed to mate with snakes, so a "tortoise egg" is a miscegenated bastard, and one of the worst insults in Chinese.) Some of these animals stand on their own merits—the soft-shelled turtle is superb when cooked right. On the other hand, the only recipe I can find for a pangolin—a scaly creature that lives on ants and termites—calls for long stewing with just about every strong-flavored item in the Chinese culinary arsenal. It seems suspiciously close to the classic occidental recipe for cooking a coot: "Put the coot in water with a brick. Boil till brick is tender. Throw the coot away and eat the brick." Only a step away is real magical practice and folk medicine. Owl soup for headache, "white crane" (egret) stew for longevity, dried sea horses, boiled nightjars for loss of some of one's soul, and other minor folk nostrums are found in the villages, and some have entered the classical Chinese herbal tradition. Their contribution to the Chinese diet is, however, insignificant.

Calvin Schwabe, in his book *Unmentionable Cuisine* (1979), comments at length on the Chinese ability to make almost anything taste good and to use almost all animals as food. It certainly makes more sense to eat pests, or at least feed them to the pigs and chickens, than it does to dump poison on them and everything else. It is also eminently sensible to make full use of the earth's resources by drawing on all possible ecological systems. Relatively free from taboos and avoidances, the Chinese have achieved a unique balance with their world, a unique success at supporting maximum populations over maximum time. As Schwabe points out, a world committed not only to using only a few animals but featuring one of the most inefficient and wasteful of them (the cow) is not destined to endure.

9 Some Basic Cooking Strategies

Batterie de Cuisine

Chinese cooking is a cooking of scarcity. Whatever the emperors and warlords may have had, the vast majority of Chinese spent their lives short of fuel, cooking oil, utensils, and even water. Nothing comparable to the huge cookware stores that now bloom in elite occidental suburbs could exist in China. Chinese ingenuity has gone in another and ecologically sounder direction: designing the most versatile possible tools that can be used for every imaginable task.

The traditional Chinese home is based around the stove, which is so important that the Chinese phrase for breaking up a household translates as "dividing the stoves." Living in Chinese houses, I learned that one has free run of everything except other families' bedrooms and stoves. The owner—if occupying the premises—reserves the right to use the big stove; renters of rooms must provide their own portable ones.

The big stove is an impressive creation. It seems to have reached its final form just before the Han Dynasty; it is seen fully developed in models in Han tombs. Standing two or three feet high and covering an area up to six feet square or more, it is a brick or adobe construction. Usually rectangular, it can also be built freeform to adapt to a rock that the house has been built against. The stove centers on a stokehole that opens onto a fuel-burning chamber. Above this are holes that serve the function of burners. Pans can be fitted tightly on them, so that no heat escapes. The brick sides insulate the firebox. Thus even a tiny amount of very poor fuel will suffice to cook a lot of food.

The traditional portable stove is similar, but made of pottery. It is now usually made in an old galvanized bucket, suitably cut up for the purpose. Other portable stove models exist. Today, small kerosene stoves tend to replace older models, and of course in Hong Kong and other affluent urban areas the full panoply of electric and gas stoves, rice cookers, and so forth is standard.

The old brick stove was a god's residence. God of the inner sanctum, tutelary deity of the household, he was a more intimate counterpart of the door god who protected the house at the front door. The stove god or kitchen god was told all the family's life events; he was the first to learn of the births, deaths, marriages, and mi-

149

nor joys and sorrows of life in the rich-textured and busy world of a Chinese family. On or around the last full moon of the year, he went to the other world in the sky to report; most families kept a little image of him near the stove and smeared its mouth with a sticky, sweet stuff (malt syrup or the like) at this time, so he would say little and that all sweet. This playful little ritual must have been the occasion for many a bittersweet meditation among women, who have charge of his cult.

The one tool that most Chinese cooks would probably single out as indispensable is the knife. The word *tou* implies a cleaver-like tool; the character was originally a drawing of one. The most common tou today is the rectangular cleaver. It comes in many shapes and sizes, from huge, thick, square, bone-hewing butchers' cleavers to tiny knives for small slicing tasks. Next most common are tou that come to a point; these are used for boning, some kinds of slicing and slitting, and other such tasks. Narrow-bladed knives like those of the West are little used; they are not versatile enough and do not pack enough mass to cut large chunks effectively. The basic task performed with the tou is chopping, but slicing is also regularly done. Chinese cooks become so proficient in both that they can cut anything cuttable into neat, even sections of exactly the desired thickness, working faster than the eye can follow. Chuang Tzu has a famous story, known to all literate and many illiterate Chinese in traditional times, of a butcher who used one cleaver for twenty years without sharpening it, because he knew so well the interstices between the joints; he merely separated bones, he did not chop them. Millions of butchers to this day follow his practice (although they do have to sharpen their cleavers).

Cutting, whether of meat or vegetables, is usually done on the bias; this creates a large surface-to-volume ratio in the chunk, permitting fast cooking and thorough coating with any sauce. Slices of meat can be "flying-thin," almost thin enough to read through. It helps if the meat is frozen and partially thawed, but traditional cooks scorn this as a modern "easy way out." The tou is also used for tasks from trimming fingernails to splitting kindling, and it can be a deadly weapon in a fight.

Almost all preparation of food for cooking can be done with the cleaver: splitting and cleaning fish, chopping meat and vegetables, scraping and peeling, skinning, mincing (with two cleavers, one in each hand), and so forth. Chopped-up material is swept onto the cleaver's broad blade to be carried to the pan. Few other tools are absolutely necessary to cooking. Probably the most widely used is a common chopstick or pair thereof. These are used as tongs, stirrers, whisks, strainers, rearrangers, and so forth. A ladle and a wire-mesh ladle (for picking things out of soup) are necessary. So is a wok shovel, a flat trapezoidal blade on a long handle that serves as a spatula, scraper, large spoon, and above all a stirrer. Finally, a chopping block, usually a tree section about nine inches wide, is useful.

The well-equipped kitchen may hold a few more tools for special functions. Among these are:

An egg whisk, a circle of spiraled wire on a handle.
A small rolling pin for rolling out won ton skins and the like, and perhaps a

few more of different sizes. There is usually no handle. The classic rolling pin is thickened toward the middle (fusiform), but routine use of lengths of dowel rod proves this is not essential. Very fancy kitchens have rolling pins with impressed patterns, like springerle pins, for rolling out small cakes with raised designs on them.

A press for moon cakes.

A press for thin cakes, two metal disks (with or without patterns to impress on the cakes), hinged, held by handles that allow them to be pressed together.

A colander.

A mortar and pestle (but most cooks employ the tou, using the handle as the pestle and any dish as the mortar).

Various sizes and shapes of cleavers, and two or three sizes of ladles, both solid and wire-mesh.

Modern kitchens will add waffle irons, rice cookers, and other exotica ad lib.

There are also pots and pans, starting with the wok. *Wok* is a Cantonese word; the Mandarin is *kuo*. The wok appears to be a rather recent acquisition as Chinese kitchen furniture goes; it has been around for only two thousand years. The first woks I know of are little pottery models on the pottery stove models in Han Dynasty tombs. Since the same sort of pan is universal in India and Southeast Asia, where it is known as a *kuali* in several languages, I strongly suspect borrowing (probably from India via Central Asia)—*kuo* must have evolved from some word close to *kuali*. The wok is virtually indispensable for stir-frying, and thus I infer that this cooking technique was a Han innovation, perhaps also borrowed or adapted from a borrowed technique. The great virtue of a wok, and its main special function in south Asia, is that when food is stewed in a wok the liquid evaporates very fast, because the surface-to-liquid ratio is high and the smooth curve of the wok sides allows flame or heated air to rise rapidly, smoothly, and evenly along all the vessel. The wok may well have evolved as a tool for making curry, in which a reduction of liquid to a thick gravy or even a crust is generally desired. The fact that the wok is also perfect for stir-frying must have been appreciated for a long time as well. The smooth, even distribution of high heat is the wok's second vital, distinctive feature. This allows, among other things, a tremendous saving of fuel—few pans are more economical.

A wok should be thick and made of a rather slow-heating substance; otherwise it is hard to prevent the food's burning to the bottom of the pan. The original woks were almost certainly of pottery; pottery pans of similar shape with wide, shallow covers are used in Southeast Asia for slow liquid-reducing stewing. Today, good woks are made of cast iron. Aluminum woks are rapidly increasing but are inferior, since aluminum transmits heat too fast. The old soft-iron wok, like its Western counterpart, the cast-iron skillet, also added a good deal of iron to the diet, since some iron dissolved into the food. (An epidemic of anemia in Nigeria was found to follow in the tracks of the aluminum pot salesman; the only good source of iron in the local diet had been soft-iron pots.) Today, a less corrosible iron or steel is used, so this dietary source has become insignificant.

The oldest Chinese cooking vessel, still used most, is a deeper, covered pot. In this one boils and steams—still the primary cooking methods in China (stir-frying is a long third) and the only regularly used methods before the days of the wok. In the Neolithic, a perforated pottery disk or shallow dish was placed halfway up or otherwise set in. For steaming, the Chinese use round bamboo trays with sides of bent wood and bottoms of bamboo slats. Dishes of food are laid in them and they are placed in the pot (over water, soup, or rice). One can also simply put dishes of food on the cooking rice, cover the whole, and make a one-pot meal of many different dishes—a neat, commonly used trick. Steamers, known as *ching-lung* (steaming baskets), come in all sizes, from a couple of inches across for individual snacks up to a meter or more for volume feeding in restaurants.

Modern pots are made of metal, but there is really no substitute for the old earthenware rice pots. Porous and highly heat-retardant, they produced fluffy, evenly cooked rice even on the uncontrollable high flames of wood and straw fires. Ash-glazed within, they still retained enough old waters in their pores to flavor rice and stew with the delicate essences of meals past; never allowed to rest long, they did not grow rancid but aged and acquired character. Known as "sand pots" from the sand tempering of their earthenware, they are still absolutely indispensable for stews and casseroles, which are always made and served in them in good restaurants and kitchens. Today, some restaurants, usually among the finest, make a specialty of sand-pot stews; only a seasoned cook (with a set of seasoned sand pots) will attempt such a subtle, gentle, slow art.

Sandy-paste steaming dishes and flat-bottomed mixing bowls will often be found as well. Completely glazed vessels like large pillboxes, now used mostly to hold dry foods, are really dishes for the very slow steam-stewing known as *tun* (a term that may be cognate with the Indian word *dum* for a very similar process). From the same material are culinary devices from spoons and ladles to pickle jars and opium pots. Their construction is simple: common clay tempered with sand or something similar, coil-built or turned on a wheel, and slip-glazed with a mixture of water, clay, and wood ashes from the kiln. The Japanese have made a true cult of derivatives of such pieces, their *raku*, *seto*, and other wares.

The typical kitchen will have a couple of small metal saucepans with covers, perhaps a few metal steamers, and other assorted minor pots. It will also have a family of jars, usually made of a modern form of the classic ash-glazed pottery. The clay is a smooth, homogeneous paste, usually glazed with a greenish rather than a natural brown color. (Green, white, and dull yellow are easy to make with ash/feldspar slip-glazes; most other colors were invented one to two thousand years later.) These jars are used to hold anything and everything. They are also used as pickling jars. The cleverest is a very ancient type—unique among early cultures—that achieves an absolutely airtight fermentation seal by fitting the cover into a water-filled trough along the rim of the vessel. This idea spread widely in ancient days, but apparently originated in China. More usually, pickles are simply covered in brine. Jars for them may hold anything from a cup to gallons.

Some pots existed for special purposes. Most widespread was the Mongolian chafing dish or steamboat, known as "firepot" or "hit-the-side stove" in Chinese. A ring-shaped vessel (like a doughnut cut in half and hollowed out) fits over a chimney that holds burning charcoal. The charcoal heats water in the pot. Diners boil thinly sliced foods in the water and then dip them into sauces and eat. At length the water turns into superb soup, which is made substantial with vegetables and eaten as the final course. This do-it-yourself dinner is regarded by many as the high point of Chinese cuisine.

A rarer specialty pot is made of solid, hard-fired earthenware. On opening it one finds a volcano within: the bottom comes up in a cone, open at the top. This pot hails from Yünnan and is used to cook chicken. The pot is covered, placed in a larger covered pot with some water in the bottom, and the whole is cooked. The chicken begins by roasting, starts to steam as vapors rise through the volcano crater, and finally boils as water percolates up over the volcanic rim.

Basic to serving are chopsticks, small bowls, and small cups for tea or other drink. The more fortunate would have larger bowls as well (for soup and noodles), pottery spoons, a teapot, a few serving dishes, and small dishes for sauces and dips. Still more elaborate service adds plates and stem-vessels for serving the rice toppings (*sung*). Varied and elaborate dishes for types of wine, meat, soup, stew, grain, and everything else have been part of elite culture since the late Neolithic. For a normal family, the teakettle, teapot, and teacups were the basics. Chopsticks, spoons, and a bowl for every member of the family were necessary. Chinese hospitality centers on tea, and the tea set was thus generally the finest thing in an old-fashioned household. People generally served themselves out of the cooking and steaming pots, but most had a big oval serving plate or two for very formal occasions. Many, but by no means all, had bigger bowls for noodles.

It was easier to eat the soup course after the rice and sung—then the soup would clean out the bowl, picking up the last of the rice and sauce and making cleanup easier. Since tea was a luxury in the old days, soup was also the daily drink. All the kitchenware could be neatly nested into a small wooden box or cubbyhole. One can easily see why an old-time Chinese kitchen could be small. A five-by-five lean-to or veranda often serves today.

Cooking Methods

Chinese cooking is primarily boiling and steaming, with stir-frying as a minor but universal adjunct. Restaurants stir-fry more than do private homes; in old days, oil was expensive, and stir-frying was practiced sparingly. Among other methods, deep-frying is perhaps most popular. Sautéing, in which food is fried in a little oil with little or no stirring, is sparsely but widely used. Roasting, grilling, and baking were once common, at least for meat, but are now primarily used for Western-borrowed foods; stir-frying seems to have replaced roasting, due at least in part to the rising price of meat as population grew denser in ancient times. Western baked goods have become popular and widespread in China, but until recently the high cost of fuel and the difficulty of finding space and materials for ovens kept baking at a minimum. Last of all, foods are rarely eaten raw. Most Chinese foods are inedible raw, and the rest are generally known to be unsafe. Even in traditional times the dangers of eating uncooked foods fertilized with night soil and irrigated with dirty water were well known.

The refinements of Chinese cooking come with the variations and combinations of these basic techniques (Francoise Sabban provides a detailed account; 1983b). In his *Encyclopedia of Chinese Cooking* (1979), Kenneth Lo lists no fewer than forty food preparation techniques, including salting, drying, and smoking. Nor is his list exhaustive—one can, for example, prepare dishes by using any combination of techniques. A well-known dish is twice-cooked pork, in which the pork is first boiled in stock and then sliced and stir-fried. In some dishes ingredients are subjected to three or four steps, or ingredients prepared in several different ways may be combined in the last stage of a recipe. The simplest and most widespread combination is almost universal in stir-frying: the food is stir-fried, then liquid is added (or cooks out of the food) and the dish finishes by boiling or steaming for a minute or two.

Chinese cooking is, first and last, materially efficient. Here as in agriculture, the one thing that is not minimized is work time. A good cook works fast and with few wasted motions, but many dishes involve complex procedures.

The first key to saving fuel is the design of the stove, with its closed-in firebox and pan-fitting burner holes. The next is the emphasis on bite-size or smaller chunks. Much care is expended producing a maximum surface-to-volume ratio. The exceptions, whole fish and poultry, are small and thoroughly opened (split and cleaned). Third, probably in response to the need to cook fast and save fuel, Chinese prefer lightly cooked foods. Chickens are served almost saignant, vegetables crisp, seafood succulent. No long-cooked foods were eaten, with the exception of the rare *tun* stews, which were kept closed and covered and simmered over infinitesimal fires. A cuisine such as that of Boston (boiled New England dinners kept simmering for hours, beans baked as long as a day) would have been unthinkable. Fourth, cooking was done over high heat, which did the job fast; slow-cooking consumes more fuel. Cooking methods that use a lot of fuel, notably roasting and baking, were virtually absent. Foods were steamed and boiled under a tight cover. Fifth, and perhaps most interesting, vessel forms were adapted to need. The earliest Chinese cooking pots had pointed bottoms and cord-markings. They were set right in the ashes, and heat flowed up the diagonal cord-markings and was distributed rapidly, thoroughly, and evenly over the vessel. The cord-markings trapped hot air and made it eddy, ensuring full benefit; a streamlined vessel lets too much heated air slip by. The advent of metal, which conducts heat faster than air (and thus reduces the need for convection) ended this particular bit of technology; but sand pots, with their rough surfaces, hark back to it.

Oil is conserved by the stir-frying technique. Salt, expensive and hard to get in much of old China, was usually used only in the form of soy sauce and pickles; thus it doubled as preservative and seasoning. Other ingredients were conserved chiefly by being used down to the last hair. Vegetables too tough to stir-fry or steam went into soup. Expensive ingredients were always dispensable; when they were used, they tended to be minor but critical and distinctive components of mixed dishes, yielding maximal salience from minimal amount.

It is possible to imagine a cuisine more efficient than the Chinese, but only by going still farther on the road they have pioneered. Cooking times could be shortened and any safe raw foods used. Fewer exotic or recherché ingredients could be employed. Such changes, however, would either have been difficult or unsafe in traditional times (e.g., eating raw foods) or would have been rather trivial in effect (eliminating the few, minor exceptions to the rules of economy, e.g., stewed foods and rare imported ingredients). On the whole, it is unlikely that any cuisine averages less use of fuel, oil, equipment, and so forth per meal. The main challengers are cuisines that have sacrificed variety and subtlety—which the Chinese have obviously not done.

All of the above, however, comes with one enormous caveat. Modern Chinese restaurant cooking is derived from the cuisine of the elite. This cuisine was, of course, substantially less economical than that of the peasants. Alcohol, meat, and other expensive ingredients are freely used; equipment multiplies; many-stage cooking increases consumption of fuel. Such cooking is probably more economical than most elite cuisines of the world, but it is far from the economy and simplicity of every-day fare.

Even in elite cooking, however, time is conserved. Perhaps the most vital and distinctive goal of Chinese cooking is to create the texture known by the word *ts'ui*, a word notoriously hard to translate. Ts'ui implies the texture of something very fresh and at its prime, cooked just enough and no more. In particular, it implies a texture offering resistance to the teeth followed by a burst of succulence. Chicken boiled a very short time so that it is just done; fresh, newly picked asparagus and similar shoots; absolutely fresh firm white fish very briefly cooked (or even raw); and fruit ripe enough to eat but not soft (as Westerners like it) are ts'ui. The opposite of ts'ui would be (on the one hand) dry and tough things like overaged vegetables, and (on the other hand) soft, mushy things like overripe fruit. Ts'ui is usually translated "crisp," but obviously this is far from an equivalence. The goal of Chinese quick-cooking is to produce the most ts'ui texture possible, while bringing flavors to their maximum, and not cooking the food a second longer. This is particularly difficult with such fast-cooking items as shrimps and small fish, about which a Chinese proverb is immortalized in the *Tao Te Ching*: "Governing a state is like cooking small fish." Knowing what to do and doing it immediately with the lightest possible hand are the requisites.

Timing is of the essence. The hissing of boiling shrimp, the crackling of frying pigeons, and other sounds are often used as cues; split-second timing is necessary in these and many other operations, and almost imperceptible changes in cooking sound are vital indicators. This is perhaps especially true in Cantonese cuisine. Another way of preserving ts'ui is to seal the juices in pieces of food, usually by plunging them suddenly into already heated cooking liquid, occasionally by use of batter or the like.

The most distinctive thing about Chinese cooking, separating it instantly from the similar and partially derivative cuisines of Korea, Japan, and Vietnam, is the flavoring mix. Chinese food is typically flavored with a rather complex and subtle variety of things, which may include onions, garlic, brown pepper, chiu, lees, various fungi, sesame oil (often added just for the flavor), rice vinegar, chili peppers (in many areas), sugar, malt syrup, five-spice, star anise, and so on. It almost always includes one or another of the fermented soy preparations. Obviously no one dish has all of the above, but many have a pretty impressive subset. The soyfoods are the most distinctive element. Black beans, hot bean paste, seafood bean paste (with chilis and dried or prepared seafood added), preparations with broad beans as well as or instead of soybeans, and several of the Chinese forms of soy sauce (especially those with mushroom or seafood flavors added), are especially distinctive. By comparison, the other three major East Asian cuisines are simpler. Korean food relies more heavily on salt, garlic, and chilis; Vietnamese uses several Southeast Asian herbs and spices not much known in China; Japanese has its own very distinctive soyfoods, as varied as the Chinese. (Japanese food also uses several items rarely or never found in China, notably two distinctive condiments: *mioga* ginger (*Zingiber mioga*), rare in China, and *wasabi* (*Wasabia wasabi*—a fine scientific name!), a horseradishlike condiment absolutely unknown on the mainland. None of the three cuisines is as apt as Chinese to use so many items, especially strong-flavored ones, in a single dish.

The last stage in food preparation is often left to the diner. Condiments, sauces, dips, and the like are provided at the table rather than used to "mask" the food (as Western cooks say, perhaps all too significantly). In some of the most popular of Chinese dishes, the firepots and barbecues, the diners do some of the cooking, holding food in boiling stock or stirring it on a brazier. Even the humble act of selecting which dishes to put on one's rice is given careful consideration; the dishes must mix harmoniously and unite to flavor the starch staple, which is after all their real purpose. The whole process resonates with Chinese philosophy, in which harmony and balance are such central concerns. The individual must actively produce order out of disparate elements, whether in eating, governing a nation, or regulating one's relationship with the cosmos. It is no surprise that won ton soup is so called; the name is derived from *hun-tun*, the original cosmic chaos when the universe was "without form and void." As the Taoists used a culinary metaphor for government, a cosmic metaphor comes to cuisine.

This concern with balanced diversity is evident in the emphasis on tremendous variety but careful coordination that is typical of both selecting ingredients for a dish and selecting dishes for a banquet. Chinese cuisine seeks out diversity whenever possible, and sometimes indulges in novelty for novelty's sake, but usually assimilates everything (at least at a given meal) into one structure.

It follows that there are rules for what ingredients go together. These are complicated and vary from place to place; it would be tedious to detail them here. Recall the Szechuan dishes with "fish flavors," cooked with the combination of seasonings traditionally associated with steamed fish: green onions, ginger, wine, oil, and a dash of soy sauce. Some cooks would add chilis, garlic, dried tangerine peel, or other items. All these eliminate or counterbalance "fishy" taste. The combination is excellent with many other foods too, but when so used it always reminds Szechuanese of fish cookery, hence the names. Sweet–sour sauce in most of China is also canonically associated with fish, and Chinese never cease to be amused at Westerners' fondness for this sauce on chicken and pork.

By contrast to Chinese cooking, Japanese cooking not only has its own distinctive flavors (wasabi, miso and other Japanese soyfoods, etc.) and textures (*konnyaku* cake, seaweed preparations), but some broader traits. One is a dedication to extremely subtle flavors. A Chinese is apt to find Japanese food insipid; Japanese often regard Chinese food as heavy-handed, with too much spice, sugar, and so on. Japanese can go into ecstasies over the taste of certain bean curds that to the uninitiated are nearly flavorless (Shurtleff and Aoyagi, 1983). Another point of distinction is the extreme attention to eye appeal that characterizes Japanese cuisine. Chinese are quite conscious of this too, but Chinese are apt to feel that Japanese sacrifice taste to eye appeal. The Chinese rarely do this (but they do it sometimes—especially when trying to impress naive Westerners, who are thought to have rudimentary taste anyway). Japanese are thus apt to feel that Chinese food looks like a mess—garish or unaesthetic. It must be admitted that neither the Chinese nor anyone else has ever even approached the sheer aesthetic experience of a traditional Japanese tea ceremony or a Zen temple cuisine "event."

On a more mundane level, Japanese cuisine runs more to soups, frying, and grilling, less to stir-frying. It uses more fish and bean curd, less fruit, and almost no wheat or meat (although wheat and meat consumption have increased enormously in the last few decades). It uses less thickened sauces and less oils (except for the frying). It is served in smaller, thinner dishes and eaten with smaller, more delicate chopsticks. For all their close relationship, a Japanese meal cannot be mistaken for a Chinese one; I think the distinction is more fundamental than can be explained by divergence. Japanese cooking preserves something from an unknown Neolithic stratum. In food as in many other things, Japanese culture shows some striking similarities to the cultures of Oceania, and many anthropologists have postulated early contacts.

Similar rules could be stated to differentiate Chinese from Korean, Southeast Asian, and other food patterns. The Chinese themselves remark on their greater awareness of food in general. Indeed, they talk about it a great deal, with a complicated and specialized gourmet language. The concept of ts'ui has been discussed. Related evaluative words in Chinese include *shuang* (resilient, springy, somewhere between crunchy and rubbery, like some seaweeds) and *kan* (translated "sweet," but including anything with a sapid, alluring taste). Fried foods should be *su*—oily but light and not soggy—rather than *ni* (greasy). Above all, foods should taste *hsien*, which means not just fresh but *au point* in general. A vegetable just picked but past its prime would be very dubiously hsien, while a ham at the proper stage of maturity would be hsien even if not literally fresh. In south and east China particularly, foods are often praised by being described as *ch'ing*, "clear" or "pure." This means that they have a delicate, subtle, exquisite flavor—not obtrusive and above all not over-doctored with spices, monosodium glutamate, or anything else that would give a heavy, harsh, or nonharmonious taste. Other evaluative words include *hsiao jou*, meat that is rich but not greasy (processed with sodium carbonate, which breaks up the fat). *Pao* is "thin", *sung* is "puffy," *neng* is "tender." A different *neng* means "tenacious." *Fen* is "mealy," *suan* "cleaning," *tan hsing* "resilient," and *chuan huo* is "mellow." Banquet cuisine is *shan*. A restaurant is usually called a "wine household" or "wine mansion," but sometimes—if very fancy—a "*shan* hall." One could continue indefinitely with increasingly arcane and refined terms. Surely few things give a better measure of the importance of food in Chinese social life than the evolution of this complicated discourse.

10 Regions and Locales

The Question of Regional Divisions

Attempts to specify the regions of Chinese cooking are subject to debate. Transitions are gradual, blends of regional cooking typical along borders. One person's subregion is another person's region, while a third may not think the area's cooking is distinctive at all.

The classical way to separate regions is in terms of cities, which gives us Peking cooking, Sian cooking, Canton cooking, and so forth. There is also a grouping of the urban cuisines into five styles or style areas: northern, focused on Peking; Honan (or central), focused today on Chengchou; eastern (or Lower Yangtze), focused today on Shanghai but earlier on Hangchou, Suchou, and Nanching; southern, focused on Canton; and western, focused on Chengtu, Chungking (in Szechuan) and Changsha (in Hunan).

This time-honored division is inadequate. First, it is too thoroughly a matter of elite cuisines. Second, it gives a wholly undeserved importance to the rather slight differences between Peking and Honan cuisines. A better division begins with the separation of the north—the region of wheat and mixed grains—from the rice region in the center and south. Mutton is the important meat in the north; dogs, cats, and snakes in the south (although these were formerly eaten in the north, too, as history attests). The fruits and vegetables are different, the north being the land of peaches, jujubes, apricots, pears, apples, and turnips (among other things), while the rice region uses citrus, litchis, bananas, taro, lotus, and so on. Southern fruits have always been northern luxuries, while the south imports soybeans from the north. Only the China-wide onion tribe and the cabbage-and-radish family transcend both agricultural and culinary barriers to become important throughout.

This division is quite different from that current in the restaurant trade. In that business, "North Chinese" cuisine is anything that is not Cantonese. A geographically comparable American division would be between the food of south Florida and that of everywhere else. Thus, "North Chinese" restaurants often serve the rice, oranges, and taro characteristic of the south. They tend to represent a cuisine of the Yangtze Valley, well north of the Cantonese homeland but south of the center of China. Moreover, in recent decades rice has invaded the north; fast-ripening new varieties are grown as far north as Manchuria. The rice-based meal is now typical of fancy cuisine throughout China. Conversely, wheat products became ever more popular in the rice region—where government policy encourages diversification—and in Taiwan, Hong Kong, and the overseas communities, whose cuisines derive from southern Chinese areas. Today, there is two to three times as much rice as wheat in the rice region, but rice makes up only a small percentage of the northern fare and is still virtually absent from remote regions.

Within the great division, there are many minor cuisines. These sort naturally into four—not five—great traditions, as Emily Hahn (1968), Fu Pei-mei (1969), and other recent writers have recognized. The north remains as a single great whole. The south is divided into three parts, east, west, and south.

The East

The east is basically the lower Yangtze Valley and the coasts north and south of it. Eastern cooking was developed in an area where land and water (fresh and salt) meet and interpenetrate; thus it is preeminent in its treatment of crabs (Chinese gourmets swear that the best in the world are the green crabs of the Shanghai area), shrimp, water plants, seaweeds, and everything that lives at the edges of great waters. A prosperous and densely populated area, it cooks with much oil, vinegar, sugar, sweet bean paste, and rice ale. Vinegar is said to be popular because it kills the taste of the bad water and can be used to wash away deposits of salts (Isabella Yen, pers. comm.). The best vinegar in China—and in the world, loyal Yangtze Delta folk would say—is that of Chinkiang and some cities near it, where some vinegars are aged for decades (allegedly for centuries) and refugees fled the area during wars with nothing but the clothes on their backs and their precious vinegar pots. (The same cult endures in Shansi, where vinegar is even more popular.)

Chinese recipes that call for generous amounts of oil, sugar, and chiu are usually of eastern Chinese origin. Sugar is most typically used in the solid, clear, crystalline form that has been called "rock sugar" in China for perhaps two thousand years. This form is supposed to be more healthful than other sugars; in traditional times it was purer and less subject to adulteration. Eastern cooks delight in making simple dishes—braised white cabbage, mushrooms, crabs, or fish slices—into complex ones by incredibly subtle variations in the quantity, quality, origin, variety, and sub-variety of oils, vinegars, and liquors. Cooking in chiu lees—pungent and unique with a slightly sweet tang—is common. Shrimp-flavored soy sauce is primarily an eastern taste.

Since it is not only the richest and most multicropped area in China but has also been the trade center for centuries, the Yangtze Delta has long had access to almost every kind of ingredient. Shellfish, fish, and the tenderer vegetables are probably the most favored items—in that order. A long tradition of Buddhism has led to the creation of superior and subtle vegetarian traditions. Almost every city in the delta has its own variant of the basic pattern and its own special dishes. Suchou and Hang-chow are the most famous among these; Ningpo is also important. Shanghai—a modern city that arose in the nineteenth century via trade with Europe and the resulting "unequal treaties" and exploitation—has developed the most eclectic of all China's cuisines, incorporating dishes and ingredients not only from every part of China but also from the West. Large British, French, and Russian colonies left their marks before being phased out after 1949; Shanghai has thus been the focus for the diffusion of bread, cakes, pies, candy, and many other Western snacks through much of China during the last century. Russian influence is probably seen in the spectacularly lavish cold appetizer platters that frequently precede (and sometimes render unnecessary) the main courses. The kitchens of the Chinese Empire produced such things, but their importance in Shanghai must owe something to the similar *zakuska* tradition. The Russians, most of whom came to Shanghai through Siberia as refugees fom the Bolsheviks, also contributed to the city's baking traditions.

Shanghai, in its early twentieth-century heyday, was a city perhaps unique in the world for its contrasts of opulence and squalor. The city's famous restaurants, such as the 3–6–9 and the Winter Garden (both of which have spawned imitators—not always worthy—in every city on earth with a Shanghainese colony), catered to warlords and international bankers, serving banquets whose cost could run into five and six figures in modern currency. Today the city is a radical stronghold and its cooking is much toned down, but it remains excellent, and Shanghainese restaurants in Hong Kong and Taiwan continue the tradition with reduced but discernible style. Shanghainese managers introduced the "eating palace," with pseudo-imperial decor and garish painted decorations running heavily to dragons, to these realms; previously, restaurants had been relatively unassuming with an ambiance of peace and quiet. Dragons with flashing red light-bulb eyes do not improve the flavor of food, although they may indicate that the restaurant has enough money to hire a good cook—if so inclined.

Outside of the Delta, eastern cuisine begins to blend into neighboring cuisines. The cooking of Shantung, north of the Yangtze lowlands, is a famous and classic tradition that long predates the rise of Peking, let alone Shanghai. Confucius, a native, left enough comments on food and manners to verify the highly developed level of both, but he does not give us much of an idea of what was served. We do learn that game, fish, vegetables, millet, and millet ale were important in his day. In modern times, Shantung is probably best known for its wheat products, especially filled dumplings; these developed long after Confucius' time. More recently, the Germans extracted a concession at Tsingtao and began a brewery there that produces much of China's beer, especially for the export market. The beer is said to have been better under the Germans. It hit a dismal low point in the early Communist years but has improved since—not enough, however, to avoid stiff competition from other and newer breweries in the major cities of China (and other East Asian countries). For the rest, Shantung cookery today is intermediate between the eastern and northern styles. One is most apt to encounter it in a Shantung chiao-tzu cafe, specializing in many different small dough-wrapped dumplings filled with chopped meat.

Inland from the delta provinces of Chiangsu and Chekiang lie Anhui and Kiangsi.

Little is known of their cuisine in the outside world. Buwei Yang Chao's deservedly famous book, *How to Cook and Eat in Chinese* (Chao 1947), is based on the food of her native Anhui; however, it reflects a generalized "Chinese home cooking" or at least "Eastern China home cooking." Northern influence extends well into this area, where the North Chinese language (Mandarin) borders on the local languages (Wu and Kan).

Down the coast from the delta is a very different and much better-known realm, the most distinctive and best of all Eastern subregions after the urban delta core. This is the Fukienese area: Fukien Province and its borderlands. Here a distinctive cluster of languages, the Min dialects, is spoken. A dialect of the Wu language of the lower Yangtze extends a bit into Fukien, and a Min tongue—the well-marked Teochiu dialect of Southern Min—is centered in northeastern Kwangtung Province, but by and large the Fukien boundaries define the area of Northern and Southern Min and of the distinctive cuisine that goes with these two languages. (The so-called "Chinese dialects" are languages as different as the romance languages are from each other. Mandarin or *p'u t'ung hua* is used in the north and west and as a national language; there are also at least seven local languages, one for each major region of east and south China. These eight are, in turn, broken up into actual dialects.) Fukienese cuisine is so distinctive and good that it has sometimes been elevated to the status of a separate regional cuisine. But Fukien cooking is distinctively Eastern.

The first important thing about Fukienese cuisine is its great focus on soups. Almost every class of soupy dish on earth is represented by numberless forms. At a banquet, people think nothing of consuming three different soupy courses and may easily manage five. These range from the thinnest of clear soups—the pure essence of chicken or fish—to thick stews. Rice is often eaten as congee (porridge). Since shark fins and birds' nests are eaten in stewed form, they are best handled in Fukien cooking. In *kuopien* (wokside) batter is cooked on the wok and then soup is cooked in this soft crust.

The Mongolian firepot chafing dish, although invented in the north, may also reach its pinnacle here. This is a dish with a central chimney stoked with charcoal and ringed by a shallow, doughnut-shaped pan. (Nowadays it can be done in any old pot on a gas burner or hot plate.) The pan is filled with stock and diners are provided with plates of raw food, which they pick up with chopsticks and hold in the stock, heated by the charcoal in the central chimney. The thinly sliced food cooks quickly; it is then eaten with sauces. The stock, enriched by all the things cooked in it, is drunk to end the meal. This dish is a complete meal in itself—about the only case in China where a full-scale banquet has only one dish. Variants include firepots or "steamboats" featuring lamb (like the "rinsed lamb" of Peking), skewered clams and mussels (Teochiu satay), and so forth. Known all over China, this arose as a winter dish, providing warmth and entertainment as well as nourishment.

Another thing that distinguishes Fukienese cooking is the widespread use of lard as cooking oil. This is virtually the only area in all East Asia where this occurs. It developed because the area is mountainous, with much fodder for pigs but little land to raise oilseeds; now it is simply a preference. Even in Fukien, it is by no means a universal rule, but when lard is routinely used to fry food, it indicates Fukienese influence.

Fukienese food is apt to be cooked more slowly than other Chinese foods: the influence of slowly simmering soups and stews has spread to other dishes. Mixed vegetables that would be flash-fried in seconds in a Cantonese home are apt to be slowly simmered in lard in a Fukienese one. At worst, this produces grease-sodden, heavy fare. Steamed and roasted foods are also taken well beyond the stage that would be considered ideal in a Cantonese kitchen. Deep frying is also relatively popular here (as in many other parts of the Eastern realm). The fat is usually brought to a very high heat and the food plunged into it, so that it sears instantly and is sealed against intrusion of the fat, thus not becoming greasy. This ideal is not always maintained.

Fukien food is characterized by a fondness for dip sauces. Many dishes have their particular accompaniments: garlic crushed in vinegar for poultry, sweet malt syrup for fried fish balls, and so on. For such things as the firepot, many different dip sauces are provided, and the diner is expected to mix and choose.

As far as ingredients go, Fukienese is similar to other Eastern cuisine, except for such minor matters as a fondness for blood. Blood is eaten in the spirit of avoiding waste. It is coagulated the way bean milk is (suggesting the origin of the latter technology), sliced, and steamed or stir-fried with alliums. Pigs' blood is considered a plebeian dish, but fresh poultry blood, served along with the bird itself (boiled or roasted), is choice.

Fukienese cooking has several marked subvarieties, which sort with dialect and subregional differences. The finest and most elaborate is the Teochiu. *Teochiu* is the local pronunciation of Chaochou, the northeastern district of Kwangtung province, centered on the rather new city of Shantou (locally pronounced something like *Swatow*, and sometimes so spelled). Chaochou is pronounced *Chiuchow* in Cantonese, and since most Teochiu cooking one encounters is in Hong Kong or in Cantonese-dominated Chinatowns in the Western world, it is often seen under this spelling. The region entered history when the great eighth-century statesman Han Yü was exiled to it for being too outspoken, and the local people asked him to give a proclamation to drive away a crocodile—believing that anyone so eminent would surely be able to sway even a saurian by his oratory. He delivered an exquisite performance, attacking his foes at court in a scathing and quite transparent satire. The crocodile duly left the area, and Han Yü's foes met a bad end, too. Since then the people have become more sophisticated; they would now no doubt convert crocodile into gourmet fare, if they could find one in this age of endangered species. Teochiu cooking has been influenced by Cantonese since the district came to be in Kwangtung. Compared to other Fukien-type cooking it is done much faster, with a lighter hand and a better sense of timing; dishes are made more flavorful and spicy, more succulent and piquant. Fried fish and shellfish balls, roasted and stir-fried poultry, stewed turtles and other water creatures, deep-fried vegetables, and thick taro desserts are among the specialties. Goose, marinated and then roasted or barbecued, is also noteworthy. Combining the best of eastern and southern cooking, Teochiu cuisine is one of the finest and most distinctive in China.

Another odd extension of Fukienese culture into Kwangtung province is found on the island of Hainan. South of the mainland, this large tropical island has its own aboriginal population, but most of the present inhabitants speak a very divergent dialect of Min. Their most famous dish is chicken rice, which is probably at its best in Singapore rather than Hainan; a great diaspora of Hainanese to Southeast Asia in the nineteenth and twentieth centuries led to the founding of countless small cafés and coffee shops. The whole bird is used, from the blood (steamed) to the cleaned intestines, and from the head to the claws. Meanwhile, rice is first fried in sesame oil, then finished by boiling in some of the stock. This is the pilaf method native to the Near East, and I suspect it is a Southeast Asian contribution, borrowed by Hainanese cooks from Indian or other South Asian peoples. It is the only extension of this method into the Chinese world; true Chinese fried rice is boiled first, dried, then fried.

Less need be said about the cooking of Fukien Province itself. It is based on pork and vegetables, of which Fukien produces an enormous quantity and variety. Southeast Asian influences have come here too, via returning emigrés to that region. One interesting case is the aforementioned Sinicization of *saté* or *satay*. Many Chinese, unaware of the borrowing process, have wondered at the odd name for a sauce that has absolutely nothing to do with either sand or tea. Fukienese cooking also runs heavily to noodles; like other easterners and unlike deep southerners, Fukienese often get half as many calories from wheat as from rice. Most of these are in the form of soup noodles, but all sorts of stir-fried noodles are popular, from wide, thick rice-flour noodles to hair-thin wheat ones. The variety of forms and names is comparable to the variation in pasta in a comparably sized region of Italy; nowhere else in China does the noodle reach such apotheosis. In most of China it is basically a fast food or snack, but in many Fukienese areas it becomes the body and bones of much of the most favored cuisine. Noodles were so loved and so constantly being devoured in one Hokkien village in Malaysia that I gave it the pseudonym "noodle village" in my writings.

Fuchou, the capital of Fukien, has its own cuisine, noted for use of rice reddened by a fungus that imparts a beautiful port-wine color to dishes but has little taste. Fuchou also produces dumpling skins made of powdered pork and other distinctive dumplings. Fish sauce (similar to *nuoc mam*) is more common than soy sauce. One dish is a sour, hot squid soup, which may include chicken and vegetables.

Most Taiwanese speak Hokkien (Southern Min), "the Taiwanese dialect." Their cooking is similar to that of other Hokkien speakers, but it uses more vegetable oil and more seafood. Its main differences derive from Japanese influence. From 1895 to 1945, Taiwan was a Japanese colony, intensively developed as a showpiece and a rice and sugar bowl. At one time there was one Japanese for every ten people on the island; most of the Japanese were administrators. Thus Japanese foods became popular and considerably influenced island cooking, making it lighter, more delicate, less greasy (less lard is used), and more oriented toward seafood. Rural areas preserve the lard and noodle heritage, however. Today there are many more Japanese than Taiwanese restaurants in Taiwan, and still more mainland Chinese ones. The mainland refugees who came to the island in 1949 disdained local cuisine and imported their own; by and large the islanders cook at home rather than for customers. However, excellent Taiwanese restaurants exist, the father of them all being the Green Leaves in Taipei.

Taiwan—and to some extent the facing coast, especially the Teochiu district—is China's fruit and vegetable capital. Some of the finest fruits in the world come from here, especially citrus. My Taiwanese field assistant in California was astonished at the poor selection of vegetables and fruits in California markets. I was surprised at this—California is America's equivalent to Taiwan in this regard—and so we counted the species in a couple of California supermarkets and then thought of all we could find at a typical Taipei street market. California scored about forty, Taipei over one hundred. The Taiwanese raise just about every fruit and vegetable in the world, except those restricted to very cold or very hot places; they have developed a major export industry for such items as asparagus and Western-type mushrooms, both virtually unknown in most of Asia. In addition, northern Taiwan and the southeast coast raise most of China's tea, though tea is also grown throughout the southern half of the mainland. The best can cost over eighty dollars a pound.

Various bean curd preparations are popular in Taiwan, especially dried bean curd, which is not only dried but often pressed to get the fluid out. It becomes almost like meat in consistency, thus is used in Buddhist cuisine, but it is really at its best as a snack in fast-food cafés, often simmered in a tea and soy sauce stock along with eggs. Eggs are cooked in the shell this way all over China—the taste but not the grease diffuses through the shell. The addition of the dry bean curd is a more narrowly Eastern, or even Fukienese, trait. Soybean milk, "soybean curd flowers" (a puddinglike preparation of undrained bean curd), soybean skin, and so on are all much used in the region.

West China

The closest relative of eastern cuisine is western; the two are linked by the Yangtze River. The west is the spicy zone in China (refuting a facile generalization that cooking gets spicier as it nears the equator). Many books ascribe this to the west's nearness to India, and there may possibly be some slight influence from that quarter, but we have ample testimony that western Chinese cuisine originated in the middle Yangtze and was spicy from the start, before India was known to the Chinese. This evidence is both textual and archeological. The main texts are the *Songs of the South*, a collection of poems from the ancient state of Ch'u in what is now Hunan. Dating to about 300 B.C., they give ample testimony of a cuisine in which Chinese brown pepper, cassia, artemisia, water pepper (a fiery water plant), smartweed, and the like figured abundantly. Later texts bear this out; Hunan had a reputation for highly spiced and herbed food by the Han Dynasty. The archeological evidence consists of the foods offered to the spirits of the dead in the well-preserved tombs near Changsha, the capital of Hunan and of old Ch'u. These tombs date from early Han times, but the people buried in them are the heirs of the Ch'u aristocracy, which was given great local autonomy and power at the time. (It was a deal. The Han couldn't subdue them effectively, they couldn't resist Han effectively.) The foods are as the texts state: rich, varied, sophisticated, and flavored with a wide range of pungent spices and herbs.

The introduction of the chile pepper in about the seventeenth century added a final crowning touch. Today, chile and garlic have replaced many of the old herbs, but brown peppers, cassia, star anise, five-spice, coriander leaves, and so on are abundantly represented in the dishes. Such uniquely Chinese and highly aromatic flavorings as dried citrus peel are particularly favored here. Food is often very delicately spiced, but on the other hand some dishes—particularly those labeled "village style"—are blazing. Similarly, the concentration of garlic can sometimes reach levels unthinkable in most of Italy or south France.

More prosaically, the cuisine's real skeleton and flesh consists of rice, noodles, pork, cabbages, white radishes, river fish (near the Yangtze and its main tributaries), and "mountain foods," which include bamboo shoots of many kinds, fungi and mushrooms, game, wild roots and herbs, and other derivatives of the lush montane forests that still survive in many parts of the region. Maize has become a major food in many areas; maize cakes or noodles with pickled vegetables and fiery sauce comprise the diet of the poorest. White potatoes, introduced in the eighteenth century by French missionaries, flourish. Among a wide range of fruits, citrus may be singled out; among the *Songs of the South* is one comparing a lovely young person to a tangerine tree. Nuts include a variety derived from conifers: pine seeds, *Torreya* yew seeds (bitter but flavorful), ginkgo nuts, and the like. (These are eaten elsewhere in China too, but they are mountain products and so most readily found in the west.) Walnuts are also common and popular, having been introduced from Iran in the early medieval centuries, and halvah-like desserts are made from them; I assume these came with the tree from the Middle East. Another Near Eastern borrowing is the broad bean, often treated like a nut—roasted for snacks.

The heart of western cuisine is the city of Changsha, the spendid capital of the ancient, rich, and powerful Ch'u state and a major trading and administrative city ever since. At the strategic and economic center of the upper-middle Yangtze drainage, it has powerfully extended its influence in all directions. The cooking of the province of Hunan serves as a base on which Changsha chefs elaborate. Hupei, the province to the north, is also rich and oriented around a great trading center (the Wuhan cities that dominate the lower-middle river) but has always been a sort of balance zone between north, east, and west, thus lacking in cultural definition, culinary or otherwise.

Hunanese cooking has now become known worldwide and has attracted a following who regard it as the finest of all Chinese cuisine. No one would deny that it is one of the contenders for the title.

Up the river from Hunan is the huge province of Szechuan, China's most populous province and one of the largest and wealthiest. With a diverse agriculture and rich mountain forests, it produces a wide range of foods, especially vegetables and tree crops. On the other hand, its rivers are fast and turbid, its lakes few, and its access to aquatic foods very limited. It bases much of its cuisine on bean products—broad beans, mung beans, peas, and others as well as soybeans. Maize is very important as a food for the poor, but nothing of culinary significance emerges from this grain. Several differences have grown up (or persisted) between Hunanese and Szechuanese food. Szechuanese dishes naturally involve much less aquatic food and more mountain products. Bamboo shoots, mushrooms and fungi, wild fruits and seeds (such as pine nuts), hill tree-crops such as walnuts, and herbs are the most significant. Game is still found locally. Szechuanese are connoisseurs of these mountain products; bamboo shoots, for instance, come in many species, varieties, and sizes; they may be young, old, fresh, pickled, dried, sauerkrauted, prepared in countless ways. Long mountain winters make pickling essential, and vegetables are pickled in many ways: fresh or dried; in brine, vinegar, bran, oil, chili, and combinations; liquid-packed or pressed fairly dry; sealed or unsealed; strong or mild. As one would expect in a mountain area, storage of meat is also important, with various kinds of sausage, smoked meat, and dried meat being prepared. However, there is nothing comparable to the riot of such products that one finds in Switzerland or Bavaria, for the Chinese here as elsewhere are basically vegetable eaters. Indeed, such mountains as the sacred Omei have long been centers of Buddhist monasticism, and much of the famous cuisine of Szechuan is strictly vegetarian.

Szechuanese cooking is, if anything, even hotter than Hunanese. Spices abound —star anise, cassia, ginger, brown pepper, and so on—and such strong herbs or herblike commodities as dried daylily buds ("golden needle vegetable") are heavily used. Garlic and chilis are, however, the preeminent spices and often seem to make up at least half the dish, particularly in small cafés. Dried chilis are often stir-fried, which brings out the full heat of the capsaicin (the spicy chemical in chilis). Won ton soup is significantly known as "red won ton" in its usual Szechuan form. Restaurant tables are adorned with crushed dried chilis, ground chilis in oil, and hot bean paste (crushed chilis mixed with fermented soybean-flour paste), to give the diner plenty of scope to add to the already incandescent food. Szechuanese restaurants in the West are based on the more subtle and less appalling cuisine of the elite and are invariably toned down for Western tastes. Even if you ask for extra spicy, you will get only what a high-born lady would get in old Szechuan, not what the porters and clerks in the markets eat. But it should be noted that not only class but also region and individual preference lend much variety to the spiciness of Szechuanese cuisine. As in Mexico, food ranges from very hot to almost bland.

Another difference between Szechuan and Hunan is the prominence of West

Asian foods in the former. These include baked goods, a mashed walnut dish closely related to halvah, and a fondness for broad beans and pastes made from them. Although Szechuan is relatively isolated in China's far interior, it has been powerfully influenced over the centuries by the outside world. This has been partly a function of Szechuan's important trade; connecting to the Silk Road by a series of passes over the northern mountains and to the Lower Yangtze via the formidable but navigable Yangtze Gorges, it has always been closely linked to China's fortunes.

Among common Szechuan dishes, two of the more famous are sour-and-hot soup and Ma Po bean curd. Sour-and-hot soup is, as the name implies, strongly flavored with rice vinegar and peppers (white, brown, and chili). The Chinese *la* means the hotness of peppers, and that is the word used here (the word for hot temperature is *je*). The soup is typically made with very thin strips of pork, coagulated duck's or pig's blood, bamboo shoots, and sometimes other mild vegetables; it is flavored with large amounts of ginger, daylily buds, and tree fungi. Garlic, garlic leaves, onions, sesame oil, soy sauce, chiu, and other common Chinese flavorings may find their way into it, for there are many variations. The variants served in restaurants in the Western world are usually very pale reflections of the real thing, which should be as thick as stew and as potent as firecrackers, but extremely subtle and rich in flavor. (If you make it yourself and can't get coagulated blood, use boiled chicken livers; it's a "legal" substitution and works fine.)

Ma Po bean curd (also known as "Ma Po tou fu," "Szechuan-style bean curd," and so on) is bean curd and minced (not ground) pork mashed up together and stir-fried in a lot of sesame oil with garlic, ginger, green onions, a great deal of hot bean paste or chilis, and often the other typical Szechuan flavorings such as chiu, soy sauce, tree fungi, or coriander leaves (added at the end as a garnish). It is subtle yet potent. I have had versions with equivalent amounts of chiles and meat. The name literally means "hemp women's bean curd"; *po* means "old woman" and is not terribly polite (it is used to refer to one's wife, as English speakers use "the old lady"). Many myths have arisen to explain this peculiar name, including: (1) the women of a restaurant family named Ma invented the dish; (2) the name is a corruption of a place name whence the dish originated; (3) the dish was invented by or for toothless, old, hemp-raising village women, who could not chew and thus needed minced meat; (4) it was invented by a pockmarked (i.e., "hemp seed marked") woman. The first is probably correct.

Another distinctive Szechuan–Hunan dish is camphor-and-tea-smoked duck. The duck is smoked for a short while over camphor chips and tea leaves as they smolder in a closed pan; then it is fried. This dish is one of the world's great poultry creations; I find it much superior to Peking duck, given equally good ducks to start with. The fame of the classic Peking duck is due to the special breed and special feeding employed. By all means get such a duck for the Szechuan dish. (I once made camphor-and-tea-smoked duck from an old semiwild mallard I had around the yard, with disastrous results.)

South of Szechuan are the remote provinces of Kweichou and Yunnan. The former is heavily inhabited by minorities. Little is available on its cuisine, although a small book of provincial recipes published in Peking some years ago includes a few recipes.

Yünnan is a large province in which Chinese were a minority until recently. Its cuisine draws heavily from Szechuan but has been influenced by local development and by the many minority groups that live in the area. It uses less spices and hot flavorings than the rest of the west and comes closer than other Chinese provinces to the Alpine preserved-meat model. The finest hams in China are made here from specially raised pigs. Usually sold whole with the leg and foot left on, a Yünnan ham commands a high price. They are frequently found in the finest grocery stores and are important gift items, being valuable and useful. Their closest analogues in the Western world are the salt-cured hams of Virginia, which are adopted as substitutes by Chinese in the United States; the Yünnan product has a stronger, meatier flavor. Yünnan also produces sausages, a headcheese-like dish, bacon, and other cured pork products. The most distinctive is the "boneless pig," made by minority peoples in the central plateau of the province. The bones and meat of a huge lard hog are removed, leaving only the thick lard layer enclosed in the skin. The skin is closed up again and the result wind-cured. This is a good way to preserve lard in the cool, dry climate of the high plateau. In the old days, boneless lard hogs could be seen hanging or stacked in well-to-do homes of the Tibeto-Burman-speaking peoples of the area.

Another oddity of Yünnan is the use of dairy products by the Chinese there, who have adopted yogurt. The proximity to India, the influence of local Tibetan and quasi-Tibetan peoples, and the important settlement of Mongols in the area in the days of Qubilai Qan probably all contributed to this situation, quite unique in traditional China. Early cultures of Yünnan, back in the last centuries B.C. when both Indian and Chinese influence was strong, were cattlekeepers with Indian-derived humped cattle. Later the plateau fell under Chinese cultural influence, but India continued to dominate the culture of Tibet and other nearby areas, and Yünnan borders on Indian-influenced Burma. This has not directly affected the food (the spiciness is a dilute reflection of Szechuan and has nothing in common with curries) except, perhaps, in this one way. Since the early centuries, India's contacts with China were primarily via Central Asia or the sea; the land route via Yünnan is appallingly difficult and was very little used, and I am unconvinced by the attempts to explain food borrowings (crops, spicy styles, or otherwise) by diffusion along this route. Mediation via Tibet is more likely. Diversity also came to Yunnan with soldiers and government officials who were sent to administer this formerly remote outpost of empire. During some dynasties, many of these were exiles (Isabella Yen, pers. comm.), often officials who were once highly placed and able to introduce elite dishes from various parts of China.

Distinctive Yünnanese dishes include "across-the-bridge noodles," in which the noodles, not quite cooked, are suddenly poured into the diner's soup to finish cooking there; and "crystal chicken," which is made in a volcano pot (see chapter 9). Other dishes include meat strips (or shrimps), fried in a rather soft batter and flavored with cassia. A cold eggplant salad with soy sauce is shared with other parts of the west. Yünnan produces good tea, including the famous "Pu-erh."

The Far South

Southern cooking means, preeminently, Cantonese cuisine, but first I will deal briefly with an anomalous ethnic group and its cooking. The Hakka moved south from central China about a thousand years ago, and their language is closer to Mandarin than to the southern languages. The Hakka have always been mountain people and have probably mixed heavily with non-Chinese ethnic groups of the high ranges of the Kiangsi–Fukien–Kwangtung border country. This might explain their delicate, fine-boned, sharp features (they are a beautiful people, akin to North Chinese, but distinctive). At present, they live scattered throughout southeast China, but their focus is at the meeting point of the three provinces just named. This is a sort of no-man's-land between the Kan, Cantonese, and Min linguistic groups. Here lies the nearest thing the Hakka have to a center: Mei Hsien (*hsien* is equivalent to county) at the northeast corner of Kwangtung.

Hakka food is simple, straightforward, and well prepared. The South Chinese emphasis on freshness is even more pronounced than usual. No exotic or expensive ingredients are typical. The Hakka are past masters at cooking tripe, liver, kidneys, chitterlings, and the like, and one of their delicacies is spinal cord of cow, chopped and stir-fried with vegetables. It is called marrow in Chinese and appears under that name on menus. The most popular Hakka dish is salt-baked chicken, which is just what its name implies. The salt seals in the flavor and juices while transmitting heat slowly and evenly. Hakka are famous for beef balls and chopped fish (which makes fish stretch far). This fish paste, which includes onion, ginger, and the like, is often used to stuff fresh or fried bean curd and can be used to stuff chilis, eggplants, bitter melon, and other vegetables. These stuffed vegetables are usually deep-fried but can be stir-fried or steamed. These stuffed items are not solely Hakka—they are widespread in the south—but the Hakka are especially fond of them. Hakka restaurants are now appearing in the United States and other Western countries.

But the true core of the south is the Cantonese. Cantonese cooking is unquestionably the one most often mentioned as the finest of all Chinese cuisines. The immortal proverb runs: "Live in Hangchow, marry in Suchou, dine in Canton, and die in Liuchou," since these cities are supposed to have, respectively, the most beautiful views, the loveliest women, the finest food, and the best coffin wood in the world. Modern Westerners, and many North Chinese, often turn up their noses at Cantonese cuisine, believing the chop suey, chow mein, and sweet-sour glop of overseas restaurants to be typical of it. Such restaurants may indicate a lamentable Cantonese tendency to seek the lowest common denominator in business practices, but they show nothing about Cantonese cooking. Unfortunately, Cantonese cooks are easily corrupted and sometimes scornful of the tastes of foreigners, and it is really difficult to find good Cantonese food away from its native home. I have never had first-rate fare outside of Hong King, Canton, and Macau. Alas, even the fine old restaurants of Canton (more correctly Kuangchou—the capital of Kwangtung province) have fallen on evil days. Moreover, dining out in Hong Kong is not always what it used to be, for the huge new "wine palaces" do not pay as much attention to freshness and individual diners as the old-time restaurants did. Pollution and overfishing have devastated Hong Kong's waters; fish tend to be caught far away and kept alive in fetid water that makes them taste as bad as frozen fish. The incomparable fresh vegetables and exquisitely flavorful rice of the old rural parts of Hong Kong have now been replaced by factories and parking lots. To balance this out, it is now possible to get acceptable Cantonese food in San Francisco, Los Angeles, New York, London, and other cities with large emigré populations.

The very best Cantonese food is found in those homes lucky enough to be run by superior cooks. A very close second is the smaller, older restaurants of Hong Kong, including the rural New Territories, which have been less subjected to the ravages of urban commercialism. But on the whole, even with well-meant recommendations of Cantonese friends (who are often overly impressed with decor, or with one favorite dish), one takes one's chances eating Cantonese restaurant food, and it is all too easy to see how the myth of Cantonese inferiority began.

But it is a myth. Cantonese food, at its best, is probably unequalled in China and possibly in the world. No other cooks insist on such absolute freshness; diners used to visit Castle Peak Bay, twenty miles by bad road, to get live fish simply because the water was cleaner there and the fish tasted better. No other cooks control cooking temperature so perfectly and maintain such split-second timing. Apprentice cooks may be upbraided unmercifully for letting shellfish remain a fraction of a second on the fire after they began to hiss softly instead of loudly—a good chef whisks them off the instant the noise softens. No other cooks insist on such quality in ingredients. Preferred species of grouper cost up to five or more times as much as inferior species (all species of grouper taste the same to me, even after twenty years of eating them), and poultry are fed on particular kinds of feed or scraps to maximize flavor. No other Chinese cooks draw on such a wide range of ingredients; Cantonese use everything Chinese, from Hami melons of Central Asia to the recently introduced guavas, bell peppers, and manioc of their own deep south. No other cooks can be so eclectic while maintaining the spirit of their tradition. European baking has been Cantonized; tomato—potato stew has been taken over and redone; and "hamburgers," made by baking an old-fashioned dumpling and inserting a flattened beef ball, have appeared in Hong Kong. No other cooks excel in so many techniques, from deep-frying (the food is sealed in a crackling, aromatic crust rather than sodden in grease) and baking (a recent Western introduction) to simmering and stewing. No other cooks produce so many dishes; Cantonese restauranteurs who listed only four or five hundred dishes on the menu have apologized to me for the small selection dictated by lack of space on the card and promised to cook anything else within reason I might want. They mean it, too, and in fact many restaurants (in Canton and elsewhere in China) do not even bother to list their specialties, on the assumption that everyone who is worth feeding knows what the specialties are, and the menu space should be saved for less obvious suggestions. Even tiny cafés and sidewalk stalls turn out literally hundreds of dishes, often superb. No culture is more obsessed with food; not even in France is so large a part of the conversation devoted to restaurants and cooking.

This is not to say that Cantonese food is superior in everything. Cantonese cooks can't touch the Fukienese and Teochiu treatment of soups; they do not like and do not excel in the extremely subtle yet highly spiced and flavored mixtures of much of the food that characterizes the Yangtze Valley from Szechuan to Shanghai; far from wheat regions, they do not do much with traditional wheat products; they do not produce vinegars, chiu, or bean pastes that approach those of the Yangtze country. Nor do they make many desserts. (No Chinese region emphasizes desserts, but the Cantonese would be even lower on the scale than the others were it not for the recent borrowings of bakery goods from the Western world.) Traditional Chinese simply didn't like sweets much, and the Cantonese were especially uninterested.

By comparison with other parts of China, the south uses fewer beans (soy, fresh, or otherwise) and more of the tropical and Western-derived fruits and vegetables special to the region. Such tropical fruits as litchis, longans ("dragon eyes," a litchi-like fruit), papayas, guavas, and citrus abound (though not as they do in the Southern Min areas, nor is the fruit so good; China's best fruit comes from Taiwan and Teochiu, not the deep south). Vegetables more common here than elsewhere include tomatoes, broccoli, cauliflower and other Westerniana. Other tropical products woven into cuisine include the Chinese olive or *kan-lan*, actually the fruit of *Canarium album*. Pickled, it is reminiscent of a Greek green olive, though the trees are not related. Better than the fruit is the kernel, which resembles a large pumpkin kernel or small almond in appearance and taste. One of the world's finest nuts, it is used rather sparingly in the south, but more commonly in Southeast Asia. It extends as far north as Fukien, but not very many trees occur north of Kwangtung. Such plants as coconut and manioc—the latter a recent import from the New World—are even more definitely tropical. An important item of not-quite-food is the betel nut, the fruit of the areca palm.

The best Cantonese cooking is what appears to be the simplest. Boiled shrimps, steamed fish, steamed or stir-fried vegetables, clear soup (such as chicken stock with mushrooms), fried oysters, dried fish roes sliced and stir-fried, boiled chicken ("white-cut chicken," boiled for a very short time and left to finish cooking in the cooling stock), and a few similar dishes make up my happiest memories of Cantonese cuisine. The secrets are timing and ingredient quality. Even relatively rich combinations, such as the famous "winter melon pond" (soup made in a winter melon, often beautifully carved; the whole melon, soup and all, is steamed in a closed container), are not as elaborate as they would be in many areas. A Cantonese cook will stick to roast pork, a bit of Yunnan ham, and a very few vegetables, letting the subtle flavor of the winter melon speak for itself. This is not to say that combinations are simple to make. The rules for what can combine with what are elaborate and demanding, specifying all the allowable permutations and combinations of hundreds of ingredients taken two, three, and (occasionally) four or more at a time. Dip sauces and flavorings extend the range; soy sauce is usual, but oyster sauce, chile sauce, very hot mustard, ground chiles, vinegars, chilis chopped in soy, sesame oil, and occasionally other flavors may be found at table, along with white pepper. As elsewhere in China, free salt was once rarely seen in traditional restaurants, though the Western custom of putting a salt shaker at each table is now almost universal. The elaborate flavorings listed above are sparingly used except in bland dishes like soup noodles.

One distinctive and common Cantonese seasoning is black beans (*toushih* in Mandarin; *taosi* in Cantonese), which are now abundant in the south but rare elsewhere. Here—as in its continued consumption of dogs, cats, and snakes, and in some language traits—the Cantonese world is conservative.

Much of what passes for Cantonese cooking in the Western world would sicken a traditional Cantonese gourmet. Canned pineapple, canned cherries, and even canned fruit cocktail; enormous quantities of dehydrated garlic, barbecue or Worcestershire sauce; canned vegetables, corn starch, monosodium glutamate, cooking sherry, and heavy doses of sugar are found in many of these bizarre creations. This fusion of pseudo-Cantonese and pseudo-Polynesian food can be traced to a renegade Cantonese chef at Trader Vic's in California. The basic formula appears to be: take the fattest, rankest pork you can get; cook it in a lot of oil with the sweetest mixture of canned fruits and sugar you can make; throw on a lot of MSG and cheap soy sauce; thicken the sauce to gluelike consistency; and serve it forth. The Cantonese regard the whole business as proof that Westerners are cultureless barbarians, but they cook it, and now even many Taiwan Chinese (having eaten Cantonese food only in cafés catering to American G.I.s) are convinced that this is typical Cantonese cooking.

About sweet-and-sour pork, the following may be said. Traditionally, this was a rare dish, and not well liked. Cantonese more often cook sweet-sour fish, especially yellow croaker. The recipe is northern and eastern in origin, though long borrowed into the south. It is best with freshwater fish in Honan. Real sweet-sour fish or pork is at least as sour as sweet and includes no fruit. Real Cantonese sweet-sour pork is a good dish, although not as good as the yellow croaker, but many Cantonese avoid it now because it is so thoroughly linked with the "barbarians."

⊢ Three other dishes that define Cantonese cuisine outside of China are more authentic, but are not the height of the true cuisine. Fried rice (*ch'ao fan*, "stir-fried rice," although it isn't always stir-fried) is a standard method of cooking leftovers, involving frying cold boiled rice with chopped-up meat and vegetables. In really superior restaurants, rice will be specially boiled and dried for this, but usually old, unused rice is served. The common (and favorite) recipe, however, is not Cantonese, but eastern, deriving from Yangchou in the lower Yangtze country; it involves mixing chopped ham, beaten egg, green peas, green onions, and other ingredients to taste, and then rather slowly sautéing the rice. The rice is neither deep-fried nor stir-fried, but *chin*—left to cook slowly in a little oil, producing a fluffy product with a slight crust. Chow mein is Cantonese *ch'ao min* (stir-fried noodles), a counterpart of fried rice. The noodles are boiled and then stir-fried with bamboo shoots, bean sprouts, slices of pork, and so forth.

Last of all, chop suey is not—as many would-be connoisseurs believe—an American invention. As Li Shu-fan points out in his delightful autobiography, *Hong Kong Surgeon* (1964), it is a local Toisanese dish. Toisan is a rural district south of Canton, the home for most of the early immigrants from Kwangtung to California. The name is Cantonese *tsap seui* (Mandarin *tsa sui*), "miscellaneous scraps." Basically, it is leftover or odd-lot vegetables stir-fried together. Noodles are often included. Bean sprouts are almost invariably present, but the rest of the dish varies according to whatever is around. The origin myth of chop suey is that it was invented in San Francisco, when someone demanded food late at night at a small Chinese restaurant. Out of food, the restaurant cooked up the day's slops, and chop suey was born. (The "someone" can be a Chinese dignitary, a band of drunken miners, a San Francisco political boss, and so on). Fortune cookies, however, are a true Californian Cantonese invention, created by a noodle company in Los Angeles (loyal Angelenos insist it was in San Francisco). They were unknown in Asia until American tourists began to demand them in the last decade or two.

None of the above dishes ranks high with Cantonese gourmets, since all are mixtures of a lot of things and none demands fresh fixings. In fact, all of them are in the nature of hash—cheap, quick, easy ways to get rid of less than desirable leftovers and other scraps. Their popularity with restauranteurs is easy to explain—all the stuff that would otherwise have to go to the animals can be fed to people. As a matter of fact, they can be excellent dishes in their own right and are widely popular, but their avatars in traditional cafés and homes in Hong Kong are very different from those one encounters in restaurants catering to Westerners.

The real gourmet dishes of the south begin with seafood. Steamed fish or whole fish quick-fried and then masked with sauce; shellfish of every description prepared in countless ways; swim-bladders, sea cucumbers, cuttlefish, squid (fresh or dried), fish roes, and every other imaginable sea product—all are treated reverently. No land meats attract so much enthusiasm or attention. Seafood is most highly regarded when alive and kept in clean water, but some of the salted products are almost as popular, especially salt-dried squid, salted dried fish roes (much like the finest caviar), and salt-hidden white croaker fish. Sea cucumbers and jellyfish are almost always dried, and oysters are not only dried or salted but boiled down and strained to make the thick oyster sauce.

Among land meats, poultry has the cachet of special occasions and religious rites, but pork is the standard meat and the one that brings out the best cooking. Whole pigs are roasted slowly with a honey or brown sugar glaze that caramelizes to a gold-red color; this makes them "golden pigs," suitable for sacrifice, the color being of religious import as the color of life and warmth. More famous is *ch'a shao, cha siu* in Cantonese, which means "fork roasted." Barbecued strips of lean pork, marinated in honey, soy, chiu, and other flavorings, are hung up on forks (or equivalent) in a special iron oven with a strong, steady, warm air flow rising through it. Poultry can be ch'a shao as well. Ch'a shao pork is sliced thin and used in noodle soups, steamed buns (the well-known *ch'a shao pao*), and other snacks and dishes.

Another class is cured meats—*laap* in Cantonese (Mandarin *la*). These include excellent sausages made with rose-flavored vodka; they are known as *laap ch'eung* (literally "cured intestines"). Pressed cured duck is, poetically, *laap aap* (Mandarin *la ya*). The strong, meaty-tasting Cantonese bacon is *laap yeuk* (*la jou*, "cured meat"). One may often see these hanging in a shady, windy place to cure; a beach with a constant sea breeze and shady trees is ideal, and swimmers may mix cheerfully with meat-curers.

The more exotic meats are not really eaten much. Dog and snake are eaten in winter to provide warmth—they are believed to be very heating, in the case of dogs because of the high amount of fat. They are not really very good, though tender young ones can be fair. In spite of all the literature on the subject I have never eaten cat or rat or seen them eaten; Cantonese known to me are repelled by the thought of eating rats. I have never seen anyone bring a live monkey to the table, cut its head open, and eat the brain out as a strengthening food, though this is done in some places. It is a medicine rather than a food in any meaningful sense. The most exotic food that is really common is frog legs, which are less popular than in France but not to be ignored. Known as "paddy chickens" and cooked as one would cook chicken, they are very good, especially chunked and stir-fried with black beans. Wild game of every sort is eaten when available and believed to be strengthening or otherwise medicinal; owls and nightjars cure headaches, "white cranes" (egrets) cure soul disorders and convey long life, and—among items that are less purely medicinal—wild ducks are believed to be tremendously strengthening, probably because the high iron content of the meat once helped many anemic persons.

The Cantonese are less thrifty than their immediate neighbors; they do not normally eat blood or relish intestines and spinal cord. They will use anything in a pinch, but on the whole they prefer the cuts used in the more eclectic parts of the Western world. One major exception is poultry feet, which are greatly loved both for making stock and for nibbling. Well-cooked duck and goose webs are considered real delicacies. I have heard that Hong Kong uses twice as many pairs of poultry feet as it does actual birds. The additional feet are imported from Canada and elsewhere. Milk dishes are found, mostly due to Western influence starting with the Macau Portuguese in the sixteenth century.

The Chinese fondness for snacks and "small eats" reaches a kind of apotheosis in the south. Substantial breakfasts of congee with peanuts, meat, fish, sauces, or similar foods are common. Noodle soups with meat (red-cooked beef or ch'a shao pork are typical) and won ton soups are even commoner. The amount of noodles per serving is large enough to make these dishes full meals in themselves. The rise of Western-type baked goods has led to a wide range of breads, rolls, and pastries that have fitted into the snacking pattern.

But the ultimate in "small eating" is the Cantonese institution of *iam ch'a* (Mandarin *he ch'a*: "to drink tea"). Drinking tea traditionally involves the consumption of snacks known as *tim sam* (borrowed into English as *dim sum*, pronounced "deem some"). This phrase (the Mandarin is *tien hsin*) means "to dot the heart," a peculiar idiom of obscure origin, meaning something like "to hit the spot." "Dot-hearts" (as Buwei Yang Chao calls them; Chao 1947) are found throughout China, but in Cantonese culture they become the sole food at huge luncheons or late breakfasts, while elsewhere in China they are definitely "small" affairs. There are hundreds of them. Many restaurants specialize in them, such as the famous Luk Yu Tea House of Hong Kong, which was one of the finest Cantonese restaurants until its recent move from tiny, aged, cramped quarters in the garment district to fancier lodgings uptown. Typical tim sam are *ha kaau* (Mandarin *hsia chiau*), based on minced shrimp and other items wrapped in thin dough skin; *siu maai* (*shao mi*), with meat filling and different skin composition; taro horns, chopped meat covered with mashed taro dough, rolled into a hornlike shape, and deep-fried; *ch'a shao pao*; other pao of many kinds; beef balls pungently flavored with soy sauce, ginger and so on; *faan kün*, oily chopped fillings wrapped in rice-flour dough skins; duck webs on rice; *tsung* or *jung*, glutinous rice dumplings stuffed with chicken or aromatic seed fillings, wrapped in lotus or broad bamboo leaves, and steamed; and anything else the cook can think of, up to and including rather substantial dishes of stew and chicken, and even suckling pig roasted and sliced. The commonest and most basic tim sam follow the pattern of some sort of starch staple wrapped around a filling of chopped meat, soy sauce, ginger, water chestnut, or similar extender and texturizer, oil and flavoring.

The ritual of iam ch'a is well established. One sits at a table in a very crowded and noisy restaurant. The waiter brings whatever tea one requests. Then one watches for the carts of tim sam being wheeled around the restaurant by young servitors. They cry out what they are bringing, contributing greatly to the high noise level of tea houses (my young son referred to them as "screaming places"). Diners take quite a while over the meal, waiting for favorite items to come round. At the end of the meal, a more senior waiter counts up the dishes and charges accordingly. More expensive dishes are on bigger plates, so charges are always figured by the number of empty plates; waiters have eagle eyes to forestall shifting of plates from table to table.

Tim sam travel fairly well—they do not depend on freshness and timing as much as most Cantonese dishes do—and there are now good tea houses in larger Western cities. The level of tim sam in Canton is also high, rather more so on the whole than the level of restaurant and hotel food. But one must still go to Hong Kong to get the good stuff; and the like of the old Luk Yu will probably never appear again.

Very common in Cantonese cooking are *ting*, dishes of mixed foods cut into cubes. Examples are chicken diced and stir-fried with cashew nuts and pork diced and stir-fried with vegetables. Stewed duck with barley, stewed chicken with Chinese medicines, and other stewed strengthening foods usually appear. Shark fins, the almost-inevitable showpiece of fancy banquets, are cooked in chicken soup or brown stock. A dish shared with the rest of South China, and rather greasy to anyone outside that realm, is slices of taro alternating with slices of fat fresh bacon in vertical array, the whole being steamed. Casseroles, cooked in the traditional sand pots, involve the tougher cuts of beef, or poultry, often with bean curd, Chinese cabbage, star anise, and soy ferments. Pork ribs are steamed with black beans; pork, chicken, or seafood is stir-fried with pungent little fermented confections. Fish is steamed with slivered ginger, green onion, tangerine peel, fungi, and a bit of chiu and soy sauce.

A strange local feast is *sik pun* ("eat from [the common] pot"). This consists of meats, fish, bean curd, and spices, cooked separately, then combined in a sort of stew. In some villages it is served at formal banquets as the sole dish when the idea is to legitimate a major social event (such as a wedding or adoption). It represents a self-consciously plebeian cuisine, leveling distinctions to involve all equally in the event. Like the socially equivalent U.S. barbecue, it is cooked by men (Watson 1985).

Cantonese cooking admits of many side-branches, but most of them are little known. The great tradition of Canton urban cooking, now established (with Western influences) in Hong Kong and Macau, tends to blank everything else. One exception is the cooking of the Sei Yap–Toisan area. Sei Yap or Sze Yap (four districts) refers to an area south of Canton where a very divergent dialect of Cantonese is spoken. This dialect, virtually incomprehensible to standard Cantonese speakers, extends through neighboring districts. The area is a rich vegetable-raising region but one in which the peasants were traditionally poor; population density and high taxes created the contrast of rich farms and poor farmers. These people lived to a great extent on mixed vegetable fry-ups and fried noodles; this is why the great focus on chop suey and chow mein in New World Cantonese restaurants—since most of the Chinese who came to the Western hemisphere were from the Sei Yap–Toisan region. Including as many as ten vegetables in one dish is standard—one ate whatever the garden was producing in surplus. Not much animal food was available, but the vegetables were unexcelled in freshness and quality, and Toisanese emigrants to Hong Kong and elsewhere spend a lot of time nostalgically recollecting them, or else become vegetable growers themselves.

Other subregions of the south are too poorly known for comment. Even the huge and populous province of Kwangsi, west of Kwangtung, is terra incognita as far as published material on food is concerned, although it has its own dialect of Cantonese and many minority languages as well. Informants say only that food was restricted by distance from the sea and from rich farming areas. Pork and mountain products were relatively frequent but fish, vegetables and many other things were hard to come by.

The North

The vast and heterogenous realm of the north is united by several factors into a single region. In this area every province has its distinctive features, but many are not particularly noteworthy. Manchuria in the northeast has yet to produce much distinctive cuisine. Shansi and Shensi in the central west are a sort of Chinese England, characterized by thrift, hard work, industrial development, and solid but stolid fare that merits little comment here. This leaves three great traditions: those of Hopei, Honan, and the northwest (particularly the Muslims).

Hopei is the province centered on Peking, although Peking is now separated in its own capital district. Peking cookery naturally dominates the province. The heir of empire, it is so elaborate as to defy description. The capital (or at least a capital) has been here since about 1000 A.D., and long before that the region was important, populous, and sophisticated. Imperial dynasties left their mark on cooking in the usual ways: cooking became more elaborate and more expensive ingredients were used. Bears' paws, camels' humps, apes' lips, and other exotica are reported in the old literature, and at least the first two were eaten in recent times at the imperial court. Bears' paws are said to be glutinous and sinewy—perhaps rather like pigs' feet on a grand scale. Much of this elaborate cuisine is dead now, lost with the world that created it. The waste and luxury of the old court were as great as one would expect; its disappearance took down with it the destructive conspicuous display.

A favorite Peking dish is rinsed lamb, Mongolian firepot with mutton. A major institution in Peking and elsewhere in the north is the Mongolian barbecue (*Meng-ku k'ao-jou*). This dish is originally Altaic—the Mongols, Koreans, and other Altaic peoples have versions—but is now quite Sinicized in its Chinese form. The barbecue is not so much a dish as a ritual, and restaurants specializing in it serve nothing else of consequence. Meats of various kinds—mutton, beef, pork, game, and whatever else may come to hand—are sliced extremely thin. The diners select these and add flavoring sauces to them: soy, chiu, sesame oil, hot pepper oil (sesame oil in which chilis have been soaked), vinegar, and so on. Slivered onions, ginger and the like may be added. The meat is borne to a conical brass grill, on which it is quickly tossed until done. Fresh hot shao-ping (the small sesame-seed-covered pocket breads of Near Eastern origin) are used to make sandwiches with the cut meat. Additional spices are provided at the table. The whole affair is very much an example of the Chinese fondness for letting the diners perform much of the artistry of the meal.

Peking is famous for its "small eats" as well as for its classic dishes. Indeed, in Peking today you can probably eat better at sidewalk stalls and cafés than at the fancy restaurants that cater to tourists. Street vendors sell fruit and wheat dumplings stuffed with sweet or savory fillings. Noodle shops abound. Chiao-tzu halls sell millions of these marvelous dumplings. They are boiled or shallow-fried without stirring, in which case they are "pot-stickers," because the bottoms toast themselves onto the pan, becoming exquisitely crisp. Many of the wheat products are made with whole-grain flour, thus are not only appealing to Western health-food devotees but also superbly flavorful. (Nothing excels freshly ground whole-grain wheat flour from the hard, red traditional wheats of Asia. The best American commercial flour cannot compete, largely because it is stored for so long.)

Honan is heir to an even longer tradition of civilization than Hopei. Of its major cities, Kaifeng was capital just before Peking was founded; Loyang was capital before that and intermittently for the previous millennium, back to 774 B.C.; Chengchou, the present provincial capital, was the seat of rule of the Shang Dynasty about 1300 B.C. Naturally these cities (and the small towns, some of which were capitals of Shang even before Chengchou was founded) look down on Peking as a mere ephemeral upstart. In my experience, the finest food in North China is to be found here; the extra millennia do seem to matter. Chengchou claims to be the native home of sweet-sour fish. The yellow croaker of the local rivers is quickly fried and then masked with the pungent, aromatic, subtle sauce. Among the countless excellent wheat products, one stands out: noodles that are made by swinging a rope of dough, doubling it over and swinging it again, keeping the noodles floured so they do not stick together. This not only makes them fine as hair, it also develops the gluten in the high-gluten local flour to a maximal degree and is an impressive performance to watch. (The stretching process of pizza crust and strudel dough is similar.) The noodles are quick-fried and serve as a bed for the fish or anything else wanting a substrate. Excellent candied apples and other fruits are made here from Honan's fine produce. Stir-frying is done carefully and gently.

Honan was the birthplace of Chinese civilization and Chinese cuisine. Recall that in Chengchou markets one can still find pottery kettles identical to those made there in the Shang Dynasty. As one would expect, the province is a meeting ground or central radiating point. All the features of Chinese cooking are found here. Skill and painstaking thought are the features of Honan cuisine, which has few local outstanding dishes (primarily because its best dishes have become pan-Chinese) but is absolutely outstanding in the creation of all of them, from the most ordinary wheat bun to the finest sweet-sour yellow fish.

China's Muslims (*Hui*) are mostly ethnic Chinese, converted or descended from part Central Asian lineages of Islamic ancestry. (The word *Hui* is derived from *Uighur*, but now refers to ethnic Chinese rather than to the Turkic folk.) Muslim cooking is localized in China's northwest—Kansu and Ninghsia—and based on the general Chinese cooking thereof, but it has spread throughout North China, since wherever they go the Muslims must have their own butcher-shops and eateries. The reason, of course, is that all regular Chinese eating places are redolent of swine, alcohol, and other fare interdicted by the Koran.

Lying near Szechuan, this area has enthusiastically adopted the chili pepper. It also makes maximal use of onions and garlic (here the influence went the other way: Szechuan evidently picked up its garlic from the northwest). The characteristic dish is thus mutton stir-fried with onions and/or garlic. Young garlic leaves, as well as the garlicky Chinese chives, are used in soups and other foods. Pocket breads and dumplings are unexcelled here, since they were central Asian–Near Eastern borrowings in the first place. The chiao-tzu are stuffed with mutton, of course, rather than pork or shellfish. Northwestern cities such as Sian feature Muslim eateries with excellent, well-cooked food, and lively atmosphere.

The Minority Nationalities

China's non-Han minorities deserve much more attention than is usually given to them. While they make up only 7 percent of the country's population, that is several tens of millions of people, dominating about half the area (much more than half until the twentieth-century expansion of the Han Chinese). There are slightly fewer than sixty minorities currently recognized, defined as groups with distinctive languages and cultures. This discussion proceeds clockwise around China.

The "Aborigines" or "mountain people" of Taiwan are speakers of widely divergent Malayo-Polynesian languages. They are primarily slash-and-burn cultivators, but settled wet-rice cultivators existed in Taiwan before the Chinese drove them to the hills or assimilated them. The aboriginal groups use rice but usually regard *Setaria* millet as their sacred food, their ancient staff of life. The commoner vegetables and root crops of Taiwan, such as taro, are grown, and chickens, pigs, and dogs are raised. Mushrooms, game, and other forest products are important foods. Food is generally very simple—boiled or cooked by methods learned from the Chinese.

Southernmost China is dominated by groups speaking Thai-Kadai languages. The Kadai languages are a tiny group, the only significant representative being Li of Hainan Island. The Li grow dry rice (hill rice) and maize in slash-and-burn fields, hunt, keep pigs, grow vegetables, and drink a great deal of home-brewed, often spiced rice beer. The Miao of Hainan and the mainland harvest glutinous or regular rice and preserve meat products. The Miao—known as Hmong in Southeast Asia and America—have taken to maize as a main crop and also raise many vegetables (Johnson 1985; Lin 1940). In short, they are typical of the up-country people of Southeast Asia, from the Philippines to eastern India. Many of the smaller Thai-speaking groups have similar life-styles. The larger Thai groups, however—speaking languages close to, but not identical to, the major tongue of Thailand—practice wet-rice cultivation and depend on rice and vegetables, eating foods broadly similar to those of the Chinese. China's largest minority, the Chuang of Kwangsi, are typical. One Chuang locality has attracted attention because of the extreme longevity of its citizens, many of whom are over a hundred years old. Almost 7 percent are over sixty-five, very old for China. The main foods here are corn, squash, hair gourd / winter melon, and wild greens; this healthy diet must have something to do with the longevity but cannot be the full explanation (*China Reconstructs*, no. 5, 1981). *Zanthoxylum* spp. similar but not identical to Chinese brown pepper is an important spice. The area of Hsishuang Panna (from Thai *Sipsong Pan-na*, "twelve states") in southern Yünnan is dominated, in the lowlands, by Northern Thais speaking the same language that is called Laotian in Laos. They depend on glutinous rice, which is rolled into a ball and dipped in very highly spiced sauce featuring chilis—adopted as enthusiastically among Thais as among Szechuanese—and *Zanthoxylum*. In Laos and northern Thailand, and so presumably in south Yünnan, another very popular sauce is made from fermented giant waterbug. Raw chopped beef spiced with brown and chili peppers is another Thai delicacy that I assume is common in the low Mekong Valley of Yünnan. Many medicinal and flavoring herbs grow in the mountains and villages of this area, as well as many Southeast Asian green vegetables and fruits.

Scattered throughout the hills and mountains of the southern half of China are Miao and Yao peoples who depend on slash-and-burn cultivation of maize and rice and on the raising of pigs, buffaloes, cattle, chickens, and dogs. They also grow vegetables, including hot chilis, and obtain much food by hunting and gathering. In Kweichow and Yünnan they border on Tibeto-Burman speakers—minorities with languages related to Tibetan and Burmese, and thus, more distantly, to Chinese. The Tibeto-Burmans of the lower, more level plateaus, such as the plateau of Yünnan, tend to be wet-rice cultivators with agriculture and food almost identical to the Chinese (but simpler). On the higher or steeper mountains, maize becomes the dominant crop, and above the maize belt is a zone of barley and buckwheat. These coarse grains are eaten in the form of thick, heavy cakes, and—with thin vegetable soup, usually involving cabbages—are often almost the only food in these regions. However, the usual animals are raised, and forest products gathered. The Nosu or Yi of Szechuan are typical, living on thick buckwheat and maize cakes and on parched oats ground and mixed with water. They eat boiled meat at major feasts. A popular dish (found widely in South China) is minced raw meat—the Nosu favor internal organs—seasoned with black and red peppers and other spices. They eat raw liver, lungs, and heart, minced with chilis. Oatmeal is used, and so is bean oil (Pollard 1921).

The high altitude agriculture of all East Asia is barley and buckwheat, grown in rotation. The six-rowed Himalayan varieties of barley extend through Tibet and much of Central Asia; two-rowed barley occurs farther north. Barley is a winter crop, buckwheat a spring one. The better buckwheat is *Fagopyrum esculentum*; higher up, *F. tataricum*, which is bitter and low-yielding, must be grown instead. Both mature quickly and survive in the very dry, windy, cold summers of the mountains; the bitter buckwheat, like the barley, grows to over 14,000 feet in Tibet. In such high altitudes, no vegetables will grow, but cabbages and white radishes flourish almost to this level. In lower parts of Tibet, along the Tsangpo (upper Brahmaputra) River and its tributaries, various cool-weather foods such as apples can be grown, and some of Tibet is even low enough for rice and maize. In high Tibet, the only meats are yak, sheep, and wild game, but in slightly lower areas there are pigs and cattle. Cattle hybridized with yak produce an animal of superior size, meat yield, stamina, and milking quality.

The staple food of Tibet is barley, parched and then ground into a coarse meal (tsamba), eaten in buttered tea. Yak butter is usually used. It cannot be kept fresh, and so is fermented into a butyric counterpart of yogurt (like the *smen* of North Africa). It is mixed into the coarse, black, brick tea that the Chinese have always palmed off on the Tibetans, and the tsamba mixed into that, to form a paste or porridge which can be eaten with spoon or fingers. Meat and vegetables are usually boiled, which means they stay half raw, for the air is so thin that water boils below 200 degrees Fahrenheit. Milk, yogurt, cheese, and other dairy products are consumed in large quantities. Tibetan elites at feasts ate a provinical version of northwest Chinese food: chiao-tzu, noodles, stir-fried meat and vegetables, good tea, fruits, nuts. The food, either emphatically native or borrowed from China, forms a striking contrast with the heavily Indian-influenced art and religion.

North of Tibet are the vast deserts of Sinkiang, Chinese Central Asia, where farming can be practiced only in oases. These are inhabited mostly by people of Turkic stock, primarily the Uighurs, but also groups known collectively as Turki. A few other ethnic groups, including some Tadzhiks speaking a language close to Persian, inhabit the westernmost oases. Food in these areas is not related to Chinese at all, except for recent superficial borrowings; it is part and parcel of the great Persian cultural area. The staple is wheat bread, sourdough-raised or otherwise leavened, and cooked in large, flat, boat-shaped or oblong loaves that puff up on baking. This provides a pocket for inserting anything one is eating with the bread, making a kind of sandwich. The loaves are much bigger and thicker than the equivalent pita breads of the Near East. They are often sprinkled with sesame seeds. Grilled meats, especially small shish kebabs, are traditional accompaniments. Boiled mutton and dairy products, primarily yogurt but also cheddarlike cheese, are common fare. Vegetables except for onions and garlic are few, but this is made up for by the incomparable fruit; apricots, grapes, and melons predominate. The finest melons of the world, according to many gourmets, are the green-and-yellow-striped Persian melons of the Hami area in the Turfan Depression in the center of Sinkiang. (The Uzbeks, close kin to the Uighurs, have a proverb: "For procreation, a woman; for pleasure, a boy; but for divine ecstasy, a melon.") Watermelons of excellent quality also abound. Apricots, mulberries, and grapes are often dried, producing a staple for winter use or for cooking with lamb. Filled dumplings equivalent to chiao-tzu are made.

The nomads of northwest China—Turkic groups like the Kirghiz and all the various Mongol tribes and linguistic groups—live on bread or porridge made from traded grain, and on dairy products. Meat is not often eaten, since animals are too valuable to butcher frequently; when old they are often sold rather than butchered at home. Yogurt is the staple. Mare's milk is typically fermented with staple yeast into kumys, which tastes like slightly spiked buttermilk. Kumys can be distilled into *ayran* or *araq*, which is said to taste like bad vodka with a little sour buttermilk added. Kumys by itself is a staple drink, indeed a staple food, for its nutritional value is higher than its alcoholic content. The nomads grill or boil meat when they do get it, and have borrowed many North Chinese and Persian dishes for feast foods.

Related to the Mongols linguistically are the Tungus peoples of northern Man-churia. The Manchu were one such group; they are now essentially all assimi-lated into the Chinese population, but other small Tungus groups still exist. Those along the main rivers live primarily by fishing, drying most of the catch and using it as the staple. Some made their clothes and tents out of fish skins until the twentieth century. Other groups live by hunting, gathering, and practicing small-scale agricul-ture. Game is still a staple food in a very few areas, incredible as this may seem in modern China with its billion people; moose (known as "elk" in the Old World) and deer are the main sources. Deer are now domesticated and farmed on a large scale. Other animals from mole rats to racoon dogs are eaten. Ginseng is an important product of these northernmost reaches of China, but it is far too expensive for most of the people there to eat in any quantity. Sorghum, soybeans, buckwheat, barley and (farther south) maize are pushing their way northward into these forest realms.

Last of Chinese minorities in our clockwise progress are the Koreans, also an Al-taic people; there are somewhat fewer than a million of them on the China side of the border. The land is basically montane there, and they live predominantly on buckwheat and barley, typically made into noodles. Maize, rice and other foods are increasing in importance; millets, soybeans cabbages, radishes, and allium crops flourish. Noodles or boiled grain are eaten with meat—beef is especially impor-tant—and fish. The fiery Korean pickles, most common of which is kimchi, are con-sumed in large quantities; they are made of cabbages, radish, or other vegetables cured by lactic-acid fermentation in very strong brine or salt, with enormous quanti-ties of chiles and garlic added. Anything and everything can wind up in the kimchi jar: chickens, fish, onion leaves, pine seeds, wild herbs, mushrooms. Pine seeds are an important food and export; the main source is *Pinus koraiensis*, the cedar pine. Other forest nuts and herbs abound, from hazelnuts to ginseng. These, domesticated deer, raccoon dogs (*Nyctereutes procyonoides*, miscalled "badger" in English; a trickster in Ja-pan, a medicinal strengthening food in China), and other forest products are eco-nomic mainstays of the Korean autonomous region. Like the other minority zones of China, this area remained backward until recently, the people treated as second-class citizens. This attitude changed dramatically during the 1950s, but the improve-ment was reversed in the 1960s and bad conditions prevailed widely until the late 1970s. At present development of minority regions is proceeding apace, and much less prejudice is seen than one found a few years ago. This has its costs: Han Chinese penetration and acculturation are increasing today.

What can we learn from this lightning survey of China's regional cuisines? First, the efficiency I stress in this book goes only so far. Cultural and subcultural prefer-ences take precedence much of the time. A clearly inferior adaptation will go to the wall, but when two alternatives are roughly equal in efficiency, the choice between them is made on the basis of cultural valuation. The Chuang eat regular rice, their close linguistic relatives of Hsishuang Panna eat glutinous rice; there is no reason ex-cept tradition and a desire to keep one's own culture, foodways, and lifestyle distinct and marked. The Cantonese avoid chiles, the Hunanese love them; chiles are highly nutritious, but the Cantonese simply cannot get used to highly spiced food. (I have sometimes treated Cantonese and Min people to Szechuanese meals; their reactions are at best polite.) Such exotica as bears' paws may persist in spite of obvious inefficiency because tradition and conspicuous consumption demand. The boundaries between staple crops—maize and barley, wheat and millet—are sharpened by ethnic and regional preference; they often stop short at a cultural boundary, instead of fading out slowly along a climate gradient. Foodways are quite resistant to change, persisting over thousands of miles and years; though acculturation is occurring rapidly now, as it has at times in the past.

Second, it is still true that much is determined by what grows best and most cheaply. Rice is always the staple in the lowland south, wheat in the dry north, barley and buckwheat in cold areas. Animals are raised where they can best be raised. These generalizations transcend cultural differences; the Tibetans may make their barley into tsamba, the Koreans into noodles, and the Chinese into pearl barley, but all raise this crop where the weather is cold and dry.

It seems that people are basically efficient and economically rational in the narrow sense, but that they will also sacrifice a certain amount to keep their cultural distinctiveness. At one extreme, the Turkic peoples of Central Asia are separated by language, religion, climate, agricultural tradition, and classical culture from the Chinese, and have quite different foodways. At the other, the Chuang live with the Chinese and farm like them, and so eat fairly similar foods. In between, religion often makes a barrier—the Muslims avoid pork even where pigs are the most efficient animal to raise—and language or dialect make barriers. The stronger or higher the barrier, the more people will sacrifice to maintain it in their foodways.

All this has led to better food, and to better use of the earth's resources, for it maximizes diversity and experimentation and provides for the retention of good ideas that would otherwise have been abandoned due to some short-term economic concern. Culture has its ecological merits as an encourager of diversity, a conserver of lore, an educational device, and a guide to protection and management of resources. Even this cursory survey should show that human–environment relations are not simple matters of either "tradition" or "environmental determinism," but a complex interplay of or accommodation between both. Long may such accommodation endure.

An interesting part of regionalism is the ways regional foods are used self-consciously as ethnic markers. Many such regional foods are quite commonly served at important and special occasions but very rarely in the home. Knowledge of regional cuisines is spread to a great extent by restaurants, but restaurants rarely serve plebeian but important and clearly regional specialties such as soured milk in west China, thick corn cakes in the west and northwest, buckwheat in the west and north, sweet potatoes in the east and southeast, millet porridge in the north, or pearled kao-liang in Manchuria. Chinese do not seem militantly supportive of their poverty foods or prone to stereotype their neighbors thereby. This is probably because poverty was until recently an all too familiar fact of life in most of China. When people are poor, they tend to think of the foods of the rich. When people are rich, they *may* afford themselves the luxury of clinging to the familiar foods of their early, and poorer, days. Soul food, for example, was not highly regarded by its creators; only when American blacks became urbanized did soul food become an institution, and then primarily among better-off and better-educated members of the community. The somewhat similar apotheosis of "bitter herbs" in Mao's China seems to have been premature. The memories it revived were *too* bitter; I have heard little about "dinners of bitter herbs" lately.

The other obvious fact that emerges from the survey is that the items are genuinely local and tend to mark off the cuisine involved. This is more true of dishes than ingredients, of which *amount* of use is important but the *kind* of ingredient rarely is. I have overemphasized the regionality of dishes by disregarding cases in which a given area is known for the especially good way it prepares a universally known dish, as for instance Honan is known for a form of sweet-sour fish. A rather more interesting case is the set of what I called *general images*, in which general taste and texture of food is stressed and a given cuisine is distinguished if it has the *most X* of the cuisines of China (*X* being, for example, one of the classic Five Flavors and/or other pronounced flavors or textures).

For a regional dish to reach worldwide restaurant fame, it must be truly regional; it must be a protein dish, including some meat or equivalent; and it should be elaborate and expensive. Ingredients and general images should be pronounced and evident in fairly sophisticated cooking, should be the most *X* in China (if possible), and should not be strictly poverty foods. The more clearly limited an item is to a given region, and the more extremely obvious its use is, the more it labels the region. What is not so obvious is why a region should be labeled by fancy foods more often than by truly typical (i.e., widely eaten) ones. The fact that most people know others' cuisines only from restaurants is only one reason; the rest of the explanation is that people tend to stress foods that they like and foods that are prestigious. Expensive ingredients are prestigious, as are complexity and skill needed for preparation.

There are interesting problems with this approximation of an explanation of why some foods become markers. First, it tends to be eaters of the cuisine in question that make a food a success, by choosing it frequently, serving it to guests, serving it at restaurant feasts, featuring it on menus if they run restaurants themselves, and so on. Second, such dishes as Ma Po bean curd and Hokkien fried noodles have some protein in them, but they are hardly the quintessence of sophisticated cuisine. Out of many cheap and available foods, why are these chosen over other foods typical of the regions they stand for? Why does Ma Po bean curd mean "Szechuan" to a world of eaters, when the equally characteristic West Chinese "home-style bean curd" does not? Why are Teochiu fish balls with malt syrup sauce served frequently at self-consciously Teochiu feasts when other Teochiu foods are not?

These foods are among those that embody most clearly the general traits ascribed to the given cuisine; they are also very popular with the people whose region they are taken to typify. But so are other foods. A food that is *particularly* striking, extreme, or common will almost always become an ethnic marker, unless it is a poverty food, but some not particularly notable foods are also labels. In these cases, I suspect that pure chance establishes them as markers. At one time perhaps they were particularly common, or particularly well prepared, or no similar foods were known.

In the actual use of these foods we come closer to a structure in the usual sense of that abused word. They stand at the head of a given section on a restaurant menu; they are criterially served at self-consciously ethnic dinners, though few have the really rigid nation/festival connection of our Anglo-American Thanksgiving menu. Chinese of a given ethnic group are faithful to their cuisine. Most of my Hong Kong informants ate in restaurants purveying their own ethnic cuisine and rarely or never tried others (although no one in Hong Kong can avoid having a good deal of Cantonese food). There was little of the experimentation with different cuisines that is characteristic of diners out in other cultures. However, it is in the last analysis impossible to separate marker foods from nonmarkers at any single specific breakpoint.[5]

11 Traditional Medical Values of Food

"It is hard to find a dish in the Middle Kingdom that is not based upon the recipe of some sage who lived centuries ago and who had an hygienic principle in mind when he designed it." So wrote E. H. Nichols in 1902, with pardonable exaggeration. The truth is, of course, less extreme, but the point is well taken: the Chinese have a complex and very ancient science of nutrition.

In the Chou Dynasty, the *Chou Li* (Rituals of Chou) prescribed that nutritionists be attached to the court as part of the highest class of medical personnel. The imperial household had a large number of specialized cooks. The high position of nutritional medicine and of culinary art, in and out of the imperial court, continued to be characteristic of Chinese civilization throughout historic times.

Chinese tradition categorizes food in several different ways. Foodstuffs are classified according to biological relationship. All these categories cross-cut; a given item can be classed under many heads, depending on context or purpose. This chapter concerns the traditional classification of the foodstuffs themselves—their traditional and folk biology. I begin with some comparisons of Chinese and English names for foods.

The earliest record of plant names from China is provided by the Book of Songs, supposedly compiled by Confucius (see chapter 3). Hsuan Keng found and identified seventy-five plant names therein. Almost all of them, and all the food plant names, are simple, basic terms. By the time of the first agricultural manuals known, in the Han Dynasty, several compound terms were in general use. Today, most common plant names are binomial compounds; scientists can readily give any plant in the world such a name. Some of the more recent coinages are complicated: kohlrabi is "ball-stalked sweet vegetable." Some are delightful: a citron that looks like a clenched fist is "Buddha's hand fruit," and so the Mexican chayote, which looks like the citron, is "Buddha's hand gourd." Some are borrowed words: fenugreek is *hu lu pa* from Arabic *hulba*. Some are translations: grapefruit is *p'u t'ao yu* (grape pomelo). Some are descriptive: fig is "flowerless fruit" (fig flowers are tiny and hidden inside the "fruit," which is actually a swollen twig).

Meanwhile, in English, someone has recently turned the luffa or silk gourd into "Chinese okra," though it is neither related nor similar to okra. Apricot kernels are used in China as the Western world uses almonds, so the former are often confused with the latter. (The apricot kernels are cooked, which eliminates the poisonous hydrocyanates and makes the kernels into a good throat-soothing food. They are usually powdered.) "Chinese artichokes" are the roots of a mint (*Stachys*) and "Chinese olives" are not related to olives. Such problems are inevitable when different languages meet. But it is a shame when they go uncorrected—especially if you are trying to make an authentic Chinese dish and the recipe translates the ingredients wrong.

Today, Chinese traditional medical and nutritional beliefs persist, and they are in no danger of disappearing. Arthur Kleinman (1980), studying a large sample of Chinese on Taiwan, found that in 93 percent of sickness episodes, diet was altered —usually the first thing done, initiated by the patient or family. My sketchier figures from Hong Kong are even higher. Certainly the vast majority of Chinese react almost immediately to physical distress of any kind by changing what they eat. Diet therapy grades into herbal medicine with no sharp separation: ginseng, white fungus, birds' nests, stewed wild birds, and the like are foods but are considered to be of almost purely medical use.

The Chinese traditional science of nutrition is based on the commonsense observation that foods provide energy for the body. Different amounts of energy are contained in different foods, and the energy takes different forms. Some foods are extremely strengthening; others are weakening, if eaten to excess. (For a very full account of Chinese nutrition and food therapy, see Lu 1986.)

The traditional word for energy is *ch'i*, which literally means "breath." Like the Latin *spiritus*, it was generalized to mean "spirit"—not *a* spirit but spiritual or invisible energy. Air and gas are ch'i as well (carbonated water is ch'i water). A "ch'i vehicle" is one powered by an internal combustion engine. Ch'i in reference to the human body, or any other natural object, usually means "energy" unless the context makes it obvious that breath or spiritual nature is meant. When Chinese talk of food providing ch'i, however, they do not mean energy in the limited Western sense. The forms or qualities of bodily ch'i are different from anything known to Western science.

The most basic division of the cosmos, in traditional Chinese thought, is between *yang* and *yin*. Originally, yang meant the sunny side of a hill—the southwest face—and yin meant the shady side. The character for yang includes a small abstract picture of a hill and the character for "sun" written over what might be a slope. Yang is thus the bright, dry, warm aspect of the cosmos; yin is the dark, moist, cool one. Note that these are aspects of a single hill (or person, or universe), not really things in themselves. Males have more yang quality, and the penis is politely known as the "yang organ"; females are more yin. However, each sex has some of the other's quality; indeed, all things have both aspects.

Another key division of the cosmos is into the Five Phases (see Liu and Liu 1980; Porkert 1974; Unschuld 1985), earth, metal, fire, wood, and water. These have been called "elements" in English, likening them to the Greek elements, but the Chinese concept is fundamentally different. The Five Phases deal with phases of the cosmos and everything in it rather than with things. (Ch'i is not a phase; it pervades everything.) The full cosmology of the phases was elaborated by Ts'ou Yen in the Warring States period and became the basis of science and cosmology, including nutrition and medicine, in the early Han Dynasty. The thinkers of those ages classified everything in the universe by fives. Preoccupation with fives has lasted to, this day in China. The compass directions—including the center—are the most classic and universally known set of five, and everything else probably stems from this basic perception; even the phases may have been set at five to fit them to the all-important directions (see chapter 3). Of particular importance for food are the Five Smells (rancid, scorched, fragrant, rotten, and putrid) and the Five Flavors (sour, bitter, sweet, pungent [piquant, "hot"], and salt). These equate with the compass directions: east, south, center, west, north. The tastes are apparently those the Han scholars found to be characteristic of the regional cuisines of those times. At least the *Yellow Emperor's Classic of Internal Medicine* (Veith 1966)—the great Han medical text—says that people in the respective regions eat foods flavored accordingly. The alternative idea—that the coding was arbitrary and the scholars merely imagined, post hoc, the regional cuisines—seems too forced even for the highly scholastic Han academies.

The Five Flavors remained to classify foods, but nutritional medicine was soon to be transformed. Sometime between the *Yellow Emperor's Classic* and the great fifth-century herbal and agricultural texts, Western medicine reached China. The nutritional medicine of the Western world at that time was based on the humoral system and was shared by the Hippocratic-Galenic, Vedic, and Near Eastern medical traditions. No one knows where or how it started; Hippocrates in the fifth century B.C. speaks of it as old. Greece, the Near East, and India all take credit for it. The Greeks have "prior publication" on their side, and the system could well have spread with Alexander's world conquests. It may have reached China from many sources, but there is little doubt that the main impetus for its adoption was Buddhism (Sivin 1980). Independent origins of similar beliefs in several places may also be involved.

The humoral theory, in its most general form, holds that the human body is affected by heat, cold, wetness, and dryness. These "qualities" or "valences" must remain in balance if the body is to remain healthy. Most illness is caused (or exacerbated) by imbalance. The model is of a person working in the hot sun and suffering heatstroke or falling into cold water and suffering from a chill. The ancient Greeks noted that illness varied with season and climate and naturally assumed that the weather had a direct effect—which was true up to a point. Lacking microscopes, they had no way of knowing how typhoid (commoner in summer) differed from heatstroke or winter pneumonia from frostbite and exposure. Another observation was that certain foods increased body heat, others seemed to make the body colder. For a long time, modern scientists thought this was all nonsense—purely arbitrary and irrational—but we now know that the ancients were really attending to something. High-calorie foods were quite correctly seen as more heating; they raise body heat in a malnourished people in winter. Perhaps the ancients saw that such foods burn with much heat when dry. Low-calorie foods don't maintain body heat in a malnourished person in cold weather (unless unrealistic amounts of them are eaten), thus such things as lettuce and cabbage were considered cooling. Salty water was seen to prevent heatstroke, thus it is classed as cooling. (The truth is that heatstroke can be caused by salt depletion through sweating.) Water itself chills the body if one falls into cold water, so it was obviously cooling (see Anderson 1980, 1982, 1984, MS.; Gould-Martin 1978).

Once these simple observations had been incorporated into a simple system, everything seemed to fit. Some foods have an effect on the skin that is similar to a burn; thus ginger, pepper, and (much later) chilis were obviously heating. The effects of alcohol make it obviously heating. A "neutral" category arose for foods that are everyday staples—bread in the Western world, rice and fish in the Eastern —these mainstays were (surely) the perfectly balanced foods. Since bread is much higher in calories than rice, bread is considered heating in the Orient; the stage is set for argument. Meat, even when not very high in calories, was seen as strengthening and body-building; so it was coded as heating, but much less so than fat or sugar. Sour foods seemed cooling (think of lemonade); bitter ones often heated. Finally, foods of hot colors—red, orange, brilliant yellow—were often coded as hot, while foods of cool colors—icy white, green—were cool. Foods of a pale brown or dull chalk-white were neutral. Some foods, of course, present mixed signals: plums are red, but sour and watery. Disagreement over such items led to locally different lists and eventually to frequent modern dismissal of the whole system as sheer superstition. We can now see that, while the system is not perfect, it was a plausible extension of real home truths. Nothing succeeds like a simple extrapolation from everyday reality. This is not to say that the full system is simple. Much remains to be learned about how and why it produces effective therapy. There are no doubt many values still to be discovered in the old hot/cold coding system (see Lu 1986), and Chinese medical research continues on it.

Wetness and dryness—obviously relevant in climate—were also seen in humans. Weeping rashes, bloating, and edema were due to excess of wetness. Dry throat, feverish wasting, and a scratchy, rough feeling could be due to excess of dryness. Foods that promoted these must be wetting and drying. In China, several foods that often cause allergic rashes—wet and succulent—are wetting; shellfish are a common example. Foods that are thought to produce a dry, scratchy feeling in the throat, including coffee and dry-roasted peanuts, are drying. This dimension was never as important as heating/cooling, however.

In recent decades, many Chinese have abandoned the heating/cooling dichotomy, although it and the related concept of "rising fire" (*shang huo*) widely persist in China and throughout East Asia.

There is a category of "cold" (*han*) foods that are quite separate from cooling foods. Several foods are both cooling *and* cold. "Coldness" is not very salient, and my informants do not have a very clear picture of the quality; such foods are thought to give one a cold feeling in the stomach or to make the body actually feel icy. They are the opposite not of heating foods in general, but of those specific heating foods that are standardly used in winter to make one feel warm: dog meat, snake meat, guava, and the like.

Remember that the actual temperature of the foods is not relevant here; their effect on the body is what counts. Cooling foods may thus be used to treat fever, rash, sores, red places, and other overhot or burnlike conditions, as well as constipation and other binding symptoms. Heating foods are used to treat low temperature (as from shock or chronic tuberculosis), pallor, frequent chills, wasting, weakness, and diarrhea. Observation often bore out the value of these cures. When people in old China suffered from chronic sores, dry skin, and redness, the problem was very frequently due to (or exacerbated by) vitamin deficiency, especially vitamins A and C. The cooling foods are usually vegetables high in one or both of these vitamins: Chinese cabbage, watercress, carrots, green radishes, and so on. Similarly, pallor and weakness usually involved anemia. Warming and strengthening foods were typically chicken stew, pigs' blood or internal organs, Chinese wolfthorn berries, and other excellent sources of iron and other minerals. On the other hand, the system sometimes had disastrous results. In particular, diarrhea is considered a cold symptom; water, vegetables, fruits, and other foods would be withheld from the sufferer, a practice often fatal. Children with diarrhea might go without vegetables and fruits and suffer from malnutrition (especially lack of vitamin C). However, on balance, the system fitted observation and cured many more people than it killed. The few deaths would likely have been among children, who in old China were almost expected to die; at least among the poor, infant mortality frequently exceeded 50 percent. The system's failures thus attracted too little notice. (Moreover, the belief in withholding vegetables and fruits was far from universal.)

By the nineteenth century, humoral nutritional medicine was believed and practiced in China, India, the Near East, most of Europe, and most of Latin America. It was widespread in the Philippines (where Spanish influences met Chinese), northern Africa, Japan (but identified there as a Chinese import), and Southeast Asia. Most of these areas' medical systems included concerns with heat and cold even before identifiable Greco-Arab-Indian influence reached them. Today, the humoral system remains the basis of folk medicine in all the less developed parts of this vast realm, and it is an important scientific field in China, Japan, and the Indian subcontinent. Modern nutritional science was not advanced enough to challenge it in the English-speaking world until the late nineteenth or early twentieth century. Indeed, a few remnants of humoral medicine are still with us—not just such metaphors as "cool as a cucumber" or the use of "hot" to mean "spicy" but also beliefs in such things as the curative value of chicken soup and the weakening effects of getting one's feet wet or standing in a draft. No medical belief system in all human history has influenced more people or lasted so long in the popular mind. Directly or indirectly, humoral nutrition affects the diet of literally every Chinese who still eats any traditional food. Indeed, few people in the world have not been influenced a bit by the system's teachings. The wide use of many vegetables, chicken soup, and several cooking herbs is dependent on it.

Heating and cooling caught on as an idea in China not only because the system worked but also because it fit so beautifully with the age-old yang and yin cosmology. Foods had been classified to some extent as yang or yin even before the Greco-Indian ideas entered. By 550 A.D., Greco-Indian codings dominated Chinese ones. But the whole logic of the system is beautifully Chinese; it stressed balance, order, and harmony, the greatest of all virtues in the Confucian worldview.

Once the system became popular, little was added to it. New foods were added; disagreements arose about the codings of some items. But the whole simply based system never changed. Significantly, the Greek concept of actual humors—sanguine, choleric, melancholic, and phlegmatic—was never accepted in Eastern Asia. Hot, cold, wet, and dry energies were enough to explain what needed to be explained. Actual bodily secretions were thought to be just secretions, and none received the special pride of place that blood, phlegm, and bile obtained in Europe.

In its final form, as seen today (and for many centuries past), the system classifies some foods as dangerously heating, to be avoided except by those in good health. These include fried and long-baked foods, strong alcoholic drinks, and hot spices. Milder heating foods are strengthening and restorative, good for those with too much cool energy: most meats, red beans, ginger, ginseng (some kinds are cooling, though), a few vegetables like chrysanthemum greens (they are spicy tasting), and so on. Neutral foods are the great mainstays, starch staples and ordinary white-fleshed fish. Cooling foods used routinely as medicine or dietary aid include Chinese cabbages, green beans (fresh or dry), radishes (green ones are cooler), watercress, and many other vegetables.

But not all diet therapy is based on the humoral dimensions. Almost as important is the concept of *pu*: "strengthening, supplementing, patching up." Such foods are initially those that promote tissue repair, cure anemia, or show general tonic action. Analysis of supplementing foods shows that they usually do have some such action, but also that they are striking in appearance. Often sympathetic magic is at work: walnut meats have a reputation for strengthening the brain because they look like a brain; red jujubes and port wine are thought to strengthen the blood mainly because of their red color. However, usually foods regarded as pu are not only appropriate but also effective. The vast majority of pu foods are easily digestible, high-quality protein. Fowl—especially wild—are probably most used. Much stronger are sea cucumbers, birds' nests, raccoon-dogs, deer antlers, shark fins, pangolins, and many other wild animals and animal products. Many of these are famous worldwide as examples of the bizarre things human beings will eat and pay high prices for.

One of the most expensive is ginseng. The plant is on the border between food and medicine, categories that merge in Chinese. It is called medicine (*yüeh*) but is eaten in quantity by those who can afford it, either cooked with foods or drunk in powder or tincture form. Ginseng's actual effect appears to be tonic. Drugs within it, including panaquin and panaquilone, have a mildly stimulating effect; the taker feels energized but not "wired" (as with caffeine). Many other drugs of tonic effect are regarded as pu, and frequently are placed—as ginseng is—in the highest class of medicines: the "heaven" or "ruler" class, which strengthens the body or increases its energy, rather than treating or helping a particular condition.

It is the combination of real effect and apparent oddness or weirdness that gives some foods their special reputation as pu. Sympathetic magic enters in ways other than appearance; for instance, the male genitalia of deer are believed to be especially strengthening to the human equivalent, doubtless because one male deer can service approximately seventy does during rut season. This is the nearest thing to an aphrodisiac in Chinese medicine; the dozens of items so listed in salacious books are all pu rather than actually aphrodisiac (i.e., directly irritating or stimulating to the sex organs), and few are specifically pu to the genitalia. Of course, all of them can work as aphrodisiacs, since nothing is more responsive to placebo effects than sexual functions. The general tonic and stimulant effects of such medicines as ginseng are obviously useful in such cases, too. But the main reason for the sexual effects of most pu foods is (I feel sure) that malnutrition rapidly and drastically weakens sexual performance and interest. Foods rich in minerals and protein were just what was needed in the bad old days. They are described as *chuang yang* (helping the yang organ), *pu shen* (strengthening the testicles), and so on.

In short, pu is a system generated by—and explicable only by—the interaction of empirical truth and psychological construction. On a solid base of observed fact, people erected a structure of extrapolation and inference. Psychosomatic effects appear to validate much of this structure; traditional Chinese medicine has never seen any reason to separate the power of suggestion from other medical powers.

Rare, exotic, and unusual foods are considered pu not just because of cost and strangeness, though these are certainly factors, and conspicuous consumption is a very major part of their use. More basic is the concept of ch'i. In the traditional Chinese worldview, bodily energy, spiritual energy, and the flow of energy in the natural world are all part of one great system. This is true of modern physics too, but the Chinese belief is more extreme, claiming that people can draw on natural energy flow by eating creatures that have a great deal of energy or even by positioning themselves in places that are appropriately located to take advantage of the flow of ch'i. The striking appearance of such creatures as pangolins and raccoon-dogs is thought to indicate great energy or unusual energy patterns. Powerful creatures like eagles—to say nothing of the sexually hyperpotent deer—are also obvious sources of energy. Unfortunately, desire for such pu items as antlers, bear gall, snake meat, and rhinoceros horn is leading to vast worldwide poaching and the extermination of many species of wildlife. Only large-scale farming or ranching offers hope for the survival and continued use of these animals. The Chinese are moving (but perhaps too slowly) in this direction.

A further powerful factor in directing Chinese attention to the vital importance of balance and harmony (*ho*, "harmony," is the term most often used) is the social importance of this value.

Other foods impart pu to other bodily systems. The Doctrine of Similarities is important here. Stewed lungs of animals improve the lungs; steamed pig or chicken or duck blood supplements the blood (which is perfectly correct if one looks at the assimilable iron value). Blood is strengthened not only by animal blood, but by port wine and many other blood-resembling items.

Almost all animal foods are pu to some degree if prepared correctly—usually by steaming or simmering slowly, especially with herbs. Essentially, all pu things are heating, but gently so; they are at the low-calorie, low-fat, low-irritant end of the hotness scale. The slow simmering is intended to reduce their heating ch'i still more. The idea is to provide a gentle warming rather than a sudden shock of heat. Prepared this way, pu foods are almost always easy to digest, by both Chinese and modern scientific criteria. They are also usually rich in protein and often in mineral nutrients. Such items as chicken are often stewed with enough vinegar to leach some of the calcium from the bones and otherwise pick up mineral nutrients. Many of the herbal items, such as ginseng, also actually have some tonic or nutrient effect. The similarity of the ginseng root to the human body is also relevant. In short, it is not enough for an item to look like an organ. The Chinese do not take the simplistic attitude once found in Europe, that any liver-shaped leaf is good for the liver, or any yellow plant is good for jaundice. They will accept an item as pu only if it does have some discernible nutrient, drug, or medical effect—though in China as in nineteenth-century America it is sometimes to be strongly suspected that the only effect of some items is produced by the strong alcohol content. (Not only port wine, but a vast variety of native wines and tinctures, are pu.)

White tree-fungus, abalone, and other anomalous creatures and plants are also pu. Such routine creatures as chickens are still less pu. It is almost safe to say that the more bizarre and striking an item is, the more pu it will be. This is an obvious instance of Mary Douglas' famous generalizations about anomalous animals, and all her comments about the pangolin in Africa are apposite—I think—in China too (Douglas 1966, 1975). My fisherman informants in Hong Kong told me that the giant grouper (which may reach five hundred pounds) often has a tiny crustacean parasite in its gills; if the grouper is caught and dies, all its ch'i goes into the crustacean, which is thus the richest possible source and the most powerful of all tonics. This is definitely a folk explanation. Although Chinese doctors educated in the elite tradition often explain pu action in terms of actual tonic chemicals alleged to exist in the foods, the folk explanation is probably the older.

Another key term in Chinese medical nutrition is *tu*. This literally means "poison," but it is used in two different senses, and almost all informants note (often spontaneously) that they are really quite distinct. One, identical to the English word, refers to things that are directly toxic if eaten, like puffer-fish liver. The other is used in reference to foods that are not poisonous in themselves but bring out or potentiate any poisons in the body of the eater. The classic foods in this category are uncastrated male poultry. In a study of cancer epidemiology, I found that cancer victims and often their entire families rigorously abstained from all poultry they did not actually see killed and cleaned, for fear of getting even the tiniest bit of an uncastrated male; they believed cancer would be stimulated by such foods. Beef is often considered tu, lamb and mutton sometimes. Several fish are poisonous in this sense, as are some nuts, seeds, and vegetables, although lists differ widely from informant to informant and in the various classical Chinese medical herbals. As Carol Laderman (1981) points out, allergic reactions—specifically hives and rashes—are often at the root of such ascriptions, especially in regard to seafoods. Since rashes are often seen as internal poisons breaking out at or through the surface of the body, responding to a food with a rash is often taken as a sign that the food is poisonous. Alternatively, though, it may indicate the food is heating and wetting, for this humoral combination brings out or stimulates certain poisons, notably those of venereal disease.

Due to the lack of agreement about what foods are poisonous, generalization is risky, but one thing stands out: the foods usually considered poisonous and/or hot and wet are either similar to or specific forms of those that are pu. Most pu foods are nonpoisonous, but the poisonous foods tend to be pu to some degree. Many herbal remedies—those of the lower herbal classes—are poisonous in their action (sometimes they act by "using poison to drive out poison," as the Chinese used to "use barbarians to control barbarians," another social-medical analogy.) The ideal pu foods and medicines are nonpoisonous, but it is clear that there is some association. Perhaps uncastrated male poultry and the like are seen to strengthen the internal poisons, nourish the cancer and give it power, for example. The tremendous amount of yang energy in a rooster or drake converts it from a gentle nourisher and cherisher of the body to an uncontrolled, dangerous nourisher of both the body and the body's enemies. I am thus tentatively persuaded—pending a much fuller study of ascription of foods to the tu category—that poison-potentiation is a logical extension of pu, or perhaps of a more general category of pharmacologically broadly effective things. Poison-potentiators are effective but hard-to-control drugs. They are, of course, conceptually very close to drugs that actually have toxic side effects.

Harder to explain are the many poisonous combinations. Here the belief is not merely that these combinations are poison-potentiating; certain foods, eaten together, are supposed to react to produce actual, virulent poisons. Gould-Martin lists "in Taiwan, crab and pumpkin, port and liquorice, mackerel and plums and, in Hong Kong, garlic and honey, crab and persimmon, dog meat and green beans" (1978:43). Very long lists of these can easily be compiled by anyone with access to informants or traditional medical books. At present I am completely at a loss to explain them. Informants tell me the combinations were arrived at empirically rather than through theory or logic; yet none of them is empirically demonstrable to be harmful in the slightest degree. No one dares actually experiment (except modern Chinese outside the traditional framework), so the belief goes untested. A delightful article by Libin Cheng (1936) recounts his daring experiments with allegedly poisonous combinations. He survived unhurt, as did his experimental animals, and he gives a good overview and summary of the whole matter. Cheng suspects the complex may be traceable to experiences with allergy, bacterially contaminated foods, adulterated foods, and the like. But why these particular combinations were chosen seems impossible to determine.

I pass briefly over such minor problems as foods said to bloat or cause flatulence—here people describe reality. One other key concept underlies the concepts of *ch'ing* (cleaning) and *hsiao* (dispelling, clearing away). In both cases, the idea is to get rid of undesirable matter or essences in the body. Ch'ing gets rid of waste products and any poisons built up in the system. One clears away (hsiao) excess wetness, "wind," and other pathogenic natural forces that have entered the body. Curing inflammation, edema, and the like involves clearing away the accumulated ill humors. Some foods, licorice and honey, for example, free one from poisons (*chieh tu*). "Dirt" (not the same thing as tu) can also be dispelled. Foods particularly good at cleaning are honey, brown sugar, and sugar cane juice (Gould-Martin 1978:40), some vegetables, a number of herbs. A very common herbal mixture, sold in all Chinese drug and general stores, is the *ch'ing pu liang* (cleaning, strengthening, and cooling) herbal tea or soup mix. *Ch'ing liang* foods relieve heat; *lin nao* foods are diuretic (often because of potassium content in the context of a high-salt diet).

The Chinese have lived with famine and malnutrition for a very long time and have accumulated countless observations connected therewith. From these they have constructed a folk nutritional science—rather, both a folk and an elite nutritional science—that subsumes the observations under a set of simple principles or concepts. Some of these broad concepts stand the test of modern science. Others merely illustrate the truth of the remark attributed to H. L. Mencken (among others) that "for every problem there is a solution that is simple, plausible, and wrong."

The study of medicinal classification has implications for the study of Chinese thought. More important are its implications for the study of human thought in general. In actual working taxonomy (so to speak), people appear to go up the taxonomic tree and then back down. They classify things by seeing some particularly important general, shared qualities. They then overgeneralize and overextend these qualities to produce a simple, grand, overarching, high-level system. They then use deduction to classify new or unusual items: if a new item has quality X, it is classified under the appropriate heading. Often the new item should not be so classified, in terms of its actual effects, but the assignment of it to a particular category is thoroughly system-driven: logic takes precedence over mere fact. On the other hand, feedback from experience guarantees that any widespread system has some truth or value. Nutritional medicine, in particular, must be grounded in experiential reality.

"Chunking" enters in that people do not generalize along a smooth gradient. They recognize the natural "chunking" of the world—for example, into biological species—and oversharpen this distinction by treating members of a chunk as if they were pretty much identical but very different from members of any other chunk. All pangolins are about equally pu. This apparently simple matter—oversharpening of some distinctions and blurring of the distinctions not so oversharpened—is at the root of many human mistakes and misperceptions (Nisbett and Ross 1980).

Last is analogical thinking. It was once said in philosophy classes that the Chinese are analogical rather than logical in their thought processes. During the critical formative period of Chinese philosophic thought, syllogistic logic vied for place with argument based on analogy. The latter won, but not without being affected by the former. Chinese thinkers recognized that there were analogies and analogies—even if you do answer Lewis Carroll's question, "why is a raven like a writing desk?" you haven't learned anything very exciting. Philosophers argued by analogy, but the one whose analogy actually included a homology (or something like one) was the winner. The idea was that if two things share a common quality, they may share a common substrate. There are qualities that are real and shared but superficial and trivial (whiteness) and ones that are real, shared, and basic (energy, in moving systems, for instance). Chinese philosophy, as it took form, focused on pragmatic, existential reality and on process. Thus, what was shared was, most importantly, certain types of effect, of energy, of transforming ability and transforming power. The Western tradition of idealism (focusing on essential reality and on unchanging, ultimate Form) was unacceptable to the Chinese, even though it was often introduced, for example with some schools of Buddhist thought, from westward.

There is little "essential" difference between logic and analogic. One can set up analogies as syllogisms:

Things that are strikingly unlike other natural things have a particular and powerful ch'i.
The pangolin is strikingly distinctive.
Therefore, it has a lot of powerful ch'i.

One can set up syllogisms as analogies:

All the people I know of who reached a great age died.
Socrates is like these other people I know of—not in everything, but in what I think are key respects.
Thus, we can expect Socrates to die too.

Either way, one carries out similar inductive and deductive processes.

On balance, Chinese traditional beliefs worked very well to keep people healthy and to keep the food production system diverse. Many plants and animals that would not otherwise have been domesticated, or kept in domestication, were grown because of their alleged medical values. While few of these were as medicinally effective as traditional doctors thought, they did provide a richer and more varied resource base for agriculture. Thus more ecological niches were used; nutrients and land were employed more efficiently, since each cultigen had its special requirements and habitat that would often have lain unused if people had wished to grow only the cheap grains. Deer and racoon-dog farms, for instance, provide a valuable economic resource in areas otherwise too cold and too far from markets to produce much. Only the high price commanded by these animals justifies cropping the areas where they occur. In the central lands, such crops as watercress and Chinese wolfthorn make efficient use of marginal bits of land. (What besides watercress would grow profitably in shallow, cold water?) Such crops also provide insurance; an agriculture that specializes in the two or three most productive crops dooms its users to famine when the crops fail. Chinese agriculture was so diverse that the people were relatively buffered against famine—or, more accurately, more people could be supported when famine struck. A knowledge of wild edible plants, gained through use thereof as medicines, also stood the peasants in good stead at such times.

But, also, the system is based on much empirical observation. The Chinese explained these observations as best they could; lacking modern laboratories and having a rather primitive, although extensive, analytic chemistry, they could not possibly have discovered those compounds and analyzed them. They thus came up with reasonable, plausible, logical inferences, which we now know to be often incorrect. But they were often very close to the truth—as in the similarity of the heating/cooling dimension to our concept of calories. (The calorie is a measure of heat.) Therefore, they worked reasonably well. To an old man who had never had much protein-rich and mineral-rich food, or for that matter to one who had been rich enough to indulge in the fatty, greasy, salty diet of banqueting luxuriants, a diet of birds' nests and sea cucumbers would be nothing but helpful.

We still have much to learn from Chinese traditional medicine and nutrition. Recent discoveries of hormones in deer velvet, stimulants in ginseng, and literally thousands of valuable drugs in Chinese herbal remedies should drive us back to the laboratories and clinical trials to see if other traditional foods have values that we do not yet know about. Mineral availability, enzyme systems, undiscovered animal medicines, and synergistic effects of various foods seem particularly promising avenues for research. I do not believe that we know all the reasons why pu foods strengthen, why cooling foods seem to heal sores, why honey seems so soothing, or why licorice seems almost magically effective at harmonizing medicines in mixed doses and preventing bad side effects. I can personally testify to such benefits as relief of cold symptoms and sore throats by loquat syrup and pear syrup. The whole concept of a medical therapy based on gentle, inexpensive, everyday means of strengthening the body and soothing its aches has much to contribute to our modern system with its powerful and dangerous remedies that all too often create iatrogenic pathologies of their own.

12 Food in Society

Social Rules and Chinese Eating

There are, in social science, two general viewpoints. One is relatively materialist, espoused mainly by those who study energetics and economics. The other, sometimes called "idealist," includes social-constructionist, hermeneutic, and phenomenological views of how humans form culture. Neither is adequate by itself to account for foodways. Everyone in every culture is constrained by the absolute necessity of adequate calories, protein, fat, vitamins, and minerals. In every habitable environment, however, many passably good solutions to this challenge may be found. Even if we restrict ourselves to broad classes of relatively optimal solutions, there are always choices. Moreover, human populations cannot expand infinitely fast. The worst famine in a generation will kill many and drive the rest to survive by eating anything and everything they can find; during the rest of that generation-long period, people will not be under such direct pressure. They can use food to satisfy their needs for variety, communication, and social contact. Thus they will socially construct foodways that conform with nutritional needs but do more than simply provide nutrients.

A materialist may look at foodways and find that they teach good nutrition, while a phenomenologist may see structures of meaning. China's traditional nutritional science serves as a case in point. The hot/cold system is explainable only as an accommodation between the facts of nutrition and the needs of information processing in a peasant society. In India, foodways have been elaborated through religion more than folk nutrition; in China, medical science proved more important than religion as a way of organizing foods.

Chinese use food to mark ethnicity, culture change, calendric and family events, and social transactions. No business deal is complete without a dinner. No family visit is complete without sharing a meal. No major religious event is correctly done without offering up special foods proper to the ritual context. Little comparative data is available from different parts of China on just what foods are appropriate to what situations, or on how people manipulate and change these customs in response to changing economic or cultural circumstances. However, we can say something about how Chinese foodways change, especially under the impact of the Western world.

Throughout this book I stress the theme that Chinese food owes much of its sophistication and elaboration to its uniquely important place in the social scheme of things. The most striking proof of this I found is a statistic from Rance Lee of the Chinese University of Hong Kong: in Hong Kong, expenditures on food as a percentage of total income actually rise as people get richer. In all other areas, Engel's Law holds: food takes less of the family budget as income increases. The reason is that Hong Kong citizens use food as the great social cement. As in much of the world, business deals, marriages, and friendly get-togethers involve food; in Hong Kong not only these but even the most trivial matters are occasions for a feast. The Cantonese are perhaps extreme in this regard. Taiwan and Singapore do not report quite such perverse violations of Engel's Law; but even in those countries, and surely in many overseas Chinese communities as well, relative food expenditure does not sink much as income rises. In mainland China, where puritanism is enforced as much as possible, the most vigorous resistance to government-sponsored asceticism has come not in the areas of corruption, reducing childbirth, or sex, but in banquets. Chinese from all walks of life persist in throwing huge banquets, and the government's principles count for little. This use of food as social lubricant, stimulus, and marker is traceable to the very dawn of Chinese civilization—and beyond, if the careful attention to beauty in the construction of Neolithic pottery means what I think it means. Food is so central that it often enters metaphoric language. "To eat vinegar" is to be envious; while in modern Hong Kong, "to eat ice cream with the eyes" means to gaze with desire at a member of the opposite sex.

In the past, as now, food was used to mark special events and to delineate the social relationships of the eaters. Nor did this significance end with the natural world: "gods, ghosts, and ancestors"—the three classical categories of supernaturals—also received their appropriate sacrifices. From earliest times, religion served as a powerful reinforcement to gourmetship, for gods and ancestors must be given the best. This situation is exactly opposite to that in the Western world, where religion so often enjoined asceticism. A basic difference in religious ideology underlies this. The Chinese otherworld was an extension of this one, not an alien or even particularly different realm. Gods liked and expected what high-status humans liked and expected, and the heavenly social order recapitulated that of earth—in historic times, the full imperial court and the local village world. In the West, and to a great extent in India, however, a great gulf separates the supernaturals—the realm of ideas and transcendent beings—from the natural. In this system, one makes oneself more acceptable to those beings by cutting ties with this world, especially the ties formed by the "lusts of the flesh." Disapproval of conspicuous waste, and even occasionally a borrowed asceticism, China certainly had (and has); but deep ethical resistance to enjoying life was foreign to East Asia. It came with invading ideologies—Buddhism, Communism—and put down wide but shallow roots. But Chinese gourmetship was not developed through the mere absence of moral opposition; it was actually morally sanctioned. Early ritual texts specify exactly what foods should go to the elderly, what to serve at particular feasts, what to sacrifice at each particular rite. There are no such canonical texts today, but unwritten law can be just as rigid.

As a marker of social status, ritual status, special occasions, and other social facts, food became less a source of nutrients than a means of communication. At formal functions, language was and is so ritualized and polite that it communicates, at best, general sentiments. The task of communicating important social facts—ethnicity, status, and so on—was carried out through food. Two guests might be addressed with the same flowery compliments, but one would be seated beside the host and served delicacies by the host himself, the other seated at a distant table where the food was lukewarm by the time it was served. Thus a consciousness of minute differences in seating arrangements, quality of dishes, and so on became highly important—sometimes literally a matter of life and death—for Chinese. Table manners took on a vital importance quite unknown in many cultures.

Every part of China has its own food rules, basically similar to those of other regions but with their own flavors and arrangements. Hong Kong in the 1960s and 1970s serves as a typical example. In traditional homes, everyday meals were rather casual affairs. The whole family sat down to dinner together, and lunch too if everyone was not otherwise occupied, but often lunch was extended and loose as people drifted in or came to a break in their work routines. Breakfast was a casual affair: children ate bowls of noodles or congee, adults foraged as they chose, and everyone was apt to eat lunch at a nearby noodle stand. Weekends, for the better-off, usually meant a leisurely breakfast of tim sam at a tea shop; even during the week, adults often ate at their favorite shops. Important local figures kept "office" hours of a sort there, sitting at their usual tables at certain times during the morning.

Between-meal snacks were frequent. Going anywhere often meant a trip to a favorite noodle stand or sweet-vendor. Marketing was not complete without a pause for tea. A major part of any all-day outing was planning where to eat—what were the specialties of the area visited, where they were best obtained, what to eat with them. Around the house, children were as devoted to small sweet snacks as are children in most other countries. They also liked spicier items, such as boiled chickens' feet and salted mei.

Even the main meal of the day could be flexible, with people eating in shifts, but usually it was taken with the entire family. Adults discussed serious matters; children were supposed to keep relatively silent, but they rarely did; young children were indulged and teased. The table was crowded with bowls: the dishes in the center for all to share and the individual rice bowls used by the eaters. Plates were mainly for the well-to-do; ordinary people made do with rice bowls, chopsticks, and spoons. Tea was drunk from glasses about as often as from cups. The man of the house might drink a beer, but alcohol consumption was rare. Mealtimes in a Chinese house were always relaxed, cheerful, leisurely occasions—unless severe work pressures or family problems interfered.

Everyday foods were, of course, rice, vegetable soup, steamed fish, steamed vegetables, stir-fried vegetables, pork, or other treats. Noodles with bits of vegetables and pork were the commonest substantial snack. If company was coming over, the mother of the family—the senior man's wife, or his mother if living—served chicken, a pork dish, perhaps another pork dish with internal organs cooked with vegetables, and proportionately less of everyday food. Large fancy-looking fish replaced the ordinary day's small fish. (But most fishermen, used to fish at every daily dinner, tended not to serve fish at a feast.)

A festival involved all of the above, the pork typically stir-fried with cashew nuts or some similarly expensive food. Chicken cooked two or more ways and/or other fowl would be served. Fruit was typical of some festivals. At New Year, for instance, tangerines were obligatory and a dish of mixed nuts and seeds traditional; all these foods brought good luck for the coming year. Large festivals always involved the sacrifice of pigs. Families ate some sacrificial pork, typically (especially for the major festivals) roasted with a gold-red glaze and called "golden roasted pork" (*kam tsu siu iuk*). Nuts and seeds appeared. At New Year, many sweets and liquors were consumed. Most foods were stir-fried and several were deep-fried, in contrast to everyday fare in which steamed and boiled foods predominated. Shrimps, crabs, and other crustaceans were typically served at festivals and sometimes for honored guests.

Even more impressive than big festivals were the life crisis rites or rites of passage —specifically weddings and the festivities thrown by a family for a man (occasionally a woman) who had turned sixty, thus completing one whole cycle of the Chinese calendar. These feasts involved all the above foods plus, typically, shark fin soup; at least one duck dish as well as two or three chicken dishes and/or a pigeon dish or two; and several dishes of pork stir-fried with the more expensive vegetables. There were always some symbolic foods: long noodles to give long life at birthdays, or at marriages a dish of lotus rhizomes, which stick together when separated and thus encourage stability of marriages. There was an emphasis at such times on rich and highly seasoned foods. Often these were heating in the humoral system, and feasts were regarded as very yang and hot affairs (Gould-Martin 1978). Memorial feasts for the dead were similar, though smaller.

Cantonese families in Hong Kong rarely cooked something special just for a treat or an intimate nuclear family celebration. Instead, they went out to eat. A business deal, contract, or other major transaction also required a substantial meal in a good restaurant. Meat dishes and expensive seafoods socially sealed the transaction.

Statistical tendencies emerge from this material. Some foods seem virtually obligatory: chicken dishes at almost all special occasions where one cooks at home; shark fin soup at rites of passage, especially marriages. Other foods are increasingly likely the fancier the occasion marked and the more spent: stir-fried and fried foods, exotic spices and flavoring agents; poultry; crustaceans, especially shrimp and crab, very highly favored in Hong Kong. Alcohol was served at major feast events, otherwise it was not common. Some foods are *less* likely to be seen at festivities: salt fish, small fish, the cheaper vegetables. (They diminish in that order—salt fish almost never appear at special occasions.) Still other foods are linked with and are markers for specific occasions: golden pork for major sacrifice rites, fruit for many sacrifice rites and some specific festivals, moon cakes for the Moon Festival, sweet snacks and nibbles such as sugar-coated seeds for New Year. Other foods are idiosyncratic: people have their likes and dislikes, and a favorite guest will find his or her favorite foods served faithfully.

The heavy, protein-rich, "heating" fare of feasts often causes indigestion, seen as the result of too much hot ch'i. Naturally, the converse is also true: bland, crisp, low-calorie vegetables, cooked by steaming and boiling, are normally cooling. They are the appropriate diet of Buddhists, people who have overindulged in hot things, people sick with hot diseases, and people too poor to buy good or special food. Buddhist devotees, as vegetarians, eat *su* (clean, vegetarian) food; meat is *hun* (unclean) to them. Cooling foods also occur at feasts, especially vegetables that are well liked and regarded as necessary to bring out flavors of some dishes; these include cauliflower, carrot, and cucumber. Heating foods are found only if they are also fairly expensive and special. In short, various exigencies of cooking and occasion-marking take precedence; a feast is not merely an array of everything heating. The relationships between medical efficacy (in folk belief), price, and special feast status are complex and there is much feedback between these properties. Group affiliation must be taken into account; one serves the dishes of the group one is in—family, linguistic group, social group.

A person planning a menu for a feast must, in essence, pick from a list of traditionally appropriate feast foods those that are fancy enough for the occasion in question but not too fancy (and/or ruinously expensive), that are more or less balanced with eath other, that are hot enough, and that are appropriate ethnically. An unthrifty feast-giver can play it safe, socially, by buying far more fancy items than he or she can afford. The present government of China has complained much about this wasteful practice but has been unable to stop it.

We should not overlook the nutritional advantages of feast giving. The high-protein foods have much nutritional value, and for a century many observers have pointed out that feasts give ordinary and poor people a chance to eat much strength-building food. Of course in traditional times the rich threw most of the feasts and the poor and malnourished enjoyed the least of this type of food, so the nutritional effects of the complex might have been only slightly positive.

There are some nutritional reasons for certain foods to be identified with special occasions. There are also social reasons. Feasts mark an occasion, do something special, leave one's guests indebted, communicate messages of solidarity (including ethnic solidarity), favor, opulence, and the like. Food is communication. There are also logical reasons for feast foods—they tend to be hot, as opposed to everyday fare. Structural considerations of complementary opposition are very obvious here. There are, of course, also reasons of taste; people eat at feasts what they think particularly delicious. (The ultimate question, though, is why some things are so considered; not everyone in the world likes sea cucumber.)

It should come as no surprise that one institution serves several relevant functions.

I doubt whether any one or even any three of these functions can predict much without the others. At base only two things are happening: feeding the body and communicating messages. The body needs nourishment and likes some foods better than others. The communication function is presumably secondary—food is such a constant that one also manages it for communicative reasons. (This is especially true since the original food of most humans, mother's milk, is by nature bound up with social and emotional messages.) In the case of special-occasion foods, however, communication is clearly the primary goal in mind when occasions are planned and dishes selected. Nutritional advantages are considered but are secondary, even spin-offs. The wide range of non-nutritious and even harmful foods involved at feasts, such as quantities of alcoholic beverages, reinforces this conclusion. But the use of foods to communicate is the central theme, although—and this is very important —one cannot predict what foods will be used at feasts on the basis of communicative value alone.

Throughout China, the same broad conclusions apply. In North China, Tun Li-ch'en's *Annual Customs and Festivals in Peking* (1965) serves as a good example of a type of book that Chinese have been writing for thousands of years. The incredible importance of food in the text is enough to make one wonder if Tun remembered that festivals have any purpose other than justifying gourmetship. Yet poems and songs, stories, and other works carry through the emphasis on food (Cheng 1954; Cooper 1985; Waley 1957; Yang 1984). In general, the points are straighforward: food is absolutely essential to all religious and social rituals, since gods and people must be appropriately entertained with the best of everything. Not only are feasts and meals important; gifts must be brought by visitors and returning travelers, and since the ritual texts of Chou, these gifts have traditionally been foodstuffs. When they go abroad, Chinese travelers seek out famous local delicacies to bring back to the home folks. This custom spread to Japan and now supports a multimillion-dollar industry around the world, where airport and midcity shops stock appropriate gift items at extortionate prices: fruit in Los Angeles, salmon and fish roe in Vancouver, steaks in Sydney.

This consecration of food and the goodness of food, this apotheosis of gourmetship into the divine and into the heart of the social (of which, the *Li Chi* and Durkheim tell us, the divine is a representation), is typical of all old civilizations. None took it farther than did China.

Chinese Food Changes: The Impact of the Modern World

Chinese food has never remained static, and it is currently changing as fast as ever in history—yet without losing any of its essential characteristics. Most of the changes are for the better as far as people's nutrition is concerned. Everywhere that Chinese have gone, they have managed to do well enough to increase their supply of food, and with affluence they choose wisely, eating larger quantities of meat, fish, vegetables and fruits. Sugar, oil, and saturated fats increase apace, unfortunately, and partially offset the improvements. Life expectancies among Chinese have lengthened enormously—from perhaps thirty-five to forty in 1900 to almost seventy now in the mainland, well into the seventies in overseas communities—but they would have increased more in the latter had not sedentary lifestyles and overrich diets brought an increase in heart and circulatory diseases. Still, the gain is incredible and can be ascribed primarily to improvement in diet.

As far as gourmetship goes, the changes have again been primarily for the better. Better ingredients, better training, and above all the increasing affluence and sophistication of the population have vastly increased the number of restaurants. Even if quality has not increased, the availability of good food to the common person is incomparably better now than in the past.

But modernization has taken its toll. The worst change, in my opinion, has been an increase in the use of cheap ingredients to bulk out or hype up a dish. Cornstarch and oil are slopped on lavishly to add calories and fill up the diners on the cheap. Salt, sugar, and monosodium glutamate (MSG) are poured into almost everything. In traditional Chinese cooking, sugar was very sparingly used, salt came only from pickled items, and MSG did not exist. Monosodium glutamate was isolated from a traditional Japanese seaweed preparation used to enhance flavor. Shortly after 1900, the Aji-no-Moto (flavor powder) Company developed and mass-produced the product. It soon spread to China under the name *wei-ch'in* or "ve-tsin," which is a translation of the Japanese. It adds a heavy, harsh, metallic taste to Chinese food and wrecks the subtle and complex blending of flavors essential to fine cuisine. It also provokes a violent allergic reaction—the "Chinese restaurant syndrome"—in many people, and the sodium is dangerous to anyone with high blood pressure. Salt, of course, is unhealthy for the same reason. Thus, quite apart from the effects on taste, these changes are undesirable from a medical point of view. Unfortunately, they come at a time when increased affluence and the rise of middle-class salaried jobs have raised consumption of saturated fat and cholesterol while lowering the physical activity of the average worker. For a generation or so, homes and many restaurants held out, and I had high hopes that the debasement was a fad that would pass. This was not to be. Fancy restaurants have been widely imitated. Those that sold to Western tourists were the worst, but did very well financially and thus set a standard. The problem is greatest in overseas Chinese restaurants, but it exists in the People's Republic as well. Then cookbooks got into the act, rushing to spread the new restaurant-banquet recipes and neglecting traditional Chinese food. The lure of the new, and the fact that the old was widely known and thus not worth bothering to write up, led to this state of affairs. Anyone following the standard modern Chinese cookbook will learn to add salt, cornstarch, and MSG by the spoonful to a dish swimming in oil and often heavily sugared. Traditional Chinese gourmets are sickened, but the new generation has learned to prefer this food to old-fashioned cooking. The rearguard action of a few stalwart traditionalists has not helped much.

There is, of course, room for debate on the aesthetics of this. I have no deep quarrel with people who prefer the new food to the old; *chacun à son goût*. They tend eventually to return to, or discover, American coffee-shop and fast-food franchise cuisine, which is even more to their taste, and thus abandon Chinese restaurants. But the health problem is really disturbing. Classic Chinese cooks depended on the finest and above all the freshest of ingredients. High-quality and completely fresh vegetables, seafoods, and poultry are now unavailable or expensive in such huge urban agglomerations as Hong Kong, Los Angeles, and Peking. This has been a major cause of the increase in salt and MSG, which hype up flavor and disguise (poorly) the lack of good ingredients. Meat is generally of better quality than it used to be, but there has been a problem with pork: the traditional pig, in which fat was sharply separated from lean, has been bred out to Western varieties in which fat is mixed or marbled into the muscle meat. This soggy, greasy pork is less than ideal for Chinese cooking by almost anyone's standards. Fortunately, this trend has reversed in the Western world and is reversing in China; lean pork is once again available, and Chinese food is improved thereby. Decline in poultry quality with the coming of mass production seems also to have bottomed out, and good restaurants are seeking out specially-fed birds.

The worst thing that could happen in the future, in my opinion, would be the disappearance of working-class street food. The street stalls and tiny hole-in-the-wall restaurants that used to make noodles, won ton, pao, congee, stuffed dumplings, steamed meatballs, fried pastries, and thousands of other snack items could be at risk in the new, affluent world of the future. They are in no danger of disappearing, but they are becoming rarer and are being influenced by the big restaurants' corner-cutting and sodium-loving ways. Much interest has belatedly been devoted to these wonderful foods, among the high points of Chinese cooking. Yet people seem less than aware of the foods in question. Chinese are apt to write them off as poverty food, and Westerners often are never introduced to them. Countless tourists have complained to me about the quality of food in the People's Republic; all of them, it turned out, had dutifully eaten only in the big West-oriented hotels and restaurants, which have altered their food to please the Western palate and which feed hundreds at a meal. I even heard that the old food stalls are gone and one can no longer get "small eats" in China. But on my travels I found that small eats existed in every form. Street pushcarts, small cafés, workers' dining halls, and snack bars sold them, as good as anything comparable in Hong Kong or Taiwan—certainly the best food I ate in China outside a few private homes.

There has been a general loss of concern among Chinese with local variation in food and other matters of authenticity. Up to a point this matters only to pedants and purists, but most Chinese cookbooks (especially those in English) passed that point quite a while ago. Substituting sherry for Chinese wine, celery for unavailable Chinese vegetables, canned water chestnuts for fresh, and other such tactics all change the flavor of a dish quite substantially. Invoke them all in the same dish and the result bears about as much resemblance to Chinese food as it does to Old Icelandic. Sometimes such dishes are excellent; a good chef will hardly be ruined by having to use celery, and creativity was ever the soul of Chinese cooking anyhow. But to assume that substituting sherry for Shaohsing wine automatically creates a good dish is not reasonable. Sherry is a completely different fluid with its own virtues and cooking qualities.

There are countervailing forces. A general worldwide ideal of gourmetship has developed in the last generation or so, based primarily on recent French attitudes. This consciousness is highly congenial to traditional Chinese cuisine; indeed, it was influenced by Chinese ideals. Newer Chinese cookbooks (in Chinese and Western languages), restaurants, and sophisticated home cooks are reflecting this new set of ideals by returning to a consciousness of fine ingredients, light touch with salt, and precisely timed cooking. Meanwhile, and far more important, both traditional Chinese and modern Western ideas of nutrition are spreading rapidly. These agree on avoidance of heavy use of sugar, salt, and oil, and on the positive values of a highly varied diet rich in vegetables and seafoods.

The thoughtful observer is struck by the extent to which these changes are driven by status emulation. Obvious matters like cutting costs and substituting available ingredients aside, the changes have generally been of two types: upgrading the food in terms of traditional Chinese standards of prestige and changing it to emulate Western ones.

I have studied dietary change in several Chinese communities: one in Hong Kong (a bit of China leased temporarily to the British), where change was within a strictly Chinese environment, and two in overseas communities where acculturation to the local dominant society was important. Accounts of these reveal more about Chinese eating than any other kind of study.

In 1965–66 my family and I lived at Castle Peak Bay in the rural New Territories of Hong Kong, where we were carrying out anthropological field research on the fishing industry and the boat people who ran it. In 1974–75 we returned for a restudy and found the area completely transformed. Rounding the last point of land on the bus route to the bay, we were shocked when a huge wall of white towers appeared suddenly before us. At first they seemed unreal—a dream city floating in the air. Yet we knew that the Hong Kong government had planned to develop a "new town"—city, actually—at Castle Peak Bay and had already housed several tens of thousands of people there. What loomed before us were the housing and commercial blocks, rising from what had been a polluted mudflat. The old gray shacks and smoky traditional-style buildings were still there, huddled below the huge new high-rise complex.

The people were the same as ever—bluff, friendly, hospitable, and open. We rented a room from an old friend, renewed old ties, and settled into the routine again, with great delight.

The routine of shopping and eating in the Castle Peak Bay community had changed a great deal, as had the area's food production. But many things had not changed much. The principal retention was a concern for *sin* or *sansin* (freshness). This was shown by the taste, texture, and appearance of a food; vegetables and many other foods were expected to be *ch'ui* (Mandarin *ts'ui*; see chapter 9), the appropriate texture for a fresh food—crisp, crunchy, succulent, or even soft and delicate. (It does not normally imply the crackliness of potato chips, although it can be used for that.) Foods were also expected to taste *ch'ing* (clear and pure), insofar as that term was appropriate to a given food category. In general, freshness could be evaluated by a number of words, but people often simply stopped at *sin*. Freshness is a virtue in foods everywhere in Hong Kong, but at Castle Peak Bay the desire for it was carried about as far as possible. In 1965–66, fish were preferred when kept alive in the sea rather than in tanks, because the water was cleaner, but by 1974–75 pollution had advanced to the point where tank-kept fish were preferred. (The tanks were kept better aerated, too.) Pigs slaughtered and vegetables picked within a couple of hours of buying were sought out. Poultry and dogs for eating were sold alive, as were other creatures when possible. Above all, everyone who could kept some poultry, so that they could have access to birds that were not only fresh but also fed and reared carefully. Certainly, poultry fed on table scraps in a backyard is far preferable in taste to battery-reared birds. Even the boat people kept poultry and—on large boats— pigs. The chickens were in small cages built out over the stern, giving rise to a Cantonese simile: "Like boat people's chickens, that see the water and can't drink." This phrase is used, among other things, to describe a person looking at and desiring a member of the opposite sex who is unapproachable. The price differential between live and dead food is high. A fish kept alive in clean water can cost ten times as much as an identical fish on ice. A frozen battery-reared chicken imported from China costs a third or less the price of a local live bird.

Between 1965 and 1974 the concern for freshness waned somewhat. People had lost all hope of getting most of their foods in an ideally fresh state. The urbanization of the area had changed supply and demand: there were very few local vegetables and many buyers. Much food was imported from China via central wholesale markets in Kowloon. Partially thawed frozen items, vegetables exposed in the sun, and other misfortunes occurred during shipment. Partially offsetting this was the improvement in preservation technology in the area. In 1965 very few families had refrigerators, let alone freezers, and transport was slow and never refrigerated. (Ice for fish, and truck-loaded tanks for live fish, were the extent of special facilities for transport.) In 1974, the rising prosperity and urbanization of the area had brought refrigerators within the financial reach of most people, and refrigerated—or at least quick and adequately iced or cooled—transport was available. Therefore, one was at the mercy of the market with regard to reliably fresh food; but one did not need absolutely fresh food to avoid outright spoiled items. As in small markets in the United States, produce and so on was not of the best quality but at least was safe.

By far the commonest complaint about the food available in Castle Peak Bay in 1974–75 was that it was not as fresh as of old. Good fresh stuff commanded very high prices, which of course took it out of the normal ken of the ordinary buyer. Therefore many households raised their own food. Everyone with a patch of ground, no matter how small, had chickens, fruit trees, herbs, or at least a vegetable or two growing. The emphasis on fresh and home-raised foods was of rural origin and background, of course, but it involved no ideology of the nobility of rural life or the transcendent value of being close to the soil. Such beliefs are not pronounced in Chinese culture and almost totally lacking in Hong Kong, where nevertheless even apartment dwellers would have small window-ledge pots of herbs.

Another vigorous holdover from the rural centuries was the standard choice of foods consumed. Our dietary surveys disclosed that in spite of the advent of many new foods and the rapid fall in their prices, the average family still ate a basic diet unchanged for a thousand years or so. Such long-established Western imports as tomatoes, potatoes, and maize were relatively little used, to say nothing of such things as broccoli, cauliflower, kohlrabi, and head lettuce, all of which had appeared in the vegetable markets by 1974 although they were almost completely unknown in 1966. Broccoli, for example, had made virtually no headway against *kaai laan choi*, although the latter—often known as Chinese broccoli—is very similar and differs primarily in being more fibrous and bitter. Butter and milk were likewise available but not much used, except in formula for babies.

Yet more interesting than the Westernization was the fact that Western foods were not accepted mindlessly. A process of Cantonization was going on. Tomatoes, potatoes, and so forth were being worked into the cuisine. There were also changes in the baked goods: sweet rolls, for example, ran heavily to coconut, peanuts, and eggs, and had less sugar than the originals. The rolls were much lighter and less floury. Affection for egg had led to brushed-on egg topping being replaced with a thick egg coating.

Soft drinks continued to prosper; the indigenous competitor, sweetened soybean milk, had about vanished from the scene. Candy and crackers, bread and cookies flourished in every home. Bread and soft drinks are probably the most widely consumed Western foods. Bread has taken the space formerly occupied by Chinese rolls (*pao*) and now competes with them as a snack, but soft drinks have been a more radical departure, competing with tea and sweet bean products. Western cuisine seems always to spread via its nutritionally most disastrous products—not surprising, since these are cheap, much ballyhooed by advertising, and easily available as minor snacks (thus not competing against the established rituals of meals). Traditional foods are abandoned in order of their cultural importance. Drinks go first, then snacks and breakfasts, then standard main dishes, and last of all the festal foods associated with ethnic traditional occasions. But Western nutritional knowledge is also spreading fairly effectively, especially via universally known and widely followed advice to give young babies a vitamin C source (usually orange juice), safe adequate formula if breast-feeding is not done, and early introduction of meat and vegetables (in order of people's answers to our questions on the subject).

In Hong Kong there are few Westerners and many non-Cantonese Chinese—especially in rural areas like Castle Peak—but the Cantonese borrow Western cuisine more than they borrow foodways from other Chinese groups. Few rural Cantonese have ever eaten more than a token meal or two of Teochiu, Hakka, Szechuanese, or other Chinese traditions well represented in Hong Kong. Western foods spread where the others do not because of the dominance and power of the West, especially the colonial power, England, but increasingly the United States and other countries. Not only are these Westerners in a position to demand and get familiar foods everywhere, they are also (as are all colonial and neocolonial powers) models for imitation.

Ethnicity is not something one is born with and always wears, but something one and one's friends and family can assume or drop at will. For example, the Teochiu population of Hong Kong exists as a separate ethnic group, but individual Teochiu often "pass" as Han Chinese. Locally born Teochiu are often more fluent in Cantonese than in their own language, and their foodways tend to imitate Hong Kong Cantonese. With Cantonese, they usually eat typical Cantonese fare and do not discuss their own. However, when they eat as families or in all-Teochiu friendship groups, they seek out Teochiu restaurants and tend toward a very fixed menu of the most widely known and popular Teochiu dishes, ritualized as is Thanksgiving dinner in the United States. Less highly regarded traditional dishes drop out; less well known ones are forgotten; but a highly formalized core persists. Often such dishes are cooked more elaborately than they were in the homeland, as if to make up for the loss of many less canonical meals.

Chinese overseas usually retain their diet longer and more faithfully than do many immigrant groups. This is true not only in the Western world, where the wide gap in diets might make adjustment more difficult, but even in Southeast Asia, where diets are quite like Chinese. Ethnic sentiments may have something to do with this. In Malaysia, where Chinese settlement goes back more than five hundred years, though most Chinese are descendants of immigrants in the last century and a half, the Chinese communities in which I lived had picked up many Malay dietary customs over the centuries (Anderson and Anderson 1972). Curries and spices, small sticky cakes, and other food items were examples of a fusion of Chinese and Malaysian cuisine that was often impossible to untangle. A syncretic style known as Nonya cooking (*nonya* is a Malay word for a Chinese lady) had arisen. But serious ethnic tension between Chinese and Malays in the 1960s and 1970s led to widespread abandonment of this style and anything else smacking of Malay influence. The Chinese turned, in food as in other folkways, away from what they associated with people they considered their oppressors. A similar process may have caused the abandonment of dairy products in the late medieval period.

In the United States, Chinese acculturate faster in dispersed situations than if they have a Chinatown at hand, and they acculturate faster if they have school-age children. Peer group pressure on children leads to insistence that the family eat instant cereal and so forth. Wang Chun-hua and I found that in Riverside, California, where the Chinese community is small and dispersed, major changes in diet occurred in only five years.[6] In San Francisco, by contrast, where the Chinese community is large, solid, and constantly renewed by immigration, generations may pass before an equivalent amount of change is seen in a family's foodways. Archeological investigations of the Chinatown that once existed in Riverside show that it was a powerful conservative force. From raising local turtles for food to selling liquors and pickles from the homeland, its stores worked to provide a traditional dietary selection. Today, families go to Chinatown in Los Angeles to shop, but this is a major expedition. And there is the constant pressure from the surrounding Anglo society. Ethnicity's outward manifestations decay and a change of self-image and personal identity is inevitable. For the Chinese, perhaps more than for any other group, food is a central feature of ethnicity, a basic statement about what one *is* (see Grivetti and Paquette 1978; Langlois 1972; Yang and Fix 1979).

Afterword

When I went to Hong Kong to study fishery development in 1965–66, I held the view that people produce food for one very obvious reason—to eat—and that in studying development I had only to see what cultural and institutional constraints were holding back the producers. This model worked well enough. In Malaysia in 1970–71, all was not so simple. Wider political considerations intervened; the Malay-dominated government, for instance, was so deeply antagonistic to the Chinese that it was willing to sacrifice development of sectors that were Chinese-dominated, including the modern fishery. I thus learned how deeply and directly government policy—including policy that has nothing to do with food production—can affect the food economy. I also saw that the demand structure of the economy is enormously important and not predictable from simple nutritional considerations. Some fish were incredibly expensive in Malaysia; others that seemed to me better both in nutrition and taste were unsalable. (This was nice for me; I got them free from the fishermen.) Subsequent field work in Hong Kong and China convinced me that, while people produce food primarily so that they and others can eat and survive, they also take into account medical beliefs, social communication, and aesthetics.

These last three matters are inextricably intertwined. Aesthetic preferences are very often determined by the other two considerations. Foods that are considered "good for you" become associated with status—they are often expensive, for example—and are then liked in accordance with the human rule that people can learn to like almost anything considered a mark of high status.

Any agricultural system is under pressure to diversify and to take full advantage of microenvironmental variation: this is the ecologically sound route. But there are even greater pressures to simplify and produce only the one or two high-yielding crops—normally bulk starches of low vitamin and mineral value—to streamline farming and maximize calorie yield per acre. This leads to an ecologically unstable and nutritionally unsound agriculture, a trap all too easy to fall into. China was unable to avoid the trap entirely; there arose monoculture of rice in the south and wheat or other dryland grains in most of the north. But enough variety was maintained, largely because of the three considerations noted, to prevent the desperate situation of, say, Ireland in the 1840s.

My study of Chinese history started with a couple of theories: (1) China's teeming millions had forced an intensive, fine-tuned agriculture on the country; (2) market forces—the "invisible hand"—had led to intensification automatically. Both turned out to be wrong. Intensification in China developed before population became dense. Population growth did lead to further intensification, but once China crossed the hundred million barrier, population size and density became as much a problem as an aid. Agricultural development began in the north, ceased as that filled, and continued in the more open south until that too grew dense. Rising numbers thus actually inhibited development. As to market forces, they were never allowed to work automatically; the hand of the government was thoroughly visible throughout.

In short, China's agriculture took the shape it did because of deliberate, explicit government policies. These remained as a steady foundation on which each dynasty rang its changes, and they are still recognizable throughout East Asia today.

Urban agglomerations, which can rise and fall rapidly, do not guarantee agricultural development. They can exist by depending in large part on long-distance importing of foods, like imperial Rome, and by forcing the masses to subsist on minimal amounts of food, as often occurred in poorer regions of China. The kind of wealth and food productivity that Marco Polo saw in Hangchou is not a mere function of urbanization or trade; it presupposes a long history of conscious planning. This came primarily from the Legalist tradition, but other inputs also figured. For the Confucians, farming produced food, the basis of life; other production was mere luxury, and nonproductive enterprises like trade and banking were downright parasitic. For the Taoists, the subsistence-farming community was the ideal: simple, natural, and free.

The other vitally important piece of the picture was a serious governmental awareness of the need for information. In the T'ang Dynasty, we find a humorous protest (by Liu Tsung-yuan in the persona of Camelback Kuo the Gardener) against the extreme oversolicitousness of officials, who drove the peasants crazy with constant advice! We have also a multitude of family manuals compiled by estate owners for their households and descendants, beginning (as far as we have record) with the Ts'ui's excellent *Ssu-min Yueh-ling* in late Han. One may hope for a great transformation of world conscience such that no one seeks profit and everyone works for sweet charity, but until that millennial day, it is useless to talk of "food for people, not for profit." Farmers too have to eat, and so do foodsellers; they have more right than most of us to enjoy the fruits of their labors.

The efficient division of labor set the framework and provided the infrastructure for successive governments. Overmanaging, whether in Sung or in Mao's China of the 1970s, produced disaster, but unrestrained private enterprise led to monopolism and exploitation. The government did best when it acted as quiet arbiter—the withdrawn ruler of Taoist writings—in a world of relatively small and relatively independent producers and distributors. Neither capitalist nor socialist extremes work well in practice, if the goal is coupling productivity with public welfare.

In the end, the most important lesson I learned from the development of China's food system is that not only man, but bread, does not live by bread alone. Ideology (both public and personal), human emotions and errors vie with rational calculus in determining behavior. Only rarely do people create such glorious syntheses as the Chinese system; all praise to the millions, named and unnamed, who have done so! Their accomplishments—and the accomplishments of all those who have fed humanity, the masses of India and Mexico, of France and Finland—are as brilliant as those of poets and artists, and perhaps even more useful. "With the deepest reverence," I think of emperors Wen and Ching, of T'ao Hung-ching and Li Shih-ch'en, and of a billion peasants whose names are lost in the black flow of time. Thanks to them, we are alive today, and we may even hope to see our children and children's children survive.

✌ Appendix:
✌ Dinner at the Ngs

It may be useful to take a look at one very traditional Chinese family at table.

In 1974–75 Marja Anderson and I returned to our old field home of Castle Peak Bay, Hong Kong, to carry out field research on Chinese food production and consumption. As part of the research, we kept a record of food consumption by our good friends and next-door neighbors the Ng family. In our earlier fieldwork in 1965–66 we had studied the boat-dwelling fishermen of the area. Most of the boat people have gone on shore now. We rented a room in the house of an old friend and informant, Mr. Chan; he and his family were rarely at home, so our nearest observable neighbors were the Ngs, who rented a small house in the same compound from Mr. Chan. The Ng family consisted of a former boat man now moved on shore, his wife, their children, and often a relative or two, usually the mother of one or the other parent. Mr. Ng worked at a fish-assembling market that bought fish from the fishermen and resold them to urban wholesale marketers in Kowloon twenty miles away. He never left the Castle Peak area on his job, but he worked long hours, usually from about six A.M. to nine P.M. or more. It was a rare treat and cause for a family celebration when he could come home early enough to eat with the younger children. The family was close, warm, and happy; mealtimes, especially with father, were times of relaxed happiness and sociability.

Most of our food consumption studies in Hong Kong were based on interviewing or interviewing plus observation, but to see what the Ngs ate we used observation alone unless we had a specific question. Over a period of five months, we observed about half the main meals (lunches and dinners) eaten (152 out of about 300). (For the other meals either the Ngs or we went out to eat.) During this time we also observed a vast and uncounted number of snacks, including breakfasts. Mr. Ng was usually gone before the children got up, and on special occasions (including most days when he stayed home later than usual) the Ngs went out to breakfast as Cantonese so love to do, so we never saw a real formal breakfast there—the morning meal was an impromptu affair with the children snacking on bread or the like. We recorded seventeen snacks, but we missed the vast majority of them or saw only part of the eating transaction and did not bother to record it. Someone in the house, usually everyone, had some sort of snack every day, in addition to breakfast. Snack foods recorded were *cha shao pao* (flour buns stuffed with roast pork filling), raisin bread, white bread with margarine, cookies, candy, small cakes, gum, and fruit (usually oranges but also apples, bananas, dried persimmons, grapes, tangerines and mandarin oranges, etc.). Breakfast and more substantial snacks often involved a bowl of rice with soy sauce. The children often bought candy, minor meat snacks such as tiny sausages, or buns from local vendors. Fruit was the major snack, however, although breakfast always involved some starch (rice, bread, or buns).

During all but the coldest days, everyone ate outside, the houses being small. The Ngs and the Andersons watched each other eat, noted what was being eaten, and asked about each other's more exotic foodways. (We lived Chinese style and ate more or less Chinese food, so there were few exotic foodways for the Ngs to see.) Our three children proved most valuable to our fieldwork. Laura and Alan were the same age as two of the Ng children and quickly formed close friendships with them and the rest of the family. They had entrée to all situations, including meals in the inner sanctums of the house where no nonfamily adults could politely enter, and they thus observed many snacks we missed. The Ng and Anderson children also continually shared food, mostly fruit.

The advantage of a purely observational approach—especially when helped by seven- and ten-year-old children—is that it produces a far more accurate record of what is actually eaten than do interviews, which are necessarily less accurate especially as to cooking method and minor ingredients. The disadvantage to observation is that one has to estimate quantities. But we did not need exact quantities, since we were interested in what people ate, not in nutritional levels (all the Ngs were clearly well-nourished and ate healthful food, and we were not specializing in nutrition). The quantity problem was made easier by the fact that food was usually bought by weight; ½ or 1 catty was the normal quantity (a catty is 1⅓ pounds). This was not true of fish or chicken bought whole, however. Most of the protein eaten came from fish that Mr. Ng acquired on the job, and this perquisite of his labors was weighed inexactly if at all. Also, weights of food bought and cooked would give a very inadequate picture of what anyone actually ate. Everyone ate different amounts from the common dish, and often much was left over, placed in the refrigerator and nibbled on later. Such nibbling was impossible to record. Rarely was a dish completely eaten at one sitting, unless it was something the children loved; but dishes never lasted more than a day. The refrigerator, a very recent addition to such working-class households of Hong Kong as the Ngs', was a supremely useful thing to have, but a bane to the anthropologist. However, we were allowed to use it ourselves, so we or more usually our children would make a point of checking it often to see what the Ngs were using it for.

The Ngs, boat people (even though now living on shore) from fishermen's families, ate a great deal of fish. They also ate rice at every real meal—in fact, a meal, here as elsewhere in East Asia, was defined as an occasion where rice was eaten with side dishes (*sung*). The adults and two older children ate one or one and a half bowls of rice at lunch, each bowl filled with 8 ounces (volume measure) of rice or a bit more, and two bowls at dinner; the younger children ate about one bowl at each meal, down to and including the baby (two and a half years old). A good deal of soy sauce went onto this rice, and often rice and soy was a snack by itself. Noodles made a rarer snack (we recorded 7 occasions).

The most important sung by weight was vegetables. At every meal except very small ones (e.g., if almost everyone was at work or at school), about 1–2 catties of vegetables were cooked up. Mustard greens were the most often used (main ingredients in fifteen dishes and several soups, a minor ingredient in several other dishes). These are the commonest vegetables in Hong Kong, and very popular. During the coldest part of the year, Peking cabbage was common (16 meals), almost always boiled with pork or fish or shrimp to make a rather soupy dish. It is strictly seasonal. A little later, lettuce came into season (8 meals; it was boiled with animal foods). Tomatoes, white radish, potatoes, bok choy, carrots, kaai choi (another kind of mustard green), bean sprouts, and pickled vegetables (of indeterminate species in the genus *Brassica* or near relatives) appeared at a few meals each (3–5 or so). Once boiled yam (*Dioscorea alata*, not sweet potato) appeared, and once Chinese arrowroot. Luffa gourd appeared once, in soup. Cauliflower, taro, and snow peas appeared once each in fancy feast dishes on holidays. The reliance on *Brassicaceae*—including the cabbages, mustard greens, and white radish—is notable; one or another species of this family appeared almost every day. Since the Chinese *Brassicaceae* include what are perhaps the most highly nutritious vegetables eaten commonly in the world, rich in vitamins A and C, iron, other minerals, and folic acid, this was a good feature of the diet.

The standard everyday condiment in the diet was salt fish. Depending on how many people were eating, about 2–6 ounces were steamed in the closed vessel in which rice was cooked, the fish resting on the rice in a small shallow dish. This amount served for the entire day. The adults, especially the women, used most of it. The children did not like it especially but ate tiny bits to add salt and flavor to the food. Salt fish appeared at no less than 111 of the 152 meals and may have been eaten more often than that, since we probably missed it a few times (occasionally it was not brought out, for instance, but snacked on from the icebox). Most of the exceptions were special meals: salt fish was considered too ordinary for most such affairs.

Fresh fish appeared steamed (usually small fish were steamed over rice) 51 times, stir-fried 16 times, minced and formed into sheets, balls or paste 3 times, and also in many mixed boiled dishes—twice in festal dishes, once in soup, and many times to flavor boiled greens. Only a few festal days were without fish. Two meals included steamed, stir-fried, and salt fish. Fish was steamed with pickled soybeans, ginger, oil, green onions, or other "defishers" or "fish flavors." Stir-frying of the tougher, stronger-flavored fish usually involved pickled soybeans and garlic. Fresh fish was liked by all. Usually the fish consisted of small and cheap varieties that Mr. Ng got at work; about ½ to 1½ catties per day were eaten.

Meat always meant pork. There were 79 servings of pork (counting multiple appearances at the same meal). The commonest form was small salami-like sausages made with Chinese grain in alcohol and called *laap cheung* (dried sausage). These were used only in cold weather; they began to appear about the middle of October and became almost daily adjuncts to the meal from November on (seen at 37 meals, probably missed a few times). One or two per day were steamed, cut up, and eaten as a sort of relish with food. The adults liked them; the children did not especially since they were very greasy. Rarely did anyone eat as much as an ounce at a meal.

More substantial quantities of fresh pork (or in one case liver) were eaten at 56 meals, about ½ catty bought at a time. More exactly, ½ catty was the standard ration except on festive occasions, when a catty might be bought, or more for company. Sometimes only ¼ catty was bought to flavor the blander sorts of vegetables. Usually the pork was lean, but almost as often—14 times—it was in the form of *p'aai kuat* ("ranked bones" or "bones arranged in ranks," i.e., spareribs). These are quite fatty and were not greatly loved by the children, who did not like greasy food; thus, only small quantities were eaten. They were usually steamed with pickled soybeans, garlic, and/or similar strong flavorings. Much less pork was used than fish, and a lot of fat and/or bone was discarded, so pork contributed far less to the diet than fish.

Chicken marked a festive meal. A bit might be bought for company, but at every major festival there was a whole chicken or more. Chicken appeared at 19 meals. Usually it was boiled; on very festive occasions it was prepared in various ways— some boiled by itself; the less choice parts boiled with other foods; some of the choicer parts fried. On the major festivals both chicken and pork were consumed, along with mushrooms (never seen otherwise) and other expensive vegetables such as the one occurrence of cauliflower. In Hong Kong, chicken is self-consciously used as a marker of a festive occasion, and mushrooms also are always classed as very special. Another festive food—seen twice, at minor occasions—was glutinous rice dumpling with meat bits in it, known as *lo maai faan*. Oysters once and lobster twice assisted at other minor festivities. Roast pork and roast duck occurred very rarely in very small quantities on minor occasions.

Eggs were moderately important in the diet. Both chicken and duck eggs were used, more often the former. Salted and dried egg yolks appeared twice each, at very casual lunches when few people were home. More important and popular were egg-and-meat dishes: a sort of stew of egg, minced meat, tomato, and green onion or a custard flavored with meats—especially strong-flavored items such as dried shrimp and squid—and soy sauce. This dish was very popular with the children, indeed about their favorite everyday fare.

The ordinary seasoning for food was soy sauce. Salt by itself was never used, nor were pepper or spices. On very rare occasions salt might be added to food, but almost invariably it was in the form of soy sauce and/or salt fish. Ginger, green onions, garlic, pickled black soybeans, and cooking oil were the only other things added to the food, except for a few cashew nuts in pork dishes for major festivals. To Westerners used to a lot of salt, pepper, MSG and the like in Cantonese food, I will mention that the Ngs were typical of traditional Cantonese households in this respect: free salt is hardly used and pepper, MSG, spices, and so on simply do not exist. People encounter them only when eating out and are not at all enthusiastic about them. For most South Chinese, soybean products are the everyday flavoring agent, with ginger a close second; the boat people add salt fish as a standard food used to add flavor.

Food was usually prepared by boiling or steaming. The rice was boiled; so were the vegetables, either in soup or in a watery boil-up with varying amounts of meat or fish. One or the other of these soupy dishes was always found at the normal meal. The bowl was filled at the end of the meal with this liquid, the last of the rice and so on incorporated in the soup, and all eaten. Like many—perhaps most—Cantonese, the Ngs did not drink tea except on social occasions, and of course they did not drink plain water. (The local water supply was unsafe, and Cantonese in general avoid plain water when possible.) Thus soup, often very watery, provided the main liquid intake.

Steaming was done in small shallow dishes on top of the rice: a one-dish meal could be prepared by steaming some fish in one dish, some salt fish in another, and a bit of vegetable in a third, all above the rice in one big closed container. The only other method of cooking was stir-frying (chaoing—some variants of stir-frying involve more or less oil and/or more or less water). An ordinary meal always included at least two dishes to eat with the rice, and usually three—ideally one steamed dish, one boiled soupy dish, and one chaoed dish, but there was no effort to conform to this pattern when convenience or cheap ingredients dictated otherwise. On festal occasions there were up to ten dishes, plus great quantities of fruit and other sweet small eats.

The determinants of this diet were many and various. Cost loomed large; small fish, salt fish, and the usual vegetables were all cheap. Yet root crops were avoided although they are the cheapest of vegetables; a good deal of pork and sausage were eaten although these were very expensive by the Ngs' standards; the seasonings used were no cheaper than the seasonings that were not; and of course everyone splurged on festivals. Family preference patterns were probably the next most important determinant. The Ngs (like most Cantonese) liked cabbage-type vegetables and hated root crops, especially yams. They all liked eggs, especially the children. The adults liked salt fish and sausage, although the children did not. Everyone loved fruit, especially oranges; the children in particular showing an almost miraculous ability to stow these away (as do almost all Hong Kong children). The Ngs all liked fish. Like most boat people, they had been raised on fish—on the boats, rice, fish, and the commonest seasonings make up most of the diet—and fish seemed almost as indispensable as rice to them. During the New Year season when they do not fish, boat people develop a real craving for fresh fish and are often reduced to jigging desperately for minnows in the harbor. (Robert Randall told me of the same "fish hunger" as a common and recognized cultural pattern among the Samal fishermen of the south Philippines, and I have found the same thing among British Columbia coastal Indians.) Only during festivals did the Ngs miss fish for a day.

Special occasions provided a source of variation in the diet. Chicken was obligatory at festivals, virtually untouched otherwise. Use of cashew nuts, mushrooms, and the rarer fruits, nuts, and vegetables was even more restricted; they appeared only at the biggest and most religiously important festivals. A lot of pork—as opposed to very small quantities—almost always meant festivity, especially when cooked in large amounts with mixed vegetables. The special importance of chicken and pork for such occasions is a sort of spin-off from their use in sacrifices; no major sacrifice rite is complete without chickens and/or swine; thus the meats thereof became associated with festal occasions even when no sacrifices occurred. The other items are festal only because they are expensive and different from everyday fare.

Medicine rarely entered into the Ngs' diets. They tried to balance hot and cooling foods (in the humoral medical system) and avoided foods believed poisonous or unhealthy, but they made no special point of it, since they were almost always in robust health. When an adult was feeling weak or "poorly," a little chicken long-stewed with strengthening medicinal herbs appeared (2 occasions were noted).

In addition to festal and health considerations, ordinary socializing entailed varying the fare. Soft drinks and tea, fruit and cookies, pork and especially time-consuming dishes, and for every special entertainment a chicken, were markers of significant social events; they are listed here in order of their importance as markers and thus of the importance of the social transactions they mark.

Much of the variety and excitement of the diet came from eating out, and the most important and significant social-eating transactions were also carried out in restaurants, so we missed these—thus more or less "cutting the head off" our survey, since we saw none of the most highly prized and highly liked meals except the main festivals. What we got was a good view of ordinary, everyday fare.

The Ngs ate extremely well for their money but did not skimp—they spent a higher percentage of their budget on food than a comparable American family would, and they did so because they wanted to: festal foods, pork, and eating out were more important to them than, say, better housing (their house was small and crowded), fancier appliances, or other alternative uses of the money. The Ngs were very well nourished, thanks to the spectacular richness in protein, vitamins, and minerals of the fish, soy products, and *Brassicaceae* that bulked large in the diet; pork, oranges, and other vegetables added their benefits to this dominant triad. Candy and cookies were uncommon; luxury meant more meat and vegetables, not more sweets.

Some other provisional conclusions can be drawn from this dietary. First, virtually all food eaten was native to China and northern Southeast Asia. Except for peanut oil used in cooking, New World and western Eurasian or African foods counted for very little indeed and made absolutely no significant contribution to the diet or nutrition. The only such food of any importance was wheat—in noodles, bread and buns, as well as cookies and crackers—hardly a recent borrowing (it spread from West Asia perhaps four or five thousand years ago). Among foods themselves (by contrast with ingredients or foodstuffs), these wheat products were the only borrowings of significance except for candy, soft drinks, and a few other sweet snacks. The Westernization of the Hong Kong diet is proceeding by way of white flour and white sugar, but among the Ngs it had not proceeded far. The poorer boat people of the rural New Territories are perhaps the most traditional—at least in diet—of anyone in Hong Kong, and their dietary reflects conditions of a thousand years ago.

In the Ngs' diet, the importance of steaming and boiling, and of soup and greens, should be noted. There is as yet no thorough study of Chinese eating patterns. Most Westerners and nutritionists seem to think of stir-frying, animal products, and bean curd as more important than they usually are—to say nothing of spices, sweet-sour dishes and such.

The importance of social and festive occasions, and their frequency, was also slightly surprising; these were important in causing the Ngs to spend a higher percentage of their budget on food than I believe most Western families would do. I was surprised to find personal likings and ancient traditions bulking so large, but usually the Ngs ate what was cheapest and most easily available.

And they were as wonderful neighbors as anyone could hope to have! Love to them all.

Notes

1 The land in one county, ca. 1228, was used thus (Shiba 1970):

	mu
Low irrigated paddy fields	39,545
Intermediate paddy fields	178,145
Hillside mulberry land	17,933
Level dry fields	35,705
Hillside dry fields	29,064
Bamboo groves	8,288
Dwarf bamboos	8,322
(Peasants') dwellings	15,222
Ponds	28,393
Miscellaneous trees	58,385
Tung-nut and fruit trees	15,699
Firewood forests	508,935
Unplanted farmland	24,685
Graves	8,013
Tea lands	146
Lime quarries	280
	Chang (Frontage)
Urban sites	20,826

Each of the ten categories of urban land seems to have been subdivided into three subcategories according to quality.

2 Several Jurchen recipes have been translated by Herbert Franke (1975:172–77). They deserve wider currency and are reprinted here, renumbered and slightly corrected. The vegetables are traditional to North China—the Chinese had in large part abandoned mallow and smartweed by this time. The underlined words are Jurchen names for the dishes, now untranslatable. "Earth pepper" is identified by Franke as *Geum japonicum*.

1. Jurchen Quail *sa-sun*

The quails are boiled until thoroughly cooked. Remove spine and bones. Chop (meat) into fine hash. Cut fine several pounds of smartweed (*Polygonum*) leaves. Mix thoroughly with bean-sauce. Prepare a juice with ground mustard, mix juice with very hot water. Season with a pinch of salt, then put into wooden pot; for serving fill into wooden bowls.

2. Jurchen Rice-gruel with Meat Hash

Take a sheep's head, boil until thoroughly soft. Pick off (meat) by hand, remove bones, and put (meat) aside together with juice. Fill mutton-tail fat mixed with sesame oil into metal pan that has been rinsed and cleaned. Fry (in pan) washed glutinous rice, let soak for a short time, then add sheep's head juice, wait until the whole is softened to a pulp. Put soft sheep's head into bowls; for serving fill these up (with the gruel soup).

3. *Ssu-la* Mallow Cold Soup

Remove the bark from the mallows. The soft interior with smaller leaves three or four inches long is then boiled until seven tenths cooked. Add again mallow leaves and let thoroughly cook. Spread out separately selected stemmed leaves that have been rinsed in cold water, arrange like the pattern of a Spring Plate, the central leaves facing each other on all four sides. Put in between shredded chicken meat and skin, shredded ginger, shredded yellow cucumber, shredded bamboo-shoots, shredded lettuce stems, shredded vegetables and shredded half-bred duck's eggs, mutton tongue, kidneys, intestines, meat with skin from head and feet, all shredded. Use meat juice and strained polygonum soup, add a sprinkle of wild red currants.

4. Steamed Mutton *Mei-Po*

Take a whole sheep, scald and clean, and remove head, feet, intestines, etc., cut up into manageable pieces. Prepare small specimens of earth-pepper with wine and vinegar, pour over the meat and let soak for two hours or more. Put into empty metal pot, build a fire with fuel-wood sticks and seal the lid with clay. Light the fire but let it not come too close. Wait until well-cooked. To be served in bowls with original juice separately.

5. *T'a-pu-la* Duck

Take a big specimen, scald, clean, remove intestines. Mix elm-seed (?) sauce and meat broth with oil in which onions have been fried, pour the whole juice into pot with some pepper-corns. Afterwards put in duck, let become well-cooked on slow fire, cut to pieces and serve filled up with soup. Geese and chicken are prepared in the same way.

6. Pheasant *sa-sun*

Boil thoroughly, use the breast meat and cut into hash. Take a few smart-weed leaves and cut them into small pieces. Mix into a juice with soy-sauce. Add powdered mustard and salt according to taste. Serve in wooden bowl. Quails are prepared in the same way.

7. Persimmon Pastry

One peck (*tou*) of glutinous rice and fifty big dried persimmons are ground together into a paste. Add dried boiled jujube paste and pass all this through a hair-sieve. Steam in a pot until well cooked. Add pine-seeds, walnut kernels and pound, form dumplings, sprinkle with honey before eating.

8. Korean Chestnut Pastry

Chestnuts, no matter whether many or few, are dried in the shadow, the husks removed, and pounded into a powder. Mix this evenly with two thirds of the amount with glutinous rice. Soak with honey-water, steam thoroughly and eat.

Gloss: Jurchen dumpling soup is the same as Mohammedan dumpling soup. Therefore they are not repeated here.

3   Marco Polo's accounts of China are too well known to warrant further attention, but a word needs to be said about his reliability. John Haeger, among others, has questioned whether Marco saw as much as we usually assume (pers. comm.). There is no question that he relied on others' accounts—usually reliable ones, but sometimes rumors—for his descriptions of some remote, off-route places, including Burma, interior Indonesia, parts of the Near East, and so on. The question is where his observations leave off and his second-hand data begin. Haeger thinks that all his accounts of South China may be cribbed directly or indirectly from Chinese geographies and gazeteers and that Marco may not even have gone back by the southern sea route. I would not be so drastic, but it does seems highly unlikely that Marco took the southwestern route he describes into Yunnan and Burma. He writes of it as if at second hand. Several Chinese cities of the north center and of the southeast (on Marco's Hangchow–Canton route) are described so cursorily and in such a stereotyped way that one must either agree with Haeger or surmise that Marco passed through them very quickly. On the other hand, the similarities of Marco's account of Hangchow to Chinese records are due to the fact that both were describing the same place from similar points of view; it does not seem to represent outright cribbing. Marco was probably not the regnant official of Yangchow, as he claimed (later accounts make him governor of the whole lower Yangtze, but this is absurd): I believe that Marco's amanuensis, Rusiciano (Rustichello), who copied Marco's account while they were in prison together, is responsible for the misinformation, adding a bit of glory by changing the words "an official" to "the governor." For his part, Marco never talks as if he had been vested with high authority. Given the Mongols' eagerness to hire all se-mu of any worth, it would have been almost incredible that Marco would *not* have had some sort of post while in China.

    For evidence of Marco's qualities as an observer, it is necessary only to direct the reader to his account of the cranes of Central Asia (Yule and Cordier 1903:1:206) —so clear and concise that it permits easy identification of the precise species of these remote and difficult to view birds. (As a veteran North American crane watcher, I can confirm many of Yule's identifications.) Marco as a political observer can be judged by his pithy comment on Southern Sung: it was "very strong by nature, and all the cities are encompassed by sheets of water of great depth, and more than an arblastshot in width; so that the country never would have been lost, had the people but been soldiers. But that is just what they were not; so lost it was" (2:145). Oversimplified, but a shrewd comment. Of Yüan food, Marco tells us a good deal, all of it confirmed by others. The importance of dairy products, especially horse milk, is clear. Dried skim milk was a staple (1:262). Wine is described as being made of rice and flavored with spices (1:441). The luxury of the Great Kaan's table service is described (1:381–83), and from Marco's note on the Yüan planting of shade trees, it seems that the Great Kaan was as industrious as the modern People's Republic in lining the highways with them. (The idea, for the Mongols, was a Persian borrowing.) Marco notes the sharp contrast between the Central Asian influenced north and the refractory south in choice of foods: in the south "they eat every kind of flesh, even that of dogs and other unclean beasts, which nothing would induce a Christian to eat" (2:187). The importance of the salt monopoly is stressed.

Marco retells the stories about cannibalism (2:235), which sound suspiciously like part of the fictional lore that eventually fed into the *Shui Hu Chuan*. This and other novels portray the Chinese of Sung and Yüan eating human flesh with enthusiastic abandon. But, as mentioned, there is no reliable evidence that Chinese ate human flesh except during desperate famines or in small quantities for medicine or revenge. The human flesh shop crops up often in Chinese stories, but it is purely fictional. Perhaps someone, somewhere, tried this dubious means of making money, but such a business surely could not have been viewed with the cheerful moral indifference of the *Shui Hu Chuan*—a book whose astonishing unconcern with murder and mayhem is comprehensible only in terms of the totalitarian, brutal society of late Yüan and Ming.

4   Chinese dishes are often imaginatively named. The apogee was reached, I should think, in a menu in a Chinese restaurant in Malaysia, on which occurred the following:

Victorious Chicken
Technicolour Cold Chicken
Sapphire Chicken
Seven Stars Accompanying Full Moon
Three Musketeers amidst Bamboo Shoots
Fried Crab Balls with Phoenix's Liver
Birds' Nest of the Southern Mountain
Crispy Pigeons of the Apricot Blossoms
Pregnant Phoenix by Dragon Fetus
Swallow Nests of the Count
Dragon's Eyeballs with Phoenix's Eyes
Happy-Go-Lucky
Spring Blossom and Autumn Moon
Seven Stars Shining over the Joyful Steamboat

(Quoted in *Far Eastern Economic Review*, June 16, 1983, p. 41).

5   The information given in chapter 10 is not intended to preempt the excellent detailed accounts of Chinese regional cuisines found in such books as F. T. Cheng, *Musings of a Chinese Gourmet* (1954) or the many cookbooks of Chinese food. Cookbooks range a good deal in quality and in faithfulness to Chinese tradition. The following is a

random selection from the better ones; I have not listed older cookbooks or those of limited availability or local distribution, so many excellent cookbooks are left out of the following list. Some of the best currently available sources for regional dishes are: Buwei Yang Chao, *How to Cook and Eat in Chinese* (Chao 1947); Kenneth Lo, *Encyclopedia of Chinese Cooking* (1979a), *Chinese Regional Cooking* (1979b) and *Peking Cooking* (1971). Among other cookbooks listing regional dishes are: Pearl Kong Chen, Tien Chi Chen and Rose Tseng, *Everything You Want to Know about Chinese Cooking* (1983); Nobuko Sakamoto, *The People's Republic of China Cookbook* (1977), which is fascinating in its translations of modern Chinese books; Mai Leung, *The Chinese People's Cookbook* (1979) which covers ingredients, terms and "street eats," and is also issued under the more descriptive title, *Dim Sum and Other Chinese Street Food*. Less clearly regional, but collectively the best guide in English to Chinese food, are Stella Lou Fessler's three books: *Chinese Meatless Cooking* (1980), *Chinese Seafood Cookery* (1981); *Chinese Poultry Cookery* (1982). There are, of course, cookbooks in Chinese for every style and region, but citation seems unnecessary here. The best is the series *Ching-kuo Ming Ts'ai Pu* (1963–65). Sakamoto translates several recipes from this. A general recent survey of the food situation in China is: Elizabeth Croll, *The Family Rice Bowl* (1983).

TABLE 1: Western and Chinese Foods Used by Chinese Residents in Riverside, California

	Recent Immigrants (under 5 years)[1] Food reported used:			
FOODS	DAILY	WEEKLY-OFTEN	SOMETIMES	NEVER OR ALMOST NEVER
Chinese				
pork	6	9	1	0
rice	13	3	0	0
tea	6	5	1	4
noodles	1	12	2	0
sweet potatoes	0	0	7	9
tofu (bean curd)	2	7	6	1
dried bean curd	1	4	5	6
k'ung hsin ts'ai	1	1	3	11
k'u kua (bitter melon)	1	1	2	12
bamboo shoots	1	4	5	6
ginger	10	5	1	0
small white cabbage	1	3	1	11
dried radish	1	6	6	3
muai (rice porridge)	1	8	3	4
yard-long bean	1	2	2	11
winter melon	1	1	4	10
Western				
hamburger	0	3	1	12
bread	7	3	2	4
coffee	3	2	5	6
spaghetti	0	3	2	11
white potatoes	0	3	5	8
cheese	3	3	1	9
milk	12	3	1	0
salad	1	5	3	7
hot dogs	0	3	3	10
tacos	0	0	0	16
TV dinners	0	0	1	15
steak[3]	0	4	3	9
canned soup	0	3	5	8
pie	0	2	9	5
doughnuts	0	3	4	9
dry breakfast cereal	3	2	1	10

TABLE 1 *(continued)*

| Foods | Long-term Residents (more than 5 years)[2] Food reported used: | | | |
	DAILY	WEEKLY-OFTEN	SOMETIMES	NEVER OR ALMOST NEVER
Chinese				
pork	5	7	1	0
rice	6	6	0	1
tea	8	4	1	0
noodles	1	12	0	0
sweet potatoes	0	1	5	7
tofu (bean curd)	0	10	3	0
dried bean curd	0	2	6	5
k'ung hsin ts'ai	0	2	4	7
k'u kua (bitter melon)	0	0	5	8
bamboo shoots	1	5	4	2
ginger	8	4	1	0
small white cabbage	1	0	9	3
dried radish	0	3	7	3
muai (rice porridge)	0	6	6	1
yard-long bean	0	2	7	4
winter melon	0	0	10	3
Western				
hamburger	0	3	5	5
bread	8	3	2	0
coffee	5	1	2	5
spaghetti	2	2	5	4
white potatoes	0	4	5	4
cheese	2	7	2	2
milk	11	1	0	1
salad	2	5	2	3
hot dogs	0	4	6	3
tacos	1	0	3	9
TV dinners	0	1	5	7
steak[3]	1	7	3	2
canned soup	1	7	3	2
pie	0	4	5	4
doughnuts	0	6	4	3
dry breakfast cereal	5	5	2	1

[1] n = 16
[2] n = 13
[3] Several of the "steak" responses probably refer to steak cut into strips and cooked Chinese style.
Source: Anderson and Wang 1980.

Bibliography

An Zhimin. 1982. China's Neolithic Period. *China Reconstructs* (June 1982):58–62.

Anderson, E. N., Jr. 1980. Heating and Cooling Foods in Hong Kong and Taiwan. *Social Science Information* 19:237–68.

———. 1982. Ecology and Ideology in Chinese Folk Nutritional Therapy. Paper, American Anthropological Association, Annual Meeting.

———. 1984. Heating and Cooling Foods Re-Examined. *Social Science Information* 23, 4/5:755–73.

———. 1987. The First Green Revolution: Chinese Agriculture in the Han Dynasty. Paper, Society for Economic Anthropology, Annual Conference.

———. 1987. Why Is Humoral Medicine So Popular? *Social Science and Medicine* 25, 4:331–37.

Anderson, E. N., Jr., and Marja L. Anderson. 1972. Penang Hokkien Ethnohoptology. *Ethnos* 1-4:134–47.

———. 1973. *Mountains and Water: The Cultural Ecology of South Coastal China.* Taipei: Orient Cultural Service.

———. 1978. *Fishing in Troubled Waters.* Taipei: Orient Cultural Service.

Anderson, E. N., Jr., Marja L. Anderson, and John Ho. 1978. Environmental Backgrounds of Young Chinese Nasopharyngeal Carcinoma Patients. De-The and Ito 1978:231–240.

Anderson, E. N., Jr., and Paul Buell. MS. Sorghum in China: A Brief Review.

Anderson, E. N., Jr., and Wang Chun-hua. 1980. Changing Foodways of Chinese Immigrants in Southern California. Paper, Southwestern Anthropological Association, Annual Meeting.

Andersson, J. Gunnar. 1934. *Children of the Yellow Earth.* London: Kegan Paul, Trench, Trubner.

———. 1943. Researches into the Prehistory of the Chinese. *Museum of Far Eastern Antiquities, Bulletin* 15.

Arens, William. 1982. *The Man-Eating Myth.* Oxford: Oxford University Press.

Baker, Hugh. 1979. *Chinese Family and Kinship.* New York: Columbia University Press.

Balasz, Etienne. 1964. *Chinese Civilization and Bureaucracy.* New Haven: Yale University Press.

Barnard, Noel (ed.). 1972. *Early Chinese Art and Its Possible Influence on the Pacific Basin.* New York: Intercultural Arts Press.

Barnard, Noel, and Sato Tamotsu. 1975. *Metallurgical Remains of Ancient China.* Tokyo: Nichiosho.

Basic and Traditional Foods Association. 1979. *Nutrition Scores*. Washington, D.C.: Basic and Traditional Foods Association.

Bastid-Bruguière, Marianne. 1980. Currents of Social Change. Fairbank and Liu 1980: 535–602.

Beattie, Hilary. 1978. *Land and Lineage in China: A Study of T'ung-Ch'eng County, Anhwei, in the Ming and Ch'ing Dynasties*. Cambridge: Cambridge University Press.

Bender, Barbara. 1975. *Farming in Prehistory*. London: A. C. Black.

Benedict, Paul. 1942. Thai, Kadai, and Indonesian: A New Alignment in Southeast Asia. *American Anthropologist* 44:576–601.

Bielenstein, Hans. 1974. The Census of China during the Period 2–742 A.D. *Museum of Far Eastern Antiquities, Bulletin* 19:125–63.

Binford, Lewis, and Chuan Xunho. 1985. Taphonomy at a Distance: Zhoukoudian: The Cave Home of Peking Man? *Current Anthropology* 26:411–42.

Binford, Lewis, and Nancy M. Stone. 1986a. The Chinese Paleolithic: An Outsider's View. *Anthroquest* 35, 1:14–21.

———. 1986b. Zhoukoudian: A Closer Look. *Current Anthropology* 27:453–75.

Bingham, Woodbridge. 1941. *The Founding of the T'ang Dynasty*. Baltimore: American Council of Learned Societies.

Bishop, Carl Whiting. 1933. The Neolithic Age in North China. *Antiquity* 7:389–404.

Blofeld, John. 1985. *The Chinese Art of Tea*. Boston: Shambhala.

Bodde, Derk. 1981. Marshes in Mencius and Elsewhere: A Lexigraphical Note. In *Essays on Chinese Civilization*, pp. 416–25. Princeton: Princeton University Press.

Boserup, Ester. 1965. *The Conditions of Agricultural Growth*. Chicago: Aldine.

———. 1985. The Impact of Scarcity and Plenty on Development. In *Hunger and History*, ed. Robert Rotberg and Theodore Rabb, pp. 185–210. Cambridge: Cambridge University Press.

Boulnois, Louis. 1963. *La route de la Soie*. Paris: Arthaud.

Boxer, C. R. 1953. *South China in the Sixteenth Century*. London: Hakluyt Society.

Boyle, John Andrew. 1977. *The Mongol World Empire*. London: Variorum Reprints.

Braudel, Fernand. 1981. *The Structures of Everyday Life*. New York: Harper and Row.

———. 1982. *The Wheels of Commerce*. New York: Harper and Row.

Bray, Francesca. 1980. Agricultural Technology and Agrarian Change in Han China. *Early China* 5:3–13.

———. 1984. *Science and Civilization in China*, vol. 6, pt. 2: *Agriculture*. Cambridge: Cambridge University Press.

———. 1986. *The Rice Economies*. Cambridge: Cambridge University Press.

Brown, Lester. 1981. World Population Growth, Soil Erosion, and Food Scarcity. *Science* 214:995–1002.

Buchanan, Keith. 1970. *The Transformation of the Chinese Earth*. London: Bell.

Buchanan, Keith, Charles Fitzgerald, and Colin A. Ronan. 1981. *China: The Land and the People; the History, the Art, and the Science*. New York: Crown.

Buck, J. Lossing. 1937. *Land Utilization in China*. Chicago: University of Chicago Press.

Budge, E. A. Wallis. 1928. *The Monks of Kublai Khan*. London: Religious Tracts Society.

Buell, Paul D. 1982. Steppe Perspectives on the Medieval History of China: Modern Mongol Scholarship on the Liao, Chin and Yuan Periods. *Zentralasiatische Studien* 15:129–49.

_____. 1987. Mongolian Foods and Recipes in the *Yin-shan Cheng-yao*: Perspectives on the Changing Foodways of a Pastoral People. Paper, Fifth International Congress of Mongolists.

Cao Xueqin. 1973–86. *The Story of the Stone*, 5 vols, trans. David Hawkes and John Minford. Harmondsworth, Sussex: Penguin.

Chan, Albert. 1982. *The Glory and Fall of the Ming Dynasty*. Norman: University of Oklahoma Press.

Chan, Marie. 1978. *Kao Shih*. Boston: Twayne.

Chang Chung-ching. 1981. *Shang Han Lun*, trans. and ed. Hong-yen Hsu and William Peacher. Los Angeles: Oriental Healing Arts Institute.

Chang Han. 1981. Essay on Merchants. trans. Patricia Ebrey. Ebrey 1981:155–160.

Chang, Kwang-chih. 1975. Ancient Trade as Economics or as Ecology. In Jeremy Sabloff and Carl Lamberg-Karlovsky, eds., *Ancient Civilization and Trade*. Albuquerque: University of New Mexico Press.

_____. 1977a. *The Archaeology of Ancient China*, 3d ed. New Haven: Yale University Press.

_____. 1977b. *Food in Chinese Culture*. New Haven: Yale University Press.

_____. 1979. *Shang Civilization*. New Haven: Yale University Press.

_____. 1983. *Art, Myth and Ritual: The Path to Political Authority in Ancient China*. Cambridge: Harvard University Press.

_____. 1986. *The Archaeology of Ancient China*, 4th ed. New Haven: Yale University Press.

Chang Tien-tse. 1933. *Sino-Portuguese Trade from 1514*. Leiden: Brill.

Chao, Buwei Yang. 1947. *How to Cook and Eat in Chinese*. New York: John Day.

Chao, Kang. 1981. New Data on Land Ownership Patterns in Ming-Ch'ing China—A Research Note. *Journal of Asian Studies* 40, 4:719–34.

_____. 1986. *Man and Land in Chinese History*. Stanford: Stanford University Press.

Chaves, Jonathan. 1975. *Heaven My Blanket, Earth My Pillow*. New York: Columbia University Press.

Chen Chi-yun. 1984. Han Dynasty China; Economy, Society and State Power. *T'oung Pao* 70:127–48.

Chen, Pearl Kong, Tien Chi Chen, and Rose Tseng. 1983. *Everything You Want to Know about Chinese Cooking*. Woodbury: Barons.

Cheng, F. T. 1954. *Musings of a Chinese Gourmet*. London: Hutchinson.

Cheng, Libin. 1936. Are the So-Called Poisonous Food-Combinations Really Poisonous? *Contributions, Biological Laboratory, Science Society of China, Zoological Series* 11, 9:307–16.

Cheng Te-kun. 1959. *Archaeology in China*, vol. 1: *Prehistoric China*. Cambridge: Heffer.

_____. 1960. *Archaeology in China*, vol. 2: *Shang China*. Cambridge: Heffer.

Chia Lan-po. 1975. *The Cave Home of Peking Man*. Beijing: Foreign Languages Press.

Ching-kuo Ming Ts'ai Pu, 11 vols. 1963–65. Peking: People's Republic of China.

Ch'oe Pu. 1965. *A Record of Drifting Across the Sea*, trans. John Meskill. Tucson: University of Arizona Press.

Chou Chin Sheng. 1974. *An Economic History of China*, trans. E. Kaplan. Bellingham: Western Washington University, Dept. of Asian Studies.

Chu Hsi and Lu Tsu-Ch'ien. 1967. *Reflections on Things at Hand*, trans. and ed. Wing-tsit Chan. New York: Columbia University Press.

Ch'u Tung-tsu. 1972. *Han Social Structure*. Seattle: University of Washington Press.

Chung-yao Ta Tzu-tien. 1979. Shanghai: Science Publishers.

Clark, Cyril Drummond LeGros. 1931. *Selections from the Works of Su Tung-p'o*. London: Jonathan Cope.

Cohen, Mark. 1975. *The Food Crisis in Prehistory*. New Haven: Yale University Press.

Conklin, Harold. 1957. *Hanunoo Agriculture*. Rome: FAO.

Cooper, Eugene. 1985. Chinese Table Manners: You Are How You Eat. MS.

Copeland, Edwin Bingham. 1924. *Rice*. London: MacMillan.

Cowgill, George. 1975. On Causes and Consequences of Ancient and Modern Population Changes. *American Anthropologist* 77:505–25.

Croll, Elizabeth. 1983. *The Family Rice Bowl*. Geneva: United Nations.

Crook, David, and Isabel Crook. 1966. *The First Years of Yangyi Commune*. London: Routledge and Kegan Paul.

Crow, Carl. 1937. *400 Million Customers*. New York: Harper and Brothers.

Crowell, William. 1979. Government Land Policies and Systems in Early Imperial China. Ph.D. diss., University of Washington.

Dardess, John W. 1973. *Conquerors and Confucians*. New York: Columbia University Press.

David, Elizabeth. 1986. Spices, Salt and Aromatics in the English Kitchen. Harmondsworth, Sussex: Penguin.

De-The, G., and Y. Ito. 1978. *Nasopharyngeal Carcinoma: Etiology and Control*. Lyon: World Health Organization, International Agency for Research on Cancer.

Dols, Michael. 1977. *The Black Death in the Middle East*. Princeton: Princeton University Press.

Douglas, Mary. 1966. *Purity and Danger*. London: Barrie and Rockliff.

———. 1975. *Implicit Meanings*. London: Routledge and Kegan Paul.

Dubs, Homer. 1938–55. *The History of the Former Han Dynasty*, 3 vols. Baltimore: Waverley Press. This primarily consists of translations of the Pan family's writings.

Durkheim, Emile. 1961. *The Elementary Forms of the Religious Life*. New York: Collier.

Eberhard, Wolfram. 1977. *A History of China*, 4th ed. Berkeley: University of California Press.

Ebrey, Patricia. 1978. *The Aristocratic Families of Early Imperial China: A Case Study of the Po-Ling Ts'ui Family*. Cambridge: Cambridge University Press.

——— (ed.). 1981. *Chinese Civilization and Society*. New York: Free Press.

Edgerton, Clement (trans.). 1939. *The Golden Lotus*. London: Routledge and Sons.

Ekvall, Robert. 1968. *Fields on the Hoof*. New York: Holt, Rinehart and Winston.

Elvin, Mark. 1973. *The Pattern of the Chinese Past*. Stanford: Stanford University Press.

Fairbank, John K. (ed.). 1978. *The Cambridge History of China*, vol. 10: *Late Ch'ing, 1800–1911, Part 1*. Cambridge: Cambridge University Press.

Fairbank, John K., and Kwang-ching Liu (eds.). 1980. *The Cambridge History of China*, vol. 11: *Late Ch'ing, 1800–1911, Part 2*. Cambridge: Cambridge University Press.

Fang Dianchuan and Wei Fan. 1986. Excavating a Lost Culture. *China Reconstructs* (December 1986):33–39.

Farmer, Edward. 1976. *Early Ming Government: The Evolution of Dual Capitals*. Cambridge: Harvard University Press.

Fei Hsiao-tung. 1953. *China's Gentry*. Chicago: University of Chicago Press.

Fessler, Stella Lou. 1980. *Chinese Meatless Cooking*. New York: New American Library.
———. 1981. *Chinese Seafood Cookery*. New York: New American Library.
———. 1982. *Chinese Poultry Cookery*. New York: New American Library.
Feuchtwang, Stephen. 1974. *An Anthropological Analysis of Chinese Geomancy*. Vientiane, Laos: Vithagna.
Fortune, Robert. 1847. *Three Years' Wanderings in the Northern Provinces of China*. London: John Murray.
———. 1857. *A Residence Among the Chinese: Inland, on the Coast, and at Sea*. London: John Murray.
Foster, George. 1965. Peasant Society and the Image of Limited Good. *American Anthropologist* 67:293–315.
Franck, Harry. 1925. *Roving Through Southern China*. New York: Century.
Franke, Herbert. 1975. Chinese Texts on the Jurchen: A Translation of the Jurchen Monograph in the *San-ch'iao Pei-meng Hui-pien*. *Zentralasiatische Studien* 7:1–186.
Freeman, Michael. 1977. Sung. Chang 1977:141–176.
Frodsham, J. 1967. *The Murmuring Stream*. Kuala Lumpur: University of Malaysia.
Fu Pei-Mei. 1969. *Pei Mei's Chinese Cook Book*. Vol. 1. Taipei: Author.
Furer-Haimendorf, Christoph. 1962. *The Apa Tani and Their Neighbors*. London: Routledge and Kegan Paul.
Furth, Charlotte. 1987. Concepts of Pregnancy, Childbirth, and Infancy in Ch'ing Dynasty China. *Journal of Asian Studies* 46, 1:7–35.
Geertz, Clifford. 1963. *Agricultural Involution*. Berkeley: University of California Press.
Gernet, Jacques. 1962. *Daily Life in China on the Eve of the Mongol Invasion*, trans. H. M. Wright. New York: Macmillan.
———. 1982. *A History of Chinese Civilization*. Cambridge: Cambridge University Press.
Gibson, Harry E. 1937. Agriculture in China during the Shang Period from Information Collected from the Inscribed Shang Bones. *China Journal* (1937):301–09.
Giles, H. A. 1926. *Chuang Tzu*, rev. ed. London: George Allen and Unwin.
Golas, Peter. 1980. Rural China in the Sung. *Journal of Asian Studies* 39:291–325.
Gorman, Chester. 1970. Excavations at Spirit Cave, North Thailand. *Asian Perspectives* 13:79–107.
Gould-Martin, Katherine. 1978. Hot Cold Clean Poison Dirt: Chinese Folk Medical Categories. *Social Science and Medicine* 12:39–46.
Goullart, Peter. 1959. *Land of the Lamas*. New York: Dutton.
Graham, A. C. 1958. *Two Chinese Philosophers*. London: Lund Humphries.
———. 1960. *The Book of Lieh Tzu*. London: John Murray.
———. 1981. *Chuang Tzu: The Inner Chapters*. London: George Allen and Unwin.
Granet, Marcel. 1930. *Chinese Civilization*. London: Kegan Paul.
———. 1932. *Festivals and Songs of Ancient China*. New York: E. P. Dutton.
Greenough, Paul R. 1982. Comments from a South Asian Perspective. *Journal of Asian Studies* 41, 4:789–98.
Grist, D. 1975. *Rice*. London: Longmans.
Grivetti, Louis E., and Marie B. Paquette. 1978. Food Choices Among First Generation Chinese in California. *California Agriculture* 32, 12:6–8.
de Groot, J. J. M. 1892–1910. *The Religious System of the Chinese*. Leiden: E. J. Brill.

Guo Xu. 1986. The Search for China's Earliest City. *China Reconstructs* (May 1986):29–31.

Haeger, John (ed.). 1975. *Crisis and Prosperity in Sung China*. Tucson: University of Arizona Press.

Hagerty, Michael. 1940. Comments on Writings Concerning Chinese Sorghums. *Harvard Journal of Asian Studies* 5:234–61.

Hahn, Emily. 1968. *The Cooking of China*. New York: Time-Life Books.

Harding, A. F. (ed.). 1982. *Climatic Change in Later Prehistory*. Edinburgh: Edinburgh University Press.

Harlan, Jack. 1975. *Crops and Man*. Madison: American Society of Agronomy and Crop Science Society of America.

Hartwell, Robert. 1961–62. A Revolution in the Chinese Iron and Coal Industries during the Northern Sung, 960–1126 A.D. *Journal of Asian Studies* 21:153–62.

———. 1982. Demographic, Political, and Social Transformations of China, 750–1550. *Harvard Journal of Asian Studies* 42:365–442.

Hawkes, J. G. 1983. *The Diversity of Crop Plants*. Cambridge: Harvard University Press.

Hayami, Yujiro, and Vernon Ruttan. 1971. *Agricultural Development*. Baltimore: Johns Hopkins University Press.

Headland, Isaac. 1914. *Home Life in China*. London: Methuen.

Herklots, G. A. C. 1972. *Vegetables in Southeast Asia*. London: George Allen and Unwin.

Hightower, James Robert. 1970. *The Poetry of T'ao Ch'ien*. Oxford: Oxford University Press.

Hill, R. D. 1976. On the Origins of Domestic Rice. *Journal of Oriental Studies* 14:35–44.

———. 1977. *Rice in Malaysia*. Kuala Lumpur: Oxford University Press in Asia.

Hinton, Harold. 1956. *The Grain Tribute System of China, 1845–1911*. Harvard East Asia Monograph 2. Cambridge: Harvard University.

Hirth, Friedrich, and W. W. Rockhill. 1911. *Chau Ju-Kua*. St. Petersburg: Russian Academy of Sciences.

Ho Ping-Ti. 1955. The Introduction of American Food Plants into China. *American Anthropologist* 57:191–201.

———. 1956–57. Early-Ripening Rice in Chinese History. *Economic History Review* 9:200–18.

———. 1959. *Studies on the Population of China*. Cambridge: Harvard University Press.

———. 1962. *The Ladder of Success in Imperial China*. New York: Columbia University Press.

———. 1970. An Estimate of the Total Population of Sung-Chin China. *Sung Studies* 1:39–53.

———. 1975. *The Cradle of the East*. Hong Kong and Chicago: Chinese University of Hong Kong Press and University of Chicago Press.

———. 1984. The Paleoenvironment of China—A Review Article. *Journal of Asian Studies* 43, 4:723–33.

Holzmann, Donald. 1976. *Poetry and Politics*. Cambridge: Cambridge University Press.

Hommel, Rudolph. 1937. *China at Work*. Cambridge: MIT Press.

Hosie, Archibald. 1910. *Manchuria: Its People, Resources and Recent History*. Boston and Tokyo: J. B. Milet.

———. 1922. *Szechuan: Its Products, Industries and Resources.* Shanghai: Kelly and Walsh.

Hsu Cho-yun. 1978. Agricultural Intensification and Marketing: Agrarianism in the Han Dynasty. In *Ancient China: Studies in Early Civilization,* ed. David Tsoy and Tsuen-hsuin Tsien, pp. 253–68. Hong Kong: Chinese University of Hong Kong.

———. 1979. Early Chinese History: The State of the Field. *Journal of Asian Studies* 38, 3:473–76.

———. 1980. *Han Agriculture.* Seattle: University of Washington Press.

Hsu Hsia-k'o. 1974. *The Travel Diaries of Hsu Hsia-k'o,* trans. and ed. Li Chi. Hong Kong: Chinese University of Hong Kong.

Huang, Philip. 1985. *The Peasant Economy and Social Change in North China.* Stanford: Stanford University Press.

Huang, Ray. 1969. Fiscal Administration during the Ming Dynasty. In Charles Hucker, ed., *Chinese Government in Ming Times.* New York: Columbia University Press, pp. 73–128.

———. 1974. *Taxation and Governmental Finance in Sixteenth-Century Ming China.* Cambridge: Cambridge University Press.

———. 1981. *1587: A Year of No Significance.* New Haven: Yale University Press.

Hubbard, R. N. L. B. 1980. Development of Agriculture in Europe and the Near East: Evidence from Quantitative Sources. *Economic Botany* 34:51–67.

Hucker, Charles. 1961. *The Traditional Chinese State in Ming Times.* Tucson: University of Arizona Press.

——— (ed.). 1969. *Chinese Government in Ming Times: Seven Studies.* New York: Columbia University Press.

———. 1978. *The Ming Dynasty: Its Origins and Evolving Institutions.* Ann Arbor: University of Michigan Press.

Jia Lanpo. 1980. *Early Man in China.* Beijing: Foreign Languages Press.

Jing Shen-tao. 1976. *The Jurchen in Twelfth Century China.* Seattle: University of Washington Press.

Johannes, R. E. 1981. *Words of the Lagoon.* Berkeley: University of California Press.

Johnson, Charles (ed.). 1985. *Dab Neeg Hmoob: Myths, Legends and Folk Tales from the Hmong of Laos.* St. Paul: Macalester College, Linguistics Department.

Kao Kuang-jen. 1978. Tawenkou: Neolithic Culture Find. *China Reconstructs* (August 1978):31–35.

Kaplan, Henry S., and Patricia Jones Tsuchitani (eds.). 1978. *Cancer in Chinese.* New York: Alan R. Liss.

Karlgren, Bernhard. 1950. *The Book of Odes.* Stockholm: Museum of Far Eastern Antiquities.

Katz, Solomon, M. Hediger, and L. Valleroy. 1974. Traditional Maize Processing Techniques in the New World. *Science* 184:765–73.

Keightley, David. 1978. *Sources of Shang History.* Berkeley: University of California Press.

——— (ed.). 1983. *The Origins of Chinese Civilization.* Berkeley: University of California Press.

Keng, Hsüan. 1974. Economic Plants of Ancient North China as Mentioned in *Shih Ching* (Book of Poetry). *Economic Botany* 28, 4:391–410.

King, F. H. 1911. *Farmers of Forty Centuries*. New York: Mrs. F. H. King.

Kleinman, Arthur. 1980. *Patients and Healers in the Context of Culture*, vol. 1. Berkeley: University of California Press.

Laderman, Carol. 1981. Symbolic and Empirical Reality: A New Approach to the Analysis of Food Avoidances. *American Ethnologist* 3:468–93.

Lamb, H. H. 1982. Reconstruction of the Course of Postglacial Climate over the World. In *Climatic Change in Later Prehistory*, ed. A. F. Harding, pp. 11–32. Edinburgh: Edinburgh University Press.

Langlois, Janet. 1972. Moon Cakes in Chinatown, New York City: Continuity and Change. *New York Folklore Quarterly* 28, 2:83–117.

Langlois, John (ed.). 1981. *China under Mongol Rule*. Princeton: Princeton University Press.

Lau, D. C. 1970. *Mencius*. Harmondsworth, Sussex: Penguin.

Laufer, Berthold. 1919. *Sino-Iranica*. Chicago: Field Museum.

Lawton, Harry, Philip Wilke, Mary DeDecker, and William Mason. Agriculture among the Paiute of Owens Valley. *Journal of California Anthropology* 3:13–50.

Lee, Mabel Ping-Hua. 1921. *The Economic History of China*. New York: Columbia University Press.

Lee, Thomas H. C. 1975–76. A Report on the Recently Excavated Song Ship at Quanzhou and a Consideration of Its True Capacity. *Sung Studies Newsletter* 11–12:4–9.

Legge, James. 1967. *The Li Chi*, 2 vols. Hong Kong: Hong Kong University Press. Originally published 1885.

Leung, Mai. 1979. *The Chinese People's Cookbook*. New York: Harper and Row. Also published as *Dim Sum and Other Chinese Street Food*.

Li Chi. 1977. *Anyang*. Seattle: University of Washington Press.

Li, Hui-lin. 1969. The Vegetables of Ancient China. *Economic Botany* 23, 3:253–60.

———. 1974. The Origin and Use of Cannabis in Eastern Asia—Linguistic-Cultural Implications. *Economic Botany* 28, 3:293–303.

———. 1977. Hallucinogenic Plants in Chinese Herbals. *Harvard University Botanical Museum Leaflets* 25, 6:161–81.

———. 1979. *Nan-fang Ts'ao-mu Chuang: A Fourth Century Flora of Southeast Asia*. Hong Kong: Chinese University of Hong Kong.

Li Shih-ch'en. 1960. *Pen-ts'ao Kang-mu*. Hong Kong: Shih Yung Book Co. Originally published 1593. This is a widespread, cheap edition.

Li Shu-Fan. 1964. *Hong Kong Surgeon*. London: Victor Gollancz.

Liang, Lucille. 1982. *Chinese Regional Cooking*. New York: Sterling.

Lin Yueh-Hua. 1940. The Miao-Man Peoples of Kweichow. *Harvard Journal of Asian Studies* 5:261–345.

Lin Yutang. 1947. *The Gay Genius: The Life and Times of Su Tung-p'o*. New York: John Day.

Ling, Shao-wen. 1977. *Aquaculture in Southeast Asia*. Seattle: University of Washington Press.

Lippit, Victor. 1974. *Land Reform and Economic Development in China*. White Plains, N.Y.: International Arts and Sciences Press.

———. 1978. The Development of Underdevelopment in China. *Modern China* 4, 3:251–328.

Liu, Frank, and Liu Yan Mau. 1980. *Chinese Medical Terminology*. Hong Kong: Commercial Press.

Liu, J. T. L. 1959. *Reform in Sung China*. Cambridge: Harvard University Press.

Liu, J. T. L, and Peter Golas (eds.). 1969. *Change in China: Innovation or Renovation?* Lexington, Md.: D. Heath.

Lo, Kenneth. 1971. *Peking Cooking*. New York: Random House.

———. 1979a. *Encyclopedia of Chinese Cooking*. New York: A & W Publishers.

———. 1979b. *Chinese Regional Cooking*. New York: Random House.

Lo, Winston Wan. 1974. *The Life and Thought of Yeh Shih*. Gainesville, Fla., and Hong Kong: University of Florida and Chinese University of Hong Kong.

Loewe, Michael. 1968. *Everyday Life in Early Imperial China*. London: B. T. Batsford.

———. 1979. *Ways to Paradise: The Chinese Quest for Immortality*. London: George Allen and Unwin.

———. 1982. *Chinese Ideas of Life and Death: Faith, Myth and Reason in the Han Period*. London: George Allen and Unwin.

Lou Sizhi. 1983. Fragrant Rice—Rare and Delicious. *China Reconstructs* (July):56.

Lu, Henry. 1986. *Chinese System of Food Cures*. New York: Sterling.

Lu Yu. 1981. *South China in the Thirteenth Century*, trans. Chun-shu Cheng and Joan Smythe. Hong Kong: Hong Kong University.

Lu Yü. 1974. *The Classic of Tea*, trans. Francis Ross Carpenter. Boston: Little, Brown.

Lynn, Richard John. 1980. *Kuan Yun-shih*. Boston: Twayne.

McKnight, Brian. 1971. *Village and Bureaucracy in Southern Sung China*. Chicago: University of Chicago Press.

———. 1975. Fiscal Privileges and the Social Order in Sung China. Haeger 1975: 79–100.

MacNeish, Richard. 1977. The Beginning of Agriculture in Central Peru. Reed 1977:753–802.

Maghbouleh, Mitra. 1979. *Psychocultural Dimensions of Alcoholism, Witchcraft, Ethnic Relations, and Asceticism: A Comparative Study*. Irvine: University of California, Irvine, School of Social Sciences, Report no. 56.

Mallory, Walter. 1926. *China: Land of Famine*. New York: American Geographic Society.

Marks, Robert. 1984. *Rural Revolution in South China*. Madison: University of Wisconsin Press.

May, Jacques. 1961. *The Ecology of Malnutrition in the Far East*. New York: Hafner.

Meacham, William. 1975. New C–14 Dates from China. *Asian Perspectives* 18:204–13.

———. 1977. Continuity and Local Evolution in the Neolithic of South China: A Non-Nuclear Approach. *Current Anthropology* 18:419–40.

Mendoza, Juan Gonzalez de. 1853. *The Historie of the Great and Mightie Kingdome of China, and the Situation Thereof: Togither with the Great Riches, Huge Citties, Politike Governement, and Rare Inventions in the Same*, trans. Richard Parker, ed. George Staunton. London: Hakluyt Society. An edition by the early British statesman in China of Parker's 1588 translation.

Meskill, Johanna Menzel. 1979. *A Chinese Pioneer Family*. Princeton: Princeton University Press.

Meskill, John (ed.). 1963. *Wang An-Shih: Practical Reformer?* Boston: Houghton Mifflin.

Meyer, Frank. 1911. *Agricultural Explorations in the Fruit and Nut Orchards of China*. Washington, D.C.: U.S. Dept. of Agriculture, Bureau of Plant Industry, Bulletin 204.

Moise, Edward. 1977. Downward Social Mobility in Pre-Revolutionary China. *Modern China* 3, 1:3–32.

Mollison, Bill. 1978. *Permaculture 1 & 2*. Berkeley: ITCI Tageri Co.

Montgomery, James. 1927. *The History of Yaballaha III, Nestorian Patriarch, and of His Vicar Bar Sauma*. New York: Columbia University Press.

Mote, Frederick. 1977. Yuan and Ming. Chang 1977b:193–257.

Moulder, Frances. 1977. *Japan, China and the Modern World Economy*. Cambridge: Cambridge University Press.

Naquin, Susan. 1976. *Millennarian Rebellion in China*. New Haven: Yale University Press.

National Institute on Alcohol Abuse and Alcoholism. 1978. Oriental Alcohol Hypersensitivity. *IFS* 51:3.

Needham, Joseph. 1956. *Science and Civilization in China*, vol. 2. Cambridge: Cambridge University Press.

———. 1976–80. *Science and Civilization in China*, vol. 5, pts. 3–4. Cambridge: Cambridge University Press. With Ho Peng-yu and Lu Gwei-djen.

Netolitzky, Almut. 1977. *Das Ling-Wai Tai-Ta von Chou Ch'u-Fei*. Wiesbaden: Franz Steiner.

Nichols, E. H. 1902. *Through Hidden Shensi*. New York: Charles Scribner's Sons.

Nisbett, Richard, and Lee Ross. 1980. *Human Inference*. Englewood Cliffs, N.J.: Prentice-Hall.

Nivison, David, and Arthur Wright (eds.). 1959. *The Confucian Persuasion*. Stanford: Stanford University Press.

Pearson, Richard. 1981. Social Complexity in Chinese Coastal Neolithic Sites. *Science* 213:1078–86.

Perkins, Dwight. 1969. *Agricultural Development in China, 1368–1968*. Chicago: Aldine.

Pimentel, David, and M. Pimentel. 1979. *Food, Energy and Society*. New York: Wiley.

Pirazzoli-T'Serstevens, Michele. 1982. *The Han Dynasty*. New York: Rizzoli.

Pollard, S. 1921. *In Unknown China*. London: Seeley, Service.

Porkert, Manfred. 1974. *Theoretical Foundations of Chinese Medicine*. Cambridge: MIT Press.

Posner, Ernst. 1972. *Archives in the Ancient World*. Cambridge: Harvard University Press.

Pulleyblank, E. 1955. *The Background of the Rebellion of An Lu-shan*. Oxford: Oxford University Press.

Qian Wenyuan. 1985. *The Great Inertia*. Dover, N.H.: Croom Helm.

Rawski, Evelyn Sakakida. 1972. *Agricultural Change and the Peasant Economy of South China*. Cambridge: Harvard University Press.

Raychaudhuri, Tapan, and Irfan Habib (eds.). 1982. *The Cambridge Economic History of India*, vol. 1: *c. 1200–1750*. Cambridge: Cambridge University Press.

Read, Bernard E. 1977. *Famine Foods Listed in the Chiu-huang Pen-ts'ao*. Taipei: Southern Materials Center.

Reed, Charles (ed.). 1977. *Origins of Agriculture*. Hague: Mouton.

Reischauer, Edwin O. 1955. *Ennin's Diary*. New York: Ronald Press.

Root, Waverley. 1971. *The Food of Italy*. New York: Atheneum.

Rossabi, Morris. 1975. *China and Inner Asia*. London: Thames and Hudson.

———. 1983. *China among Equals*. Berkeley: University of California Press.

Rossbach, Stella. 1983. *Feng-Shui: The Chinese Art of Placement*. New York: E. P. Dutton.

Rosman, Gilbert. 1982. *Population and Marketing Settlements in Ch'ing China*. Cambridge: Cambridge University Press.

Rozin, Elizabeth. 1973. *Ethnic Cuisine: The Flavor Principle Cookbook*. New York: Greene.

Sabban, Francoise. 1983a. Cuisine à la cour de l'empereur de Chine au XIVe siècle. *Medievales* 5:32–56.

———. 1983b. Le système des cuissons dans la tradition culinaire chinoise. *Annales* 2:341–68.

Sahlins, Marshall. 1972. *Stone Age Economics*. Chicago: Aldine.

Sakamoto, Nobuko. 1977. *The People's Republic of China Cookbook*. New York: Random House.

Sauer, Carl. 1952. *Agricultural Origins and Dispersals*. Berkeley: University of California Press.

Schafer, Edward H. 1954. *The Empire of Min*. Rutland, Vt., and Tokyo: Charles Tuttle.

———. 1963. *The Golden Peaches of Samarkand*. Berkeley: University of California Press.

———. 1967. *The Vermilion Bird*. Berkeley: University of California Press.

———. 1969. *Shore of Pearls*. Berkeley: University of California Press.

———. 1977. T'ang. Chang 1977b:85–140.

———. 1980. *Mao Shan in T'ang Times*. Berkeley: Society for the Study of Chinese Religions.

Schlepp, Wayne. 1970. *San-ch'u*. Madison: University of Wisconsin Press.

Schurmann, Franz. 1956. *Economic Structures of the Yuan Dynasty*. Cambridge: Harvard University Press.

Schwabe, Calvin. 1979. *Unmentionable Cuisine*. Charlottesville: University of Virginia Press.

Shangraw, Clarence. 1978. The Beginnings of China's Painted Pottery Tradition. *Oriental Art* 24:60–69.

Shiba, Yoshinobu. 1970. *Commerce and Society in Sung China*, trans. Mark Elvin. Ann Arbor: University of Michigan, Center for Chinese Studies.

Shih Sheng-han. 1962. *Ch'i Min Yao Shu*. Beijing: Sciences Press.

———. 1974. *On "Fan Sheng-chih Shu"*. Beijing: Sciences Press.

Shurtleff, William, and Akiko Aoyagi. 1976. *The Book of Miso*. Berkeley: Ten Speed Press.

———. 1979. *The Book of Tempeh*. New York: Harper and Row.

———. 1983. *The Book of Tofu*. Berkeley: Ten Speed Press.

Sima Qian, 1974. *Warlords*, trans. William Dolby and John Scott. Edinburgh: Southside Press.

Simon, Julian. 1985. The Effects of Population on Nutrition and Economic Well-Being. In *Hunger and History*, ed. Robert Rotberg and Theodore Rabb, pp. 215–40. Cambridge: Cambridge University Press.

Sinoda, Osamu. 1977. The History of Chinese Food and Diet. *Progress in Food and Nutritional Science* 2:483–97.

Sivin, Nathan. 1975. Shen Kua. *Sung Studies Newsletter* 13:36.

———. 1980. Science in China's Past. In *Science in Contemporary China*, ed. Leo Orleans, pp. 1–29. Stanford: Stanford University Press.

Skinner, G. William. 1964–65. Marketing and Social Structure in Rural China. *Journal of Asian Studies* 24, 1:3–43, 2:195–228, 3:363–400.

———. 1986. Sichuan's Population in the Nineteenth Century: Lessons from Disaggregated Data. *Late Imperial China* 7:1–79.

———. (ed.). 1976. *The City in Late Imperial China*. Stanford: Stanford University Press.

Slicher von Bath, E. H. 1963. *The Agragian History of Western Europe, A.D. 500–1850*. New York: St. Martin's.

Smil, Vaclav. 1984. *The Bad Earth*. Armonk, N.Y.: M. E. Sharpe.

Smith, Thomas C. 1959. *The Agrarian Origins of Modern Japan*. Stanford: Stanford University Press.

———. 1977. *Nakahara*. Stanford: Stanford University Press.

Snellgrove, David, and Hugh Richardson, 1968. *A Cultural History of Tibet*. London: Weidenfeld and Nicholson.

Solheim, William. 1970. Northern Thailand, Southeast Asia, and World Prehistory. *Asian Perspectives* 13:145–62.

Sowerby, Arthur de Carle. 1940. *Nature in Chinese Art*. New York: John Day.

Spence, Jonathan. 1974. *Emperor of China*. New Haven: Yale University Press.

———. 1977. Ch'ing. Chang 1977:259–294.

Spence, Jonathan, and John E. Wills, Jr. (eds.). 1979. *From Ming to Ch'ing*. New Haven: Yale University Press.

Staunton, George. 1797. *An Historical Account of the Embassy to the Emperor of China*. London: Stockdale.

Strickmann, Michel. 1979. On the Alchemy of T'ao Hung-ching. In *Facets of Taoism*, ed. Holmes Welch and Anna Seidel, pp. 123–92. New Haven: Yale University Press.

Sun Shouduo and Guo Dashun. 1986. Hongshan: A Lost Culture. *China Pictorial* (August): 2–7.

Sung Ying-hsing. 1966. *T'ien-kung K'ai-wu*, trans. E-tu Zen Sun and Shiou-chuan Sun. University Park: Pennsylvania State University.

Swann, Nancy. 1950. *Food and Money in Ancient China*. Princeton: Princeton University Press.

Symons, Van Jay. 1981. *Ch'ing Ginseng Management: Ch'ing Monopolies in Microcosm*. Tempe: Arizona State University, Center for Asian Studies, Occasional Paper 13.

Torbert, Preston. 1977. *The Ch'ing Imperial Household Department*. Harvard East Asia Monograph 71. Cambridge: Harvard University.

Tregear, T. R. 1980. *China: A Geographical Survey*. London: Hodder and Stoughton.

Tuan, Yi-fu. 1969. *China*. Chicago: Aldine.

Tucci, Giuseppe. 1967. *Tibet*. New York: Stein and Day.

Tun Li-Ch'en. 1965. *Annual Customs and Festivals in Peking*, trans. Derk Bodde. Hong Kong: Hong Kong University Press.

Twitchett, Denis. 1962. *Land Tenure and the Social Order in T'ang and Sung China*. London: University of London.

———. 1963. *Financial Administration Under the T'ang Dynasty*. Cambridge: Cambridge University Press.

_____ (ed.). 1979. *The Cambridge History of China*, vol. 3, pt. 1: *Sui and T'ang China*. Cambridge: Cambridge University Press.

Twitchett, Denis, and Arthur Wright (eds.). 1973. *Perspectives on the T'ang*. New Haven: Yale University Press.

Unschuld, Paul. 1985. *Medicine in China: A History of Ideas*. Berkeley: University of California Press.

_____. 1986. *Medicine in China: A History of Pharmaceutics*. Berkeley: University of California Press.

Veith, Ilza (ed. and trans.). 1966. *The Yellow Emperor's Classic of Internal Medicine*. Berkeley: University of California Press.

Waley, Arthur. 1931. *The Travels of an Alchemist*. London: Routledge and Kegan Paul.

_____. 1939. *Three Ways of Thought in Ancient China*. London: George Allen and Unwin.

_____. 1957. *Yuan Mei: Eighteenth Century Chinese Poet*. New York: Grove Press.

_____. 1958. *The Book of the Way and Its Power*. New York: Grove Press.

_____. 1963. *The Secret History of the Mongols*. London: George Allen and Unwin.

Wallace, D. Mackenzie. 1881. *Russia*. New York: Henry Holt.

Wang Shou-Wu and Zhao Zong-ci. 1981. Droughts and Floods in China, 1470–1979. In *Climate in History*, ed. T. Wigley, M. Ingram and G. Farmer, pp. 271–288. Cambridge: Cambridge University Press.

Wang Shou-wu, Zhao Zong-ci, and Chen Zhen-hua. 1981. Reconstruction of the Summer Rainfall Regime for the Last 500 Years in China. *GeoJournal* 5, 2:117–22.

Wang Zhongshu. 1982. *Han Civilization*. New Haven: Yale University Press.

Warriner, Doreen. 1939. *Economics of Peasant Farming*. London: Oxford University Press.

Watson, Burton. 1965. *Su Tung-p'o*. New York: Columbia University Press.

_____. 1967. *Records of the Grand Historian*. New York: Columbia University Press.

_____. 1974a. *Chinese Lyricism*. New York: Columbia University Press.

_____. 1974b. *Courtier and Commoner in Ancient China*. New York: Columbia University Press.

Watson, James L. 1985. From the Common Pot: Feasting with Equals in Chinese Society. MS.

Watson, William. 1969. Early Animal Domestication in China. In *The Domestication and Exploitation of Plants and Animals*, ed. P. P. Ucko and G. Dimbleby, pp. 393–96. Chicago: Aldine.

_____. 1971. *Cultural Frontiers in Ancient East Asia*. Edinburgh: Edinburgh University Press.

Weltfish, Gene. 1965. *The Lost Universe*. New York: Basic Books.

Wen Dazhong and David Pimentel. 1986a. Seventeenth Century Organic Argiculture in China, pt. I: Cropping Systems in Jiaxing Region. *Human Ecology* 14, 1:1–14.

_____. 1986b. Seventeenth Century Organic Agriculture in China, pt. II: Energy Flows Through an Agroecosystem in Jiaxing Region. *Human Ecology* 14, 1:15–28.

Wheatley, Paul. 1959. Geographical Notes on Some Commodities Involved in Sung Maritime Trade. *Journal of the Malayan Branch, Royal Asiatic Society*, 32, 2:1–140.

_____. 1971. *The Pivot of the Four Quarters*. Edinburgh: Edinburgh University Press.

Whyte, R. O. 1972. *Rural Nutrition in China*. Hong Kong: Oxford University Press.

————. 1974. *Rural Nutrition in Monsoon Asia*. Kuala Lumpur: Oxford University Press.

Wilhelm, Helmut. 1962. Yueh Fei. In *Confucian Personalities*, ed. Arthur Wright and D. Twitchett, pp. 146–61. Stanford: Stanford University Press.

Will, Pierre-Etienne. 1980. *Bureaucracie et famine en Chine en 18ème siècle*. Paris and Hague: Mouton.

Willets, William. 1965. *Foundations of Chinese Art*. London: Thames and Hudson.

Williamson, H. R. 1935–37. *Wang An-Shih*. London: Probsthain.

Wittfogel, Karl. 1957. *Oriental Despotism*. New Haven: Yale University Press.

Wittfogel, Karl, and Chia-sheng Feng. 1949. *History of Chinese Civilization: Liao*. Philadelphia: American Philosophical Society, Transactions, 36.

Wong, Chimin, and Wu Lien-Teh. 1936. *History of Chinese Medicine*, 2d ed. Shanghai: China (Republic), National Quarantine Service.

Worthy, Edmund. 1975. Regional Control in the Southern Sung Salt Administration. Haeger 1975:101–141.

Wright, Arthur. 1978. *The Sui Dynasty*. New York: Knopf.

————. 1979. The Sui Dynasty. Twitchett 1979: 49–149.

Wu Ch'ing-tzu. 1957. *The Scholars*, trans. Hsien-li Yang and Gladys Yang. Beijing: Foreign Languages Press.

Yang, Billy Wen-Chi. 1984. *History of Chinese Food Culture and Food Industries* (in Chinese). Peking: Agricultural History Press.

Yang, Grace I-Ping, and Hazel M. Fix. 1979. Food Habit Changes of Chinese Persons Living in Lincoln, Nebraska. *American Dietetic Association Journal* 75, 10:420–24.

Yoon, Hong Key. 1976. *Geomantic Relationships between Nature and Culture in Korea*. Taipei: Orient Cultural Service.

Yu, Ying-shih. 1967. *Trade and Expansion in Han China*. Berkeley: University of California Press.

————. 1977. Han. Chang 1977b:53–84.

Yuan, Tsing. 1978. Continuities and Discontinuities in Chinese Agriculture, 1550–1700. *Ming Studies* 7:35–51.

Yule, Henry, and H. Cordier. 1903. *The Book of Ser Marco Polo*, 2 vols. London: John Murray.

Zelin, Madeleine. 1986. The Rights of Tenants in Mid-Qing Sichuan: A Study of Land-Related Lawsuits in the Baxian Archives. *Journal of Asian Studies* 45, 3:499–526.

Zhang Jiacheng. 1982. A Colder or Warmer World? *China Reconstructs* (May): 34–35.

Zheng Gouqing. 1987. "Mao Tai Town." *China Pictorial*, Feb., pp. 40–41.

Zhong Yao Da Zi Dian. 1979. Shanghai: People's Press.

Zhuan Han-Sheng and R. A. Kraus. 1975. *Mid-Ch'ing Rice Markets and Trade: An Essay in Price History*. Harvard East Asian Monograph 54. Cambridge: Harvard University.

Zohary, Daniel. 1973. *Geobotanical Foundations of the Middle East*. Stuttgart: G. Fischer.

Index